A
GOOD
PLACE
TO
LIVE

TERRY PINDELL

HENRY HOLT AND COMPANY
NEW YORK

A GOOD PLACE TO LIVE

AMERICA'S LAST MIGRATION

Henry Holt and Company, Inc.
Publishers since 1866
115 West 18th Street
New York, New York 10011

Henry Holt® is a registered
trademark of Henry Holt and Company, Inc.

Published in Canada by Fitzhenry & Whiteside Ltd.,
195 Allstate Parkway, Markham, Ontario L3R 4T8.

Library of Congress Cataloging-in-Publication Data
Pindell, Terry.
A good place to live: America's last migration / Terry Pindell
—1st ed.
p.   cm.
Includes bibliographical references and index.
1. United States—Description and travel.   2. City and town
life—United States.   3. Community life.   4. Pindell, Terry—
Journeys.   5. United States—Social conditions—1980–   I. Title
E169.04.P55   1995   94-43680
973.929—dc20   CIP

ISBN 0-8050-2352-6

Henry Holt books are available for special promotions and
premiums. For details contact: Director, Special Markets.

First Edition—1995

Designed by Katy Riegel

Printed in the United States of America
All first editions are printed on acid-free paper. ∞

10 9 8 7 6 5 4 3 2 1

For my mother,
whose ancestral search
inspired this one . . .

CONTENTS

PREFACE

The true story of America is an unfinished quest for place and community. Our continental heritage is a history of spasms of migration toward or away from someplace, beginning of course with the flight from the Old World to the new. When there was frontier land, we occupied it hoping to make a better living than we could in the cities we had just corrupted back East. When life on our farms and in our heartland small towns became mean and limiting, we flocked to the cities searching for opportunity. When the cities seemed overcrowded and dangerous, we invented the suburbs. When we rebelled against the sterility of our suburbs and found that they had also ruined our cities, we headed back to the land.

We on this continent have never resolved the problem of place, partly because we have seldom stayed in our places long enough to get them right and rarely apprehended the connection between place and human community. It shows in locales with few physical edifices that last beyond a generation or two, as if all we know are beginnings, and so we frenetically tear down and pave over every last generation's best effort. It shows in the cities that the middle class has abandoned to the rich and the poor. It shows in the fallen suburban ideal where we lived an isolated existence remote from the settings of human intercourse. It shows in the countryside where the farms have been sold to mall developers and the roadsides strewn with ticky-tacky cinderblock retail outlets that change hands almost annually, and where it is difficult to know when you have actually left Farmington and entered Pleasantville. It shows in the dying small-town Main Streets and empty village greens; in the thriving shopping malls, fast-food chains, and gated developments; in the waning art of public conversation and fast rise of the cellular phone and video culture—mass paradigms of our acquiescence in the failure of American places to promote a sense of community. James Howard Kunstler has recently described American communities as a "geography of nowhere" dysfunctionally contoured by the relentless drive of the individualist American dream and our intoxication with the illusion of freedom provided by the private automobile.

Now, in the nineties, Americans are on the move again, this time in a migration whose motivation is not economic and whose direction is not focused on any particular geographic arena of opportunity. The last migration is plainly and simply the search for a good place to live in a land where such places are perceived as increasingly rare.

This book is a record of my own deliberate participation in that search. For three years I traveled the continent, stopping off for extended sojourns in places that are frequent destinations in Americans' contemporary quest for a good place to live—places characterized by substantive alternatives to the way of life in Anyplace, USA.

It is a report of surprisingly good news. The last migration is onto something. There are more good places to live in North America than there were ten years ago and there will be even more of them a few years from now than there are today. Some fine awakenings are newly abroad in the land, and the recurring themes running through these stories are fragments of common human wisdom as old as the drinking cups that archaeologists unearth from ancient trading centers.

ACKNOWLEDGMENTS

I would like to thank the following people who helped make this book possible:

Peter Ryner, long-suffering, beleaguered, and underappreciated city planner for my town of Keene, New Hampshire. It was his influence that convinced me that there might be reasons, rationale, and even science behind what makes a good place to live. And it was his suggested bibliography that formed the foundation of my reading for this project.

Pat MacQueen, long-suffering, beleaguered, and underappreciated city manager for my town of Keene. He showed me that city bureaucracy can and should be an agent of vision and decency.

Jane Sheffield, director of Inherit New Hampshire and former Main Street director for Altoona, Pennsylvania. She is the ultimate "new person," one who comes into a region from somewhere else and sets the place afire with revitalizing energy. Her friendship and activism during the final phases of producing this book kept me believing in what the book was all about.

Kennedy Smith, director of the Main Street Program of the National Trust. In so many good places I visited I found her footprint, and when I finally heard her speak when she was working to found a

Main Street Center in New Hampshire, I knew the movement back to the center would not lack for leadership.

Nancy Vincent and the staff of the Keene Public Library, who again enabled me to do the research for a book within the comfortable realm of my hometown.

My editor, Bill Strachan, who continues to defy the common wisdom that sooner or later there need be conflict between writer and editor.

Darcy Tromanhauser, assistant editor, for assistance with all matters great and small.

My agent, Joe Spieler, who continues to jump into the breach and justify why writers need managers.

My copy editor, Sandra Dhols, whose patience with my impatience at the copy editor's role is greatly appreciated.

Community leaders named throughout the book, who shared their visions and offered blueprint details about how to replicate their accomplishments.

Nancy, Molly, and Katie, for their continued support.

We shall not cease from exploration
And the end of all our exploring
Will be to arrive where we started
And know the place for the first time.
                                    —T. S. Eliot

Sometimes you want to go
Where everybody knows your name
And they're always glad you came.
        —Theme song from "Cheers"

It's time in this country for an end to the
politics of division and a renaissance of
American community.
                        —President Bill Clinton

INTRODUCTION

For twenty years I had lived in Keene, New Hampshire, a small city with a picture-postcard New England downtown and a huge old white church at the head of the square. Keene is commonly considered a good place to live. Friends from New York or Pennsylvania come up for weekends and swoon over our autumn maples; our perfect snowfalls in winter woods; the stillness of our summer lakes, where you can really hear the fish sucking in flies; and the wisps of wood smoke that hang in our air. Many of us don't lock our doors here, there is no interstate buzzing threateningly just outside of town, and so far the closest thing to a modern shopping mall in Keene is the tasteful redevelopment of a century-old mill as a marketplace. We have two colleges in town and a school system that sends most of its students on to higher education. And Boston is just two hours' drive away.

But after twenty years, I found myself dissatisfied with the way we lived, even in Keene. I was tired of making calendar appointments to see friends, chafing at Keene's lack of arenas for spontaneous social contact, and frustrated at the need to drive out of town for stimulating entertainment or cultural excitement. I was angry at the prevailing community values with which I wrestled as a member of the city council, where a lust for the quick-and-dirty economic fix threatened what we had, and an obsession with custom thwarted what we could become. There was a dumb malaise behind the Potemkin facade of our cute downtown, where our teenagers hung out on Central Square scheming illicit parties in the woods because there was nothing else to do. A great quietness hung over our public life, punctuated mainly by the occasional outbursts of one faction perceiving another somehow getting ahead.

Keene was a sleepy town, people liked to say, and many thought they liked it that way. But our community was terribly divided, and a serious gap had begun to open between our economic means and the cost of the community amenities that we had come to take for granted. Placid as it seemed, our community, like most American places, was troubled, and it was headed toward the more obvious traumas of less blessed places all across the continent.

Fully cognizant that there were lots of places in North America far worse off than Keene, I set out to see if I could find better ones—or at least to learn what it would take to make the one I had, whose rudiments were so attractive to those visitors from downcountry, more satisfying with the richness of human possibility.

At the start of these journeys, I quickly discovered that I was participating in a widespread contemporary phenomenon—and that my own yearnings were representative of those of thousands of my generation who constituted a new American migration that began in the late eighties and is continuing into the nineties. I met people searching for a good place to live everywhere I went—on trains and planes and buses, in bars and roadside diners, in real estate offices and at chamber of commerce desks, and on street corners of communities large and small all across the continent. The great surprise and the genesis of this book was the fact that initially everyone seemed to be talking about the same handful of places—a couple dozen or so sites were on everyone's shortlist.

The new migrants came from a variety of environments: crime-ridden cities, suffocating small towns, stultifying suburbs, and, newest on the list of broken dreams, the rural settings of the post–Vietnam War "back-to-the-landers." I came to think of them as members of a "last migration" because so many of these searchers believed they might be participating in America's last chance to secure the blessings of community before some sociological apocalypse obliterated the existing foundations on which they might build.

Participants in the last migration had three things in common: they all had the means, either through income level or, more commonly, through the increasingly mobile nature of today's occupations, to live almost anywhere they wanted; they had undertaken the search for a good place to live with the same rational, thoughtful sense of purpose that other generations had put into scheming financial security; and they were generally fleeing, and therefore seeking, the same kinds of things.

What were they looking for that led them to their shortlist of good places? Besides the usual concerns about crime, taxes, bad government, and traffic (the last migration is less obsessed with climate than was the Sun Belt migration of the seventies and early eighties), there were several overwhelmingly consistent complaints about the places left behind that defined the positive qualities of the "good places" sought.

First was the void that I felt so strongly myself in Keene—the lack of community gathering places where you can walk in at almost any time and be assured of either encountering old friends or making new ones. Such places are the balm of life to the social being, the third piece of human wholeness after the realms of family and work. Thus Ray Oldenburg in *The Great Good Place* calls them "third places" (after the first, home, and the second, the workplace). Other societies with more functional communities than ours are built around them: the pubs of England, the bistros of France, the biergartens of Germany, the coffeehouses of Vienna, the piazzas of Italy, and plazas of Spain.

Unfortunately, American social history has not been kind to the third place, from Puritan strictures against revelry to the misevolution of the American bar as a place of disrepute to the modern constriction of social life to the individual home. The convivial taverns that once spawned a democratic revolution are now tourist attractions and the small-town Main Streets that perpetuated it are deserted for malls built on the outskirts. In America the scarcity of the third place is more than an obstacle to good community, it is a threat to the democratic pluralism that we cherish, since it is in third places that people rub shoulders regularly with folks they don't work with or invite to dinner.

But perhaps Oldenburg's obituary to the American third place was written a year or two too soon. Participants in the last migration are spawning a revival of social gathering places, ranging from the obvious brew pubs, coffeehouses, and sidewalk cafés to such innovations as the deli bookstore, the pizza and beer Laundromat, the health food fitness center, and the river walk. The downtown itself is being redefined as a place to meet with people rather than to shop for merchandise. Architects, planners, and developers have finally caught on to the wisdom of Jane Jacobs, Lewis Mumford, and William Whyte in creating public spaces that bring people together rather than force them apart. Towns and cities whose social life coalesces around such places rather than the country club and the private home meet the first criteria for people looking for a good place to live today.

The new migrants' second criterion developed in reaction to our national romance with the automobile and the associated rise of the suburban lifestyle. Most of our current community structures were based on the myth that the mobility provided by the private car made quiet streets, distance, and isolation from the forums of human contact desirable. We created the suburban housing development where there is nothing within walking distance of home but other homes. To go to work, shop for groceries, see a doctor, buy clothes, pick up household necessities, visit a library, pay a bill, or find some center where people gather requires getting in a car and driving. Offices moved to corporate parks on the outskirts, malls took the retail world out to the exit off the interstate. The great dispersal of our communities away from their centers spelled their doom.

Leaving aside the ecological consequences of our overreliance on automobiles, there is a growing consensus that the necessity of getting into the hermetic enclosure of the private automobile and pulling out into traffic to go anywhere at all is profoundly disruptive to the sense of connection between home and anyplace else that matters. It breeds a condition of isolation and militates against a feeling of membership in community. Kunstler has cataloged, in addition, the dozens of ways that shaping places toward the needs of automobiles misshapes them as habitats for people. We paved paradise and put in a parking lot.

Architects Andres Duany and Elizabeth Plater-Zyberk describe the curse of the suburb as follows:

> The classic suburb is less a community than an agglomeration of houses, shops and offices connected to one another by cars, not by the fabric of human life. . . . The structure of the suburb tends to confine people to their houses and cars; it discourages strolling, walking, mingling with neighbors. The suburb is the last word in privatization, perhaps even its lethal consummation, and it spells the end of authentic civil life.

Whether chosen out of an apprehension of life dominated by the madness of traffic or out of a desire to escape the personal isolation of suburban living, the destinations of the last migration tended to be places where people could live adjacent to the center of community or where it was otherwise possible to move from home to centers of human intercourse with minimal reliance on their cars. The last migration was particularly attracted to small cities (and a few exceptional large ones) fortunate to have a substantial ring of decent, middle-class residential neighborhoods immediately adjacent to a thriving downtown and the resources and will to fund micropolitan public transit operations. The new home seekers wanted urban living in cities that felt like small towns. They sought a return to the center.

A third concern of the last migration was the juxtaposition of two often mutually exclusive features. Modern North Americans grew up believing that one had to make a painful choice between unspoiled environments with attractive natural amenities and centers of thriving human culture. You could live in the pristine mountains of Vermont or you could enjoy the theater and nightlife of New York City; you could walk along the surf of Big Sur or cruise the clubs of L.A. But you couldn't have it both ways.

With the emergence of the great cities of the naturally spectacular Northwest and the recent cultural renaissance of small cities in a variety of beautiful locations (often promoted by the influx of the last migration itself), the new home seekers realized that they could demand a minimal level of both natural and cultural amenities. It didn't have to be "Rocky Mountain highs" and the Bolshoi Ballet. But they did want attractive rural or wilderness country just outside of town, clean air, and communities with enough sophistication that not having the *New York Times,* a theater or performing arts center, decent restaurants, and places to go at night for music and dancing was unthinkable.

Finally there was the question of the placelessness of so many American communities—the phenomenon one writer has called the McDonaldization of America. Even before the franchise chains, the national myths of newness and the melting pot had long conspired to mold generic places that look and feel the same wherever they may be. The chain establishments of today merely cast in concrete, fiberboard, and plastic a careless, thoughtless habit of communal conformity that has been evolving for decades.

In response, the last migration wanted communities colored by a strong, unique, and even idiosyncratic sense of place—places that might not invoke Gertrude Stein's condemnation of Oakland: "There is no there there." The new migrants searched for sites that were either downright un-American or so profoundly proto-American that they bore little resemblance to Anyplace, USA. The roots of Someplace, U.S.A., might be local geography, history, politics, economics, or demographics. But its flowering in the face of the national winds of homogenization and thoughtless development depended on a strong community sense of identity and local pride—and sometimes plain dumb luck.

Once I realized that people were finding what they were looking for, I became fascinated with the preconditions and process by which places came to meet their requirements, and by the fact that discovery by the last migration tended to be a key element. I developed my itinerary by reviewing the "places rated" guides, magazine surveys, publications of city planners, extant "good place" literature, and, most of all, my notes of the considerable oral testimony I had recorded during my travels for this and previous projects. I spent a lot of time in bars, coffeehouses, and public spaces. I liked having company; it changed the nature of the quest from one characterized by alienation to one of camaraderie—the boon that we questers of the last migration set after in the first place.

By the time I finished the project, it was clear that the last migration was only half of the story. Equally important were those people who stayed put in their own communities and worked with the new-comers to engineer a renaissance of community by promoting an economic, social, and cultural return to the center. Bankers, develop-ers, entrepreneurs, city officials, newspaper publishers, arts people, social activists, and visionaries from many walks of life found they could work together, sometimes amid great controversy, once some critical mass of perception had been reached. It was a perception of impending loss. The movement, and that's what the return to the center surely is, became a classic historical response to challenge.

These journeys were carried out during the recent recession that gave America a new president and perhaps a new model for American life. I didn't always find felicity. Even the best of reviving communities were often deeply troubled, and their greatest successes stood before a backdrop of apocalyptic national headlines that underscored just how tenuous these new beginnings toward better living might turn out to be. But I did find communities whose people convinced me pro-foundly that they had found and nurtured a better life in a better place. And their renaissance always turned out to be the touchstone to a new prosperity that enabled them to crawl out of the eighties reces-sion ahead of their less enlightened counterparts elsewhere.

For the most part these North Americans were full of good will, energy, and hope rather than the anger, cynicism, and fatalism that had soured our communal life for at least a generation or two. They welcomed change and initiative while valuing the historic foundations of community upon which they might build. They liked people and were not fearful that the public world was a threat to their private worlds. They had rediscovered that old American confidence that the task could be done. What they had wrought, in many places in less than a decade, was something new under the sun—a return to the center that set a pattern for an American renaissance of community in the 1990s.

1

ROOTS

The sign hanging over the sidewalk at the corner of San Francisco and Galisteo streets in Santa Fe read EVANGELO'S COCKTAIL LOUNGE, and the dented blue double doors at the entrance sported an ugly padlock till after two in the afternoon. The place didn't fit in with the cheeriness of the trading post shops, art galleries, and Southwest cuisineries that lined the street so fiercely awash with that pure, piercing Santa Fe sunlight that had enchanted seekers from D. H. Lawrence to Eric Sloane to Bruce Springsteen. As one of the few establishments in downtown Santa Fe with a northeasterly streetfront, Evangelo's seemed to lurk in rare shadow like a dive that some drug lord or merchant of illegal work flesh had held out of the tourist gentrification market as an operational headquarters. No respectable bar outside of a hotel called itself a cocktail lounge anymore. And no place in Santa Fe would be deliberately done up in the Polynesian decor I could just barely discern when I squinted through the diamond windows at the murkiness inside. I noticed that the brightly clad tourists thronging San Francisco Street this golden April afternoon took one look in those windows and passed on by, while a different, dunner selection of people came and went through the double doors, materializing seemingly out of nowhere and then evaporating just as inscrutably when they departed. Surrounded by the correct and trendy shops of the 1990s surface of Santa Fe, Evangelo's teased me for two days before I went inside. It turned out that pushing open that ugly blue double door was like opening the gate to a secret city.

Inside Evangelo's there were fishnets, tortoise shells, bamboo, glass floats, grass mats, and coconuts—all of the trappings of a tropical seaside bar in a city a thousand miles from saltwater. Behind the bar, a grim, beady-eyed man with a dark beard, wearing a spotless white fedora, poured drinks. The patrons gathered at the bar and around the tables looked tough—a variety of ages, some leather, some denim, and some wool, all in earth colors, none of the flashing hues of tourists. A room downstairs clicked with the sounds of people at pool tables. There was a jukebox playing at low volume but no live music. And no food was served, not even chips. It was darker than most popular bars these days. It seemed like a good place to score cocaine or illicit documents.

"Evangelo's is a drinking bar—straight, traditional," said Nick Klones, the man in the white fedora whose family had owned the bar since 1971, when I asked for a bar menu. He turned and wandered back down to the far end of the bar and watched me drink the bottled Bud he had poured for me. Soon he strolled back to my end and offered another little sound bite, "When you drink you're supposed to talk—good conversation is what a Greek bar is all about," and wandered away again before I had a chance to take him up on his suggestion.

At his next pass, I asked him why the Polynesian decor in a Greek bar in Santa Fe. "Papa [Evangelo] was sick of all the adobe shit. So he made a Polynesian-Greek bar." And to prove that Evangelo wasn't crazy, Nick pulled a book off a shelf—*Barhop USA,* Awesome Wells's survey of the one hundred best bars in America—tossed it to me, and meandered off again to talk to a tough-looking woman at a table across the room. There in the book was Evangelo's, ranked at number thirty-one, complete with a description of Nick and his hat.

I had to begin with Santa Fe if I wanted to be absolutely sure that my first stop was not Anyplace, USA. I could have gone to Key West or New Orleans. But there's only one city in America older than Santa Fe and, despite the tourists, none that has remained so original against the forces of homogenization. Then there was that sun, the breath of the Sangre de Cristo Mountains looming just to the east, and the five-hundred-mile vista across the Rio Grande valley to the west. Santa Fe was on the shortlist of practically every good place searcher I had ever met.

Yet travel writers love to hate Santa Fe these days. On the plane I read an article in the *New York Times* travel section advising serious seekers of interesting places to visit that Santa Fe had sold its soul, lost its charm, and become common with chain franchises and swarms of the meaner sort of tourists.

The first couple of days I spent there tended to confirm that judgment, despite the sun, the vigorous altitude, and the most amazing eruption of colorful old American earth anywhere on the continent. Though the city had scrupulously preserved by ordinance the adobe Santa Fe–style architecture, so the downtown certainly didn't look like Main Street, Anyplace, USA, I met no one at first but other visitors moving restlessly past the shops on the plaza and San Francisco Street, where spectacular and beautiful things were displayed for sale and merchants were happy to accept MasterCard and ship to almost anyplace on the globe. There were the Pueblo and Navajo Indians, of course, lined up under the portico of the Governor's Palace selling their handicrafts; but in a place so crammed with tourists, they seemed like Disney employees. The disturbing thing about downtown Santa Fe was that there seemed to be no places left for the people who actually lived in the city.

But there was one.

Nick Klones made several more passes by my stool in Evangelo's that third afternoon, dispensing tidbits about the bar and asking me a few blunt questions about who I was and why I was sitting at his bar with a notebook in front of me. Finally he seemed to make some kind of calculation and settled down on a stool beside me, now downright verbose in his willingness to satisfy my curiosity about the place.

Evangelo's was the last of the old Santa Fe bars, he told me. Everybody else had sold out as property values shot up from out-of-town money moving in to milk the tourist trade with galleries and shops. But Nick was less and less inclined to follow suit, because as the competition had disappeared, his place had turned into a gold mine. "It's the only place downtown where the real Santa Fe people can go," he remonstrated. "And it will survive for the same reason Santa Fe will. As there is less and less of what makes the magic, there's greater value to what's left—till you get to a point where one way or another, you're apple pie and motherhood."

Santa Fe had felt like a city under siege during the past few decades. "Big money has found Santa Fe," he went on. "Of course we've always had some glamor passing through. But in the seventies we got rich Texans till their oil went bust, then we had the New Yorkers in the eighties till the market crashed, now we're getting the cock-sucking Californians. The money drives up the price of everything—young people can't find housing, and old downtown businesses can't keep up with the rents."

I asked him if that meant that Santa Fe was losing its identity, and before disappearing into a back room for the remainder of my stay that afternoon, he advised me that a Spanish historian named Pedro Ortega liked to drink beer in Evangelo's. He could best answer that question for me.

While I talked with Nick at the bar, I noticed a handsome young black man with reggae-style dreadlocks whom I was sure I had seen somewhere before. He seemed to be noticing me in the same way and finally gestured for me to join him and the woman with whom he was seated at a table near the stairs leading to the pool room. Ramon Isaacs and his girlfriend Dolores, who was from Switzerland, had drifted through a lot of places all over North America before getting snagged by something they couldn't define about Santa Fe. Dolores said, "Santa Fe is the end of the world."

Ramon countered, "No, Taos is the end of the world. Santa Fe is the last way station." Dolores had come here for the space, the sunshine, the spirit, and the mountains. She made silver jewelry. Ramon played in a reggae band.

We spent some time comparing itineraries but couldn't figure out where Ramon and I had met before. Before I left to find some supper, he invited me to come see his band play the following night at another bar, Comme Chez Vous, where he guaranteed I would meet scores of locals.

When I got back to my motel room after supper and asked my portable computer where I had met Ramon Isaacs, it said, "Vancouver, B.C. Drummer in a reggae band, Feb. 14, 1990." I took it as an omen. I had felt a lot of intimidation back East about daring to pick a

first site in my search, and the tourist craziness of the past two days
was not encouraging. But meeting an acquaintance from beautiful
Vancouver here in Santa Fe was one of the little serendipities and
lucky coincidences that are the needles to the travel writer's compass. I
had taken a reading through beer glass and computer hard disk and
determined that, despite the tourist deluge, I was on course.

It took some doing to hold the heading for the next day or so. In
the plaza I picked up discouraging sound bites—an out-of-work Hollywood actress returning to her family ranch: "The real Santa Fe is
found at the dinners of people with grand houses in the foothills"; a
D.C. lobbyist driving cross-country on a beltway getaway: "Santa Fe
used to be the perfect antidote to reality, but not anymore"; and a
saleswoman at one of the expensive shops: "Santa Fe is the capital city
of a third-world country."

Though spectacularly located on the high shoulders of the Rio
Grande Valley, with the peaks of the Sangre de Cristo to the east and
north, Santa Fe was not particularly well-endowed with the downtown
"third places" I was seeking. Besides Evangelo's, which was a little
rough for many people's taste, there was only the upscale Dragon
Room at the Pink Adobe Restaurant on the Old Santa Fe Trail and a
curious place called El Farol over on Canyon Road, the thoroughfare
of artist galleries.

I started Friday evening at Comme Chez Vous, a spiritless restaurant with wall-to-wall carpeting where Ramon Isaacs's reggae band
worked valiantly to fill the void. The consensus seemed to be that for
ordinary people like those assembled here—nurses, construction
workers, teachers, waitresses, service employees, government workers
—Santa Fe was a hard place to live. Middle-class people struggled
mightily to hang on and sometimes wondered why they did it. The
city offered few services—no buses, no trash collection, schools of
widely varying quality depending on the neighborhood in which they
were located, no long-term plan for dealing with the increasingly in-
sufferable tourist-induced traffic problems, no downtown amenities
for residents, no emissions testing for autos because the poor then
couldn't afford cars. Residents did their shopping at widely scattered
locations in malls on the periphery. There was a rising crime problem,
with break-ins becoming increasingly common. And the poor here
had nothing to do but drink and drive. A fellow who overheard one of

these conversations leaned in and said, "You're talking about the disillusionment of Santa Fe."

But despite all of these complaints, the denizens of Comme Chez Vous presented themselves as prime examples of the folk who would struggle mightily to hang on by the fingernails in Santa Fe, often taking second or third jobs in the service industry to bring in the necessary income. Typical was a friend of Ramon's, a divorced mother of three children, who cleaned rooms and made beds at a local hotel every day before her shift as a nurse at the hospital.

"The whole world passes through Santa Fe," she said. "And some of the most interesting and creative people anywhere get hooked and stop off here. Where else could you live in a city that still feels like a small town and meet people that you'd expect to find only in New York or L.A.? It's a place where the cream rises, and in America, that's a rare and good thing."

And others rhapsodized about the land—the enchantment of the New Mexico high country, where the light and altitude and natural austerity taught newcomers to see colors they'd never seen before. If residents of Santa Fe liked it here, I thought, they sure complained a lot before saying so.

At the Dragon Room, a watering hole for decidedly more upscale Californian and New Yorker recent arrivals, I heard more consistently positive sentiments with emphasis on the miracle of Santa Fe's small size and its remoteness from the craziness they had left behind. Here I met Robin West, a recent transplant from the advertising world of Manhattan. Robin and her husband, Jim, an emergency room doctor, had come to Santa Fe as a result of a conscious and meticulous search for a good place to live and were prime examples of the affluent immigration that was driving up the cost of everything for the long-time locals. She wanted to learn to be a good Santa Fean but admitted that she was not off to a very good start. When she returned from a visit to New York, she found no mail in her mailbox. My God, she thought, they steal your mail here. I'll have to get a lock for the box. It turned out that her next-door neighbor had taken in her mail and had even picked up some things for her at the grocery that might come in handy. "People just don't do that for you in Manhattan," said Robin.

The following afternoon, I drove with Ramon and Dolores out to a place that they insisted was pure contemporary Santa Fe: 10,000

Waves, a Japanese establishment with hot tubs that overlooked spectacular mountain views out on the road to the Santa Fe Ski Resort.
There were private tubs where you could go to be alone with a partner
and a public one where strangers soaked naked together. "It breaks
down barriers," Ramon had said. "You might have a hippie outlaw
sitting next to a lawyer or a movie star. People reveal their real selves
in Santa Fe—nothing held back. Ten Thousand Waves makes it
tangible."

We pulled into a dirt parking lot, above which a wooden building
rambled at odd angles and multiple levels around a huge outcropping
of rock. From the road you couldn't see any of the bathers. Inside we
paid our money (eighteen dollars each for the communal tub) and a
young Japanese woman in a kimono guided us to locker rooms, where
we were provided with robes and optional swim suits. Ramon insisted
that we dispense with the briefs and do it right. The tub, located on an
outdoor deck with a spectacular view of the mountains to the east,
was about the size of a small swimming pool and contained half a
dozen cheery patrons, two of them women, all of them probably in
their thirties, none of them wearing the optional cover-ups. Thick
billows of steam rose from the water, and more kimonoed attendants
took orders and brought colorful drinks in nonbreakable glasses right
to the side of the tub.

We dropped our robes and eased our way in. Those already present interrupted their conversations to introduce themselves and ask us
our names, just as might a friendly group at any sociable bar—no
averted eyes or bashfulness whatsoever. All of them were, like Ramon
and Dolores, relative newcomers to Santa Fe. The women were nurses;
three of the men were teachers and one a building contractor.

It was amazing to me how quickly the spell of the hot, bubbling
water, the bracing mountain air, the sense of space in the vista beyond, and the fruity beverages banished whatever inhibitions I might
have had. Soon I was holding forth grandly on the search for a good
place to live. My tubmates thought we should devise some kind of
system for rating the places I visited.

They understood that I didn't want to mimic the systems of the
various published rating guides with measures of the usual concerns
such as good schools, low taxes, low crime rates, affordable housing,
and plentiful jobs. Anyplace, USA, could all too easily score high

under that regime, we decided. The good life was not based on bread alone. And anyway, it seemed plausible that places that were good places to live in a more fundamental sense would find ways to generate good qualities of the conventional sort. Consensus all around the tub.

Instead we turned to the four persistent qualities mentioned by the seekers of good places that I met everywhere I went. First there was that need for social libido characterized by the presence of good "third places" and a feeling of communal openness. We decided to call this the Cheers Factor. Second was the yearning to escape the suburban paradigm with a lifestyle where one could come and go without having to crawl into a private automobile. This would be the Foot Factor. Third was the desire to have one's cake and eat it too concerning the combination of cultural and natural amenities. Thus, the Cake Factor. And finally there was the issue of local identity, uniqueness, and the sense of not being Anyplace, USA. This would be the Someplace Factor.

But there was one conventional concern that we decided I could not duck. A community that measured up to our new set of standards could generate many of the traditional qualities rated in the guides, but good climate could not be created. I feared I might regret this somewhere down the road in some wonderful place that had terrible weather. Nonetheless, we added a Comfort Factor for weather that was moderately warm and dry or seasonally interesting without being uncomfortable.

Last, there was the possibility of surprises—remarkable pluses or minuses resulting from something unanticipated. Since we already had cake, we decided I had better have a Fudge Factor. I would assign ratings to these six factors ranging from one (a failing grade) to five (a perfect score). Thus we devised the 10,000 Waves Alternative Places Rated Scale.

There ensued a spirited debate concerning how to rate Santa Fe. All agreed that for Cake, Someplace, and Comfort the city rated pure fives. But there was no consensus about the others as my tubmates argued over some of the complaints that I had heard the night before. As long, black, late afternoon shadows began to creep up the red mountainside before us and the buzz of the 10,000 Waves experience warmed the very marrow of my bones, I didn't care. At the moment the best place to live in the world was right here in my corner of the convivial hot tub. "Does anyone ever fall asleep and drown in this thing?" I asked Ramon when it finally registered that the other six had gotten out, said their good-byes, and headed home.

I met Pedro Ortega the fifth night in Santa Fe. He was sitting at the bar in Evangelo's wearing a cowboy hat, glasses, a woven vest, denim, and boots, and when I walked in, Nick Klones just nodded toward him. Pedro was fair-skinned, sported a short-cut white beard, and spoke with a slight Spanish accent that got a little thicker as he quenched his thirst. He talked quietly and earnestly and with a patience that suggested a habit of firm command. His family, Ortegas and Riberas, did indeed come to this country from Spain via Mexico in 1598, twenty-one generations ago. They had a mandate: conquer a people and settle. In an imperial policy emulating the Roman legions, Spanish conquistadors of that time were exiled from their homeland once they conquered a new one. It guaranteed their commitment to holding the new additions to the empire.

Though the Spanish intermarried with native peoples throughout the Caribbean, Central America, and South America, the missionaries in central New Mexico forbade unions with the Pueblo people there (I would discover later that the Pueblo had a different explanation for how the segregation was maintained). The result was the fair-skinned Castilian character of many of Santa Fe's Spanish that is the most remarkable first impression about them today. Pedro estimated that there were around 150 families still in Santa Fe who went back that far. They were very "genealogically minded," even if their current station in life was humble, as it was for many. Pedro's family had members in all walks of life, from hotel employees, craftsman wood-carvers, and weavers to teachers, writers, and historians like himself. They were also the founders and owners of Ortega Taco Shells and Mexican Food Products.

I asked him how people with roots like his dealt with the radical force of change. He answered that change was inevitable. "None of this getting angry," Pedro said. "Long-term survivors like us have to be able to roll with the punches." He explained how it had all happened before. "It's a matter of adapting where you can and holding on to what you must. Ortegas have always been bilingual, at least. We depended on the Indians for food, so we became Indianized. We later depended on the Anglos for trade, so we became Anglicized. Today we depend on the tourists for jobs. But always we have remembered who we are—God has granted us our prayer: the patience to accept what we cannot change, the courage to try to change what we cannot accept, and the wisdom to know the difference."

Pedro insisted that the tourist trade insinuated itself as more significant than it really was and cited the retirement community, the art community, and the construction economy as mainstays that were just as important. When I asked what drew people here his answer was instantaneous and firm: "This country has always been a uniquely spiritual natural environment. Like it says on our license plates, the enchantment here is in the land, not the works of man. Even without the history, the religion, the art, the magic remains here. It is in the dirt."

But there were threats to the magic, and they came from humans —erosion was the worst. "It's an austere, unforgiving environment," Pedro said, "where you can't tear down the mountain trees. The animals and flora survive here and show us the way." He was heartened by a proposed city ordinance to prevent construction on the hillsides. "We've aggressively protected the historic areas of town, now we will do the same for the natural surroundings. You destroy thirty to forty piñon and juniper trees for every house built. This will stop." He had a sublime confidence that the city would respond to the challenge. "We have no choice, we have to use our minds. Plus I'm an optimist because of my faith." He recommended that I interview a city councilor named Debbie Jaramillo who was a crusader for preserving Santa Fe for the Santa Feans.

Author of *Christmas in Old Santa Fe* and a dozen historical monographs, Pedro did his work at a 1753 adobe fortress his family owned at Truchas, up in the Sangre de Cristo Mountains. "Washington has been trying to get its hands on the place as a historical monument," he grumbled. "But I tell them, 'I don't want you bastards to come in and ruin it.' " He had turned the place into a historical research center and would spend summers up there until the weather sent him back down to Santa Fe in late fall.

But he considered himself a resident Santa Fean. I asked about all of the new people who wanted to earn that status. "New people can't remain tourists for long," he believed. "They have to be assimilated; it takes about two to three years. You have to be a good person and be proud of who you are. Don't apologize for your own culture. If you are English, don't try to be Spanish, be proud of being English. When you hear my prejudice against the English, stand up to it with dignity and pride and I will respect you more and modify my prejudice. We like people who know who they are."

As the evening wound down, Pedro kept coming back to the question of being a good person. I asked, "What is a good person?"

"One who is willing to listen, to share, to give. Tomorrow I will show you. I will invite you to my house and prepare for you a simple meal and sit with you and listen. That's the best one can do."

It snowed heavily in the mountains that night, and in the morning clouds swept the peaks that towered to the east above Santa Fe while passing drizzles muddied the red dust in the streets. I walked past the row of art galleries on Canyon Road as their proprietors were opening shutters and sweeping off stoops. Well-dressed men and women walking well-fed dogs stopped now and again to chat. Fires of piñon wood had already infused their nearly smokeless scent in the otherwise pristine mountain air, delighting the nose. Downtown, with its shops and gaudy tourists, seemed miles away rather than just blocks.

Before going to Pedro Ortega's house for lunch, I wandered into the Linda Durham Gallery, a large Victorian brick house on the corner of Canyon and Garcia, and there sat Linda Durham herself, ready to schmooze with buyers. I had already heard several references to her as the epitome of success in the Santa Fe gallery world. Linda was tall, flamboyantly red-haired, spangled with noisy, heavy jewelry, which she readjusted regularly as she struck dramatic poses in conversation on her divan, and dressed in a short, tight-fitting red skirt. But the art on her walls was even more outrageous. Perhaps she presented herself as she did to be able to coexist with the kind of work she sold.

"Call me a world-class adventurer," she said when I asked her about herself. In another life she had been a New Yorker working in theater, in television, and as one of the original Playboy bunnies. She married a man who brought her here to a ranchette on a quarter section in 1966. They had kids before they divorced, and now Linda was eternally grateful to the man for bringing her to a place where she could pursue her great adventure and then releasing her to do it.

"But when I first came here, I wasn't so positive. I felt like a fish out of water," she said. "I couldn't imagine how people here didn't know what they were missing—Santa Fe was pretty provincial in those days. I didn't think I could survive without the theater, the *New York Times,* the bright lights and action. But I changed and so did Santa Fe."

The change for Linda was learning how to see, and that was what led her to the world of art. "I started out thinking everything here was shades of brown—depressing, lifeless. Then I was out hiking in the desert one day and suddenly I saw it—lavender, orange, yellow, magenta. The colors were there all along, of course, but I didn't have the visual language to apprehend them. When I weaned myself from New York, the earth shifted. I learned to be visually hungry—to see all of the things you don't see in New York."

She still needed the New York connection for a time, but eventually the trips back became more and more infrequent. She rattled off some of the cultural amenities that had accumulated: the Santa Fe Symphony, the Orchestra of Santa Fe, the Santa Fe Opera, half a dozen ensemble and chamber music groups, several concert series organizations attracting world-class talent, the Prince State Ballet, the New Mexico Repertory Theater, and more than a dozen other dramatic or performing arts theaters. "Where else could you live in a city of fifty-some thousand, light years from a big city, and have all that?" Linda asked.

Santa Fe's art galleries, whose tradition traced back to the beginnings of the century, experienced a boom during the years when Linda was making her name, and her success followed, more or less, that of the art world here as a whole. But her specialty was still unique. "My artists do not fit the mold of Santa Fe art," she insisted. "Though the traditionalists do wonderful stuff that transcends the kitsch of the old days, people come in here and say, 'My god, we're in Santa Fe and look what we're seeing.'"

As she guided me through the art in her rooms, Linda stressed that there was a lot of variety in the contemporary work hanging on her walls. "But what they all have in common is the willingness to take extraordinary risks to create something that never existed before." One piece that candidly demonstrated the theme of Linda's gallery was a sculpture of a ladybug, realistic in every detail except that the wings opened up on hinges to reveal an intricately furnished dollhouse interior.

We talked about some other places Linda had lived and the type of vision they provoked. She had spent some time in Charlottesville, Virginia, one of the places on my itinerary. "The woods there are nice to walk in," she said, "but you can't see far. Seeing far creates expansiveness—physically, emotionally, and spiritually."

Virginia was a disappointment to her after having spent some time in my own New England. "New England, of course, has the same problem of trees and not being able to see far as Virginia [does], but the winter is a compensation. Cutting firewood and then burning it in your fireplace while the snow piles up outside changes all of the rules of seeing. You learn to see inward and turn introspective." Of course, Santa Fe was superior to either place because you could have that introspective winter experience here as well as the experience of seeing differently and for great distances.

I asked Linda if she thought that the boom she had participated in threatened the magic of Santa Fe. Echoing Pedro Ortega, she answered, "The magic resides in the dirt and won't die. But it can be endangered—by things like ersatz adobe houses, the proliferation of T-shirt galleries, the overlay of the tourist superficiality." She was concerned about the tourist trade's tendency to homogenize, about people who come in and aren't happy unless they can find a McDonald's—or, for that matter, a Talbot's or an Ann Taylor.

On a larger scale, she feared that as Americans we were losing the sense of being a nation of individuals: "That's why I live in Santa Fe, because it's one of the last places where you can still be an individual —where you have to be. The homogenizing thing here is still just tourists, not the people who live here yet. It still takes a daring person to live here, and as long as that's the way it is, I'll be here and happy to be here."

I left Linda to pursue the business of selling something to a man from California who had come in during our conversation. As I walked to Pedro Ortega's house on Garcia Street just a few blocks up the hill from the galleries of Canyon Road, the cool, damp grip of the early spring day and the scent of burning piñon from the chimneys turned my seeing inward, just as Linda had said New England winters did. The houses in these neighborhoods were surrounded by traditional vine-covered adobe walls, but their gates, more often than not, stood open and conveyed mental images of domestic interiors connected to, not isolated from, the surrounding community. I liked that; but still, when I tried to picture myself living here, I realized with trepidation what a huge leap of daring was involved in the decision to pick a place and move there without any of the traditional inducements and securities. I decided I would look up Robin West, the recent New York transplant, and visit her and her husband at their home as soon as I could.

Pedro's house was small, humble, and set back behind others more grandly fronting the street. Pedro welcomed me formally and led me into his kitchen, the only room he kept warm enough for company on days like this. The rooms had the cluttered look of the place of a man living alone—papers and books on the tables in layers, spices and cooking utensils scattered on the countertop, sweatshirts and jackets hanging from hooks on the doors.

When I mentioned the delightful smell of piñon in the air today, he explained that the Spanish believed that piñon was one of the few softwoods worthy of burning for heat. Piñon trees looked very much like junipers but were somewhat smaller. He didn't know whether the wood really created more heat than other softwoods; perhaps the ambience it radiated did as much to warm a person as did real Btus. He offered me some piñon nuts—brown and pistachiolike with a musky taste almost like coffee. The Indians showed his ancestors how to harvest these by shaking the tree and gathering those with the right color.

While Pedro cooked at the stove, he told me a story about Spanish pride. The emperor Charles V was known as a master of many languages, and this caused a problem for members of his court, who were always asking him which language they should speak in his presence. After a day particularly heavy with such inquiries, he took them aside and explained, " 'I like English for the hunt, it is a blunt language worthy of the chase and good for commanding the dogs. When I whisper to my lover, I use French, it is the language of love. When I address my cook, I speak Italian, the language of food and pleasure of the senses. But when I talk to God, I have to speak Spanish.'

"That is how one should feel about his own culture and language, whether it's Spanish, English, African, whatever," Pedro believed. The loss of cultural identity was the great tragedy in the otherwise magnificent American adventure. He was not a fan of the myth of the melting pot. "Nothing is worse than people who have no roots in tradition or their past. So many Americans actually work at denying their pasts or trying to escape them by accumulating wealth or power. When you have no basis for your pride, you do terrible things."

For lunch Pedro had made "New Mexican spaghetti" with tuna and ground chilies, and spinach sauteed with onions, garlic, bacon, and more chilies. He explained that the Spanish palate was very demanding of vegetables and that nearly all of the vegetables he cooked had to be prepared this way in order to have enough flavor to satisfy.

He showed me a Baggie of freshly ground chilies, bought from a local market. It was dark, deep red with a pungent earthy aroma. "We couldn't have survived here in North America without [the] chili," he said. "The chili and the tomato are brother and sister, so we put them together." But he emphasized that there was a difference between Mexican food and New Mexican cooking. "First of all, the soil of northern New Mexico gives our chilies a different flavor, richer and more nutlike, so that we can even use it without the tomato, as I have with the spinach. And second, we apply the traditional Mexican flavors to a wider range of American foodstuffs—things that are not essentially Mexican or Spanish, like potatoes or spinach."

We bowed our heads and Pedro prayed before eating. Even more important to Pedro than food, or his Spanish heritage, was his religion. It was an integrated part of every moment of his life, and he strove to emulate St. Francis. "My goal is to die poor, and I am achieving my dream very quickly." Besides passing on his wealth and property to the church and the next generation of Ribera-Ortegas, Pedro believed that, as a historian, he served God by forging a link between people and their past.

We ate in silence, and afterward he said, "Everything changes; that's why it is so important that there be people like us Santa Fe Spanish, who maintain human continuity." Pedro believed that his Indian brothers, the Pueblo, were another people who had accomplished the same thing: "They are still the same people my ancestors met twenty-one generations ago." They had survived better than other native North American nations, such as the Navajo, because they still lived where they always had and kept their traditions sacrosanct.

It was raining more heavily outside when I left Pedro on his doorstep. I asked him which Santa Fe season he liked best. "Spring, today," he answered without hesitation. "This rain is blessed. But the buds on the trees remind you that you have to let go of every season and that it's smart to love summer more. It will soon turn dry and warm and then summer will be best, until autumn, which is better still. Of course, then winter and Christmas in Santa Fe will be the best of all, until spring, when we'll get this blessed rain again."

It was a catechism of the faith of a survivor.

Much as I was learning that the real Santa Fe existed away from the plaza, I kept drifting back there after every foray into more remote locales. One afternoon when the rain had stopped and the clouds broke up, revealing larger cones of white on the peaks of the Sangre de Cristo, where winter was not yet ready to yield, I again strolled the plaza, drawn by its superficial magnetism, and sat for a while on one of the benches opposite the portico of the Governor's Palace. A woman about my age and her teenage daughter were seated near me, and I couldn't help overhearing their conversation. The woman had the long dark hair and fair complexion that Pedro had told me were characteristic of the Santa Fe Spanish, like himself, with deep roots.

The daughter was earnestly seeking her mother's help in dealing with a dilemma: at fifteen, she was sure she was the last virgin in her grade at school. She had felt she could deal with it as long as it was only a peer pressure issue, but now she was experiencing—and here she paused and searched for the right word—". . . a hunger . . . Mom, I'm getting really horny."

The two suddenly began giggling and then noticed me listening and laughed even harder. "Do you have a teenage daughter?" the woman said to me.

"I do, two of them."

"Well, Father, what should I say to her?"

Maria Braun, still bearing the name of the German husband from whom she was now legally separated, was indeed Spanish and very Santa Fe. Her father had brought her up in Mexico while he pursued "a playboy life," which Maria believed included running drugs, but she never knew for sure. Her mother had then brought her to Santa Fe to get away from him, and she had since lived in Spain, Portugal, and South America. But Santa Fe was home.

We chatted for a while about the effect that place had on raising kids. Her daughter wanted to know what the kids were like in New Hampshire. We concluded that the problems of drugs, drinking, premature sex, and peer pressure were pretty much universal. But Maria insisted, and her daughter agreed, that Santa Fe at least provided different paths that pressured kids could turn to: the mountains, the desert, the different native and Spanish cultures. "Do your kids in New Hampshire have all that?" she wanted to know.

I couldn't say that they did.

The daughter soon spotted some of her peers and tripped off with them, telling her mother that she would be home by eleven. "Have you been to El Farol yet?" Maria asked me. I hadn't, and so we agreed to meet there that evening for tapas.

El Farol was a low wood-frame-and-adobe building on Canyon Road that had been there since 1835 and had functioned alternately as a barber shop, a hardware store, a liquor store, a cathouse, and now a bar and restaurant. It was rustic, with a softwood plank bar, 1920s vintage glass cabinets, a bartender wearing a sailor's uniform, and a large German shepherd lying in the middle of the floor. We were met at the door by owner David Salazar, who was happy to sit with us and tell us stories of the tapas, El Farol, and Santa Fe.

David Salazar had come to Santa Fe from the small northern town of Hernandez, where Ansel Adams shot one of his most famous photographs, and took credit for reviving El Farol's modern reputation with the tapas menu. Four hundred years ago, drinkers of sweet wine in Spain had a problem: the little Iberian flies would be attracted to the wine and find a way to drown themselves in it while the drinker's attention was distracted by conversation. You could drink fast, or hold your hand over the glass, or try to wave them away and risk spillage. Then some enterprising hosts devised the trick of serving toasted slices of bread to place as tops—tapas—on the glasses of wine to keep out the flies. The practice caught on, and soon chefs were decorating the toast with toppings, providing not only fly protection but hors d'oeuvres, which became immensely popular. Rival chefs competed through the creativity of their toppings until some were concocting dishes that didn't fit on top of a wineglass. Eventually the tapas evolved into the tradition of "little dishes" that had nothing to do with a piece of toast or a wineglass. Diners would make a meal out of a communally shared combination of half a dozen or more of them.

For our tapas meal we chose oysters and mushrooms, snails and garlic, ham and rice, curry chicken, beans and mesquite beef, and a quesadilla. David brought us his house version of the traditional sweet Spanish wine and a musician played Spanish and sixties folk music on guitar. It had become drippy again outside, but inside, the music, the scent of the piñon in the fireplace, and the dramatically varied flavors of the tapas provoked a spirit of conviviality and civility that contrasted sharply with the rough edges and high-alcohol sheen of Evangelo's. The patrons wore the same earth colors and coarse textures as the folks at Evangelo's, but nobody was on the make here. Everyone danced to music that was never really meant for dancing, and David kept coming back to our table to pour more wine and tell me more stories of the Spanish experience of Santa Fe.

Like Pedro, he insisted that the secret to Santa Fe's resilience in a world of change was the force of continuity. That's why he brought the ancient tapas menu to El Farol before it became a national culinary fad and why he provided an atmosphere that people could come back to and count on being the same as it was a year ago.

During the Carter administration David had left New Mexico to work as assistant secretary of agriculture. He thought he was just one of many Hispanic New Mexicans who had gone into the world beyond the mountains, seen what was out there, and been drawn back with a sense of mission to perform in Santa Fe.

He explained that the members of old Spanish families here often had very little but their heritage, that a chambermaid at my motel might be a fifteenth-generation descendant of an imperial governor. "They haven't bought into the American dream of living on credit and depending on the talents of others—they build their own houses, fix their own cars and drive them till they're decrepit, barter for what they can't do for themselves, and work in the service sector, government, or Los Alamos, since they don't have the land they need to do what their heritage has prepared them for." But a curious recompense

for the loss of their ancient land and money had appeared. Many of
the moneyed Anglo "movers" in town had become connected by marriage with some of the old families.

After we left El Farol that evening, Maria showed me the house she
and her husband had built themselves on a hill overlooking the lights
of the city, just a few blocks from the plaza. She fit the description of
the local Spanish that David had presented, right down to the bit
about marrying Anglo, or in this case German, money. She confessed
that her divorce gave her the chance to have it both ways. Now if she
could only find a lovable Spanish man.

I went the next afternoon to visit Robin West and her husband,
Jim, at their house on Garcia Street, just a few blocks from Pedro
Ortega's place. Like Pedro's, their house was set back behind houses
immediately on the street, but theirs was huge and finished with all of
the right amenities—not the abode of a follower of St. Francis. They
sat me down in an airy, white-walled sunroom and poured me some
tea. Jim West had grown up in an Oklahoma small town, completed
his medical training in Wisconsin, San Francisco, and Kansas City,
and then married and settled in New York. "I was a boy from the
prairie who wanted to immerse myself in the Big Apple, the city that
never sleeps, all that stuff. But it was wrong right from the start." The
marriage lasted a year.

He might have left New York then, but he met Robin. They dated
for six years, married, and then stayed there five more years. She
worked in advertising, came from a New York family, and regarded
any place beyond New Jersey as primitive territory. "When I saw the
city's emergency medical system where I worked breaking down," Jim
explained, "it was emblematic of what I had always sensed about the
whole city. I wanted out." Together he and Robin embarked on a
search for a good place to live.

Where to go. They eliminated suburbs right off, certain that Robin
would go stark raving crazy in such sterility. The only other cities they
could countenance were San Francisco and Washington, D.C., and
they didn't want to be isolated out in the country in some small town.
"But the possibility of particularly unique small cities intrigued us,"
Jim went on. "We wanted a tolerant attitude, a certain liberalism,
good countryside, physical attractiveness, some nightlife, a decent

bookstore or two, theater would be nice, and the climate had to be moderate."

They thought about New England but "never got a warm feeling there." They couldn't think of anyplace down South beyond Charlottesville, Virginia. The rain of the Northwest turned them off. Texas was full of Texans. It came down to Santa Fe, Charlottesville, and a small city midway between San Francisco and L.A., San Luis Obispo, which happened to be the next stop on my itinerary. "We checked out SLO and really liked it—though climate hadn't originally been a big factor, we had no idea how good a climate could be till we spent some time there." But a job opportunity for Jim brought them to Santa Fe.

"We found that buying a lot or a house in town was pretty expensive," Robin said. "And we hated the 'Happy Valley' developments on the outskirts with the fake adobe. Gave me the creeps." But they discovered that renting in town was the secret to living in Santa Fe. At half of what they had paid for an Upper East Side apartment in Manhattan, they found this huge real adobe house just off Canyon Road and within walking distance of the square.

Initially Jim was nervous about being trapped in a regime of trendiness. "I was afraid we'd be surrounded by neighbors with crystals and horoscopes," he recalled. "We heard that the woman next door had done interior decorating for Jane Fonda. But she turned out to be a casual earth mother type whose own house needed a decorator." The most difficult adjustment was living among people who considered it an insult if you didn't walk into their house once a day.

Jim concluded that Santa Fe was turning out to be what San Francisco used to be, "a last refuge for characters and eccentrics—people who just don't fit in anywhere else"—and he liked that just fine. Robin seemed to agree, but the New Yorker in her was still strong. I told her about Pedro Ortega's belief that the true Santa Fean is one who becomes part of the community without losing the identity she brought with her. She liked that and said she would invite this man to dinner soon.

By the end of my visit, I asked them about the anxiety I had felt that day walking to Pedro's house, at the prospect of pulling up roots and moving to a place simply because it was a good place. "You're not ready yet," said Jim. "When you are, you won't feel that way."

Jim had one lingering concern, "the possibility that there might be some other place even better. If you get to San Luis Obispo and it's better, don't call, don't write. I don't want to know."

It was time to meet the mayor. I had devised a rule for these travels about dealing with local politicians: never talk to them until you feel like you've gotten inside the place without their help. Otherwise they have you at their mercy. A corollary of this rule is that you visit chambers of commerce only to collect printed matter; never talk to anyone there.

Mayor Sam Pick looked, talked, and gestured like a Texan—a real western kind of guy—right from the moment I walked into his office. He saw himself as an unabashed promoter of the greater glory of Santa Fe "and I don't apologize to anyone for it. Oh, I get some flak, but I keep on winning."

Economic development was the goal as far as the mayor was concerned. "People worry about preserving the character of Santa Fe, and so do I," he argued. "But how can you hope to do that without a robust, growing local economy? We don't have a lot beyond tourism right now." Pick pointed to the relocation of *Outside* magazine from Chicago to Santa Fe as the kind of return he wanted on his investment in promotional work.

His nemeses in Santa Fe were the "close-the-door-behind-me" people from New York and California who formed an "unholy alliance" with radical Hispanics like City Councilor Debbie Jaramillo, whom he accused of unfairly injecting a racial issue into local politics that wasn't there naturally. "I don't buy that Hispanics have been pushed aside by our promotional efforts. I want to keep the Spanish here by providing low-income housing and jobs. People complain that the downtown has been lost to the Spanish, but it was actually Jewish and Greek before the big tourist boom anyway. The Spanish always had the government jobs and still do, and [they] always were a minority in business."

Pick didn't believe that the promotion of tourism had disrupted the identity of the community. "It's difficult to get other kinds of industry in here, like electronics, for instance," he said. "There's the cost of land, the lack of the right kind of workforce, our transportation is considered inadequate. So we dance with who we brought." He conceded that the downtown had changed radically in the last ten years. It used to cater more to locals, but Pick maintained that people's shopping habits had changed. "Those who complain don't realize that the average American housewife would rather go to a mall to shop," he figured. "Sam Walton has changed the way Western cities work."

The mayor wanted me to understand that the city was sensitive to the issue of uncontrolled growth. The rate had been maintained at about 2 percent per year largely through building regulation. The Santa Fe style of architecture was protected within the city by strict ordinance. A new escarpment ordinance would protect ridge tops from harmful development. And, he said, "[although] we can't do rent control, because that's not the free enterprise system, we do have ways to encourage developers to build affordable housing." Santa Fe's water supply was in considerably better shape than that in much of the Southwest, and the Growth Management Task Force was charged with keeping it that way. And even the much-maligned downtown had world-class museums, churches, and remnant hangouts like Evangelo's and restaurants like Tía Sophía's that would keep the Santa Fe identity intact.

"There's one more thing that the people who want to close the door forget," he added. "It has been newcomers to Santa Fe like themselves who have traditionally identified what we ought to preserve, what we are doing wrong that is done better elsewhere—and you don't get new people if you don't have growth."

"What about those who have been here for generations?" I asked him.

"Well, I don't really have as much of a problem with them, they think they're protecting their heritage. There." He laughed, gesturing that the interview was over. "That's nicer than anything Debbie Jaramillo will say about me when you talk to her."

I went to the home of City Councilor Debbie Jaramillo for coffee the next morning. She and her husband, a vigorous couple in the prime of their lives, had spent ten years building with their own hands the beautiful adobe house they lived in on a southerly hillside in an old barrio on Bob Street. Like Maria Braun and hundreds of other residents of Spanish descent in Santa Fe, this was the way the Jaramillos got themselves a home of a quality beyond the meager earnings that they and many of their fellows could make here. Their project was different from the hand-built enterprises of back-to-the-landers (like myself in one phase of my life). These people had always made their own homes here, for fifteen generations.

The house combined traditional Spanish rooms and interior decor with modern architecture and technology. It had passive solar collectors with heating pipes embedded in the tile floor. The most difficult trick of the design was to conceal the hot water pipes in walls built around exposed wooden beams. There were gallery rooms flooded with sunlight from high southerly windows and others nearly windowless to create the deliberate interior darkness that the Santa Feans prized equally for its sense of domestic retreat.

"It was the house that started it all," Jaramillo said as she showed me around. As good jobs became scarce and taxes and the general cost of living went up, many of her Spanish-descended brethren had been forced to sell homes they had put their lives into and move to cheap housing or mobile homes in little towns out in the country. "I said, 'No, I won't do that. This is my city. I'll run for office instead.'"

Debbie Jaramillo's insurgency just about coincided with the past dozen years of Santa Fe's boom growth. Before that the city had what she called a "healthy intracommunity growth" and a traditionally slow rate of overall evolution. But the eighties changed all that: a mayor's committee of the national League of Cities voted Santa Fe America's best small city to live in; Mayor Pick was elected; and the assault was on. Speaking as if she were a Pueblo, she said, "This time we were conquered by money and education." Until 1990 Jaramillo was the lone vote on the city council against what was going on.

Santa Fe needed growth but had gotten the wrong kind—all geared toward wealth. Rents went up, and the Spanish population began moving out, often back to ancestral towns like Hernández or bastions of cheap housing like Rio Rancho. The 1990 census showed the Hispanics to be a minority for the first time in the history of Santa Fe.

A large mall on the south end killed the mom-and-pop stores downtown. The last one was a barber and boot repair shop that closed because of increased rents last summer. There were petitions and editorials and call-ins to the radio shows, but all to no avail. "Then in come the galleries and Ann Taylor, never mind the architectural ordinances," Jaramillo said. "People say we lost our downtown, but I say we gave it away. We painted it brown but moved the brown people out."

For the Spanish families that did manage to hang on, life in Santa Fe had become a matter of dwindling expectations: "It's not the Spanish way to compete for the almighty dollar," Jaramillo explained. Working in government used to be the route to comfort for Spanish-descended residents till pay increases of 1 and 2 percent began lagging far behind cost-of-living increases of 7 to 10 percent. Many ended up in service jobs. "They move out of town and commute to clean bathrooms," she said.

Ironically, though, it was largely the influx of newcomers that had enabled Jaramillo's insurgency to become the threat that so concerned Mayor Pick. "It never was a Spanish versus Anglo thing," she explained. "Sure the goal was to keep the Spanish able to live and thrive here. But some of the Anglo newcomers, the ones Mayor Pick calls the close-the-door people, recognized that we are the heart and soul of what attracted them here in the first place." Thus Jaramillo's basic Hispanic constituency was bolstered by a large bloc of well-heeled Anglo votes. "It drives Sam crazy." Now the council was evenly split between the mayor's and Jaramillo's supporters. Only two members were Anglo. For the moment the mayor still ruled because he voted to break ties.

There were other newcomers who were a problem: "It's those in the gated communities who contribute nothing but their tax—who come here once or twice a month from L.A. to breathe some fresh air, who bring their BMWs but not their banks or businesses."

The fundamental plank in the insurgent platform was to replace the old anything-goes growth mentality with a procommunity mentality that would attract developers interested in making money while contributing to the community. Debbie pointed to the example of a genetics company, Vivigen, that came in and opened a child-care program for its employees, offered on-site technical training to bring local workers up to speed, and provided expanded health coverage on its own initiative. "City hall should be trumpeting this company's praises," she said. "Instead Sam Pick compliments himself on stealing *Outside* magazine from Chicago when we have no idea yet what kind of neighbor they are going to be."

Jaramillo recognized that she was wrestling with intangibles that presented a daunting public relations struggle. She was trying to tone down her "anti-everything" image with the press by going out to realtor dinners and service club socials and chamber of commerce events. After one speaking engagement, a local businessman came up to her and said, "After what I had read about you, I expected you to have horns. But you're alright. You just want to save the soul of the city."

At the end of our talk, I suggested that her successes seemed to vindicate Pedro Ortega's passive faith that everything would be OK. She knew Pedro, of course, and had tremendous respect for him. "But that's part of our Spanish problem. The church has taught us a kind of complacency that our people misapprehend. It teaches us to turn the other cheek, but it didn't say to lay down and die. Sure, God will provide, but he gave us a brain to use."

My last day in Santa Fe, I bought a silver bracelet and hair pin for one of my daughters and then sat down beside the vendor on the stone floor under the portico of the Governor's Palace. Glenn Paquin grinned and offered me his heavy hand. He was a handsome fellow with his long black hair held back by a pin similar to the one I had just bought.

We talked and I asked him about Pedro Ortega's belief that the Pueblo were the least disrupted of all Native Americans, and he agreed that it was true, though he didn't give the credit to the Spanish. "Our women wouldn't go with them. And we Pueblos have always had a very conservative, very diplomatic philosophy of life. We always had to live with the aggressive Navajos, even before the Spanish came." Though they could be very tenacious in defending their homes, the Pueblos were never great warriors, and they knew it. "So we never subscribed to the individualist ethic that became the American way, nor to the warrior-hero version of so many other native nations that amounted to the same thing." It was tribal communalism that enabled them to preserve their cultural bonds and resist the corruptions that have decimated other nations.

Glenn believed that the conservative, communal character of the Pueblo was evident in the craft art on display here under the portico. "It is austere, like our way of living, less flamboyant and egocentric than the heavier Navajo work," he explained. "Just stone and silver from our native earth, put together in patterns that represent our way of living on it—like sculptures of Native American existence."

Glenn hadn't always made his living as an artisan selling his wares under the portico. After graduation from the University of New Mexico, he worked in law and order, directed a Head Start program, and then became active in Indian affairs.

"But I was looking to do something different and authentic," he explained. "I wanted to pass on our tradition and be a good example to my children." He had found all of the usual factors of job satisfaction here under the portico. "It is a good place to talk; I've had good talk with people from all over the world here. The world comes to me. And then they walk away with a piece of my life in their hands." He'd been here now for thirteen years and believed he had a happiness that you couldn't measure in terms of money. I asked him if he thought Santa Fe was a good place to live. He replied that it was certainly a good place to live near, and he thanked history for plunking it down right next to his family's millennia-old home ground.

I drove out of Santa Fe on the high road under a big sky filled with exploding white clouds that looked like gods. On the ground were colors that initially struck me as red and green—the red of the rocks and soil, the dark green of the low junipers and piñon, and the lighter, almost beige green of the sage and mesquite. But ten miles out of town, where the colors were draped over ragged hills, canyons, and arroyos, I could also see magentas, blues, and yellows vibrating like peyote auras in the margins between the more obvious hues. I stopped several times to try to identify the individual sources of these other colors and did find little flowers and small shrubs that weren't really recognizable in the panoramic perspective. But some of the colors vanished when I tried to approach them along the roadside—nothing more than the interplay of the light with the fundamental reds and greens.

As I drove, I tried out the good place rating scheme we had devised at 10,000 Waves. As a relatively closed community (which it had to be to survive the tourist onslaught) not particularly well-endowed with third places and whose downtown was owned by tourists, Santa Fe rated only a two for Cheers.

The city wasn't exactly a refuge from the automobile, either. Too many neighborhoods had been built on the outskirts and there was no public transit system. But there were fine old neighborhoods like Garcia Street and modest barrios like Jaramillo's enclave within walking distance of the heart of town, so I gave it a three for Foot Factor.

For Cake, Someplace, and Comfort, Santa Fe got fives—indeed, it would become the standard against which I measured all other places on those scales. I thought it was quite possible that I would never find another place in America that combined flourishing culture, spectacular landscape, and ravishing climate with such a profoundly rooted sense of place.

That's why Santa Fe held on to a slot in the good place seekers' shortlists, despite its poor Cheers Factor, a flaw that would eventually eliminate other places as I learned more about the importance and potential of public downtown living. But Santa Fe was still an original in a nation where such a thing was antithetical to the prevailing national spirit. It showed the power of roots to hold a sense of place against winds of change, profit, and exploitation. It had been a good place to begin, but it was not representative of the places where I would spend my time for the next two years.

At least not at the time of my visit. I telephoned Debbie Jaramillo one morning in March of 1994. Her answering machine clicked on and I heard her voice saying, "Congratulations! We did it. Thanks to one and all." I called again later and reached Jaramillo herself.

"I heard your message," I said. "Are you mayor?"

"Yes, I am," she said. "Officially as of seven o'clock last Tuesday. We're going to reclaim Santa Fe for the Santa Feans. We're going to bring it all back home."

Add a Fudge Factor of four or five.

2

HOTEL CALIFORNIA

In every western place I visited, I found the story of southern Californians immigrating in numbers enough and with money enough to cause disruptions in the local quality of life and a widespread prejudice against them as a group. Despite its continued glamorization by Hollywood, southern California generally was one of the places people were abandoning, every bit as much as New York or Detroit. Many of those southern Californians who were so reviled for invading other places were of course prime participants themselves in the last migration. But these people were widely believed to have a bad habit of bringing with them the very values that had turned their old homes into places from which to flee.

And yet there was one unspoiled jewel literally in southern California's northern backyard. San Luis Obispo, a small city of about 55,000, is sited in a notch of the Coast Range near the Pacific shore exactly midway between San Francisco and Los Angeles, four and a half hours' drive from each.

The first fact of San Luis Obispo's attractiveness was climate—by just about everybody's statistical rule, it was the best in America: little rain or cloudiness, no snow, summer highs around eighty, winter in the mid sixties, and clean, smogless air. San Simeon, the site chosen by

William Randolph Hearst for his paradise castle and immortalized as Xanadu in the film *Citizen Kane,* was near here. So too were California's best uncrowded beaches: Pismo, Avila, and Morro Bay.

San Luis Obispo's second virtue was its reputation for taking a very different path with regard to growth from most southern California places. It had leaped very quickly from obscurity to stardom and then suddenly clamped on the regulatory brakes to keep itself at that stage. I would find other places further down the road where the task was to find ways to stimulate certain kinds of growth. But SLO was hot enough that its negative antigrowth stance was actually a place-shaping proposition, like the pruning of an extravagantly growing hedge.

Besides the recommendation of Robin and Jim West of Santa Fe and many other seekers, G. Scott Thomas had put SLO on my map with his number-one rating in *Life in America's Small Cities,* based largely on its spectacular score for climate but also on strong ratings in all of the conventional considerations except for proximity to a large urban center. Somehow the trash-and-burn development of the Sun Belt migration of the late seventies and early eighties had missed SLO. What attracted people here was plainly and simply the hope of renewing the California dream at one of the last unspoiled sites where it might be possible to prevent the nightmare of southern California's sprawl, auto congestion, materialism, pollution, and nasty demographics.

I had been here before, as had anyone who ever traveled on Amtrak's Coast Starlight, which made a stop here long enough for passengers to step off the train, take a hit of sun and clean air, and prick their fingers on the cacti that grow along the tracks by the charming Spanish stucco station. From San Francisco and the north, you ride through the green irrigated agricultural country of the Salinas River valley—hundreds of miles of broccoli and spinach and lettuce. Then the tracks turn west, climbing through the tan, dry mounds of the Coast Range and descending through several tight horseshoe curves into a crack between the mountains that widens into a platform, where things turn green again. The wide streets and stylish, tile-roofed buildings of SLO come as a bit of a surprise after the long stretch of rural empty spaces.

If you approach from L.A. and the south, the effect is even more impressive. After Santa Barbara the tracks run on the cliffs above miles of empty beaches past Point Conception and along the barren shoreline of Vandenberg Air Force Base. Then the train rounds a rocky promontory and rises through the foothills of the Coast Range until suddenly it skirts a mountain and slows for the stop at SLO. Despite a five-year drought, the city arrives like an oasis. Take a 365-day growing season and add people, and things turn up green, even when there isn't much water.

Besides greenery, SLO astonished me with its melange of curious architecture. Of course there was the Spanish style in the old Mission San Luis Obispo de Tolosa and a scattering of adobes. But there was also a significant number of Victorian structures, many sided with clapboards painted in bright primary colors and some fitted out with New Orleans–style ironwork. There were whimsical pastel-colored art deco buildings dating from the 1950s, such as the marqueed Fremont Theater, and granite block churches reminiscent of New England. And finally, a handful of downtown buildings had recently been redeveloped with an overscaled style that I had seen in shopping malls, in big-name theme parks, and here and there in other fashionably renovated downtowns—I call it "theme mall monumental."

In all, I found this a pleasant mix, despite the out-of-scale stuff, delighting the eye with surprise at the turning of every corner and lending the town a through-the-looking-glass quality of pleasing dissonance. In the heart of the downtown, there was more automobile traffic than I would have liked, to be sure, but it was balanced by a healthy density of pedestrians bustling about at almost all hours of the day, the prime measure of the health of urban areas according to writers like William Whyte and Jane Jacobs. And no matter where you were in town, you had only to raise your eyes to see the streetscape framed by the sugar-loaf shoulders of San Luis Mountain and Bishop Peak.

I was also impressed by SLO's chamber of commerce brochure. Not only was it composed by someone who could write in complete, even sonorous English sentences, it also expressed a philosophy unlike any chamber of commerce tract I had ever seen. Though it had become common usage for chamber literature to make token abstract statements about the community's efforts to preserve its quality of life, usually the thrust was still toward growth dynamism and enterprise opportunity. Not so in SLO, where the chamber theme was firmly and unequivocally about preservation and conservation, not only of lands but of buildings.

> After World War II, when many places became sprawling suburbias laced with freeway networks, shopping centers and fast-food outlets, we took a different route. We preserved our open spaces. We didn't carve up our beautiful peaks and open our farmland into subdivisions. . . . We didn't demolish our distinctive commercial buildings and homes. . . .
>
> It wasn't easy. Many times it would have been . . . more cost effective to tear down and start from scratch, to pave instead of plant, to wreck instead of restore. . . .
>
> Many cities are just now becoming aware of the need to live in balance with their surroundings. San Luis Obispo always has. We know we have a beautiful environment. We preserve it, we protect it, we celebrate it!

They didn't talk like that in the chambers of commerce where I came from.

A less agreeable element in first impressions of SLO was the citywide smoking ban. There was actually an ordinance in place prohibiting smoking indoors anywhere in the city except for the privacy of one's own home. It wasn't that I felt a personal need to smoke so much as it was a sense that the absolute ban signaled a hostile political correctness—an intolerant mean-spiritedness that ran contrary to the accepting and nonjudgmental community values I sought.

I was wrong of course, as I should have been able to tell that first Friday evening from the liveliness of so many good third places in the heart of the downtown. There was Linnae's Coffee Shop, with its alternative lifestyle patrons and their earnest conversations; the Earthling Bookstore, where readers congregated around an open hearth and guitar players wandered in to sit down and quietly pluck their strings; the Network, an outdoor plaza where a demographic cross section gathered to eat and drink and listen to live folk-rock; the SLO Brewing Company, whose brew master and chef were good enough to make the place extremely popular despite its upstairs location; and a score of other thriving bars, cafés, and restaurants along and just off the main drag, Higuera Street. Eventually I found that the antismoking ordinance actually aided in the social process, especially in a place where people spent so much of their time out of doors. Outside every establishment there were little knots of smokers always open to the spontaneous entrée of a friend or a stranger asking for a light.

The second day of my visit, a strange thing happened in San Luis Obispo. It rained. I was curious to see how people in such an arid place reacted to rain, and I was surprised that they did not take to the streets to splash around in it. Instead they did what everyone everywhere did when it rained, though perhaps enjoying it more. They hunkered down in their homes and withdrew into a domestic mode. It made sense, really, people used to living out in the streets under warm sun rediscovering the pleasures of the inward-turning eye.

I went to visit Mark and Kathleen Michelle, two artists I had met at a show in the SLO Brewing Company the day before, at their home on Fixlini Drive. Though it was a good walk to the downtown, their neighborhood was definitely "in-town," not suburban, and they could easily survive without their car. But what caught my eye, even on a rainy day, was that the neighborhood had the look of a suburb, but in the positive sense—quiet streets, nice, big lawns and shrubbery, a clear sense of property and privacy—proof that, at least here in San Luis Obispo, you could have the advantages of suburban life without living in suburbia.

Over coffee and cookies Mark and Kathleen explained that the rain was the key to the truth of San Luis Obispo. "We've had five years of drought," said Mark, "and decisions being made now about water will chart the future of this town." The big debate was whether or not to accept the state program for bringing in water from dammed rivers in the northern mountains. There was tremendous growth pressure on SLO because it was one of the last places near the coast that had a lot of prime farmland that could be exploited for residential and commercial development. The people who were concerned about impending growth and loss of farmland had allied themselves with environmentalists opposed to the damming of the mountain rivers. Thus the water issue was a litmus test of the great divide in San Luis Obispo. If you wanted to preserve the quality of life in SLO, the Michelles believed, you had to be against the state water program.

Kathleen said that longtime SLO residents lived in a false sense of security about the four-and-a-half-hour driving time to Los Angeles. "People think we're too far away to be exploited and ruined. But that's what people in Santa Barbara thought before the growth marched up the coast and they had to enact all those awful ordinances to keep people out." She believed that the constellation of places around SLO —Atascadero, Pismo Beach, Arroyo Grande, Oceano, Nipomo—could coalesce into a megacity with all of the sprawl and eventual dysfunction of Los Angeles itself.

"The world has discovered SLO in the past five years and the boom is on," Mark said, "though people here don't realize it." Recession and drought had so far blunted its impact, and, citing the water issue, the county had turned decidedly antigrowth and placed a moratorium on new building permits in SLO itself. But the growth pressure worked into other channels—the buying up of agricultural land for development investment and the redevelopment of downtown properties.

When the Madonna Shopping Plaza was built, it drew a lot of businesses out of the downtown, and many of those that stayed behind failed. Soon there was a move afoot to redevelop the downtown. Kathleen thought that should have been a good thing, but as an architect, she didn't like what she began seeing as some of the stores were made over with inauthentic materials and styles and then turned to selling T-shirts, posters, and cards.

"But businesspeople always convince themselves that growth is the way out of a recession," added Mark. "And since they can't currently build much of anything new, the developers are in a frenzy to rebuild everything that already stands."

"That contradicts the whole theme of your chamber of commerce brochure," I observed.

"And our whole history since World War II," he said. "That's the point; this was something new, and we've recently had to scream bloody murder to keep the town true to its principles."

Mark was an art teacher at the Community Art Center located next to the old mission downtown. He loved SLO because it supported the kind of place where he worked and because of the good in-town neighborhoods like the one he and Kathleen lived in. But he felt that an influx of new money threatened to price SLO out of the market for people who valued what was best about the community. I asked where the new money was coming from.

"Cal Poly," he said. "This may be the only town you'll ever see where property values go up when students move into a neighborhood rather than down. The reason is that they can afford to pay top dollar for whatever they want." It was the fear of every neighborhood. One group would decide to buy a house on the block and then others would follow. Some neighborhoods had been entirely taken over by students. "They're not good neighbors—just partying and spending their way along the fast track to yuppiedom." Mark and Kathleen's neighborhood was relatively unscathed, though there had been an obnoxious bunch next door for a while. The upshot of all of this was an ordinance currently in city council that would limit the number of students per house to five and another that would attempt to zone where students could buy.

Mark pointed out, however, that there was also an intense student counterculture. There had been radical protests against everything from the Diablo Canyon nuclear power plant to U.S. aid to the Nicaraguan contras to the prospect of offshore drilling for oil. "But the people carrying those signs are not the same ones you see driving the Corvettes and buying up neighborhood bungalows."

The Michelles thought that grassroots preservationist activism, working through local government, was the key to SLO's future. "The art community hangs on and many of the newcomer professionals do come here for the right reasons and become involved in keeping SLO sane," Kathleen said. "And our city and county politicians have been pretty cautious about opening the floodgates." Her landscape architecture firm was currently doing almost all of its business out of town because developers couldn't get building permits in SLO, and that suited her just fine.

Mark walked me to my rented car after the rain had stopped and the clouds overhead were breaking up. I could feel warm drafts of dry air wafting in from the hills to the southwest. "Looks like this one isn't going to end the drought," Mark observed. "I guess we're safe from the onslaught for a little longer."

I found a different viewpoint one evening at the bar of SLO Brewing when I talked to Mike Hoffmann, owner and founder of the place and the man who donated his wall for the use of the art show that Mark and Kathleen had been part of. Patron of the arts that he was and sincere believer in the importance of the arts community to SLO, Mike didn't concur with some of the views my artist friends had expressed to me. "That's the trouble with so many people, they want to close the door behind them once they get settled in here. They don't want any change. Hell, I thought this was California—we're supposed to welcome change and innovation and new ideas here."

Mike believed that the current crop of local politicians was anti-growth and antibusiness. But he perceived a change for the better in the business community in just the past few years. "A lot of un-progressive businesses bombed out and have been replaced by people who keep up with the times," he said, clearly referring to the down-town renovation about which Kathleen Michelle had expressed reservations.

Mike Hoffmann was originally a wine maker from a local wine-making family. His family's vineyards folded, so Mark went off to Wenatchee, Washington, to develop another winery and eventually returned to work for Ballard County Winery with a renewed apprecia-tion for San Luis Obispo. "SLO is an open, accepting place. People may have their disagreements, but they don't retreat into combative corners and glower at each other the way they do in so many commu-nities where different ways of life conflict."

He wanted to do something in his own downtown—maybe a fish market or a deli. And then he heard about the 1982 change in the law that allowed establishments to serve beer made on the premises that jump-started the whole brew pub phenomenon. So he went back to the University of California to learn to be a brew master and started SLO Brewing.

Just when he got established, the antismoking ordinance went into effect and he was sure it would kill him off, with his upstairs location and no patio. It was begun by a councilman, Jerry Reise, ". . . who wanted to make a name for himself. No one took it very seriously at first, and then suddenly the medical profession, the American Cancer Society, and outsiders with an agenda—you know, like lawyers with cases against cigarette companies—and the national press descended on us and the thing became a monster." Mike was interviewed by

Time magazine, there were public hearings, and a group was organized by downtown restaurateurs to fight with a petition, but it didn't even get enough signatures to be put on the ballot. "We never had a chance. Not many people smoke in this community anyway. It's, you know, the California ethic, health consciousness, vegetarians. Besides a few of us restaurateurs and bar owners, there just wasn't much opposition."

Like most of the businesspeople I talked to, Mike had accommodated himself to the fact of the smoking ban and his place had thrived despite it. But he didn't like government meddling in business, expecting the businessperson to police the issue and carrying out busts and levying fines against proprietors who weren't vigilant enough.

I watched SLO Brewing fill up for the after-work and dinner hours that evening. It was a big space with hardwood floors, a vaulting warehouse ceiling, lots of tables, and a very long bar. But it attracted enough people that it felt small and intimate. I liked the mix of people coming in here. They were friendly. The testosterone level was low. People didn't segregate themselves by trade. Here the lawyers and accountants bellied up to the bar or slouched at tables alongside electricians and plumbers. Conversations were not continuations of what had happened at the office, and people were fresh, curious, eager to lift that first pint with a new friend as if this were a great new day. Ray Oldenburg would be pleased.

I talked to a man who drove a delivery truck in nearby Atascadero rather than here in SLO because the local police were so strict about ticketing trucks standing on the streets that he had just given up on it. "But I live here," he said with some pride. "It takes some doing, I have to count my pints and live on a budget, but it's worth it," and he gestured toward the roomful of people who all seemed to know each other or, if they didn't, seemed determined to remedy that condition before the day was out.

A black lawyer in an impeccable suit and wearing an L.A. Raiders cap cheerfully explained the white Californian backlash against his team. Since so many gangs had adopted the Raiders for their colors, there were some bars that forbade the wearing of the black and silver as a way of discouraging gang activity on the premises. "The white middle class in California doesn't cheer for the Raiders anymore;

they're either 49ers or Rams fans. It's harmless and sort of amusing. Because this year the Raiders are our only winners—I wear the cap with pride."

I met one of Mike's cooks who turned out the tasty Mexican and California dishes that first brought people up the steps and into the bar. His name was Walt and he had begun his adult life as a Hell's Angels enforcer. But it was also in that life that he learned the talent of pulling together the ingredients for decent road grub in circumstances about as chaotic as working in a popular bar kitchen. Eventually the bike life passed him by and dumped him in SLO, where he became a well-known street person. Mike picked him up and gave him work at SLO Brewing, and today he was an established folk fixture here.

I decided it was safe to visit the mayor the next day. Ron Dunin was an anomaly. He was short, spoke with a heavy Polish accent, was one of the few local politicians to come out strongly against the no-smoking ordinance, tended to oppose the antigrowth majority on his city council, and wanted to keep the heavy hand of government off the backs of the businesspeople who were the local engines of prosperity. But he was no Sam Pick.

"We have a medium-quality-of-life city," Dunin said when I sat down in his cluttered office in city hall. "We try to improve the cultural offerings, we try to deal with environmental concerns like the creek and greenbelts, we try to preserve our historical and architectural heritage, like the Mission. We have some successes, but I wouldn't consider that we stick out as a spectacular place. SLO is a middle-of-the-road town. We're not full of cultural amenities but have enough to sustain a good life."

It was the creed of a modest man coping with rocketing expectations. When he came to SLO twenty-five years ago, it was a sleepy motel stop for people traveling U.S. 101 between L.A. and San Francisco, with a population of only twenty thousand. Besides the nearby beaches and its proximity to the Hearst Castle at San Simeon, its only claim to fame was that the first establishment to call itself a motel was located here.

Dunin was born on the Black Sea, where his parents had been deported during World War II. He was living in Britain when his daughter, who had immigrated to Seven Oaks, California, wrote to him and told him about this quiet California town with the beautiful weather and spectacular coast where she had stopped off for a night during a trip to San Francisco. "You have to come and see this place," she wrote. So he came here to buy a business.

There were only three businesses for sale when he arrived: a liquor store, a nursery, and a motel. He bought the motel, the first one he had ever stayed in. He did well enough with it that he was soon able to buy a second business, Schinsheimer's, an old-fashioned general store, which he remodeled and turned into an apparel and gift store.

"My pappy always used to say that if you ever go to a new community and the community accepts you, you must give back as much as you got," he explained. So he got involved in the downtown association, helped organize Obispo Beautiful, a downtown beautification project, and became active in the chamber. Eventually people started telling him to go into local politics. He ran for city council in 1977 and for mayor in 1985. He never lost an election.

During most of the years up until the time he became mayor, SLO remained the little-noticed, drowsy place it had always been. It had virtually no industry. The economic mainstays were tourism, the university, a nearby army camp, agriculture, shopping—SLO was the retail hub for the county—and a state prison (I learned from an ex-con on a later train ride that well-traveled California convicts employed byzantine legal machinations to get themselves sent to the SLO prison, "the best place to be incarcerated in America").

Dunin didn't know whether art discovered SLO or whether SLO discovered art. But he thought it was the sudden proliferation of cultural action that seeded the bloom of today's SLO. The university had a lot to do with it, despite the fact that many residents today stereotyped Cal Poly students as the antithesis of everything cultural in SLO. The SLO County Symphony located here with its internationally renowned Mozart festival. Actors immigrated from L.A. and set up thriving local theaters. The city, university, and community groups formed a three-way partnership to build the Performing Arts Center. The Mission Arts Center and plaza, where Mark Michelle taught, were built under city auspices. A children's museum was established through an all-volunteer effort.

When these things started happening, SLO awoke from its long slumber. People wanted to come here and there was a lot of new residential construction. G. Scott Thomas named SLO the best small city in America. Developers began remodeling the downtown. "Ironically, we lost our position as retail hub during this time as the general rush to the area fueled commercial development in all of the surrounding towns," said Dunin, "especially those along the coast. But it didn't seem to matter; the growth pie was big enough for everybody." And somehow the recession had yet to really take hold in SLO, even during my time there.

But the mayor was nonetheless a worried man, coping with a five-year drought that he feared could have the same effect on his city that the recession had on so many others. County and city governments had established growth moratoriums for the duration. But people were still in a lather to support all kinds of government initiatives to enhance SLO's status as a good place to live. "There is a lack of understanding that the time is not always ripe to do what you may not be able to afford," Dunin fretted. "People want to do too much too quickly." SLO had rapidly invested in free public bus transit, free parking, and extensive greenbelts and parks, and was considering a plant to recycle water to the drought-stricken Laguna Lake. But the mayor hastened to point out that these things are not free and that the issue could very quickly shift from the community's willingness to pay to its ability to pay.

At the same time, Dunin was concerned about the additional costs of the antigrowth movement currently in vogue. "We wouldn't have the things we've been able to do if we hadn't had the robust growth of the past ten years. Those who want to stop it are activist newcomers. But they're the ones who appreciate most the infrastructural and cultural things that growth has enabled us to do. They are highly motivated, organized, and have tremendous political leverage. They control city council; I'm the odd man out, not because I am foolishly progrowth, but because I am cautious. People here expect too much of their government."

And now the antigrowth forces were exploiting the water issue to promote their program. "It is absolutely indefensible to play with a life-giving resource to extort an antigrowth program," Dunin argued with some heat.

While he was on a contentious roll I thought I would bring up the antismoking ban, knowing that he had opposed it. He had offered a series of amendments to make it less draconian, but they had all been defeated. "It was a motherland and apple pie issue, and any attempt to modify it was viewed as an attempt to wreck it." Dunin believed that it unfairly impacted some more than others. Places with an outdoor patio, easy ground-floor access to the street, or a location just outside city limits were suddenly given a marketplace advantage by an action of government.

But the issue didn't get the mayor riled as did the question of water. "People enjoy having a meal without inhaling smoke. Smokers have adjusted. You've seen the sociable little curb gatherings. We may amend it sometime, but it's here to stay."

Eventually the drought-induced moratorium on growth would end, Mayor Dunin hoped, and he wanted to see cluster development on marginal agricultural lands as the key to SLO's economic future. Government would be heavily involved in protecting prime agricultural land and ensuring that the cluster concept really would guarantee permanent green spaces elsewhere. He foresaw further change coming to the downtown, buildings going to two and three stories to curb sprawl and architecture reverting to turn-of-the-century styles. The city would develop an adequate water supply one way or another. "No destination" traffic would be prohibited in the downtown and residential zoning would be revised to do something about the student intrusion issue while allowing for mixed-use development as people rediscovered (with the help of fax machines, computers, and telecommunications) the advantages of working out of or in close proximity to their residences. The "holes" in the downtown, vacant storefronts or failing businesses headed in that direction, would be filled in by the growing arts, entertainment, and culture industry. All of this from a man concerned about high expectations of government.

Dunin walked me out to my car and we watched the bustle of shoppers, professionals, and working people simply out for a sociable lunchtime stroll along Palm Street. "Looks like your town has the formula just about right as it is," I commented. "Maybe the government-activist, antigrowth people are on to something."

He shrugged his shoulders and smiled. It was the only conversation I ever had with a mayor of an American city where I had the last word.

There was a man in San Luis Obispo whose name came up in virtually every conversation about the character of the place, albeit sometimes with a snicker or tongue in cheek. Alex Madonna's name was all over the map—there was Madonna Road, the Madonna Construction Company, Madonna Mountain, and, most notably, the Madonna Inn. He was the current scion of an old local landowning family who had become a rich developer. But his fame, or notoriety, came from his chef d'oeuvre, the Madonna Inn. Depending on whom you were talking with, the Madonna Inn was a heroic stand against the uniformity of contemporary American construction, a temple to bad taste, the genius of a man who invented camp long before its brief ascension in the late sixties, or a grotesque extension of the motel culture that had founded modern SLO.

Sprawling haphazardly at the base of Madonna Mountain on the western edge of town, the Madonna Inn certainly looked like a Disneyland cartoon from the outside, all fantastic curliques and cutesy European schmaltz, done mostly in pink and white. Inside, three-foot tree trunks, deep shag carpets, plastic hanging lamps, wrought iron work, and a million decorative gizmos assaulted any eye lacking a sense of humor. No two rooms of the inn were alike, and the same was true of plumbing fixtures, doorknobs, and windows. The Caveman Room was hollowed out of a solid rock ledge. The urinals in the public men's room were man-made waterfalls.

I met Alex Madonna at the offices of his construction company down the road, where once inside I found touches of the same extravagant style as at the inn. The floor of the lobby was made of lacquered cross sections of tree trunks embedded in concrete. He was a quiet, soft-spoken man who didn't smile or make small talk, conveying the distinct impression that I had been granted a rare opportunity to talk to him.

His father had owned the ranch that later became Camp San Luis. Alex converted family land into capital for his construction company and his company's profits into investments in more land and development. But his passion had always been the inn. It was inspired by trips to Europe, where he was charmed, he said, "by the towns built helter-skelter with something of fresh visual interest at every corner. We wanted to do that in California, with novelties new and old at every turn."

According to Alex, the inn was built in twenty-foot modules, one per day. The plan for each day's work was sketched out on a napkin the day before. The materials were pulled from a stockpile of curiosities that his men had been gathering for a year before work began. "People come here from as far away as Japan asking help to re-create the Madonna Inn," he proudly stated.

Alex thought there was no secret to SLO's success. He named climate; the proximity of the ocean, mountains, and open agricultural country; and the location midway between California's two great cities as the keys to the town's popularity. People would have discovered the place sooner or later regardless of the cultural influence of the university or the good works of the city government.

But the university certainly did change the town. Before it became so dominant, the people who ran things were born and raised in the area. That had changed, Alex believed, and he launched into a discourse of opposition to the new regime. "Outsiders who want to close the door on others like themselves have become a problem. They all vote, and the politicians know that, so they have to take a stand against growth to get elected. All except for Mayor Dunin. We need four more on the council like him.

"It's nice to try to keep a small-town atmosphere, but people have a right to live where and how they choose. People want to be able to live here and get up in the morning with a job to go to. A million and a half people come through the Madonna Inn every year and most would give their eyeteeth to live here. I don't know how you're going to stop them."

Though clearly a proponent of growth, Alex Madonna stressed his concern about automobile pollution. His argument was that by restricting growth here at the center in SLO, current policies were stimulating car-dependent sprawl growth farther afield that would create just the kind of southern California environment people were so concerned about preventing. He thought it was particularly foolish to force growth out into the agricultural lands. "Here we are in prime California agricultural country, and we're increasingly dependent on trucking our food in—more trucks to add to pollution.

"It's a shame we can't build on the mountains right here in town," he went on. "It's the only direction we have left to go." He had twenty-two acres on the sides and top of San Luis Mountain. "We wanted to do a beautiful project on it—another inn with a funicular running to the top to keep cars off the mountain. But the thing became front-page headlines every day. People thought that God gave them that mountain to look at. The project died because it wasn't worth the hassle."

Throughout our conversation, Alex took calls from subordinates working on multimillion-dollar projects as far afield as Eureka and Lake Tahoe. He answered questions and issued orders in the same quiet, unsmiling tone with which he talked to me.

When I took my leave, I commented that his construction business seemed to be thriving, but he shook his head and complained that he needed some really big jobs right here in SLO. It wasn't a question of making more money, but of taking part in the great adventure that SLO had become. He was a builder besieged during exciting times in his hometown by an antigrowth regime.

I went to church one Sunday morning and found myself immersed in the regime that Alex Madonna had decried. It was the Michelles who had suggested that at the Unity Church I might find something of the new California spirit as applied in the SLO renaissance. Not to be confused with a United Church or the Unitarian Church, Unity was a Christian organization dedicated to the proposition that one could have religion without dogma, ritual, or creed. But it wasn't the theory that intrigued me so much as the congregation itself. The modernist chapel was packed that morning, standing room only. And as I looked around, I recognized dozens of faces I had seen around town during my visit, including city hall employees, artists I had met at the show, young women I had seen dancing in the bars, two city councilors, and various proprietors of downtown establishments. Whatever else it was, Unity Church was a true third place.

As people mingled in the lobby and the parking lot out front after the service, I was impressed by the earnest conversation and authentic warmth these people shared with one another. And everyone seemed to be banding together into little groups that would take the connectedness of the morning out to the beaches, mountains, and coffeeshops for good human cheer the rest of the day. A young black man I had briefly spoken to one morning in Linnae's remembered my face and asked me if I had been to the ocean yet. I hadn't, so he invited me to come along with him that afternoon to Pismo, where he would meet some buddies and check out the surf.

Lew Apollo was a demographic composite of some of the people who were changing SLO. A graduate student in architecture and city planning at Cal Poly, he had come here on scholarship from L.A. as an undergraduate art major and was a leader in the small but zealous student environmental movement. He was also a surfer, and he planned to stay in SLO to make his life.

As we drove in his little Toyota convertible four-by-four through the dry coastal hills on U.S. 101, he remonstrated against one aspect of his identity: "I'm not one of those BMW students, man. I hate that stereotype."

"But from what I've seen and heard, many Cal Poly students are rich and apolitical. Guys like you seem a minority here."

"Talk to me about minorities," he said with a laugh. "SLOtown, what a place, where a black homeboy from L.A. can be accepted in any neighborhood in town as long as he's not a student. But yeah, most Cal Poly students are assholes—Ron Reagan's favorite kids."

He believed that what attracted people here was what complicated life here. "Everybody wants the perfect place in the sun, and too many come here with a lot of bucks and an attitude that would trash it." Despite his love of surfing, Lew insisted that the climate and location were minor considerations in his decision to live here. He had studied community and environmental planning and believed that most attractive small American cities evolved through stages of obscurity, discovery, and boom, leading eventually to dissolution. "It's the American way, man, don't stand in the way of progress; if something is good, exploit it till it isn't anymore."

He believed that the trick was to find a community in the first blush of discovery, raise its consciousness of what it had and what it stood to lose, and work to break the cycle. "You can't just find a good place and settle in, or you become part of the problem. You've got to make connections with enough people who want to preserve what they love about the place that you become a force—a force against all those destructive forces that push a place along the road to ruin."

"You mean that once you get in, you conspire with others to close the door behind you."

"Yeah, I know that's what they say about us. But in a society where the growth force is so unbalanced, maybe that's what you have to do for a time while you work out a whole new way of providing jobs and housing for people. You know, man, it's not that we want to close the door on people, just on the instinct to make a lot of money at the expense of the environment where the people will live."

Echoing Mark Michelle, he thought it was also a matter of who was attracted to settle here. "There is a segment of the population looking, not so much for the community of a good place to live, but for a good place to attempt to privately enjoy their money. That's who we don't want."

I was familiar with the people to whom Lew referred. I had met them on the road and listened to their testimony about the search for a good place to live, a very different testimony than that which had inspired the 10,000 Waves Alternative Places criteria. In response I had bypassed or made very brief stops in several other high-profile places besides southern California (central Arizona and its AARP golf course culture, Orlando and the Florida Gold Coast, Aspen, Atlanta) that were big draws for the gated community crowd. They would like SLO, but not if the activism of Lew Apollo and Mark Michelle had its way.

The waterfront road into Pismo Beach was strip developed with small commercial and service establishments. But side streets provided easy access to the beaches and there were frequent unobstructed views of the water and spectacular undeveloped headlands in both directions up and down the coast. "Now this here could have been planned a lot better, but it isn't bad yet—you're not cut off from the ocean by a wall of high-rise resorts and condos." His statement conjured up in my mind an image of spoiled shore places I knew in Florida—Fort Lauderdale, Marcos Island, Naples—and again I knew exactly what it was he wanted to close the door on.

We met his four friends at the pier, where they were waiting with surfboards stacked in the back of a pickup truck. Only one besides Lew was a Cal Poly student. The other guys all supported their surfing and activism habits by working in the service sector—a waiter, a hotel manager, a bartender. Lew introduced me as someone who would help publicize the "right" side of SLO.

Just twenty minutes from downtown SLO, here we were at the edge of the Pacific—open water before us all the way to Japan, ragged coastal mountains at our backs, and the world's finest vegetable-growing valleys behind them. The beach was broad with hard-packed fine sand. It was cleaner than beaches I knew on the East Coast and far less crowded this seventy-five-degree Sunday afternoon than its eastern equivalent would have been. It was easy to see why so many people had for so many years become fevered with the California dream.

The surf was up and I got a sunburn along with my first surfing lesson. I never did get the knack of it. The waves were tall, and pitching off the top of one into that six-foot gulf below was a little like skiing a double diamond slope that wouldn't stay still. Eventually I gave up and resigned myself to the role of spectator.

I learned very little about the clichés of surfing that day on the beach—in fact, the day became a refutation of stereotypes. All afternoon the talk during breaks was about the community life in SLO—speakers at the Unity Church, art exhibits, cultural offerings at the university, bands playing that week in the bars, the doings in city council, and, of course, upcoming exercises of environmental activism. Lew and his friends gestured frequently to the roiling green ocean before us and urged me to conjure up the dire consequences of oil drilling just off this shore. Then I was asked to imagine this pure white beach blackened with tar as far as the eye could see up the bight in both directions toward the headlands in the distance.

Riding back to SLO with the top down on Lew's Toyota, I could feel the slight change in temperature when a hill blocked the warmth of the sun sinking out over the Pacific. But even in the shadows the air was balmy and soft this late April evening. I asked Lew about being black in SLO. It was an overwhelmingly white town and I hadn't heard him or his friends mention issues of race once all afternoon.

"Sure there's racism here," he answered. "It's everywhere. But SLOtown is an easy town. Like you can live here and come and go with the same feeling of tolerance that you get in a resort hotel where everybody's welcome as long as you pay your bill. It's Hotel California. Maybe it helps that it's all so new—there aren't a lot of folks with a bigoted sense of title to the place. And the climate casts a spell where it's hard to be uncomfortable enough to get angry."

Under California's political system, county government played a much larger role in community planning than it did in the Northeast, where I lived. There was one county commissioner whose name had come up in several of my conversations with people on both sides of the growth argument. Alex Madonna had described her as a go-slow environmentalist, while Lew had seen her as a force in favor of growth and business interests. I went to see her on my last day in SLO at the county government offices.

Ruth Bracket was surprised to hear that anybody had described her as an antigrowth environmentalist but was pleased that she wasn't pigeonholed as a boom-growth promoter either. "I work for a balance between healthy growth and preserving the small-town environment and wide open spaces that people have always come here for," she explained. "But under the current climate I find myself acting often as a defender of property rights. The pendulum has swung too far. People want government to control too much too fast."

She had trouble with SLO's smoking ban, for instance, though she appreciated its effects. "People said it was a legitimate exercise of government to regulate a behavior which has consequences that cost the taxpayer." She recognized the logic of the argument but believed that government erred when it proscribed choice without offering something compensatory.

Bracket was upbeat about SLO's future. She believed that the place had some organic advantages that would help it keep its character through times of bad economic or political weather "without Herculean efforts of government activism." Obviously the climate and coast would always attract a few tourist dollars. There was also the fact that SLO had a large number of government jobs—as a county seat, a Polytechnic college site, and a governmental focal point of the central California coast. Then there was the public utility at Diablo Canyon. Controversial or no, it was a significant stabilizing factor for employment and cash flow in the region. And finally, and perhaps most important, Bracket believed that the beleaguered agricultural sector would remain a much stronger force than some would have had me believe. People could talk all they wanted about the importance of the art infusion or the aesthetic of the recent land buyer, but SLO's future was still firmly rooted in the land, as it always had been.

"People think of this land as broccoli land, and much of it is," she explained. "The lands that are prime for vegetables, where farmers can still make good money growing broccoli, will be preserved in that state by economic factors as much as through county land-use regulations. The issue is the marginal land, which is a large percentage, where growing broccoli or grazing cattle no longer makes sense. These are the lands where the owner is tempted by developers wanting to build tract housing. We have to encourage the conversion of these lands to proven high-productive crops like wine making and fruit if we want to keep them rural in character."

Here she invoked the Williamson Act, the California measure that, in exchange for tax advantages, essentially forced landowners to declare their intent to subdivide ten years in advance. Bracket believed that it operated as a stabilizing force, encouraging farmers to make the transition to crops that could make it in this age rather than sell out to developers. And she could trot out a pretty substantial list of successful wine and fruit growers to prove her point.

But the state legislation was just a starting point. Bracket warmed to the topic of how the county intended to preserve the agricultural base of its identity, and soon it was easy to forget that I was talking to an official who had begun the conversation with misgivings about how active government ought to be. There were minimum parcel sizes for subdivision that varied according to the agricultural use of the land: three hundred acres for rangeland, twenty for grapes and row crops. Thirteen of these categories were defined by the character of the land itself rather than by arbitrary zoning decisions, and the rules for development within them varied considerably one from another. "The point," said Bracket, "is to guarantee that land that is particularly good for growing broccoli will be used to grow broccoli, but [it's also] to recognize that other lands may have radically different potential uses."

Commissioner Bracket also saw a role for the county in controlling urban sprawl. Thus cities that wanted to annex lands beyond their current boundaries had to make a proposal to the county for permission. "What we look for is to prevent long fingers of development that encourage wasteful low-density infill. We require that the urban area remain compact and have the ability to provide all foreseeable services. And each city or town relies on the county to preserve green spaces and belts that separate places and preserve community identity."

She was particularly excited about a long-range scheme that would retire development rights from highly developed or sensitive locations and transfer them to other areas where new development would be desirable. In practice this meant that when the government deprived a property owner of development rights through growth-control regulation, it would compensate not with money but by granting development rights somewhere else. In order to do this, of course, government would have to have a bank of parcels where it owned development rights. These would be acquired through purchasing easements to the rights and through trade-offs with landowning developers seeking governmental waivers and fast-tracking of their projects.

Concerning the water issue, Bracket agreed with Mayor Dunin: "Battle lines over growth have been drawn in the wrong place and are corrupting the whole separate question of how we will provide water for our children." Her solution was for the county to get into the state water program as a whole and hook in various communities when they were ready to accept it.

I commented that some might charge her with hypocrisy concerning her philosophy about limiting government—that a cynic might say she was simply advocating greater power for her particular governmental jurisdiction. She countered, "That's where government does have a legitimate role, to bring order into a chaotic situation and play referee."

Commissioner Bracket ended our conversation by returning to her theme that government should stay out of the way of property owners and free enterprise as much as possible. And yet, to this visitor from the "Live Free or Die" state, every idea we discussed represented some aggressive and innovative exercise of government in those arenas. I didn't doubt the sincerity of her self-description. Rather I was moved to contemplate relativity—how what was considered radical governmental activism in one place was merely thoughtful responsibility in another. It was an illustration of the power of place—and an affirmation of other, more personal but equally revolutionary transformations that one might effect in oneself by the simple expedient of moving on.

I spent another week in SLO trying to get a grip on the soul of the little city. I visited a county alcoholism treatment program that had recently adopted acupuncture therapy with results surpassing any of the traditional approaches. Many of the patients were attractive, well-dressed women. Meeting them on the street, one would never guess that they were alcoholics who could describe sleeping under bridges and vomiting through their nostrils.

I attended performances in clubs and bars of some of the region's up-and-coming alternative bands—Giant Sands, Mobile Hombres, and others. The music was strange, sometimes downright ear assaulting, but the lyrics were intelligent and sincere, slicing through the worldview conventions of my generation's rock music like a hot knife through butter. We had failed to make the world a better place, they seemed to say to me. Now get out of the way and let a new generation just do it.

At times I felt like a voyeur peering through cracked doors in the halls of Hotel California with all of the fringe ferment that one might expect to find in the West Coast experience. But there was a common homely ground beneath it all. Government, either state, county, or local, was almost always there, providing subsidies, facilities, coordination, or assistance with publicity. In my own New Hampshire, government was viewed as an ad hoc function invoked as rarely as possible to perform only an absolute minimum of services and preserve a superficial sense of public decency. Here it was like hotel management, catering fastidiously to the diverse fancies of a demanding clientele.

My last day in SLO was a Thursday, and as I wandered about the downtown, seeking final impressions, I found a swirl of activity different from anything I had yet seen. It seemed as though every store were intent on emptying its contents into the streets. Workmen wrestled with staging and platforms and stands. A cavalcade of pickup trucks laden with farm produce rolled into town.

By evening the police had closed off Higuera Street and signs and banners went up proclaiming this Farmer's Market Day. The usually clean air was pleasantly fouled by smoke from scores of makeshift barbecues, where cooks basted racks and racks of pork and beef ribs. Clowns, mimes, magicians, and musicians had set up shop on street corners. And there were more people in the streets than there had been on the college students' Saturday night out.

The SLO Thursday night farmer's market was founded by the downtown merchants' Business Improvement Association and supported by city hall. I knew that towns all across the country had instituted various kinds of farmer's market days, but SLO's was something else entirely, almost like a county fair that happened weekly.

The entire downtown became one great third place where even a visitor of just two weeks spotted acquaintances and mingled with them for good cheer long into the night. Lew Apollo was here, and the Michelles, even the mayor and Alex Madonna, eminently pleased with the proceedings, despite their sense that their town had gotten away from them.

The next morning on the Amtrak train bound for San Jose, where I would catch a flight back East, I tried to score SLO on the 10,000 Waves Alternative Places Rated Scale. It did better for Cheers Factor than Santa Fe had, a three or maybe a four; I had visions of fives down the road that offered a level of spontaneity and social comfort that I knew might turn out to be a pipe dream. Despite neighborhoods like the Michelles' and the city's generous support of a bus system, too many people still lived in their cars here. Give it a two or three for Foot Factor. SLO had potential for Cake, with its beautiful Pacific beaches nearby and the rolling productive agricultural farms inland. But despite the activism of local government in promoting culture, this was as yet no Santa Fe, and San Francisco was, after all, four and a half hours away—a three. Though it could hardly be mistaken for Anyplace, USA, SLO had only a nascent sense of identity threatened by growth pressures that were unabating—thus a three for Someplace. Of course for Comfort, SLO was a pure five, and since it was one of those rare places that seemed to actually deliver on the promise offered by Sun Belt sites, I thought it deserved a Fudge Factor of four.

SLO was still young and its identity and future were still undecided. If the preservationists had their way and a few more cultural institutions and enlightened industries located here, the scores might improve dramatically and quickly. For a speculative good place seeker, SLO might turn out to be a great bet. So far it had survived a decade of high-test development pressure, and the only secret to success I could find here besides temporary remoteness was the tenuous stance of government. After all, this was a city that had outlawed smoking in bars and growth in the midst of a recession—and gotten away with both. This was a place where complaints about the expansion of governmental power came from elected officials concerned about the aggressive activism their constituents demanded of them. This was a city whose chamber of commerce talked like historical preservationists elsewhere.

Despite the protestations of Commissioner Bracket, it seemed to me that SLO had few organic defenses against the exploitation and dissolution that surfer Lew believed were usually the final phases in the evolution of North American communities in highly attractive sites. Cal Poly was no Cornell, whose role I would later find to be so significant in Ithaca, New York. There was no enlightened economic muscle like Nike, Cornerstone, or Hewlitt-Packard, as I would later find in the Willamette Valley of Oregon. There was not yet any benevolently despotic Christian Brothers or Mondavi, as there would be in Napa.

But there was a clear track record of a community determined to aggressively preserve and protect its quality of life through grassroots activism working with local government. SLO illustrated a new definition of the necessity of government in America that went against the common wisdom on both sides of the great ideological divide in other places. It was a last resort—a preservation of the good life by other means.

3

AMERICAN EDEN

NAPA, CALIFORNIA

"Welcome to hell, now go home," read the only legible graffiti on the brick wall along the tracks as my Amtrak train from the east rolled into Oakland on a warm July evening. The rest of it was hieroglyphics that only gang members could read. Earlier I had seen the bumper-to-bumper traffic on the freeways we bridged back near Sacramento—and of course the endless wasteland of commercial strips that line highways and encircle towns throughout America. But the Oakland train station was surely the Dantean extremity I would have to pass through before emerging into the light of better places to live. The main building was now closed up because of security problems with gangs in the area, and passengers were unceremoniously hustled off to buses or taxis by burly cops carrying sputtering radios.

My taxi driver wheeled through the slum streets surrounding the station at fifty miles per hour and slumped down in his seat with his eyes darting right and left. I wanted to ask facetiously if he was afraid of stray bullets, but just then his radio squawked a warning of a shooting on Front Street. "That's just two blocks that way," he said, pointing as he turned the car squealing onto a street headed in the opposite direction.

And then suddenly we were driving down a thoroughfare that

reminded me of New York's Fifth Avenue and pulling up in front of the Park Hotel, where a stiffly uniformed doorman with a heavily affected English accent opened the door with white-gloved hands and offered to take my bags to the Hertz car rental desk. Inside, business-people talked in the lobby, buying and selling the world while all hell went down just a few blocks away.

Despite my agreeable visits to Santa Fe and San Luis Obispo, it was hard to imagine as I drove onto the freeway entrance ramp after Oakland that there could be more places in America with the characteristics for which I was searching. Places like inner-city Oakland give the sense that some inevitable historical tide will eventually deluge everything in chaos. But traveling changes perceptions, even in a rented Chevy Geo driving on I-80 past the Berkeley hills and over the Carquinez Bridge. I marveled at the California terrain, golden with cheat grass in the late afternoon sun, spotted here and there with seemingly deliberate, well-defined clusters of dark green California oaks.

The southern approach of California 121 into Napa, my first destination of a long summer sojourn through the Northwest, was predictably lined with retail plazas, though here the landscaping seemed a little cleaner and greener. And then there was something different, like the flotsam that once signaled seafaring explorers that they were near land: a little brown sign that directed me away from the outskirts and down Third Street to the downtown historical district. Crossing the Napa River and turning onto Main Street, I quickly saw why filmmakers came to these northern California towns when they wanted to shoot something in a fifties period setting. Here were marquee theaters still showing current movies, soft ice-cream drive-ins, and art deco storefronts.

At the corner of Main and Second was a place called Willett's Brewing Company with a beer garden separating the checker-tiled building from a small, grassy Veterans Park and a bandstand by the banks of the river. A waitress carrying pints of dark beer smiled cheerfully at me as I drove by. It was late and I was tired, hungry, and thirsty, so I decided to go in.

"Everybody in Napa is from somewhere else," said a fellow at the bar after I had wolfed down a Mexican burger and begun to sample the local lager. The music of R.E.M.'s "Losing My Religion" mixed congenially with the hubbub of a couple dozen patrons, ranging from hip twenties to tweedy middle age, who all seemed to know one another. Three or four sociable women moved around from group to group. It was clear that this was a place dominated by regulars, where the tourist or visitor like myself began as a decided outsider. So far it was exactly what I was looking for.

Willett's rough-plastered barroom was a narrow space. Above the bar and its wooden swivel stools hung cabinets for wine storage, and I noticed that the bartender had to chin himself up there to get at the bottles. He wore a T-shirt that read REEDUCATING WINE DRINKERS SIX DAYS A WEEK. Behind the bar were rows of pint glasses in a refrigerated case. Above, there weren't any of the usual racks of hard liquor. Willett's did not serve hard liquor. It didn't serve bottled beer, either. Besides a few Napa Valley wines, Willett's offered just the dozen varieties of beer brewed on the premises and drawn from taps on the back wall.

Around the corner from the bar I found the brewery, four large vats behind a tiled kneewall, and, up a few steps beyond that, the restaurant, whose windows overlooked the Napa River. Behind a door marked EMPLOYEES ONLY, I could see the cold room with its fermenting and aging tanks. A door off the barroom led to the beer garden and the park, where a blues band played for a gathering of maybe seventy-five people sprawled in the grass. Along the river several fathers and sons fished.

The friendly fellow at the bar told me about the worst place to live he had ever seen: Lubbock, Texas, where Marriott had sent him for two miserable years. "It's typical of the Bible Belt," he said. "There are no places in town to have a drink with friends, so you have to drive out to these drive-in liquor stores that are beyond the city limits. There's one on every road out of town. So the idiots have their dry town but create one of the worst drinking-and-driving problems in the country." His favorite country-and-western song was about the joy of seeing "Lubbock fading in the rearview mirror." He was glad Marriott had given him the chance to come back to Napa, where he could walk six blocks from home to places like Willett's.

The morning of my second day in Napa began with a cool mist draped across the valley. Dave Oster, the proprietor of the Elms Bed and Breakfast, where I was staying, explained that the mist would burn off in a few hours for a dry, warm afternoon and that this kind of weather was part of what made the valley so fruitful for wine making.

The B and B was recently built, and it was my first encounter with something I would become accustomed to in the Pacific Northwest: recently constructed establishments combining modern and antique notions of grace. Sometimes northern European, sometimes Mediterranean, sometimes Georgian, sometimes Spanish, sometimes even New England in ambience, these places cumulatively created an authentic West Coast architecture that merely borrowed from the older world without imitating it. There was always something Californian about them, like the Jacuzzi located on an open veranda just off the lobby of the otherwise Georgian-style Elms. They were like so many of the people I would meet, people who had come here from other places with a commitment to live more broadly and eclectically than they had elsewhere.

I drove west that morning on California 121 and then California 116 to see what lay between Napa and the Pacific. Just a few miles out of town the road began to wind and rise. I passed a vineyard, Domaine Carneros, the first I had seen up close. With its European-style central chateau and surrounding vineyard lands, the place conveyed a sense of the medieval—a novel feeling for an American standing on American soil.

Then the road curved past an old gingerbread Victorian schoolhouse, over the ridge of mountains that defined the western rampart of Napa Valley, and down into Sonoma Valley. These wine country valleys all ran southeast to northwest, with ridges of mountains separating them. Both the valleys and the ridges were narrow and tightly defined, resulting in a complex sorting out of the moisture-bearing westerly winds rolling off the Pacific and producing the radical microclimates for which the region was famous. Napa Valley was kept relatively cool and moist by sea winds off San Pablo Bay whereas the hotter, drier Sonoma Valley was affected more by winds that came in over land and several mountain ridges.

Beyond the western ridge of Sonoma Valley, California 116 approached the small city of Petaluma. I was mildly curious about Petaluma because I had read about its creative zoning policies. But the

first things I saw were miles of walls surrounding housing developments. About eight feet high, they were built of some kind of cinder
brick, and behind them one could just see the rooftops of the houses
inside. The downtown didn't seem like such a bad place and had some
period charm. Banners over the street announced THE PETALUMA RIVER
FESTIVAL. *American Graffiti* was filmed here, as were Ronald Reagan's
1984 "Morning in America" ads. It didn't seem like the kind of inner
city that would intimidate the residential neighborhoods on the outskirts into surrounding themselves with walls.

But then I drove under the U.S. 101 freeway. Unlike the country
roads that led slowly to Napa, 101 was a high-speed pipeline right into
downtown San Francisco. Its presence opened this third valley to
high-pressure development and a bedroom community lifestyle, as
well as the possibility of invasion by the kinds of people that some
built walls to keep out.

Beyond Petaluma, the county road was the kind that automobile
manufacturers love to feature in their ads. And since there was little
traffic on it, it was a rare opportunity to really enjoy the American
machine the way we think we do in the myth. These hills rose sharply
from the ravine wrinkles between them up to rounded tops, and the
road twisted with the contours of the land. The highway engineers
here must have had a rare concept of road standards and little interest
in making cuts and fills.

The mist and low clouds that had been clearing as I left the Sonoma Valley now intensified as I approached the Pacific. Then the
road descended into the crack of the San Andreas Fault separating the
mainland from Point Reyes National Seashore. Here cows grazed placidly on ground that could open up any minute and swallow them.
Point Reyes Station itself, with its brick-and-log buildings, had the
look of a far northern outpost, but the place was less than an hour
north of San Francisco.

That was the lesson of the day's drive. Winding on another sports-
car road from Point Reyes to Bodega Bay, I marveled at the miles and
miles of undisturbed natural landscape just a stone's throw from one
of America's most booming metropolitan areas. And this wasn't fal-
low farm country, either. This was land simply not yet touched by
human hands.

I drove on from Bodega Bay to Santa Rosa, a city of more than a hundred thousand, bursting at the seams from the development and population that followed U.S. 101 up from San Francisco. As I schemed the fastest way in and out of the traffic-congested town, I remembered a woman from Santa Rosa whom I had met on the train. She didn't want me to write about this place and attract a lot of people to it. Someone should tell her that word has already leaked.

I drove through Sonoma and got back to Napa in the late after-noon convinced of two reassuring things. First, with the exception of the U.S. 101 corridor, Napa was located in the midst of a region precious with undisturbed scenic resources. And second, of the towns I saw in the region, Napa, with its progressively preserved art deco–era downtown and adjacent middle-class neighborhoods, appeared to be the most attractive.

Back at Willett's for supper, I ate at the bar with off-duty bar-tender Paul Henkelman, born in nearby Vallejo, raised in Napa and so the closest yet to a true native. Paul looked like a high school basket-ball player with a marine's jaw and haircut. He talked with a rasp in his voice that he said was the permanent effect of a devastating chest cold he'd had last spring (though barroom gossip speculated that it might be a deliberate addition to his persona as a macho bartender). But he brought a sense of mission to his work that put some substance behind whatever twenty-something vanities he chose to indulge.

"All my life I can remember thinking that there were too many people around me who didn't know how to have fun," Paul told me. So he decided after high school that he would make his living helping people learn how to do that. He was drawn to the places where people gathered, starting out as a waiter, a sports counselor, a cook, a restau-rant manager. Then two years ago he hitched up with Willett's as a bartender. "The two guys who own this place were after something more than just making money," he said. "They had this dream to make Willett's a focal point of people's lives in this town."

I explained to him Ray Oldenburg's concept of the third place, where people gather spontaneously to enjoy the pleasures of social contact. "That's exactly what Willett's is all about," he enthused. But he argued that my source was all wrong about third places being a dying phenomenon in America. And to prove his point, he disappeared behind the bar for a moment and returned with a copy of a paperback book entitled *On Tap*, a 1991 catalog of brew pubs throughout the country.

A quick skimming of the book revealed two significant facts: more than half of the brew pubs of America were located in the three Pacific states—California, Oregon, and Washington—and almost all of them were founded since 1986.

"It's a movement," said Paul. "What it's all about is the return to respectability of social-drinking places. The secret is to not serve hard liquor." For a twenty-six-year-old without a bachelor's degree, Paul was surprisingly well-informed about American sociological history. "First there were your New England Puritans, then Victorians raving about 'demon rum,' then the turn-of-the-century temperance movement getting all tangled up with women's suffrage, then prohibition, then the fifties, and most recently the alcohol-free movement of health nuts and PCs. Americans have always found some excuse not to have fun. But on the West Coast in the past few years, we've started turning that all around. I think people just got tired of making lots of money and not enjoying it."

As the evening livened up at Willett's, Paul introduced me to more of the other regulars. There was Marc Alther, a plumber, who was very close to native status because he had come here from Arcata, near Eureka, just a few hundred miles up the Pacific coast. Arcata was one of those North Pacific Coast places "permanently enshrouded in fog, where you never saw anybody you didn't know." His parents had chosen Arcata as a reaction against the crowds of L.A., and he subsequently chose Napa as a reaction against the isolation of Arcata.

"Napa is a good place to be a plumber," he said. "People are always renovating their houses, putting the kitchen where the living room used to be, installing hot tubs and swimming pools. Sure it's a pretty expensive place to live, but you can make more money here too —enough that you can afford it, just barely. My kids go to a good school and my wife works in a bookstore because she wants to, not because she has to."

And there was Douglas Rennie, a cooper originally from Scotland. In his first years in America, he had coached soccer in Florida and managed a golf course in Arizona. But in Napa he found a place that put some real value on his antiquated barrel-maker's art. The Seguin

Moreau Vineyard paid him well enough that he could afford an apartment just a few blocks away from Willett's on First Street. "Most
coopers consider themselves lucky if they get a job in a theme park or
historical museum. Here I get to do the real thing for an industry that
considers my work a critical part of their quality."

The next evening, on Marc's recommendation, I checked out another Napa third place. Overlooking the Napa River about a dozen
blocks north of downtown, Harry O'Shortal's had a parking problem
so severe that the management hired a woman with a golf cart to
shuttle patrons from a nearby plaza parking lot. Inside there were
several TVs over the bar tuned silently to baseball games and tennis
matches, and windows with placid views of the river along the opposite wall. The wall behind the bar was spangled with taps—Sierra
Nevada, Hubsch Brau, Red Tail, Devil Mountain Railroad Ale, Wid-
mer's, and at least a dozen others. A tap at the lower-right-hand
corner of the display offered "training beer"—Budweiser.

The TVs were soundless tonight because a performer was playing
sixties folk-rock music on the stage. But what was most enchanting
about Harry O's was the presence of children. In most bars, whether
by law or by social convention, children, and sometimes even wives,
are banished, contributing to bars' reputation as antifamily institutions. I had seen, of course, that this did not have to be, from visits to
pubs in England and taverns in certain parts of Canada. But how
refreshing to find whole families in a tavern in America.

Most of the kids, six or seven of them, were gathered at the circular booths in front of the stage and the musician, and indeed, they
seemed to be the ones who were making the requests the fellow was
playing. Their parents were at the bar, several of them celebrating the
birthday of the mother of two of the kids. There was interaction
between the generations, the parents commenting on the kids' requests for music, the kids asking the parents for money for more pizza
or soft drinks.

During his break, the performer, Calvin Jo Ross, joined me for a
pint at the bar. I asked him if this all-in-the-family-style bar was
common on the West Coast, and he said that Napa was a bit unique in
that respect. "A lot of places, you'll see kids in them once in a while,"
he answered. "But it's not usually encouraged as it is here."

He had played in brew pubs and taverns all over the Northwest

and agreed with Paul at Willett's that the brew pub was spearheading
a revival of drinking places that perform a respectable social role.
"They're not places for the old man to go belt down some high test
and escape the wife and kids he can't stand to be around. Nobody sits
alone nursing a Manhattan at these places. People talk, laugh, sing.
And here at Harry O's they bring the old lady and the kids and they all
have a good time."

We talked about the future of the small cities he knew so well
in this region. "It's only a matter of time, all of the other places
north of San Francisco will be ruined soon," he believed. "People
will just pour up those valley highways and the small places will
soon all be like Santa Rosa and Santa Rosa will be like Santa
Clara." But he believed that Napa would escape. It was protected
by its location in between the main valley corridors to the east and
west. "But more important, the wine makers and vineyards have
got control of the land. What they don't own themselves is tied up
in the tightest land-use laws in the country. Development could roll
up the Napa Valley from the south, but it would stop dead in its
tracks at the southern boundary of the city of Napa."

Calvin had seen the power of the wine interests firsthand. Up the
valley, he formerly ran the Yountville Restaurant and Coffee Saloon,
where he had begun offering dinner theater, folk performers, and rock
groups. But behind his place, there was a small but exclusive residential development in which the houses weren't selling well. First the
county forced him to allow a road through his parking lot to provide
better access. Then he began getting complaints that the noise from
his rock music was preventing the houses from selling. "Next thing I
knew they had passed an ordinance requiring a license for electrically
amplified music. And they simply wouldn't give me one. That shut me
down and I had to sell out." But Calvin thought the neighboring
housing development had been a red herring. "You couldn't even hear
our music in that neighborhood. The county supervisors don't even
unzip their flies without permission from the winegrowers. That's
what did me in."

It was another of those ephemerally misty Napa mornings when I
walked downtown to Ed Huber's jewelry store. Ed was a city councilor
and longtime veteran of Napa city politics. From my own experience

as a city councilor in Keene, I had some idea of the various approaches that different elected local officials took toward their jobs.

There were the demagogues, who got on the council because they had some axe to grind. There were the concerned citizens making their sacrifice of time to keep the city running smoothly. There were the city hall buffs so fascinated by the workings and personalities of local government that they developed a manager's level of expertise on every nook and cranny of city hall. There were the one-issue people, on the council just to promote their pet concerns. There were behind-the-scenes manipulators, those with a stronger belief in their own ability to quietly steer things than in the workings of public democracy. And there were the fixers.

Fixers tended to be older men and women cut from the mold of the traditional ward heeler politician. They had only incidental interest in the broad strokes of legislation or community policy. They were more concerned about assisting individuals with a specific interest or grievance on a case-by-case basis. Their phones were ringing continually and city government for them was primarily a process of crisis management.

Ed Huber was a fixer. Before I had a chance to finish introducing myself, we were interrupted by four telephone calls, each involving at least ten minutes of talk ranging from loud denunciations to whispered confidentialities. Each ended with Huber's promise to talk to this or that person to see what he could do.

Huber was a gruff, phlegmy man with white hair and a smoker's rasp. He began by deflecting my questions with suggestions of various other people to whom I should talk who might be more helpful than he could be. I pressed him to tell me what was the most controversial local issue recently, and he said probably the Wine Train.

The Wine Train was the dream of San Francisco magnate Vincent DeDomenico, former owner of Golden Grain, Rice-a-Roni, and Ghirardelli chocolate. When he sold those enterprises to Quaker Oats for $275 million, he had the stake needed to make his dream come true, a historic re-creation of a luxury passenger train running through the wine country and serving its customers world-class food and wine. Most places would have welcomed an innovative attraction that promoted the local claim to fame. But Napa had a rare conception of what was authentic and fit. To many, the wine train was neither and thus provoked an outcry of protest from interests all up and down the valley. The wine makers had spent some $180,000 on a campaign of opposition.

DeDomenico countered that his train had taken 200,000 polluting automobiles off of the valley's California 29, that he had sold 7,000 cases of his critics' wines, that his company's payroll in the valley was in excess of $2.5 million, and that it contributed more than $300,000 to the local tax base.

"You'll have to talk to people up in the valley to get their concerns," Huber dodged when I pressed him on the reasons for the opposition. Many in Napa saw the Wine Train Station as a valuable attraction for the downtown.

Huber thought Napa's downtown was the product of anticipated floods and earthquakes. "All of our plans for continuing the revitalization of the downtown get tangled up in flood prevention and earthquake design," he said. "We have a lot of old buildings, and nobody wants to tear them down and build new ones."

The result was the preservation of distinct mid-century architecture by market forces responding to both the downtown's historical designation status and the strict requirements for new construction. Huber seemed to feel some ambivalence about the fact that in Napa there was usually someone who would come forth with big money to renovate the old buildings, as was currently happening with the old opera house on Main Street near Willett's. Perhaps it was the elected politician's unease at sharing power with forces whose clout didn't come from the ballot box.

Throughout our conversation, Huber continually suggested that I talk to one of the county supervisors, and I remembered from my visit to San Luis Obispo that the California city politician had to share power with the county to an extent that was unheard of back in New England. "They run everything out beyond the city's incorporated limits and have a lot to say about what we do here, too," he lamented.

The county passed a proposition at the last election called the 2020 initiative that, in effect, locked up all land beyond the city limits till the year 2020. "It was passed by the voters overwhelmingly," Huber conceded, adding, "because the winegrowers poured a lot of money into the campaign. But the result for us is that it puts all of the developmental pressure on the city. And now the county wants to take a lot of our downtown parking for their employees at the county offices." Huber never said there was conflict between the various power centers here. He just presented his view of the facts and let me draw my own conclusions.

I asked him what was the biggest change in Napa in the years he had lived here. He said that besides population growth, it was the number and power of the wineries. Once there were just six, putting out cheap jug wine. Now there were 150 vying for world prominence. Huber found my questions about guarantees by the city and county against invasion by large regional shopping malls quaint. "The wine-growers own all the land and make all the rules. And they don't like shopping malls. But if they ever decide they do, we'll have one."

Back at Willett's for lunch, I found Brian Hunt, brew master and part owner, inventorying his brewing supplies. Brian was a tall, forty-ish fellow who wore his remaining hair tied back in a ponytail. He was attired in a Willett's T-shirt, blue jeans, and boots. He had a sparkle in his eye that brightened further whenever he talked about brewing beer. He and his partner, Chuck Ankeny, were models of the young downtown entrepreneurs who were spearheading the renaissance process in small cities all across the continent.

Brian's interest in brewing began during high school in Sacramento when he read about fermenting mead from honey. He tried it and offered small libations of the product to his friends at parties. When his dad heard the bubbler in his room, he was busted, but he knew by then that he wanted to be a brew master. So he went to the University of California at Davis, the only place in the western hemisphere that offered a degree in brewing.

After college, Brian went to work for Schlitz in Milwaukee, "when they still made good beer. Before they made the fatal attempt to join the trend toward Bud-style beer." When it came, the new regime sickened him. "Here I thought I had found a place where I could be part of a big-time brewery still making decent beer." But instead he participated in the introduction of a recipe for the more watery, more heavily carbonated brew that Americans in the seventies were being taught by the Budweiser ad men to accept as beer.

"It was all in the advertising—that and the fact that you were supposed to drink it so cold, you couldn't tell whether it tasted good,"

Brian explained. Schlitz never got the advertising or the recipe for the Bud-style beer right, so it went out of business. But not before Brian had cut himself loose.

Chuck Ankeny contacted him in 1988 about starting a brew pub in Napa. Great-grandson of brewer Theodore Hamm, twenty-eight-year-old Dartmouth grad Chuck Willett Ankeny grew up in Minneapolis, where he came from a long line of old-time American brewers. Working for a Napa Valley winery, he got the bug to start a brew pub and spent a year and a half looking for the perfect building. It had to have good visibility, had to be historic, had to contribute to the redevelopment of a downtown, and had to have the potential for outdoor dining.

Brian and Chuck found this building, which had fallen in the earthquake of 1906 and been rebuilt in 1920, and went to work. The place was a financial success within a year or so. Unlike my own state of New Hampshire, which still had blue law restrictions that made it difficult to start up a brew pub, California "bends over backward to help you to help them to make money off of the liquor taxes you will pay them," Brian said. The state saw early in the brew pub movement that these places would become cash cows.

Brian was happy to have found a place where one of the obstacles to success wouldn't be the traditional American hangups about drinking. The wine culture here had already created an environment in which you could make good beer for people who would appreciate it properly. "Beer drinking is one of the oldest and highest forms of human social intercourse, not to mention gastronomic delights," he said.

And then his eye began to twinkle as he launched into a monologue about brewing. "I take the same attitude toward brewing that the vintner of fine wines does to his work. You're taking natural materials from the earth and artfully transforming them into something that brings joy and gladness to the palate and soul.

"Beer should be barley, hops, yeast, water, and some carbonation," he declared. "For eight thousand years it's been made that way and there are infinite variations of those basic ingredients—enough to satisfy anybody's need for creativity or novelty." He had a new brew almost ready for drinking as we talked, a black beer made with malt roasted so deeply that it was almost burned. He was currently trying to think of a good name for it.

Brian told me that there were numerous people living in Napa who had moved there as a result of a conscious search for a good place to live, without any economic or employment incentive. He gave me the names and number of Len and Hilary Zunin, who invited me to their home after supper for tea and talk.

They lived in a quiet enclave of attached units along the river a few blocks from Harry O's. The immaculately kept interior was expensively furnished with modern and antique pieces, all chosen for their idiosyncrasy. There were clocks that did not look or sound like clocks and tables that looked like planar crystal sculpture, and as we settled ourselves in the living room, Len lit things that turned out to be candles with a black object that turned out to be an electric lighter.

He hadn't always had the fine things around him that he did now. He was born in a lower-middle-class section of Brooklyn, where his father was a pharmacist. Tormented by asthma as a child, young Len took the cure in Tucson when he was seven. His improvement was so dramatic that his family relocated there soon after. He concluded, "I guess that experience was where I got the idea that you could improve the quality of your life by finding a better place to live."

Len became a psychiatrist and, after getting drafted during the height of the Vietnam War, wrote his best-seller, *Contact: The First Four Minutes,* a popular psychological study of human greeting behavior. Then, with the means to go anywhere and experience anything, he spent three years in a Buddhist monastery in Nepal, where he learned that "a place is just a place; it doesn't have to be a home having emotional roots. Thus there is no reason to ever put up with living in a place that isn't a good place to live."

When he returned to America, he met Hilary in Seattle at a wine tasting and knew he would marry her. Hilary was from Port Chester, New York, where her family had lived since the 1880s. "But in my generation," she said, "part of what you do in Port Chester is leave as soon as you can." She came to Napa during the seventies, when she was working her way up and down the West Coast skydiving as a federally licensed parachute rigger.

The couple spent the first few years of their marriage traveling the country searching for the best place for them to live. "We had the means to live wherever we wanted; there was no need to be limited. This is the only life we've got," Len explained. They liked Sedona, Arizona; the Hudson River valley of New York State; northwestern Connecticut; and Seattle. But Napa, where each had touched down once before, turned out to be the place.

They liked Napa's size. "It's a large enough town. It has interesting demographics, a wide variety of entertainment, good social-gathering places, and you can have anonymity here if you want it," noted Len, citing the reason they rejected the small-town ideal for which some others were searching.

"You don't have to go out of town for shopping, you're in the midst of beautiful country, but you're less than two hours away from a world-class city," added Hilary. And, of course, there was the wine industry. It wasn't just that it gave the place a notable, valid identity. It also provided a link between the economics and the quality of life of the place. "Too many places have become economically dependent on enterprises that are antithetical to their community identity," she believed.

I asked about the interesting demographics Len had mentioned. He explained, "Twenty-five percent of the names in the local schools are Hispanic, but there is no Hispanic neighborhood in town. There's a remarkable homogeneity of neighborhoods, not just ethnically, but also economically." I had noticed already, driving around the city, that there were no poor neighborhoods, though there were what the locals called "low-wealth" homes scattered throughout, including one of a poor Mexican family next to my own lodgings.

Len's final suggestion to me as I left was that I should visit the historical society and look into Napa history. I hadn't done that in Santa Fe because its unique history was so well known, or in San Luis Obispo, which was so new that it had little history of significance beyond what Mayor Dunin could relate firsthand. I followed Len's advice at the city library the next day.

Like the Zunins, people had been coming to Napa looking for a good place to live longer than they had been making wine here. That's what the first Napa Valley pioneers were after; there was no gold, no trade crossroads, not even a Spanish mission. Father Jose Altimira had checked the place out in 1823 as a possible mission site but chose nearby Sonoma instead. The first white settler, the American George Yount, wrote in his diary the day he entered the valley, "In such a place, I would like to clear the land and make my home; in such a place, I would like to live and die." When he arrived in 1831 with a land grant from Mexican general Mariano Vallejo himself, there was nothing here but a small community of Wappo Indians, vast meadows of wild oats, streams full of fish, and hillsides teeming with deer and bear. He planted some crude vineyards, but only as part of the agricultural amenities he thought necessary for civilized living on the California frontier.

In the next twenty years, he was followed by a handful of pioneers looking for California homesteads away from the madness of the gold fields. Many followed Yount's example and included small vineyards in their agricultural schemes. By the time of the Bear Flag revolt in nearby Sonoma, rough wine making was already established as a key element of the good life in the valley. The revolt opened huge acreage previously tied up in Mexican land grants and attracted large numbers of a new generation of settlers, now looking for a good place not only to live, but also to make wine on a commercial scale.

First was the German Charles Krug, who in 1858 launched the winery that still flourishes under Mondavi ownership today. Through the latter half of the century, familiar names like Jacob, Schram, and Beringer established Napa wines with a predominantly Germanic character. Belatedly, miners found what they were looking for in the Napa Valley during these same years. Quicksilver (mercury) needed for the gold-extraction process was found northwest of Calistoga in the 1860s, and silver was mined at the famous Silverado in the 1870s. But fortunately, the ores were too few and the wine making too well established, and by the beginning of the twentieth century, wine was firmly entrenched as the valley's economic base. The impressive buildings and cellars of Inglenook and today's Heublein are opulent remnants of this era.

Prohibition had a devastating effect on wine-producing areas in California and elsewhere. But Napa survived relatively unscathed because of its small population and its ability to use the fertile land for other agricultural products, particularly raisins and prunes. Thus Inglenook, Beringer, and Beaulieu were well positioned for the repeal. Dozens of new wineries were founded in the post-Prohibition rush but only a few of the new ones thrived in an era of overspeculation in the industry: Christian Brothers, Louis Martini, and the Mondavi family.

World War II brought the first diversion to the valley's economic direction since the discovery of quicksilver back in the 1860s. Housing was needed for booming naval shipyards at Mare Island in the nearby bay, and thus the little city of Napa was radically transformed from a bucolic agricultural town into a municipal center of substantial population. Threatened with the possibility of Napa becoming a bedroom community for the Bay Area, wine makers rallied in the fifties to establish the valley as the dominant wine-producing region in the country. By the late sixties their success set them to planning and planting for the world-class varietal wine culture that now thrives in the valley. As part of that vision, the wine makers set out to extend their influence over everything from land-use planning to population growth to cultural establishments in the city of Napa.

Thus there had always been a connection between good living and wine making in Napa Valley. Forged in the days when the first pioneers found life here congenial enough to cultivate one of the "finer things" in the wilderness, the correlation continues with the insistence of modern wine makers that a certain quality of life must be preserved (by ordinance if need be) to guarantee the production of a world-class product.

A few days after my visit to the Zunins, I returned to Willett's, where Paul invited me to join the crew and a few of the regulars for a Napa institution, late night volleyball under the lights at a place called the Tom Foolery. The Foolery, as everyone referred to it, was a restaurant and bar with lighted sand volleyball courts and an outdoor bandstand and dance floor on the north side of town by the river. Its regular clientele were gung-ho volleyball teams and dancing singles who competed at their respective sports with equally intense fervor. But late at night, for the duration of my visit, it was invaded regularly by our contingent from Willett's. I was becoming a regular.

One morning there was a message for me at the Elms's desk. The mayor had called. Apparently my queries had worked their way into the Napa political grapevine. He wanted to see me in his office at noon. I went to Willett's for brunch before seeing the mayor. Brian Hunt came in carrying rubber boots and a wineglass with a little water and a freshly picked thistle blossom inside. It was a brewing day and he liked to begin his work with a thing of natural beauty casting its spell over the proceedings.

Because of a state alcohol tax increase, the cost of a pint was going up at Willett's from $2.25 to $2.75. "So this is Death and Taxes Black," he said as he drew me a small glass of his new black beer.

Brian donned his rubber boots and then began his day's work, crawling up into the attic, where he slit the burlap bags of barley and fed the grain into a mill that ground it and dumped it into the lauter tun, a large vessel with a stainless steel mesh filter at the bottom. Then he pumped the hot water from the heating vessel into the lauter tun. Most of the remainder of his day's work was a matter of hooking up hoses and clamps and moving liquids. He could have installed a setup where this work would be done by turning valves, but he preferred the aesthetics of the hoses. By noon the aroma of the wort was in the air. People came in for lunch and asked about the pleasant, warm smell— "Is it hot Grape Nuts or some other kind of cooking cereal?" That's exactly what it was.

I left Brian to his task and walked to city hall for my appointment with Ed Solomon. Solomon was a bespectacled, distinguished-looking elderly gentleman who, like myself, had made a transition from educator to local politician. He was not born here.

"In the late fifties and early sixties, Napa was going to be a big city," he began. The city's general plan, based on the World War II housing boom, called for a population of 120,000 by the year 2000, and zoning laws allowed an extensive ring of commercial development around the outskirts of the city. By 1968 business was fleeing to the outskirts, the downtown was becoming a ghost town, and the public mood had changed. A ballot plebiscite that year calling for a growth cap of 75,000 by the year 2000 won by a huge majority. Only 22 percent of the voters had gone to the polls and the wine makers had put a lot of money into the campaign, but the decision shaped Napa's planning and has ever since.

"Instead of population," the mayor believed, "what we need is more tourism. People used to tend to drive through Napa toward the wine country up the valley. What we have been doing is to get them to stop and spend a night or two in Napa."

In the meantime, Solomon pointed with pride to some of the progressive accomplishments of the city under his leadership. New housing developers were required to build a percentage of "low-wealth" housing for every project given approval, and the city had been careful to perpetuate the tradition of spreading low-wealth housing throughout the city, not concentrating it into ghettos. "The result," he said, "is a city that is not factionalized."

He had helped to promote the active Napa Renaissance Group and the Downtown Redevelopment Association, which assisted projects like the proposed opera house renovation and gave merchants incentives to provide the goods and services that would bring people to the downtown.

Solomon's dream was to exploit the riverfront, as San Antonio had done, to enrich the Napa experience. "We still need a boardwalk, the opera house, a performing arts center, a wine and cuisine center—enough action in the heart of town to keep our residents here and bring in tourists to join them."

Solomon viewed his role as mayor as a matter of holding forth a dream before the community and curbing the political fractiousness that can shatter such dreams. Enforcing a less contentious and more cooperative regime within the city council was his proudest accomplishment.

At five o'clock Brian was still brewing back at Willett's, where he had cooked the beer, added the hops, and run the wort (cooked beer) through the lauder tun screen. Now he was cooling the wort in preparation for adding yeast, assisted by the waitress whose smile had brought me into Willett's that first day. Petra Van Winden offered the tale of her father's immigration to Napa from Holland after World War II. He had come here at age eighteen because his mother died of anxiety during the Nazi occupation; "he just kept moving west till he found a place where he felt safe." Now the Van Windens ran the biggest horticultural nursery in Napa, and Petra was the youngest of seven beautiful blond daughters courted by guys from all over town.

Eventually I drove up California 29 through the heart of the wine country to meet County Supervisor Mel Varrelman in St. Helena. Heading north, the valley narrowed, and I was struck by how quickly I had passed from city to country. There was no sprawl on the wine makers' side of town, only mile after mile of sunny vineyards with rows of grapes stretching from the roadside all the way to the verge of the valley on either side. Mounted on towers, curious machines that looked like airplane propellers stood ready to move the air should the Napa climate fail.

Each winery had a central manor house whose style suggested another era. Small signs announcing tasting hours directed visitors up graceful drives through hanging willows and towering palms. Along the road ran the tracks of the Wine Train, and the only hints of disturbance to the medieval placidity of the valley were small signs erected like parking signs on the properties along the tracks: NO WINE TRAIN.

County Commissioner Mel Varrelman had his CPA's office on a side street in St. Helena, a busy little town with lots of flowers and a distinctly European feel. Varrelman was of a slightly younger generation than Huber and Solomon and greeted me in the style of a man confident and in control. He seemed to have no political fear of publicity, evading none of my questions.

I asked him to describe what he thought were the keys to the quality of life in Napa Valley. "Certainly the wine industry provides a unique economic base," he answered. "But we have taken the issue of rural growth control to an ultimate level. And that is the key."

It all began with the state's Williamson Act of 1966, which I had heard about in SLO, allowing tax credits to people who put their land into agricultural preservation for ten years. "It's similar to the current-use legislation you have in New England, with one huge difference. The contract rolls over every year, so the land is always guaranteed to be in agricultural preservation for ten years." In effect, if you wanted to get out, you had to announce your intention ten years ahead of time. "That's what makes it work in a way your current-use laws back East never have."

Then there was the Agricultural Preservation Act of 1968, and this was unique to Napa County. In areas where the soil types had been identified as "prime agricultural," large minimum lot sizes were enacted—first twenty acres and more recently forty acres. Thus any subdivision required at least eighty acres.

I protested that rural zoning with five-acre-lot minimums had been attacked in my part of the country as being elitist—saying in effect, that you can have a home in the country only if you are affluent enough to afford a big lot. Varrelman countered, "But we're not interested in people building homes on prime agricultural land at all, at any level of affluence. The criticisms of your five-acre minimum are correct—all it accomplishes is to guarantee to the established neighbors that only homes of a certain wealth level will be built. But our forty-acre minimum is based on what you need to have a working small vineyard. You can farm five tons of grapes per acre at $2,000 per ton—that means $400,000 gross on forty acres, which is what it takes to make a living growing grapes. Of course, the importance of the wine industry here is what makes all this possible. We couldn't do this if we raised broccoli."

Varrelman's concern was that the forty-acre minimum wasn't large enough. "Outfits come in and buy thousand-acre spreads and develop these ranchettes on forty acres each and sell them to wealthy customers who have no intention of growing grapes. So now we're considering a 160-acre minimum. Over in Sonoma they have a 360-acre minimum."

But he conceded that there was the same danger here that there was with the five-acre minimum. "The larger your minimum, the faster your land gets gobbled up as long as there are people with enough money to build homes on the lots. You still get sprawl, only at a lower and even more wasteful density. The key is [to] find a size large enough to stop the process entirely. But until you get there you play a dangerous game of chicken with your remaining land."

"Where are people supposed to live?" I asked.

"Not in the agricultural zones," he answered firmly. "That's what we have cities like Napa for."

"What about commercial development?"

"Not allowed, period," he answered. Except for one small industrial park near the airport, all commercial and industrial development in the county was zoned by law within city corporate limits. The city shared tax revenue from such development with the county so that there was no incentive for the county to cave in to developers for tax base purposes. The result, Varrelman believed, was a guarantee of discrete population centers and definite boundaries between the urban and county landscape instead of the low-density sprawl afflicting the countryside between cities in so much of the nation.

To Varrelman, the biggest problem facing the county and the valley was the city of Napa. "They made three horrendous mistakes down there," he said. "The first was to allow too much commercial development in the outer ring that sucked the economic life out of the down-town. The second was to cut in half the city's projected population ceiling. The third was to try to revitalize the downtown by building a downtown mall. The result is they've got a city with a commercial establishment designed to serve twice the population they mean to allow. I don't care what Ed Solomon says, that's still a troubled down-town."

What Napa needed, Varrelman believed, was more population, preferably in high-density developments in or adjacent to the town center. Like all downtowns, Napa's downtown needed to stop trying to compete with the plazas and malls for the commercial dollar. Instead the emphasis should be on cultural, entertainment, and service estab-lishments like the opera house, the Mondavi wine culture center, a performing arts center, and the river park.

Finally I asked Mel Varrelman about his biggest headache here in St. Helena. Wasn't the Wine Train the same kind of creative business proposal for the county that he urged for the city of Napa? Here Varrelman's tone shifted from one evincing strong personal views to one of objective reporting about the views of his constituents. He chose his words more carefully.

"People in the valley see the Wine Train as basically a way to drop 400,000 people a year off in St. Helena. St. Helena can't accommodate that level of tourism. Plus many see it as a kind of Disneyland activity, out of the class of the valley. The valley's future is based on making world-class, high-quality wine. The Wine Train and balloon rides and other things like that are seen as extraneous profiteering. Many don't believe that's what this valley is all about."

Back on Main Street in Napa that evening it was hard to imagine that there was a quarrel anywhere in the valley. People were gathering on the lawn of Veterans Park for a concert. Mark, another of the bartenders at Willett's, had just finished his shift and joined his wife and two energetic young boys frolicking in the grass. I asked him, as one of the older members of the Willett's crew, if he intended to stay at that work for a long time. "Why not? I can sleep late, play with my wife and kids a lot, and walk a couple of blocks to a job I love. I could make more money doing something else, but would I be as happy?"

Down the block from the park and Willett's, I found another kind of third place, the Napa Valley Coffee Roasting Company. It was a small place with just a few tables where patrons could sip their coffee while reading the newspaper, dandling kids on knees, or socializing with acquaintances coming in through a door that never ceased swinging. Managers Marilyn Wiskus and Alison Denefrio, evening regulars at Willett's, explained that places like this had enjoyed a West Coast renaissance even before the brew pub trend. "The two are part of the same phenomenon," said Alison. "A simple desire to live well. Part of living well is being able to spontaneously stroll downtown and talk with acquaintances over coffee or beer." More people than usual were out doing precisely that this evening. Marilyn said it was because tonight was the opening of the Napa Town and Country Fair.

Later Paul and some of the Willett's crew invited me to tag along with them to the fair, reminding me of another phenomenon I was coming to appreciate in Napa. There were no age barriers here, no generation gaps. Provided one was willing to sip a glass or lift a pint, to dive in the sand for the volleyball or clamber aboard the roller coaster at the fair, to talk hearty, and to pursue the serious business of enjoying life with zest, the youth regime of this West Coast city issued a standing invitation to shed the years and join in the fun.

During the next week, I began to see this for what it was—just one of the many effects of living in a town with a strong third place tradition. People lived publicly in Napa and the result was the general lowering of all sorts of social barriers besides age. College professors discussed physics with carpenters in Willett's. Young black rappers queried white middle-aged lawyers about how to dig big band swing at performances in the park by the river. Local writers discussed Central American politics with recent arrivals from Mexico at the Coffee Roasting Company. Kids and their parents listened to the music at Harry O's. Lawyers and college kids contended at the nets in the sand late nights at the Foolery.

My last morning in Napa, I drove to the Silver Oaks Winery up the valley in Oakville to meet wine maker Justin Meyers. I chose Silver Oaks because it made cabernet sauvignon exclusively and its 1986 vintage had just been named Best American Cabernet for the third straight year in the American Wine Competition. Word on the street in Napa had it that Silver Oaks was among those leading the valley's assault on the beleaguered French wine industry worldwide.

The winery was located in the old Oakville Dairy, just a short drive down a narrow road from California 29. Inside, the hospitality room was a dark, almost cavelike chamber paneled in redwood from old barrels. I was directed up a flight of stairs to an office room clicking and buzzing with desktop computers and modern communications equipment. Two opposing glass walls overlooked the warehouse aging rooms with their hundreds of barrels, spic and span, high and dry, and displayed under bright light. No dank, musty aging cave here.

I was shown into a private office with windows overlooking the vineyards outside. Justin Meyers rose from his desk to an impressive height and shook my hand with a grip that I imagined could be useful to convey anything from hearty commitment to brutal intimidation. With a bald pate and full beard, he might have looked a bit like a seaman but for his impeccable attire and manicuring.

"What does it take to get to where we are?" he asked rhetorically before I had a chance to pose a question. "Places that make world-class wine are blessed with soil and climate. You can make it work or botch it up. There are technical aspects, business aspects, and, frankly, being aggressive enough to generate good publicity."

Otherwise Justin believed that the long-term health of the wine industry here was dependent on a continuing struggle for control of the land, how it was used, and how people lived on it. "Santa Clara is an example of every Napa wine maker's nightmare," he declared. "Once the land has houses on it, the blessing we have here is lost forever. Making good wine requires living a good life. It has to be rural, free from other commercial distractions, it has to be rich with culture, intelligence, tradition, and plain, simple joy. Here we can live like that. They live like that in Bordeaux."

Justin differed strongly, however, with Mel Varrelman over who was responsible for preserving the land and the quality of life in Napa Valley. He believed that it was the private enterprise wineries, not government, that had created and preserved what everyone cherished here. "The Williamson Act is a joke," he scoffed. "It has so many hooks in it, nobody uses it. The forty-acre-minimum lot size has failed because the people who want to build in Napa have enough money to buy that big. And this talk of increasing the minimum would prevent the kid with a degree in wine making from starting up a new winery on a small vineyard. That's me twenty years ago.

"I didn't become conservative till I had something to conserve," he went on. "And I don't mean money. I mean a way of life and a valued product. I haven't abused the countryside for profit and I resent the county government's assault on the landowner's rights."

It was Justin's contention that government created sweepingly foolish ordinances as a reaction to somebody doing something badly. Why didn't they just deal with abusers, he wanted to know, rather than creating blanket legislation that deprived everyone of the opportunity to do some innovative things right?

He talked about the future of Napa. "As long as grape growing makes sense, the land and the way of life will be preserved. The big question is who is going to control the land—those who use it, or those who are elected by voters who live on it, or those from the outside with money enough to buy it? Our democratic tradition says it should be the politicians. But experience shows that it has to be those who use it or the outsiders will take over and turn it into condos and strip malls."

I asked him if he thought the Napa experience offered any instruction to less blessed communities elsewhere in America. He answered, "A lot of places are blessed with something. When an industry that recognizes the blessing develops it and becomes a success, you have the potential for a good place to live. I guess the real lesson of Napa Valley is to promote an industry that strives for a product that is the best in the world. If you think about it, that's what America did across the board back in the days when there were lots of good places to live in this country."

As I drove back down the valley, it seemed to me that the medieval motif of Napa Valley was more than just an image. In order to compete globally, the wine barons had found means to subvert democratic government with a benevolent despotism that generated a way of life far superior to the usual contemporary American way. Besides the obvious five for Comfort, I knew I would rate Napa a five for Someplace and also for Cheers. There would be a four for Cake and a Fudge Factor of four, acknowledging the remarkable degree to which wine makers and local government had succeeded in preserving the valley's quality of life, despite their disagreements. Only for the Foot Factor would Napa get a mediocre three; it was, after all, another sprawling western town where people spent too much time in their cars.

While Santa Fe had shown the value of community roots and identity and San Luis Obispo showed that with a little aggressive activism, Sun Belt sites didn't have to be exploited to despoliation, Napa offered several lessons applicable, I thought, to places elsewhere.

First, there was the land of Napa Valley. Its rural character had been preserved and would continue to be preserved because it was actively used, as Justin Meyers had argued, by an industry whose interests lay in keeping it rural and whose economic clout was enough to guarantee it. Commissioner Bracket in San Luis Obispo had talked about wine making and fruit growing as industries that would keep her county's marginal rural lands off the auction block. In both places, minimum lot sizes were established according to the minimum required for a landowner to utilize it for its best rural use. Perhaps dairy country lands elsewhere should have minimum lot sizes appropriate to dairy farming. It certainly made more sense than the standard five-acre minimum so common in places whose rural land was rapidly disappearing under pavement.

The county's absolute insistence that residential and commercial development be channeled into the urban areas made sense too. Rural sprawl not only destroys the countryside, it enervates the cities and towns. For three thousand years human evolution has led us to congregate in various-size urban settings. How foolish to think that the development patterns of just the past forty years should change the functional underpinnings of that history. William Whyte has shown that many of our cities and towns today are actually well below their ideal density levels, with numerous vacant buildings, huge spaces devoted to parking lots, and low-density sprawl beginning relatively close to the center. Thus significant commercial and residential growth that might otherwise destroy the countryside can be accommodated with urban infill. Whyte has also shown that when push comes to shove, relatively small expansions of cities at their periphery, *developed at a truly urban density,* can accommodate significant growth. These principles hold true for cities of all sizes as well as for small towns. The planners in Napa Valley apparently had read Whyte's book.

Despite Commissioner Varrelman's concerns about the health of Napa's downtown, there was no question that it was bouncing back from the stagnation it first experienced when the city erred in allowing commercial growth appropriate for a much larger city (and Napa might yet become that larger city). Its historical designation status protected its funky old buildings from the wrecking ball and attracted businesses owned by people who yearned to be part of something richer than just the ringing of cash registers. Further, it demonstrated that at least one critically located third place could lead the way in making the downtown a place for people to gather and live publicly. Willett's Brewing Company, sited at the key intersection beside the park and the river, was the first and one of the best of many such models I would find in subsequent travels across the continent. It didn't have to be a bar and restaurant; it could have been the coffee shop it spawned just down the street, or a deli bookstore, or some other imaginative development from a new generation of downtown entrepreneurs—like Brian Hunt and Chuck Ankeny—possessed by the vision of making their livings by making the downtown a better place to live.

The people of Napa were its other strength, so many of whom had come here from someplace else with what I regarded at this point in my travels as a West Coast penchant for living well. I wouldn't know till later visits to places back East that the influx of newcomers determined to live more freely, youthfully, and gregariously was a hallmark of renaissance towns generally, regardless of location.

Back in town, I drove around Napa's remarkably homogeneous neighborhoods before heading for Oakland, where I would catch a train to Oregon. The Mexican family next door to the Elms gathered around one of their cars at streetside with an ease and security that their counterparts in Oakland couldn't imagine. Just a few blocks one way, bartender Mark would be strolling to his evening shift, and a few more blocks in the other direction, the wealthy author of a best-seller would be having cocktails in a place he had studied to find. Nearby, the Van Winden family and their seven lovely daughters would soon be sitting down for supper before the evening ritual of gentlemen callers from seven walks of Napa life.

At Willett's, Brian Hunt was brewing creme ale. Death and Taxes Black was already a huge success. In reference to the government deficits that provoked the alcohol tax increase, someone had written on the chalkboard above the bar: DRINK TO THE DEFICITS! A new fellow from out of town sat at the bar with an ale that Paul had just poured for him, looking through a local realty magazine. "Look at this," he said. "Nice homes for under $150,000. I could afford to live here."

"Do you like to play volleyball?" asked Paul.

4

GETTING IT RIGHT
THIS TIME

The fellow with the straw hat held the pin while his white-haired partner lined up a ten-foot putt. Dew sparkled under a platinum sun this cloudless Oregon summer morning. "You'll have to give it some extra kick," said pin holder to putter. "This green's still wet." The putter clicked and the ball rolled, and curved, and pin holder pulled out the pin. "Not bad, ol' buddy—two pars before eight in the morning. Not bad at all."

I watched this little golfers' scene as I sat sipping my coffee on the back porch of Sparks Abed and Breakfast, just a few feet from the sixth hole of the Country Club Golf Course in Corvallis, Oregon. Herb Sparks, my host, identified the golfers as a professor from Oregon State University and a retired executive of Hewlitt-Packard, "the two main reasons," he said, "besides the climate and country, why Corvallis is such a good place to live."

For a few minutes, the golfers set aside their clubs to join us for Mrs. Sparks's coffee. They pointed out Mary's Peak to the west, the highest mountain in the Coast Range and possessed of a virgin meadow on its flat top with "the most spectacular sunset views in the universe," and the line of purple Cascade peaks far to the east across the flatness of the Willamette Valley. They explained that the pleasant breeze that tinkled through the wind chimes on Herb's back porch almost never ceased and that this part of the profusely beflowered valley got far less rain than did Seattle. "Can you imagine what the old pioneer settlers must have thought when they found this place after the sufferings they went through to get here?" asked one of the golfers. "Musta thought they had died and gone to heaven."

Corvallis was indeed right in the heart of the Oregon country sought by wagon trains following the Oregon Trail in the 1840s, and that was one of the reasons I had come here. The other was the fact that the Willamette Valley, and the cities of Corvallis and Portland in particular, were now the object of a new migration 150 years later. Corvallis had just been ranked number two (after San Luis Obispo) in G. Scott Thomas's *Rating Guide to Life in America's Small Cities,* and Portland had gained distinction as a city whose crime rates had actually gone down in the past decade. At populations of 44,757 and 437,319, respectively, the two cities offered two poles of successful, modern American, urban experience.

Mrs. Sparks called from the kitchen that breakfast was ready, so the golfers returned to their game and Herb and I joined three other boarders at the dining room table. Over fresh homemade muffins, fruit compote with whipped cream, sausage kishke, and strawberry pie, Herb explained that he and his family had lived in Seattle, where he worked for Boeing. "I know everybody says Seattle's a wonderful place to live, but there were just too many people. When I got laid off, it was a blessing in disguise." He came to the Willamette Valley with his family in a true pioneer spirit. He had no job lined up; he just knew he wanted to live here. And when he did land a job, it was only temporary, until the last of his five kids graduated from high school. What he and his wife really wanted was to make a B and B out of the large empty nest when the kids were gone. "Now our guests are our family and our excuse to live the life we want where we want."

Besides myself, the Sparks's guests at the table that morning included a couple from Coos Bay who took the weekend to sojourn inland and escape the coastal rain, wind, and fog and see a little sun. There was also a young mother who lived in Corvallis but was taking a weekend getaway from her family at Sparks's. "This is what a sensible mother who doesn't work does to prevent child abuse, affairs, divorce —you know," she said. "I just take a weekend every month or so and crash here at Sparks's."

That's what she liked about Corvallis—that you could do that kind of thing without raising any eyebrows. "It's a family town and people are pretty creative about alternatives to the usual pattern of living just for your kids, being married to your automobile, your calendar, and slowly going stark-raving bathouse." She recommended that I begin my exploration of Corvallis at a coffeehouse called the Beanery.

The Sparkses' place was on the outskirts of the city, but in less than five minutes' drive I was cruising downtown First Street. I noticed on the way into town that the boulevards had wide, grassy verges with dedicated bicycle paths and I saw nearly as many bicycles as cars.

The downtown was a five-by-nine-block grid with north-south streets numbered in the western fashion and east-west streets named after presidents. There was Whiteside's Marquee Movie Theater, a bustling farmer's market, and dozens of thriving shops and restaurants. The Beanery was a prime specimen of the Northwest coffeehouse. But unlike most, which tended to be so small that they only just barely achieved the critical mass for good social ferment, the Beanery was huge, like a beer hall without beer. With wooden floors at several different levels, large windows on the street front, wooden tables with lots of freestanding chairs (including rockers), and two serving counters, the Beanery was designed to maximize public comfort for a good number of people. You could curl up in a rocker with your coffee and newspaper alone, or you could join acquaintances at a table, or you could carry your coffee and move from group to group. And, of course, the coffees and their aroma warming the room were excellent.

I took a table by the window and looked out at the clearly healthy downtown, with clean streets, lots of large, leafy trees obviously planted some years ago, and no empty storefronts. The awning-covered sidewalks thronged with people. And most curious, a fact I had noticed immediately as I entered the town yesterday, there was absolutely no graffiti.

"Why would anyone want to mark up such a good place?" said a gray-bearded fellow sipping his coffee next to me. "People here believe they live in the perfect spot, far enough from Portland so we're not a bedroom community but close enough to take advantage of it. We're close to the ocean one way and to Mount Hood the other. Good climate year-round, a good diversity of people. We've got Asians, Moslems, Europeans, Africans—all because of the university, of course."

When I asked if there were other places as good elsewhere in the Willamette Valley, I provoked a lot of head shaking among a group at another table beside us. A woman who worked for the state in children's services was adamant: "In many places, the valley is no 'pioneer paradise,' I'll tell ya. Too much dependence on a hurting industry, logging, and pulp. Albany's a depressed place. Salem's just a bedroom community for Portland. And Sweet Home—good name, huh?—it's the child abuse and wife-beating capital of the world. Police break up bloody fights on the street there every night. No, it's just Corvallis, and Eugene further up the valley—they have the University of Oregon there."

"But Eugene's not like Corvallis," the gray beard interrupted. "Too radical for my taste. There's a conservative ethic here—not politically, but in terms of people's behavior. People look out for each other and they don't do things to aggravate each other." I was advised to approach people in Corvallis cautiously, not just because of that conservative nature but also because there might not be a lot of enthusiasm for letting the news get out that the city was such a good place to live.

Saturday evening I set out to see if Corvallis had night spots as cordial as the Beanery. People I'd met there had given a rough-looking downtown tavern, the Peacock, mixed reviews: it was a bikers' bar, it was the fundamental local institution of the working middle class, it was a tough singles' place, it was a place for couples with some spunk in their lives, it was a pool hall, it was the best blues club in the Northwest, and, according to Herb Sparks, it had "maybe more local color than you might want."

Parked along First Street out front, there were indeed a half dozen big, gleaming Harleys. But the fellow with long salt-and-pepper hair taking the cover charge at the doorway gave me a friendly invitation to come in and check out the music before paying. Inside, the place was cavernous and more brightly lighted than I had expected. There were at least a dozen pool tables and all in use. In one corner a blues band, Bill Rhodes's Party Kings, played while half a dozen couples danced western-rock style in the space before the stage. At the other side of the room stretched the longest bar I had ever seen, with maybe fifty patrons seated or leaning at it. Though the ambience was blue jeans and flannel, boots and leather, there were three or four men in jackets and ties and a few women dressed for dinner. Two beefy bouncers wearing black Zig Zag T-shirts just cruised around the room with bare tattooed arms.

Just a couple of doors down the street from the Peacock, I came upon the Majestic Theatre, where a performance of *A Funny Thing Happened on the Way to the Forum* was in progress. Liz Hogan, house manager, explained that the theater was a vaudeville house in the thirties, then a movie house. In 1986 a group of local theater aficionados decided that Corvallis needed a performing arts center that wasn't associated with the university. "It wasn't a matter of competing with the university," Liz believed. "People just felt that the town was culturally fertile enough to sponsor its own theater to complement what the university offers." The result was a grassroots effort to raise the money to rehabilitate the house and to bring in a local theater troupe that had been performing for twenty-five years in a barn.

The house was full of well-dressed white heads this night, while out front, three or four tough-looking bikers chatted quietly beside their machines. "Sort of a queer juxtaposition of establishments," I commented to Liz.

"I have to come out to close the doors some nights because of their noise," she answered. "But you'd be surprised what good neighbors they usually are. Most of them routinely walk their bikes down the street before starting them up when we've got a performance going."

On Sunday I moved from Sparks's Abed and Breakfast to an inexpensive motel right downtown. Sparks's was the place I would stay if I came back here on vacation, but I feared that if I stayed out there by the golf course, I might miss something vital in the heart of town. I spent the morning walking to places near my new digs—Central Park, with its immaculately maintained lawns and gardens, where kids climbed on an elaborate Big Toy and families picnicked in the grass; Martin Luther King Grove, "dedicated by the citizens of Corvallis to the principles of peace, freedom, justice, and equality"; the Southern Pacific Railroad tracks, where a thirty-car freight train rolled through just for my delight; and the unfinished river park, where bike paths and benches lined the bluff above the shoreline. The bike paths of Corvallis were so inviting that I decided to park my car for the remainder of the visit and rent a bicycle.

In the afternoon I rode over to the Peacock to see Tommy Connors, the owner. I noticed two other bicycles parked in front alongside a trio of Harleys. Tommy believed that the key to the Peacock's success as a gathering place for a cross section of Corvallis was treating everybody the same. "I don't care if you sleep under the bridge or make a million bucks, treat me right, have a good time, be responsible, let it roll." His clientele included preppies, bikers, loggers, ranchers, metalworkers, and college professors—"people making anywhere from four figures to six figures."

Though the business was good enough that Tommy didn't have to work behind the bar himself, he liked doing it. "You run a bar like you run a family," he contended. "[The] bar's my household, see, and the patrons are all my kids. I have a responsibility to take care of 'em. It takes personal contact—you can't run a family if you're never at home, and you can't run a bar unless you're in it."

I asked Tommy why he thought Corvallis was such a good place to live. He began to tick off the points. It was the only town he'd ever lived in where he never locked his door. It was a great place to raise kids. It was a town where people cared about one another. "My kids will usually tell me where they've been, and if they slip up, my friends will tell me," he said.

Tommy was no college man, but he respected what the university did for the town. Since its roots were the old ag school, he believed that Oregon State University had always been more a part of the real community here than colleges in many places. He thought the public schools in Corvallis were the best he had ever seen—teachers were paid higher salaries than other teachers nationally, and the school district had a reputation for not tolerating teachers who didn't deserve the high salary.

As others had, Tommy described the people of Corvallis as conservative—in a behavioral rather than ideological sense. "People here want to live a good life," he believed, "rather than make a lot of money or get on some L.A.-type power trip. They're pretty tolerant—we got Muslims and Buddhists and all kinds of races. But there's one thing we don't like: people who deliberately try to antagonize, whether its antiabortionists or radical feminists. You got the right to do almost whatever you want, but you don't have the right to be an asshole."

Wherever I went in Corvallis, there was a lot of talk defining the "conservative" nature of the town. Corvallis was a place with a thriving underground music scene, where racially mixed couples and gay couples strolled the downtown sidewalks without eliciting a glance from passersby, where taxpayers tolerated huge property taxes with little complaint, and where everybody acknowledged the blessing brought to the town by the university's academia. Yet people still insisted on calling the place conservative. I decided to track down a real conservative in hopes of getting a different articulation of this paradox.

I was told that the local newspaper was more conservative, in an ideological sense, than the town as a whole and that Tom Watson, publisher of the Corvallis *Gazette-Times,* was the man responsible. I visited him in his office after deadline the third day of my visit.

Tom Watson was a veteran newsman of thirty-one years' experience in Missouri, Texas, and California, but after only two and a half years he hoped that Corvallis would be his final posting. "Climate, westernness, and an intellectual community—that's what I like about Corvallis," he said.

I asked him why he was considered the town conservative. He laughed. "I guess they call me that because I give the elitist crowd a hard time. There's a frame of mind in Corvallis that thinks you can preserve what we have here and promote expanding social services without adding to the economic base."

Tom believed that Corvallis was blessed with spectacular good fortune but was threatened by "elitist complacency" and certain hostile elements in the larger state political environment. Besides the wonderful land and climate, the first key to success was the university. The town grew up around it and there was universal recognition of its importance—never any of the kind of town-gown conflict he had seen back in Columbia, Missouri. The university and the community worked together to promote events like the annual da Vinci Days cultural fair in summer. For two weeks everybody from semiconductor engineers to the children of country logging men would explore music, sculpture, biology, and physics in high-tech, hands-on exhibits, and enjoy live performances, dancing, and a cornucopia of fine food and wine. There were also joint community development endeavors, such as the Madison Avenue project, which would establish a landscaped corridor between the downtown and the university.

A second blessing was Hewlitt-Packard, Corvallis's largest employer. "The beauty of HP," Tom said, "is that it creates all of these little spin-off industries when their people go off and start their own little computer-related businesses. Between the university and HP, you couldn't ask for a healthier, more enlightened basis for an economy."

I asked him about the threat he had mentioned.

"Oregon has bigger problems than people realize. We're hurting for money and we have the highest property taxes in the country—$3,500 on a $100,000 house. So since the state won't do the job with its taxes and expenditures, people stop the buck at the local property tax. The result when things get tight is that education, which is so critical to a city like Corvallis, gets screwed.

"Then there's this war between the environmentalists and the timber industry that has sapped the regional economy and put everyone in a mean disposition. Corvallis is an island of success in a sea of trouble."

Despite his complaints about the elitist crowd, Tom had no quarrel with Corvallis's basic commitment to strong city planning. In fact, using Palm Springs as a model, he thought there were ways the city could be even more aggressive, such as by banning neon signs and considering the effects of shadow lines in reviewing the architecture of new building projects.

"You can't argue with success," he conceded. "We have a healthy downtown, and you won't find many cities where beautification has become such a part of the community ethic. Show me another town where the Burger Kings do the landscaping they do here."

His comment reminded me of the lack of graffiti, and I asked him about it.

"We have the same psychology here that they do at Disneyland, where there are people running around constantly keeping the place clean—result, people keep a clean place clean. There's an occasional act of vandalism, but we fix it immediately. We sweep the streets—there's no more false economy than to garage the street sweeper. Everybody knows the old saw that if one property owner lets his go, the one next door will too. But the opposite is also true. People take care of their property—it's expected."

Tom insisted that it wasn't really conservatism that people were talking about when they described the community, it was goodwill. "There's a certain sense of classlessness here that makes people behave well, or at least gives them no excuse not to," he contended. "Because of the university, we have significant minority populations here—the largest is Asian, not black or Hispanic—without the usual conflicts. I suppose it helps that we're off the interstate corridor and so a lot of the migrant types tend to bypass us."

Tom Watson ended our discussion with another reference to the danger of complacency. "There is a demographic change taking place here that could upset the apple cart: Californians. They sell their expensive California houses and come north, where they get too much equity. They bring too much money into the market and skew the lifestyle. As a result, they're resented for it. They're the first minority that has ever provoked a backlash—and once people learn to feel that way about one group, well. . . ."

The session with Tom was another lesson in West Coast relativity. Here was the so-called conservative publisher of the local paper concerned about antiminority backlash, underfunded education, and zoning regulation that didn't go far enough.

That evening I stopped by the Peacock and ran into Tommy Connors and his son, who were heading out to do their laundry. It was eight-thirty in the evening, an odd hour for such a chore, but Tommy promised that if I tagged along, I would see why it made sense.

We drove a few blocks in his car and pulled into a place called the Suds 'n' Suds, located beside a Woodstock's Pizzeria. Inside, the laundry opened into the pizzeria and out back was a small, convivial bar and a little beer garden. I had seen the slick national chains of combination launderette-bars catering primarily to young singles. But Suds 'n' Suds wasn't like that. Most of the patrons here were families; the kids would head next door for pizza while Mom and Dad, after loading up the washer, would settle in at the bar for a pint of one of those good northwestern microbrews.

A long-haired fellow with thick eyeglasses who worked behind the bar befriended me as soon as I bellied up. Dave Mellish described himself as a former biker-hippie learning to be a good liberal citizen of the best place to live he'd ever seen. He had come to Corvallis with his wife after two years of hard living in the saddle of a Harley David-son. "What makes Corvallis so good is the radical mix of people you get here in such a small city. You get button-down computer engineers and their families rubbing shoulders with guys like me, and no fric-tion."

I asked him about the conservative theme. "People here appreciate what they have," he said. "Maybe that's conservative. I think it's kind of hip myself."

He talked about the natural amenities that moved people from all walks of life to settle here—the nearby ocean, the mountains, the climate. "Wednesday night we're going up to the meadow on top of Mary's Peak to watch the Perseid meteor shower," he said. "If you want to really understand the Willamette Valley life, you should come with us."

In the morning I went to city hall, passing a brick wall.that dis-played the first piece of graffiti I had seen during my visit here. STOP GREED was all it said. The mayor was unavailable, but Neil Mann, the director of community development, was happy to talk to me. Com-bining the duties of city planning, development regulation, industrial recruiting, and city engineering, his department worked to oversee both public improvement and private investment, with a mission to ensure that new growth was consistent with a community vision.

He then ticked off the elements of the community vision he was charged with implementing: maintaining population growth at 1.5 percent per year through limited construction of new housing, siting small high-tech industries on lands set aside for that purpose, chan-neling all major commercial development into the downtown, devel-oping small "pocket" commercial zones in residential areas and within walking distance of private homes, confining strip development to the one north-south corridor where it was established years ago and absolutely prohibiting it from the pristine east and west entrances to the city, cooperating with the university on development and land-scaping to further integrate it with the city, and planning for capital improvement projects to support the desired growth. Later that after-noon he had an appointment with the CEO of a communications company he was trying to lure to Corvallis.

I was intrigued because in my city, like most in New England, we had no equivalent to the integration of community development functions inherent in Mann's broad-reaching mandate. Back there we relied simply on a planning department to regulate development in a primarily negative manner. The idea was that if city government confined itself to thwarting harmful development, the market could be relied on to bring us the things we did want. The closest we had come to actually directing development was to fund a private industrial recruitment corporation.

Our method didn't work very well. We tended to get the things we didn't want anyway, and development proposals truly consistent with our community goals were few and far between. And the activities of the private industrial recruiter continually struck sparks from competing land vendors and developers, who criticized him for coziness with certain private sector players.

"That's right," said Mann. "We believe it takes an aggressive, proactive stance in city hall itself to attract developers interested in building what you want to see built and to avoid manipulation by private interests." But at this he demurred that we were now into politics and out of his depth. He sent me down the hall to talk to the city manager.

The position of city manager is one of the hottest seats in America. Instituted in many small cities as part of the depoliticizing of city hall administrations following the depression, it put the day-to-day operation of city government in the hands of a nonelected trained professional who was hired by and served the will of an elected city council and nonadministrative mayor. Besides taking management out of the hands of elected figures subject to the temptations of politics, the motivation was to ensure professional competence for handling the increasingly complex mechanism of modern city government.

Though the city manager form of government has become the norm in small cities, it has had a stormy history. City managers can wield enormous power, sometimes even manipulating and controlling their elected bosses, and some constituents have never accepted the undemocratic nature of the institution. But because they can be fired on the whim of a majority of the council, city managers are often the subject of vicious attack by private interests who believe they are disadvantaged by city policy. As a result it has become common wisdom that city managers rarely last more than a few years before moving on.

The most successful ones, in addition to demonstrating extraordinary skill, tend to be low-profile reflections of the mainstream of their communities.

So it surprised me when I entered the office of Gerald Seals, city manager of a town that described itself as conservative, to meet a robust, outspoken African-American. He didn't want to talk much about himself but he had a lot to say about how city government worked in Corvallis. He saw his job as one of making public administration a customer-oriented business. It wasn't enough that people had the chance to elect their political leaders. "They have to share in the process of government, particularly in the area of community planning," he said. Thus the city engaged some years ago in a "visioning process" in which every resident was invited to participate through flyers sent out with the local newspaper. The result was "Vision 2010," a community goals statement that had guided planning ever since.

Corvallis's formal commitment to planning was established only a little more than a decade ago, relatively recently compared to many communities nationwide. "But planning has roots in Corvallis that go back to its founding. People who came here, even in pioneer days, did so as a result of bad experiences with communities back East," he said. Locals told a story about those early Oregon pioneers and the legendary intelligence they brought with them. According to the story, there was once a sign posted just west of South Pass in Wyoming where the California and Oregon Trails diverged. It was a square sign with no arrow or pointer shape, and it read, OREGON TRAIL TURN RIGHT. Thus only those who could read came to Oregon.

Seals insisted that the Oregon idea of "getting it right this time" was no myth and that even in the old days it established a pattern of de facto or "volunteer" planning. Cities like Corvallis had always been cautious about development, even during the boom years of the sixties, when places like Napa opened the floodgates to commercial development.

"And so we have the space along streets to put in bike paths today, fifty miles of them as established city policy," he said. "We have them because the city fathers who laid out the town anticipated some such need—they didn't know it would be bike paths, but they knew it was a good idea to leave that kind of space."

I asked him my usual question about protecting against the incursions of regional mall developers and he gave me a novel answer: "Malls are made possible only when you already have a deteriorating downtown—deteriorating downtowns lead to malls, not the other way around, as the common wisdom would have it." He thought that the city had to make a commitment to partnership with a downtown association of merchants that operated almost like mall management. Government could help with traffic patterns, pedestrian friendliness, parks, benches, and other infrastructure, he said, "but you need an association to combat the hideboundness of downtown merchants who are always their own worst enemies. It can teach merchants not to try to compete with the plazas for every need. Merchants err when they focus too much on retail and not enough on amenities, services, and entertainment. This is the key to healthy downtowns in micropolitan communities—to get away from high-tech and into high-touch."

Corvallis was a national innovator in the business of downtown associations. With nearly 100 percent membership, its downtown group taxed itself to pay for the association and was headed up by a full-time executive officer with powers almost like those of a mall director. "She educates merchants on how to make their piece of the downtown work and can offer carrots or sticks to make sure they apply what they have learned," Gerald explained.

The issue of weather protection for customers (he refused to call them shoppers) illustrated the limits as well as the possibilities of the concept. Anticipating the advantage that a competing enclosed mall would have in Oregon's sometimes rainy climate, the downtown association conceived the idea of constructing a continuous sidewalk awning along all of the downtown storefronts. When volunteerism fell short of 100 percent participation, they turned to the city for an ordinance and funding. The proposal was turned down by voters, but the idea caught on anyway. "Most of the sidewalks are now covered, and the merchants whose aren't face a market incentive during the rainy season, as well as peer pressure, to get their act together."

Seals mentioned mass transit as an example of how the city had followed the lead of its downtown association. An excellent bus system, a rarity in micropolitan cities, was funded by a property tax surcharge specifically approved for this purpose by voters in a referendum proposed by the association. "That's what it takes in a micro-politan to get mass transit," said Seals. "It can't be assumed as it can in a big city. You have to get a mandate from the public."

But Seals believed that you could sit in his seat and get sucked into thinking that government can resolve all issues. "Our West Coast community ethic lets us do more than can similar communities in your part of the country, maybe, but we feel our way pretty carefully when we get into economic issues. If we're going to be activist, we had better do it after learning some lessons from the private sector."

I mentioned my earlier interview with Tom Watson, and Seals concluded our talk by saying it was probably healthy to have a pub-lisher in town more conservative than his readership. "Oregon has a history of people willing to innovate. But the same concerns about the limits of government that swept the country during the Reagan years are beginning to emerge here. Watson's scrutiny has prepared us for this."

My last night in Corvallis I met Dave Mellish, the bartender from Suds 'n' Suds at McMenamin's after supper. Tonight was the peak of the Perseid meteor showers and he had been serious about his pro-posal to view them from the meadow atop Mary's Peak. Our group included his roommate, his ex-wife Donna (still a good friend), a woman who bartended at McMenamin's, and two other guys from Suds 'n' Suds. The plan was to spend the night on the mountaintop and drive back in the morning.

I was struck by the simplicity of our preparations for a mountain-top overnight: a flashlight, a tape deck, a few blankets, some munchies, and a half dozen pint-size canning jars of McMenamin's brews. There was no need for mosquito netting or insect repellent because there would be no bugs. The evening's weather report guaran-teed that clear skies could be relied on to render unnecessary the precautions of tents, tarps, or rain gear. This was Oregon.

We drove west on Oregon 34 and fifteen miles out of Corvallis turned onto the winding Mary's Peak Road. Through hairpin curve after curve we rose to an altitude we could sense only through the pressure in our ears, since the road was bordered by tall forest most of the way. We slowed twice for deer.

At the top the trees abruptly disappeared. We parked in a paved lot surrounded by maybe fifty acres of open meadow. To the west a subtle purple haze still lingered along the Pacific horizon where the sun had set two hours earlier. To the east and far below sprawled the bright lights of Corvallis, and farther, the twinkling of places along I-5.

Walking through the thick grasses of the meadow took some doing. Dave explained that this was virgin meadow weed, never cut or cultivated by human hands. I wondered how it had survived the surely frequent incursions by folks like us. Dave explained that the state simply closed off the road when the meadow needed rejuvenating.

We spread our blankets, drank our beer, and watched the streaking sparks in the skies overhead. We talked of community and I asked these people, whose lives moved far from the circles of city hall, what they thought of city planning and tax increases. It was the bartender from McMenamin's who responded after a long, thoughtful silence. "Those aren't hostile issues here," he said. "People look at how well the town is doing and remember what it was like in other places they've lived. I don't know how city hall works, but they seem to get it right."

In the morning I woke to discover that I had used somebody's foot and some empty corn chip bags as a pillow. But I was quickly distracted from the pain in my neck by the brightening lavender in the eastern sky, sculpted underneath by the ragged skyline of the Cascade Mountains. Then the first arc of sun broached the gaps and the lavender flashed to blue with golden highlights on a few scudding clouds.

Considered in the light of the 10,000 Waves scale, Corvallis was a quiet, unspectacular town whose advantages were subtle. I couldn't rate it a five for any category, though it earned strong fours for Comfort, for Foot Factor, and, maybe, with Portland so nearby, for Cake. If there was a weakness it would be as Someplace. Besides the legend of its being a town where people behaved well and strove to get it right this time, Corvallis hadn't the bedrock sense of identity that Santa Fe or Napa had. One wrong move by voters, government, or the private sector and much of what it had gotten right could be lost.

We gathered up our blankets and trash, and within a half hour I had dropped off my fellow meteor gazers and was packing my bags for the drive to Portland. I took a detour on my way out of town and stopped by Sparks's Abed and Breakfast. Again there were early morning golfers gathered on Herb's back porch for his wife's coffee, two former systems analysts from New York who had retired to Corvallis. I asked them why Corvallis instead of Florida or Arizona. "Real life, real people, real surroundings," said one. "In those places it's all props and special effects."

I drove out of Corvallis and took another detour to cruise the Main Street of Sweet Home, confirming that it was the most inappropriately named place in the country. Too many of the businesses not boarded up were bars, and the men hanging out at their entrances glared menacingly at me as I drove slowly past, looking for some kind of invitation. It appeared that the trash along the street hadn't been picked up for weeks.

As I-5 approached Portland, the signs of economic health returned. Parking lots were full of cars, smokestacks made smoke, men maneuvered big iron machines carrying anything from logs to packing crates, and the train tracks at crossings were worn clean of rust. There were none of the empty ex-urban office buildings that would become monuments to the eighties.

But Portland was a big city, complete with big-city traffic, and my first contact with it behind the wheel of a car produced frustration and deletable expletives. So it was quite pleasing when the receptionist at my motel explained that I probably would not need my rental car for the duration of my stay in Portland—that I could catch the Max, a light-rail mass transit train, just a block from the motel and walk from its stops to almost anyplace in downtown Portland. "Portland is the most pedestrian city in America," he boasted.

I had stood on the balcony of this same motel one night two years ago during a train trip stopover and discovered that from here I could see virtually all of the heart of the city. The blazing spires of its tallest buildings downtown were set amid the twinkling of lights in the taller residential hills to the west. Atop the clock tower of Union Station, a blue-and-yellow neon sign flashed GO BY TRAIN. Chains of bluish vapor lights lined the bridges across the dark river, where moving red-and-green navigation lamps marked the stately progress of boats on the water. Somehow Portland's builders had managed to create an urban esthetic perfectly consistent with the Oregon spirit I had witnessed from the top of Mary's Peak. Tucked with incredible compactness into a narrowing of the Willamette Valley before the river emptied into the Columbia, Portland was a great city small enough to be graspable, knowable.

I took the motel receptionist's advice and walked to the Max stop near the twin glass needles of the new Portland Convention Center. In just a few minutes the inbound Max hummed to a silent stop, and as I boarded, a fellow actually moved over to make room for me to sit down. I said to him, "That's not how they do it on the subways in New York."

He laughed and answered, "Well, you're not in New York. Welcome to Portland." For the duration of the short ride across the river and into the heart of downtown, he talked with me and touted his city. He recalled how all of Portland had stood at windows and on rooftops to watch the laser show in the twin glass towers climaxing the inauguration of the Convention Center, as if it had been Fourth of July fireworks. He described how the river filled with a promenade of boats during the annual Rose Festival, a week celebrating the city's claim to being the rose capital of the world. He pointed out the Saturday market in the old town, where cheerful crowds swarmed vendors of produce from the rich Willamette Valley soil.

The Max ride was a nice introduction to the city but nothing compared to the experience that awaited me after I got off at Morrison Street and headed toward the riverfront. Suddenly the streets and traffic were behind me and I emerged into an open world peopled by others like myself, on foot. As far as I could see along the graceful curve of the river in either direction, there was nothing but a wide band of grass, a few trees, walkways, and people—moving slowly and casually, gathered here and there into little knots of sociability. Beyond the grass, the river formed a band of sparkling water where a few pleasure boats coasted by, and across the water a distant city backdrop like the one I had just stepped out from, but far enough away to be unintimidating. I felt a paradoxical sense of ease and excitement I knew I had felt somewhere once before and quickly remembered that it had been my first foray out of Chicago's downtown and into the Lakefront Park.

To the north the park and its pathways continued out of sight around a westerly bend in the river under Burnside Bridge, beckoning me to walk that way to see what might lie hidden from view. To the south the river curved smoothly to the east, but gentle contours in the landscaping obscured parts of this shoreline as well. In both directions the pathways were elevated above the river, and sweeping views developed as one rounded knolls or clumps of trees so that there was a continual sense of prospect.

Hundreds of people, maybe thousands, were out strolling this warm Saturday summer evening but the space was so large that there was no sense of crowds. The width of the walkways varied as one moved along, bringing one closer to other people one moment and then allowing more personal space. I liked the way people were dressed, casual and loose with lots of color and few power suits to be seen.

Walking south I passed a plaza, the Salmon Street Springs, where dozens of children of several races frolicked in the high-powered spray of the fountains while parents lounged nearby on benches or in the beer garden of McCall's Restaurant. Later I would discover that some distance to the north I would find the Old Town district, which also bordered on the park and offered another center of refuge.

At its southern end the park culminated in Riverplace, a recent development featuring nightclubs, sidewalk cafés, shops, restaurants, a marina, and some pricey apartments. Though there were large numbers of people all along the waterfront, the concentration here made it clear that this was the anchor—the focal point of the social phenomenon and minor miracle of Portland's Tom McCall Waterfront Park. In no place where I had arrived as a stranger had I ever felt so welcomed, so comfortable, so sure that I was going to like being there. Of course, I had no idea at the time that the feeling I experienced had been carefully planned and choreographed.

Tony Hiss's 1990 book *The Experience of Place* applied recent research in environmental psychology to suggest that when a human-made environment combined certain elements, it produced a change of perception and mood in its visitors remarkably like what I experienced that first day in Portland. He cited the work of Dr. John H. Falk, suggesting an atavistic human affinity for expanses of grass and a similar attraction to water. The work of the Kaplans found in humans a common appreciation for settings with a little bit of mystery; they demonstrated that people's curiosity will lead them to explore places obstructed from view as long as the overall geography promises they won't get lost (a characteristic the Kaplans called legibility). The British geographer Jay Appleton had research showing a human preference for sites combining broad vistas with places of refuge.

When I read Hiss's book six months after my visit to Portland, I recognized the elements of the McCall Waterfront Park in his discussion: grass, water, beauty, mystery, legibility, prospect, and refuge. Of course, by then I knew that it had been planned that way.

At the Riverplace development there was a sidewalk bar called the Patio where I sat and watched the people passing by. Initially the scene here reminded me of Fisherman's Wharf in San Francisco, the first place tourists head for when they hit town. But there were too many casual greetings by people who knew one another; it was clear that besides tourists, Riverplace attracted a lot of Portland residents out for a stroll looking to meet familiar faces.

There was also some singles action going on here. A fellow at the table next to mine smiled at a woman walking by; she stopped, sat down, had a drink with him, wrote her telephone number on a napkin, and then looked at her watch and left. He had noticed me watching, and when she was gone, turned to me with the cryptic comment, "Not a bad start; maybe this won't be so bad after all."

As it turned out, Rick Smart was a thirty-year-old English teacher who had just been ditched by his longtime girlfriend. "Came back to my apartment last week and all her stuff was gone. Next day she calls and says she's sorry, but she's got another guy." I offered my condolences and bought him a beer. "Looking for a good place to live, eh?" he said. "Well, you've come to the right place." Shortly it was agreed that I could move out of my motel and crash in his ex-girlfriend's room for the week of my stay.

Rick's apartment was located in the McCormick Pier development at the north end of the McCall Waterfront. Resembling building blocks stacked atop one another all akilter, McCormick Pier Apartments lined a grassy greenway with pedestrian walks along the river. Perched above the water here and there were gazebos where joggers and walkers could stop to rest or to escape the frequent Portland shower. Behind lay the tracks and terminal of Portland's Union Station Amtrak terminal. Rick paid eight hundred dollars a month for his two-bedroom apartment overlooking the river in this perfect spot.

Each morning of my stay began with the twenty-block walk along the waterfront to Riverplace for coffee and bagels before Rick would catch a city bus to his classes at Lincoln High School. Often we were joined by Vicki, a handsome middle-aged divorcée living across the hall, who took a motherly interest in our two quests—one for a new girlfriend, the other for a good place to live.

Both of my morning companions had come to Portland by chance and been hooked by its warm, fuzzy allure. Rick was from fast-lane L.A., where he had grown up believing that he would find himself a place beside a river in the country and never live in a city again. Vicki came from Spokane via Seattle, a bad marriage, and a plane crash. Each had found in downtown Portland an unexpected haven from past trouble and, in Vicki's words, "a setting where it was always easy to find friends or make new ones."

With that cue, I explained one morning the third place concept. Of course, it was exactly what each had been talking about. "But in Portland it's not just that there are lots of little places like that," Vicki said. "That's the spirit of the whole city—especially downtown at Pioneer Square and here along the riverfront."

Rick thought it was also a Northwest ingenuity for having fun and went on to catalog unique places I should enjoy during my stay: the Baghdad Pub Theater, where you could watch a movie seated at counters at which pitchers of good Northwest microbrews and pizza were served; the Veritable Quandary, a vintage First Street pub where a conflict between old-timers and new yuppie patrons had been turned to advantage and institutionalized in the layout, decor, and name; weekend concerts on the grass of McCall Waterfront; Shanghai's at Riverplace, where you could eat for under three dollars and dance till two with partners met along the river walk or at the concerts; and lots of great brew pubs and coffee shops, like the East Bank Saloon and the Roast Room. By the end of my stay, Rick or Vicki would take me to each of these places, but my favorites were those on the waterfront—the concerts and Shanghai's, which became my focal place in Portland.

I met Rick there for supper my third evening in town. He introduced me to a bartender named Jeff, and while Rick and I enjoyed a three-dollar bar dinner of bean soup and enchiladas, Jeff related the legend of Portland that I would hear confirmed again and again in a kind of local oral tradition. "It wasn't always the town that it is now," Jeff began. "Ten years ago the Crips and Tongs were coming up from L.A. The city was pretty rough already what with the port and the railroad terminals. But we had an urban renaissance program under way. And when gang trouble started hitting the headlines, the whole city got on the bandwagon."

Rick agreed. "It seemed like somebody had a plan," he said. "The city is divided into four quarters. And one by one you'd see the police move into each one and get really aggressive at about the same time that the construction people went into action." First it was the southwest, including most of the downtown. Then it was the northwest. Now it was the southeast, including the area around the Convention Center, the Coliseum, and my Red Lion Motel, where I had noticed a strong police presence. That first night in town I had spotted a hobo on top of a boxcar beneath my motel vantage point, and soon the whole area was crawling with flashlights and police, both uniformed and plainclothes.

Quarter by quarter the community of Portland had reclaimed its streets, and at the time of my visit only the northeast, where a few gangs were still rumored to be active, lay beyond the pale. Statistics from city hall confirmed that Portland was America's only major city in which crime rates had declined—dramatically—in the past ten years. Local polls showed Portland to be that rarity where residents perceived their city to be safer today than previously. And it wasn't because Portland was somehow off the beaten path. Immigration was running about a thousand people a month, though even at that rate it would be nearly another ten years before Portland would match the population of Seattle at the time of my visit.

I remembered the lesson of Napa and asked if there was some key economic power that was behind the Portland renaissance. "Real estate people, I guess," answered Rick, "who saw they could make a lot of money off of saving a city. There's also Nike shoes and the computer software guys, who help set a kind of classy tone, but the real activists have been the developers working in partnership with the city." It was a novel answer for one of my experience, accustomed to viewing the real estate developer as the natural enemy of the landscape we New Englanders wanted to preserve.

Later in the evening in Shanghai's I met Laura Jacobsen, a family therapist who lived in Seattle after having gone to college here in Portland, now here for a weekend nostalgia visit. Laura was the only person I met in Portland who had good things to say about Seattle, despite its having gotten more immigration than it was prepared for in the past ten years. She urged me to visit the city later and let her show me why it was still a good place to live.

In the meantime I met her and her large German shepherd, Talker, at the Riverfront Coffee Shop the next morning. Laura was one of those people who really got to know the places she lived in.

We walked downtown through Pioneer Square and the central shopping district. The sidewalks here thronged with the rich pedestrian culture William Whyte saw as the hallmark of successful cities, including food and flower vendors, handbill passers, schmoozing businesspeople, and soapbox speakers, as well as thousands of people going about their city business on foot. There were big trees and long benches, frequent pocket plazas, ledges that invited sitting, and attractive patches of grass and gardens. There were almost none of the blank walls so common in modern cities. Instead so much glass lined the sidewalks that the interiors of banks, offices, and stores appeared as inviting extensions of the street scene itself. The timing of crosswalk lights created a further impression that this was a place designed for people on foot.

We explored more of the city by hopping buses. The Twenty-first Street–Twenty-third Street neighborhood where Laura had lived in her college days had become gentrified since then but still was marked by heavily tree-lined streets and corner third places reminiscent of New York's Greenwich Village. We rode up the western hills to the Japanese Gardens and the Rose Gardens, where I first encountered the biological symbol of the Northwest, the five-inch green slugs that were one of the few pests in a land seemingly without bugs.

Then we headed out to the southeast quadrant, where modest, old middle-class neighborhoods ran for dozens of blocks. At Oaks Amusement Park, Laura showed me the Ladybug Theater, where children's drama groups were active every summer. Along the river we saw people living a novel lifestyle in pricey houseboats evoking the waterfront, if not the poverty, of the real Shanghai.

We rode through the affluent neighborhoods of Palatine Hill on the southern West Side, where the streets were in a state of desperate disrepair but where Portland's wealthiest families lived in spectacular settings of dense woods, ivy, rhododendron, and alders. In Marquam Hill, another West Side neighborhood farther north, the houses were more modest, places I might aspire to myself. They ran along steep slopes facing east with spectacular views of Mount Hood, Mount Adams, and Mount St. Helens ("the one with no top"). Again there were dense, tall woods—and no lawns. Ten minutes away by bus, however, residents could find all the grass they wanted at McCall Riverfront Park.

There were suburbs farther out, to be sure, where the usual American auto-dominated life prevailed. But Portland itself was the first large city I had ever explored where there seemed to be no excuse to live that way. There were thriving neighborhoods aplenty with either the pedestrian proximity or safe, quick mass transit connections, so that downtown was always just a few minutes away.

With a promise to help me explore Seattle, Laura and Talker returned to her car at Riverplace and I sought out the offices of Cornerstone Columbia Development Company, recommended by Rick as a place where I would learn some of the secrets of Portland. A receptionist asked if she could help me, and when I explained my curiosity about how the riverfront had been developed, she showed me to the office of Ellen Gyllstrom, formerly of the Portland Development Commission and now a marketing officer for Cornerstone.

Ellen, a thirty-something surefooted veteran of both the public and private sectors, verified the local legend. The quarter-by-quarter reclamation of the city was indeed the result of a plan. Portland's urban renewal initiative began in the mid-seventies—late by national standards, but the city's small size had allowed a peaceful slumber till people woke up one day to find gangs on their streets. Community leaders saw what had happened to other cities and came together determined that it wasn't going to happen here. Since then, to live in Portland was to witness a city successfully being born again. Portland was fortunate to come late to the urban renewal party because it could learn from the wrecking-ball mistakes of the first wave and could incorporate state-of-the-art research in planning and environmental psychology. The state's establishment of urban growth boundaries was another boon, fixing a firm definition to the urban area and keeping the city's redevelopment compact. In effect it legislated the concept, long advocated by urbanists, of development through infill.

The first key was to avoid the trap of the traditional planning regime: emphasis on negative regulation to keep out what the city didn't want, as if some magical market force would then come along

and miraculously provide what the city did want. Instead the Portland
Development Commission researched what Ellen called "the best and
the brightest thinking and scholarship on the subject of making a
modern city livable and nurturing for human beings." She showed me
a bibliography of titles constituting the research base for the commission's work—Michael Corbett, Tony Hiss, Ada Louise Huxtable, Jane
Jacobs, Lewis Mumford, William Whyte, Frederick Law Olmsted, Cal-
vert Vaux, and so on. Portland was to be the place where cutting-edge
thinking would be applied.

"All of the research concluded that the major disruptive force in
great cities today is the private automobile," Ellen expounded. "Right
from the start our guiding principle was to make Portland a pedestrian city." It helped that Portland was the home of Nike shoes, which
played a role here not unlike that of the winegrowers in Napa. The
commission determined that the city should discourage auto traffic in
the downtown (during one errant foray out in my rental car, I had
seen for myself how this was done: through astronomical parking fees
and limited spaces), develop innovative mass transit (including free
downtown buses and cheap, safe, aboveground light rail), establish
extensive parks and greenbelts linked by walkways, plant more street
trees, and put brick underfoot for pedestrian friendliness. Design
guidelines focused on making the street level an attractive environment for people on foot by maintaining the integrity of the two-
hundred-foot block and requiring building fronts to be visually active
with sidewalk views into all interiors. Zoning encouraged mixed uses
where commercial, financial, and service activity coexisted within
walking radii of downtown residential sites, bus stops, and Max stations.

"But the centerpiece was to be the riverfront," she went on. "You
can make a city as pedestrian friendly as you want, but it doesn't work
till people have someplace to go that's easier to walk to than to drive
to." So the multilane Harbor Drive was demolished in 1976 and an
old plywood mill was moved out to make way for the Tom McCall
Waterfront Park at the river boundary of the downtown. Here planners applied the classical precepts of Frederick Law Olmsted and Cal-
vert Vaux, the architects of Manhattan's Central Park and Brooklyn's
Prospect Park, as well as the emerging work of the environmental
psychologists and geographers summarized in Tony Hiss's recent

book. The result was the sense of release and ease I had felt that first day when I emerged on foot from the trafficked city streets into the broad expanse of water-bordered grass.

The key to bringing the social aspect of the park to its critical mass was that there had to be people residing there. Thus the city awarded a partnership to the developers who built the McCormick Pier Apartments at one end of the park and then selected Cornerstone to design and build Riverplace at the other end. The commission was impressed with what Cornerstone promised, and Ellen was personally so excited by the project that she left the commission to work with Cornerstone on it.

As the focal point of the city's larger vision, Riverplace was planned as a mixed-use residential, commercial, and "urban resort" area anchoring the southern end of McCall Waterfront. The goal was to create from whole cloth a residential and recreational neighborhood that would attract people to the South Waterfront area year-round. For its half of the bargain, the city provided a tree-lined boulevard leading from Front Street to the site, ornamental lights, street furniture, pedestrian walkways, a meadow between the boulevard and the seawall walkway, breakwaters for the marina, and a five-acre terrace bowl just north of the project (where the concerts and festivals were held). It struck me that these were the kinds of amenities that cities in the budget-strapped Northeast had increasingly been requiring developers to create in recent years. The difference, of course, was that here the city could require a developer to build a project to the specifications of the city's vision rather than to his or her own whims and private perceptions of market opportunities— because this was where the action was. Developers were lined up at the door, drooling for the chance to get a piece of the pie.

Cornerstone's design began with a hotel whose turn-of-the-century seaside resort architecture set the theme for the rest of the development. There was also an athletic club; a marina; a floating restaurant on the river; a nightclub restaurant (Shanghai's), coffeeshops, open-air bistros, and retail stores along a waterfront esplanade; 190 condominium units (including middle-income housing in the $75,000 range); 47,000 square feet of office space in a low-rise complex behind the esplanade shops; and a parking garage. Ellen believed that Cornerstone had met every expectation in terms of function. "It's like *Field of Dreams:* if you build it, people will come. They have come. And this has gone against the grain in the decade where new real estate projects stand empty and breaking the banks all across the country."

I asked her the Napa question, if there was a particular industry or force in town that was the mover behind all of this, such as Nike. "Well, it didn't hurt to have Nike supporting our pedestrian city theme. And companies like Microsoft certainly employ lots of people with the sophistication to offer public support." But the real force in Portland, Ellen thought, was a remarkably enlightened real estate and development community. "Downtown in Pioneer Square you'll see another miracle project pulled off by the Rouse people. For over a decade now Portland's dominant industry has been the rebuilding of Portland."

After my interview with Ellen Gyllstrom, I had another three-dollar supper at Shanghai's and then walked the length of the water-front back to Rick's apartment. For the first time, I really noticed another feature of the park—homeless people. I knew from previous trips to the West Coast to expect large numbers of them in any of the big cities where railway terminals, ports, and a mild climate conspired to attract them. But what I noticed now was that they seemed to blend into the general crowd of people in a manner unlike what one sees in New York or elsewhere back East. A homeless man might be parked at one end of a bench while a mother attended to her children at the other. A bag lady would ask a jogger for the time and get an answer as well as some pleasantries about the weather. College kids playing Frisbee would invite hobos to join in their game. So many places in North America shrank from offering effective pedestrian amenities in their public spaces out of fear of domination by "undesirables." Portland's riverfront and downtown showed that if you attract the mainstream of people, the so-called undesirables simply become a well-behaved part of the scene.

The final weekend of my stay in Portland was the occasion of the Rose City Blues Festival, a three-day extravaganza of music in the terraced bowl of McCall Waterfront. There was something going on here almost every weekend; the previous weekend was a country-and-western concert and the next would be the Last Chance Summer Dance, for teens about to go back to school. But this weekend the headliner was Bo Diddly backed up by blues groups from New York to L.A. to Montreal.

The festival was a benefit for the homeless sponsored by something called the Sunshine Division and the Urban Entertainment Coalition. Upon investigation, the Sunshine Division turned out to be a volunteer arm of the Portland Police Department that fed, clothed, and sheltered the homeless. Admission for the day was two dollars plus a can or two of food for the poor or five dollars without the food.

Rick and I walked to the bowl from his apartment on Saturday afternoon. We had watched the preparations for the event during our morning walks over the past week but were struck by what an extensive commercial venture it was now that everything was in place. The bowl was lined with mobile beer concessions, vendors hawking sausages and hot Mex, T-shirt outlets, and souvenir peddlers. The musicians performed on a stage built at the north end of the bowl, and the vast grassy center was crammed with people sprawled on blankets and lawn chairs. Though the atmosphere was laden with the smell of spicy fried food, and copious quantities of beer flowed freely, there was no rowdyism, absolutely none. The music was amplified to a level that flooded the bowl with impact but allowed space for conversation, while boats drifted by on the river and the crowds of people on foot kept coming through the gates with their cans of Spam, tuna, and Chinese vegetables. There was plenty of room to sit and lots of people ready to welcome and talk to a stranger. Down front near the bands, barefoot couples danced in the grass. If not heaven, this was at least the front porch.

Rick and I cheered Bo Diddly and danced with some friendly married women to a rocking band from British Columbia while their husbands watched us with bemused, tolerant grins from their lounge chairs. I got into a conversation with one of the husbands, an off-duty cop, about the Sunshine Division. "It's the best thing we ever did," he said. "Our role in the urban renaissance could have become a war with the street people and the kids. But the Sunshine work made all the difference. When you feed people, and find them shelter and get them to a doctor when they're sick, they see more than just that blue uniform."

Back at Rick's apartment afterward, we flipped on CNN. A grainy video portrayed a half dozen cops savagely beating and kicking a black man who writhed on the ground as other cops stood idly by. Rick cursed breathlessly as we stared in horror.

Since then, like millions of Americans, I have been sickened again and again by the tape of Rodney King's brutal beating. But I first saw it in Portland, a city where cops fed and clothed their potential adversaries, where citizens felt safer and more secure with each passing year, where I had seen a better way.

At Portland Union Station, waiting for my train to Seattle, I participated in a scene where the Portland penchant for planning and getting it right didn't work. Several trains going in different directions all arrived at the same time, and the result was a crowded station where no one seemed to know which train he or she was about to get on.

But even amid this chaos, the genius of Portland still seemed to prevail. Waiting for my train, I met a dozen friendly fellow travelers eager to help me rate Portland on the 10,000 Waves scorecard. It surely deserved fours or fives for Cheers, Foot, Cake, and Someplace factors. With the mild, rainy climate, Comfort was good but not great —a three. Applying a Fudge Factor was difficult and depended on how seriously you took the remaining big-city trouble in the northeast quadrant and the mysterious local rumor about organized crime figures settling their families in this good place to live. But this was a large city that scored as high or higher than cozy Santa Fe or Napa. I never did find an American city this size that rivaled it.

Leaving the Willamette Valley, I didn't feel the usual sense of casting off moorings that one feels when leaving most places after an extended stay. Instead I felt like a pedestrian, getting up from a pleasant park bench and walking on to see what lay around the bend of a grassy hill. It seemed that, at least in the two cities I visited here, people were getting it right this time, while they were still getting it so wrong elsewhere, even on the West Coast.

5

THE GREAT NORTHWEST
GOOD PLACE BUST

PUGET SOUND, WASHINGTON

At well over half a million in population, Seattle was substantially larger than Portland, and felt even bigger as I drove my rental car through the darkened streets of Capitol Hill looking for the address of a fellow writer who had consented to let me use his apartment while he was away. Whatever else I learned about Seattle, which had been America's darling city long enough that it had begun to lose some of its allure, I never got away from that feeling that this was a truly big city.

Locating the Thomas Street apartment wasn't difficult, but finding a place to park the car was another matter. I finally parked on the dirt between the sidewalk and the curb about three blocks away from my digs.

My Seattle residence reminded me of friends' places in Manhattan —a cozy bookcase-walled living room separated from a tiny galley by a bar in an interior open windowcase, a cramped bathroom, and a postage-stamp bedroom down the hall. There was a futon on the floor of the bedroom (a double bed wouldn't have fit) and a writing desk in front of a living room window with a distant tree limb–framed view of the Space Needle and the Olympic Range beyond the sound. But mostly the apartment was dominated by books, periodicals, video and audio equipment, and cooking paraphernalia. Like city dwellers everywhere, my host obviously compensated for the lack of personal space with stimulation of the mind and senses. But unlike citizens of Manhattan's Upper East Side, he paid a rent of only six hundred dollars a month. That was the second lesson of Seattle: you could still live here in decent, inexpensive neighborhoods closer to the heart of the city than you could anywhere in New York City.

In the morning I went to look for my rental car and couldn't find it at first. I remembered that I had parked it between the curb and sidewalk on a block where many other cars were parked the same way. The problem was that my car was the only one left on the block, and so I didn't recognize the setting. Everyone else had moved their cars earlier in the morning. Mine had a twenty-eight-dollar parking ticket tucked under a wiper blade.

I drove around Lake Union, which was really a bay in the channel linking Lake Washington to Puget Sound. I was hoping to find some kind of public promenade but was disappointed to find the lake lined with commercial marinas, warehouses, and private residential developments of some sort. No McCall Waterfront Park here.

That evening I went in search of the next best thing: the blues dens on Pioneer Square. Seattle natives were quick to advise me that Portland's Pioneer Square was ersatz, whereas this was the real McCoy. By the time I got there, a Mariners game had let out and the square was flooded with crowds such as I had seen only at a Times Square New Year's Eve celebration. There was great food and music at places like the Old Timers, New Orleans, Larry's, the Merchants' Cafe, and JM, but the crush made it tough to appreciate.

I finally gave up and went looking for my rental car. Again I couldn't find it. It wasn't just that I had forgotten where I had parked it. It was my fourth rental car of the summer and frankly, I couldn't remember which car I was looking for. In the end I took a cab back to Thomas Street and in the morning got out my rental agreement, called the police, and asked about cars that had been towed during the night. Sure enough, my little white Le Mans had been picked up. I now owed a fifty-dollar towing bill and another twenty-eight-dollar parking ticket.

That afternoon I headed back to the waterfront, but transportation again became an issue. I didn't have a bicycle and the transit system was more daunting than Portland's. So, a slow learner, I drove down to the waterfront and left the car in a parking garage. Strolling the piers with crowds of mostly Japanese tourists, I checked the locations of the ferries to points across the sound, bought a crabmeat sandwich, and boarded a waterfront trolley to the base of the steps leading up to Pike Place.

Pike Place was the setpiece downtown development in Seattle, like Faneuil Hall Marketplace in Boston or Rouse Harbor Project in Baltimore. It was considered a success because locals, as well as tourists, thronged the place looking for bargains. But Pike Place had failed in one respect. It was meant to attract customers as pedestrians. But instead it attracted cars, thousands of them, enough that it had become the source of Seattle's first serious downtown traffic jams. Despite my initial trepidation, Seattle's fine mass transit system should have been adequate to offer a viable alternative. But it was simply still too easy to get around Seattle by car. Seattle wasn't small enough, as was Portland, for improvements in pedestrian access and limiting parking to discourage auto traffic. It would take a crisis in auto traffic itself to change public habit.

I found a little grassy square with a totem pole that I remembered as the focal point of the downtown from previous visits. Dozens of people sprawled in the grass soaking up the warm, sunny afternoon. A few were tourists, but most were residents who worked downtown and routinely stopped off here during their breaks to admire the spectacular view across the sound toward the Olympic Mountains.

But the space was small and there were also a few particularly deranged street people who injected an unwelcome note of tension into the scene. One man shouted, moaned, jumped around, pounded his head, and tried to strike up conversations about the ghosts on the green. People moved away from him but there wasn't much place to go, so most of them ended up leaving the park entirely.

A fellow on his lunch break from his job in a bank three blocks away told me that everyone in downtown Seattle was attracted to this little park but that it didn't work because it was just too small. It was the only grass anywhere on the downtown heights overlooking the sound. I mentioned the McCall Riverfront Park in Portland and he said there was nothing like that along the waterfront here, though there was something like it surrounding Green Lake in the north end

of the city. "Of the two cities," he said, "Seattle has the more spectacular natural site. But Portland has done so much more with what they
had to work with." The crazies who had just disrupted this place
would have been buffered and unobtrusive in the space and numbers
of people in McCall Riverfront Park.

When I returned to the parking garage to retrieve my car, I was
shocked to see that it had cost me eight dollars for less than two hours
of downtown parking. When I found a parking spot back on Capitol
Hill, I made a final resolution to leave the blasted thing there as long
as I could.

One afternoon I joined the stream of gays, hipsters, and outrageous folk promenading down Broadway, Capitol Hill's main drag,
headed to the Deluxe Tavern to meet a fellow I knew from a writers
conference. My friend, Peter Blue, had published short stories and was
living in Seattle because he thought it was the place to launch a career
in fiction. He had grown up in Connecticut and left college early to
travel the country, hopping trains and picking apples, cherries, and
peaches. "I didn't know I was looking for a home," he said. "I thought
I was looking for adventure."

Peter's search led to a stint working cruise boats around the Pacific
until he found a job in Samoa as editor of the *Samoa News*. Then,
after a brief interruption to finish his college education, he settled
in another island community and worked for another local paper—
this time it was Orcas Island in the San Juans, north of Seattle.
"After a few years, though, I started feeling too removed from the
world," Peter said. "I wanted to see what life was like in America, so
I came to Seattle. I wanted to live in a place where a major newspaper was delivered to my doorstep every morning." He traded his
battered old car to a friend for help fixing up an old house in a
neighborhood near the University of Washington. Since then he had
made his living remodeling houses, as his readers had done on Orcas.
It was a good balance of mental and physical work, and there was
the option of pursuing an advanced degree and writing in an academic setting.

I asked him what he liked best about Seattle. "Livable neighborhoods in the heart of a big city," he answered without hesitation. That
was the big plus for Seattle, against a rising tide of negatives in a place

that had become too fashionable too quickly. But by shedding the car entirely, as Peter had, one could still live subversively apart from the city's emerging auto-congested reality.

One evening a few nights later, I walked a dozen blocks east to the house of a friend of my host for dinner. One block across the glitz and frizz of Broadway, I entered into the quiet, middle-class residential neighborhood along Republican Street. The bungalows were all well maintained and people here obviously spent time and money on their shrubbery, gardens, and little lawns. Republican Street itself was designed with forced turnouts every few blocks, instead of intersections, so that through traffic could not penetrate the neighborhood.

Doug Nufer, a cheerful, quick-witted fellow in his upper thirties, met me on his front porch. His house did not have one of those tiny lawns—instead it was surrounded by what looked like a section of profuse rain forest bog somehow lifted out of the Olympic Peninsula and transplanted here on a rise along Twenty-second Street. Next to the front steps was a little sign identifying Doug's yard as a federally certified wetland. Doug explained that it was the project of his wife, Kathleen Skeels. "She filled out the federal forms and everything," he said. "We just didn't want to mow and water a lawn. It's done with sunken bathtubs and layers of impermeable plastic under the soil. Holds moisture well enough that even when there's a drought and others have a dead lawn, we have a live bog."

We sat in the clutter of Doug and Kathleen's dining room while Kathleen cooked and Doug told me how he had come to Seattle. He was from New Jersey originally and determined never to live the hell on earth of his father's life, planning three hours a day to commute to and from work. He went to school at the University of Virginia in Charlottesville and got a taste for living in a better place.

After four years and a failed marriage in North Carolina, he broke free to write several unpublished novels and got serious about searching for a place to live that was different from anywhere else. It had to be a city, but it couldn't be as big as New York. It had to be on a coast. It had to have major league baseball and a racetrack. His plan was to explore from east to west hugging the coasts and living in various places until he found what he wanted. After trying and rejecting New Orleans, San Diego, L.A., San Francisco, and Portland, he settled at his last stop, Seattle.

Seattle had big league baseball, a real big-city feel, and neighborhoods in the heart of things where he could afford to live. "And I've
learned I can live here without a car," he said. "Though Seattle's not
quite the pedestrian city that Portland is, here serious bicycling is the
alternative transportation ethic. Why should I spend two thousand
dollars a year so I can drive to the Oregon coast or Yakima twice a
year? It's easier and cheaper to rent a car for trips like that."

He got rid of his car when he got a job working in a Seattle
tradition, as a bicycle messenger. He made a hundred dollars a day, a
big deal at the time. "That was a crazy life," he recalled. "Bicycle like
hell all day long—there was competition to be the best, and I was, at
one point. After work I'd drink beer, eat, and then drink Irish coffee
till the alcohol would send me home to sleep. The caffeine would kick
in in time to wake me up at 5:00 A.M. to write. It was a kind of cocaine
existence without the coke." As he grew older he just got tired and
wanted to do something with his weekends besides sleep, but it was
from this life that he learned the reliance on the bicycle for transportation that had kept him auto-free ever since.

At the time of my visit Doug managed a wine store and bicycled to
the racetrack or, less often, to Tacoma for ball games. He had finally
published a book, *The 1990 Guide to Northwest Minor League Baseball.*
We sat for dinner at a picnic table under a grape arbor in the backyard
bog. Doug took me on a tasting tour of some of the more interesting
wines he sold in the store. We began with a bottle of Washington State
wine, Badger Mountain Vineyard Pinot Noir, 1988. Doug said it was
from the last batch before the winery got its all-organic certification.
Badger Mountain was supposed to begin producing all-organic wine
in 1987, but a crop duster hit the vineyard by mistake and delayed the
certification for a year. Our bottle was basically organic, but once-
dusted, wine.

Kathleen had a theatrical bent to her conversation and gestures
and would frequently pop off with some fanciful leap in our conversation accompanied by quirky little looks and poses. She took me on a
tour of her bog. "Everything in here is reclaimed from someplace
else," she announced with a wave of her hand toward the city beyond
the hill. The bathtubs, the stone and brick of the walkways, even the
plastic liner underneath came from demolition sites. The mosses,
shrubs, ferns, flowers, and trees were all transplanted from someplace

where they were endangered. Migrating birds, hawks, and rare species like the Wilson warbler had landed in her city backyard. Racoons showed up here. The one creature that was not welcome was the huge green Northwest slug. "They can totally waste a garden as small as this," she explained.

Over our after-dinner coffee Kathleen talked about some of Seattle's problems. "The city's not handling its attractiveness very well and things are getting out of hand," she believed. "It's just been in the past couple of years that traffic has become the problem that it is now." The schools were bad and more and more people were sending their kids to private institutions. The California invasion was driving up the cost of living and sullying Seattle's legendary civility.

There had even been several highly publicized stories recently of police brutality, in particular one of a tourist who was beaten for jaywalking. As shootings and gangs and crack dealers became more common, the police came to behave more and more like what one heard about in L.A. "But somehow the neighborhoods do seem to hang on," she concluded.

I had approached Seattle in a different manner from that of my previous stops. Because it was such a big city, rather than relying on chance meetings in third places, as I had in Napa, Corvallis, and Portland, I made sure I had a number of contacts ahead of time. Such arrangements were easy because everywhere you went you met people who ended up coming to Seattle during these recent boom years. On a bright Saturday morning I went to visit a Chinese-American I had first met at a New Year's party at a house on the shore of a fishing lake back in New Hampshire many years previously. His Seattle address was a houseboat on the eastern shore of Lake Union.

"No, you can't use my name," he said as he met me on the long pier that served as the neighborhood lane for the little houseboat community he lived in. "But in exchange for that kindness, I'll answer the questions that nobody else will. Just call me the philosopher—the philosopher of paradise."

His houseboat was at the end of the pier, commanding a spectacular 180-degree view of the lake, the opposite hill layered with condos, and the Seattle skyline to the southwest. "Once there were thousands of these houseboats on Lake Union and they were the cheapest place to live in town—two hundred dollars a month," he said as I got down on my knees to see how water, sewage, and electricity were channeled through pipes attached to the underside of the pier. "But alas, under the old regime they were a source of terrible pollution in the lake and the city moved to eliminate them. When there were only six hundred left, someone recognized that they were an important part of Seattle's heritage and the city grandfathered the remainder in with strict requirements for proper sewage hookups." Now they rented for as much as eighteen hundred dollars a month, but there were still families and kids and dogs.

"It's a real community," said the philosopher as he served me tea in the plush glass-walled living room of his houseboat. "You have to walk down the pier past all of your neighbors, you don't just get in your car and go. So you get to know them like an extension of your family."

Besides Seattle, he owned houses in five or six other places and had sojourned in many more. "Don't go to Bremerton," he said, referring to the small city across the sound that had been named best place to live in America by *Money* magazine the previous year. "There's nothing there. A gas station, a drugstore. Residents have to cross a bridge to another town to do any shopping. And to do anything else they have to endure the hour-long ferry ride across the sound to Seattle."

In a former life the philosopher of paradise was a Chinese immigrant who came to America to pursue the dream. As a young man he founded a company that made him a fast millionaire many times over. Then he struck midlife shoals and commenced the ten-year voyage that made him the philosopher of paradise. He sold the company and got out. "In my field, once you're out of doing it full-time, you get behind very fast. Let the younger ones do it now." But still youthful and vigorous, he traveled the world looking for the perfect place and collecting homes in those that felt especially comfortable. He never found paradise and gave up looking; instead he found his wife and his current philosophy of living rootlessly.

He had a launch tied up outside his houseboat and invited me for a ride around the lake before lunch. The boat, actually newly made, was a long, elegant wooden masterpiece reminding me of something out of an F. Scott Fitzgerald novel. He ran it with a handheld remote control keypad, so we sprawled on cushions halfway back to the stern.

He knew my town of Keene, New Hampshire, because a mutual friend with whom he had gone to school lived there. As we silently motored around the lake he said, "You live in paradise, don't you?" I said I didn't think so. Otherwise I wouldn't be looking for a good place to live. "But that's exactly why you're looking for a good place to live," he answered. "Keene is paradise for you and our friend because you have been there so long, you are so settled there. You had a job, a family, local friends, and nothing to challenge your soul. It is so easy you could sleepwalk through your life. It is your home. You're safe and secure and don't need to risk anything."

"Then why am I dissatisfied?" I asked.

"Because your father died and freed you. Because you are too alive now to settle for those things. Because you know about the downside to paradise—that to really live you need to take risks and make mistakes. In paradise you can't make mistakes, it is the one thing that is forbidden on pain of the most horrible penalties."

I asked the philosopher of paradise if he knew these things because he was rich and had concluded his long-running midlife crisis. "Who can tell when it is concluded?" he answered. "But yes, it is because I am rich and because I made the choice to leave paradise. That's why I live in so many different places. It's how I stay free of the usual sense of home. Home isn't a place. It's wherever I am as long as I am not lonely."

"Like a citizen of the world?" I asked.

"Yes—no. It's simpler than that. Like an adult. Paradise is for children."

I had to see for myself who was right about Bremerton, the philosopher or *Money* magazine. So I took a bus down to the waterfront and the forty-five-minute high-speed foot ferry across the sound.

Approaching Bremerton, the ferry wound through some tight channels backed by dense primordial forest. The Seattle skyline was now far from view and the fir trees had a tranquilizing effect. Along the shoreline I could see homes like those described in *Money* magazine's review of the place when they named it number one. They were affluent middle-class houses, the kind you might find along the fairways of any garden-variety country club. They had docks on the water and it was easy to picture the seaside barbecue scene described in the magazine.

At Bremerton the ferry pulled into a concrete dock protruding from a shoreline of parking lots, corrugated metal warehouses, and military naval docks. An old destroyer was parked just offshore. I walked three blocks to the city hall past the waterfront parking lots, some tough-looking bars, a few vacant storefronts, and cheery signs waving from every lamppost proclaiming Bremerton the best place to live in America. Little had been done in the way of downtown beautification and it was clear that the city didn't have much of a sign code.

My Bremerton contact, a fan of my rail books, asked not to be named because of his position in city hall—call him Tim. We had lunch at a place called Sinclair's and he told me what he knew about the genesis of Bremerton. The town was founded around the turn of the century by one Ambrose Wykoff, who started a merchant marine shipyard when land here could be had for fifty cents an acre. It was a pretty rough place—seamen's bars, corduroy roads, knife play, and callous prostitutes. The Bremer family saw greater potential for the town as a naval base and bought up most of the present waterfront with that purpose in mind. As the Japanese threat grew in the thirties, so did the naval establishment in the now-named Bremerton.

The Northwest border region had a history of dependence on boom-or-bust single-industry economics. First there was gold in British Columbia, then timber on both sides of the border, then hydropower, and now the military industry, with the naval installation in Bremerton, a submarine base at nearby Bangor, and of course Boeing in Seattle. It was never a matter of limited alternative opportunities. But beginning with gold, the Northwest had been blessed (or cursed) with a series of such prolific cash cows that a habit had been ingrained. Seattle had learned from its history, Bremerton had not.

After World War II Bremerton declined as the nation's naval needs shrank. But the cold war brought the navy contracts back, and during the sixties and seventies residents felt that Bremerton's place in a regime of international military confrontation was secure.

In 1982 a mall developer launched a project at nearby Silverdale rather than at Bremerton after a nasty property lawsuit with the Bremers. Soon there were boarded-up storefronts all over downtown and unemployment was rising. People left for better employment opportunities associated with the submarine base over at Bangor. The local schools developed a bad reputation when the junior high went on double shifts because of revenue shortfalls. But few acknowledged at the time that the real cause of the local recession was, once again, a decline in the activity of the naval installation. Then came the Reagan six-hundred-ship navy, and the town was pumped up to the point where *Money* magazine would eventually take notice. Taxes and unemployment were low and earnings and growth were strong. During the upswings of the cycle, people did credit the role of the military establishment and showed pride in their navy connection.

But as I spent the rest of the day touring the town with Tim, it was hard to see what all the excitement was about. There were still too many boarded storefronts downtown, the waterfront was a parking lot, and the only visible focus of community spirit seemed to be the ever-present naval caps, ensigns in windows, and signs welcoming back the USS *Backlash*. Tim said there were ambitious plans to revitalize the downtown and turn the waterfront into a military theme park linking the existing naval museum to the mothballed USS *Turner Joy* at the end of a catwalk just offshore.

Only when Tim told me the selling prices for abandoned downtown buildings (the old art deco Roxy Theater had recently sold for just $65,000), whose buyers had grand schemes for redevelopment, did I begin to understand the interest of *Money* magazine. I remembered that, when I had first been elected to the city council in Keene in 1985, all candidates made ritual pledges not to let Keene become like Nashua, New Hampshire—at that time a city of abandoned mills (available for prices like the Roxy in Bremerton)—which had suddenly experienced a rat race of chaotic growth spurred by the nearby economic engine of high-tech Massachusetts. *Money* magazine named Nashua its best place to live in America that year, provoking the same bewilderment in Keene that Bremerton's triumph did now in Seattle.

Like Bremerton, Nashua then had a city government ill prepared and ill disposed to manage growth with some kind of positive community vision. Both, at the time of *Money* magazine's interest, were wide-open places on the verge of redevelopment with huge opportunities for cheap, bare-knuckles interests to come in and make piles of money without long-term commitment to the community. I have since confirmed the pattern in other places that have received the nod from *Money* magazine. Few places have ever stayed at the top of *Money*'s list for long.

I returned to Seattle that same afternoon following an admittedly quick visit, but I had seen absolutely nothing to hold me. On the ferry ride back, two Bremerton men sat behind me reading the evening paper headline GORBACHEV OUSTED IN MILITARY COUP—TANKS ROLL IN MOSCOW with apparent satisfaction. I turned and asked them if they didn't find the news disturbing. "It just goes to show ya can't ever trust 'em," said one. "And trouble with the Russkies means fat paychecks in Bremerton," added the other. I had spent the day of Gorbachev's ouster in one of the few cities on the globe that cheered the event.

Back at the apartment on Capitol Hill, there was a message for me on my host's answering machine. It was Laura, the Seattle woman I had met in Portland. When I called her back, she promised to pick me up at eight and show me a place where I would find what I had failed to find along the shore of Lake Union.

We drove north on I-5 over Portage Bay to Green Lake, a real lake surrounded by trees, grass, and walkways on all sides right in the heart of the city. Across the street that bounded the lake were appealing neighborhoods and frequent eating and drinking establishments. We had excellent Northwest chowder (like New England chowder but spiced up with green peppers, tomato, oregano, and coriander) at the Chowder House and then walked the circumference of the lake.

Laura was a family counselor and therapist whose dedication to the West Coast ethic of a life of freedom had kept her single till her recent engagement at thirty-five. She had jumped out of airplanes, bicycled through Europe, ridden on the backs of killer whales, hitchhiked through Mexico, and skied the dust slopes in summertime. But despite the bravado of some of her exploits, she was a soft-spoken, gentle soul who saw herself primarily as a nurturer and a protector who fulfilled that identity in her work with disturbed families. Living and working in a city was trying to the spirit. "That's why Green Lake is so important to me," she said. "I come here nearly every day. I couldn't live in a city where there wasn't a place like this where you could walk till way after dark and feel safe."

As we strolled the paved walkways we met dozens of joggers, even after the sun set. Couples cuddled on blankets in the grass and children climbed in the trees. We passed through certain parts of the park where there were tall bushes and few streetlamps. I kept hearing what I thought was the sound of a dog's chain collar tinkling near us, which stopped every time we stopped. But it was only the sound of Laura's large, mobilelike tin earrings, and she laughed at my unease when I mentioned it. "You put out a lot of negative energy when you're nervous," she said. "You're not really a happy city camper yet."

The walk around the refuge of Green Lake was calming, but the place didn't serve the same function as the riverfront in Portland. It wasn't at the nexus destination in the heart of downtown, and you had to be told you were safe there after dark; it wasn't patently apparent.

For the next few days I continued to cast about the Puget Sound area. First I drove out to the suburban town of Bothell, uninteresting except as an example of how small companies locate. My deceased father had cofounded a pharmaceutical research company called Panlabs, whose administrative offices were located in Bothell. Panlabs was the kind of industry that every community wanted to attract— clean, high-tech, high-pay. My dad and his partner, Joe Lein, realized that they could run their business just about anywhere they wanted. My father didn't care where that was, so Joe undertook his own good place search and ultimately the company was based in Bothell, near Orcas Island, the place where Joe wanted to live.

It's just one business story of thousands, with an anecdotal lesson for industrial recruiters in small cities everywhere. Many of the small, high-growth industries that most communities would love to attract are no longer moved by the traditional business considerations in the information age. They are located where the officers who run the company want to make their lives. William Whyte's research has shown that this is the primary motivation for the majority of companies that have left New York City for places like Stamford, Connecticut.

In the morning I headed for Port Townsend, on the Olympic Peninsula. After an expensive car ferry ($6.50 each way), I hit terrible traffic on the peninsula highways. There were few opportunities to pass on these winding two-lane roads, which reminded me of one of the most frustrating things about New Hampshire. In fact, a lot of what I saw reminded me of home. The landscape was primarily impenetrable forest, and the steep-roofed buildings had that North Country look so cultivated in the mountainous regions of New England. In the little towns like Port Gamble, the freshly painted clapboard houses could have been from Vermont. Where the road bounded the rocky waterfront of Puget Sound, I could have been anywhere along the Maine seacoast.

But then I approached the opening for the bridge over the Hood Canal and two things smacked me with reminders of how far I was from home. First was a state highway sign declaring it illegal to drive with five or more cars backed up behind you. Slow drivers in Washington were required by law to pull over to the shoulder to allow others by on roads too curvy for passing lanes. What a refreshing breath of common sense! What a clear departure from New Hampshire logic where a place on the road and the ability to regulate the speed of those impatient atheists behind (probably liberal flatlanders from Massachusetts or New Jersey) were God-given rights!

The second reminder was the spectacular view of the glacier-draped Olympic Mountains above vast stretches of blue water. We don't have that combination in New England, and as I drove across the bridge, I determined that it made a difference. With vistas like this a part of everyday existence, no wonder northwesterners were capable of leaps of innovation at which folks in less emancipating environments could only shake their heads.

But as I approached Port Townsend there were other messages: the nauseating smell of a pulp mill and huge gashes on the mountainsides denoting clear-cutting of the forests. A reminder, if I had needed it, that there was no such thing as paradise.

The town was really two towns. There was one along the waterfront that was quaint, cute, and permeated with tourist culture. The other was the real town, up on a plateau above white clay bluffs. Here were real neighborhoods with plenty of locals walking about. At the Uptown Pub a patron told me that the real natives were being squeezed out fast by people wanting to make money off of tourism and people who already had money and wanted to live in a picture-postcard place.

Uptown also featured a spectacular golf course with views of the Olympics, and the steam-billowing pulp mill down in the hollow, from every hole. I was surprised to find that it was not a country club but a public park supported by local taxes. There was also a real municipal bus service in this town of seven thousand, less than a third the size of Keene, where we believed we couldn't afford such a luxury.

This was what you could do in a place of booming tourism and why the tourist siren call was so alluring to communities with otherwise better sense all across America.

I drove from Port Townsend farther out on the peninsula to Port Angeles, ranked seventh in the nation in G. Scott Thomas's *Guide to Life in America's Small Cities,* the same book that had ranked Corvallis number two. The high ranking was mainly the result of spectacular scores for climate and urban proximity. Located on the Juan de Fuca Strait north of the Olympic Mountains and considerably farther west of the Cascades than Seattle, Port Angeles had Northwest temperatures without the Northwest rain that fell mostly to the southeast. Like British Columbia's Vancouver and Victoria, Port Angeles was the beneficiary of the warm Japanese current that made it warmer in winter than places farther south, like Portland. Sea breezes kept the summer temperatures cool, however, averaging just sixty-nine degrees.

The score for urban proximity, I concluded, was positively misleading. Looking at a map and considering the reputation of the Puget Sound region for reliable ferry service, one might conceive that Port Angeles was close to Seattle. It wasn't. When traffic was bad, as it was during my visit, the town was well beyond the two-hour limit.

Port Angeles was the official gateway to Olympic National Park, and the towering peaks visible from any point in town were its most impressive feature. Besides park management and tourism, the local economy was based on plywood, not pulp, and I was told by folks on the street that this made a considerable difference. Plywood mills don't smell. I verified that this was true. And they were somehow supposed to be more immune to boom and bust cycles than pulp mills. This I took with a dollop of doubt. It seemed to me that the construction industry's need for plywood would be more affected by recessions than the media's need for newsprint. But in Port Angeles it was an article of faith that the town's continuing high personal income rate had something to do with the fact that they made plywood here rather than pulp.

Housing was expensive because people had the money to buy. Otherwise the architecture of the residential sections of town, as well as the downtown, for that matter, was nondescript. Aside from the Lincoln Marquee Theater, the construction in Port Angeles was ticky-tacky modern, and there was little evidence of investment in parks and constructive open space. Perhaps the towering Olympics made such amenities seem superfluous.

Still the most important thing I learned about Port Angeles was how awfully far it really was from Seattle's cultural beehive. That was the lesson of my peninsula tour, especially after the frantic drive back to try to make the five o'clock ferry when, common sense signs or no, long lines of maddened drivers crawled along behind slow tourists while watching frantically for opportunities to pass. The good place literature had it that Olympic Peninsula locations were idyllic communities amid spectacular natural splendor with the bright lights and humanity of Seattle just a stone's throw away. But what I saw was that the imagined proximity of Seattle had perhaps led to a neglect of the social and cultural life that might have been established locally, that residents contended with a tourist traffic invasion that was more than just a nuisance, and that the whole business of getting to and from Seattle could resemble all too vividly the worst of a Connecticut or New Jersey commuter existence.

I was nearing the end of my stay in the Puget Sound region and felt frustrated that it was the first place I had come to where I didn't find much of what I was looking for. Sure Seattle had the houseboats and those wonderful inner-city neighborhoods, but I liked Portland better, and none of the other highly touted locations in the area had caught my fancy. As I started making my telephone calls to offer thanks and farewells, I got one final piece of advice from Laura Jacobsen. Laura knew Portland, of course, so she wasn't surprised at my feeling, but she urged me to follow through on my plan to visit one more place highly recommended by some patrons of Willett's back in Napa. "Check out Bellingham," she said. "You like good downtowns. They have four of them there."

The morning I drove to Bellingham, Thursday, August 21, 1991, the radio was full of the news that the Soviet coup had failed. I listened to the reports on National Public Radio and marveled at the steepness of the slopes of the mountains bounding I-5 north of Seattle. Snowcapped Mount Baker loomed up on the right through several propitious gaps in the forested mountain wall, and the Northwest summer sun was high and bright.

I exited off I-5 and drove down Lakeway and then Holly Street into the heart of downtown Bellingham. Already this little city was different from any other Puget Sound place I had visited. Large trees and sidewalk cafés lined the streets. There were well-preserved Victorian buildings, and clearly well-conceived architectural and sign codes had been applied. And best of all, there were lots of colorfully and smartly dressed pedestrians, families, collegiates, thirty-something professionals, and sprightly seniors. The place and its people simply looked good. One street, Railroad Street, had been set aside as a pedestrian mall, but otherwise light traffic flowed smoothly through a traditional grid and I could see no empty storefronts. Bowls of flowers hung from double-globed turn-of-the-century streetlamps.

I had lunch at a sidewalk table at the Paradise Café and Coffee Shop, which seemed to be a midday gathering place for people at work as well as those out for a casual stroll. I particularly liked the mix of women dressed in shorts and sandals with others dressed in classy business suits and fresh, lively dresses. It was breezy but warm, a place where you could take off your jacket, but not because you were sweating. Two couples seated at the table beside mine were discussing the apparent outcome of the coup in Moscow. One of the women said she hadn't watched the news with such anxiety since the sixties. Ditto for the rest. But the news was good. Earth generally was becoming a better place to live.

After lunch I drove across town to the Bellingham Athletic Club, where I found Scott Grier, a friend of one of the waitresses at Willett's who had gone to college in Bellingham and liked it so much that she intended to move there as soon as she saved up enough money. Scott was the manager and had the bulk and vigor of someone who spends a lot of time in training. While people pumped iron and sweated around us, we sat over coffee and he told me why he lived in Bellingham. Originally a native of Seattle, he had come to Bellingham six years before to get his teacher's certification at Western Washington University. "It was a good place to be a single male grad student," he said. "Mount Baker is nearby for skiing and mountain climbing, northern Puget Sound is the best place to sail in the world, and nightspots like Up 'n' Ups are world-class college bars. And the town appreciates its college culture."

He thought he'd be here only six months, but then he got a teaching job. "I had moved into a new phase of maturity, I guess. Stopped

going to college bars and discovered that Bellingham already had another scene ready for me to slide into," he said, gesturing to the gym
and health food bar around us. "That's the thing I've discovered about
Bellingham, there are a variety of lifestyles flourishing here, each one
tuned to a different phase of your life. I've put down roots now and
intend to stay here."

I asked him why he thought that phenomenon existed here. "Location, location, location," he answered. "Here we are an hour and a
half from Seattle one way and less than an hour from Vancouver, B.C.,
the other. Five minutes to the east from downtown you've got state
parks that are really pristine. And across the water to the west is Orcas
Island and the San Juans. Bellingham's right in the center of the most
diverse world imaginable and yet it's just a small city of about fifty
thousand. You can be a cosmopolitan person at any age and still enjoy
a saner, slower lifestyle than you can in one of the big cities."

He thought it was also a matter of a unique demographic balance.
Bellingham was a college town but also a significant center for elderly
retirees, who made up 20 percent of the population, having been
noted by *RSVP* magazine as one of the top five places to retire in the
United States. And in between there were the "prime-of-life people"
managing the strikingly diverse industries of the local economy. There
were fishing, logging, shipping, and plywood here. But there were also
three oil refineries (Arco, Tallco, and BP) nearby, GP Chemicals, the
big-time alternative lifestyle Dharma Juice factory, Mount Baker Vineyards, a Prudential Insurance branch, headquarters for outdoor outfitters the Great Adventure, the terminal for the Alaska State Ferry,
numerous art galleries, a significant but not stifling tourist trade, and
of course the university. Despite the large number of relatively low-
paying jobs in logging, shipping, and fishing, Bellingham still boasted
an average income of about thirty thousand dollars and one of the
highest ratios of doctors and dentists per capita of any small city in
America.

Scott had witnessed an economic and cultural boom in Bellingham during his six years here. "It began when Californians who had
been immigrating to the San Juans discovered Bellingham and began
moving here instead. They brought money and a spirit of innovation
that really kicked this town into high gear," he said. I mentioned that I
had visited other places where the Californian intrusion was widely

despised. He knew about that. "But so far they've filled a population and economic gap," he contended. "We needed them. Plus we think our Californians, the ones who come this far north, this close to Canada, are a better breed than most—mostly ex–northern Californians, not L.A. people."

The other key to Bellingham's recent success, Scott believed, was the paternal guidance of one large, progressive developer, Trillium Land Development. "They developed a mall on the outskirts but were simultaneously heavily involved in the redevelopment of the downtown. They planned the two to be complementary, not competing. The mall caters primarily to the Canadian dollar, while the downtown has shifted away from nuts and bolts and focuses on entertainment, specialties, and arts, catering primarily to locals." There was still undeveloped land five minutes from the downtown, and Trillium had worked out with local government a long-term plan to maintain the city's vitality but to guard against premature overdevelopment.

Before I left him to drive around exploring, Scott recommended a number of third places I should check out in Bellingham. I confirmed what Laura Jacobsen had told me, that there really were four downtowns, all thriving and each located within walking distance of its own constellation of neighborhoods. The reason for this unusual arrangement was that Bellingham was actually an almagamation of four original settlements: old Bellingham, Whatcom, Sehome, and Fairhaven.

A visit to the local library shed a little light on why this community was so different from others in the Puget Sound area. British captain George Vancouver named Bellingham Bay during a voyage charting the area in 1792. Coal and waterpower for sawmills lured the first settlers here in 1852. The settlement of Whatcom was named for an Indian word meaning "noisy waters," referring to the waterfall on the creek that connected a large freshwater lake to the sound. It was the 1858 Fraser Valley gold rush in British Columbia that put old Bellingham on the map as a port and staging area for miners, ten thousand of whom camped on the shores of the bay during those years. Men who found fortunes and turned them into substantial, continuing business empires by the late century founded Sehome, a community of beautiful, sometimes extravagant Victorian homes on a hill overlooking the bay.

But the jewel of the four settlements was Fairhaven, originally founded by a smuggler known as "Dirty Dan," who put his ill-gotten gains into cutting a town from whole cloth. His scheme might not have amounted to much but for the fact that one James Hill was building a railway across the northern tier of the country from the Midwest, and no one knew where its Pacific terminus would be. Speculators watched how Hill, a Canadian expatriate himself, hugged the border as he built through Montana and concluded that Fairhaven was the place. As the railway approached, Fairhaven became a boom town as fortunes were invested in creating a town worthy of its anticipated status. As it turned out, Hill went to Everett and Seattle instead, and the boom fizzled and fortunes were lost. But the place was established, with architecture that has survived and given it status as a national historic district today.

As I walked around the center of Fairhaven, I quickly saw that it had become a fashionable gathering place for artists, tourists, fans of alternative rock music, literati, and colorful students of all ages. There was a combination bookstore-café, where I found a young man with a long ponytail leafing through a copy of a book I had written. Chad Meyers was a college student with a double major in history and music. In return for my signing his purchase, he offered to be my tour guide for the remainder of my short stay in Bellingham.

We strolled the streets of old Fairhaven while Chad recited the local history of the dozen Victorian buildings that had been preserved as historic landmarks. "Fairhaven was going to be the next Chicago till Jim Hill headed south," he explained. But I was less intrigued by the history of the places than by the fact that each was today the site of flourishing commercial enterprise—bars, restaurants, a clothing shop, a barber, a bakery.

We went for supper to a place called Bullie's for crab-and-shrimp stroganoff—another Northwest innovation (and another good Northwest dinner for under ten dollars). Chad thought I might also like the red-checkered tablecloths and the microbrews on tap: Full Sail, Flagship, T. Kemper, Pike Place, Red Hook, Big Rock Buzzard Breath, Alaskan Amber, Pyramid Wheaten, and Ballard Bitter. The door here was wide open and there was no screen, either, another testimony to the lack of bugs in the Northwest.

I bought a paper and after supper we headed across the street to Tony's Coffeehouse. Besides the small shop, the property included a brick terrace backed up by an old railroad caboose. There were a couple dozen people at the tables outside, all either young or old, nobody in between. One very old fellow with long white hair and a full beard stained with tobacco juice around his mouth seemed to be a regular. He wore a work cap over a wool seaman's cap, suspenders, and purple jeans and had a little puppy with him, which seemed to be his link to the younger set, who would pet the puppy and then talk to the old man. Most of the coffee drinkers were reading. I saw *On Being and Nothingness, The Hobbit, Rise and Fall of the Third Reich,* the *Seattle Times,* the *New Republic,* and several alternative-style periodicals whose titles I did not recognize.

In our own paper, Chad and I perused the latest from Moscow. The coup had failed, Gorbachev was back in the capital, and Boris Yeltsin was a national hero for his heroic stand at the White House. Another story described a new expansion at Boeing, based on commercial rather than military sales. The old man with the puppy was talking about world peace with a pair of young men at the table next to us. "I will see it in my lifetime," he rejoiced. The two young men ·raised their coffee cups in a toast, joined by several others nearby: "Peace in Pop's lifetime," they said. Somewhere between Bremerton and Bellingham, I had crossed a great divide.

Chad took me to several of Bellingham's bars that evening. I particularly liked the Chat Noir, a classy upstairs bar in one of Fairhaven's heritage buildings, with a semicircular oak bar, etched glass on the doors, Toulouse-Lautrec prints on the walls, and French lamps at the velvet-draped windows. In the Bellingham Bay Brewing Company, a brew pub featuring, on this night, an open mike routine, I found all of the elements of an ideal third place—and great pizza to boot.

Throughout our evening, Chad had entertained me with his idea of a Northwest philosophy of life that reminded me of the way that Laura Jacobsen had talked. "You can have all the good physical amenities in the world, mountains, parks, good gathering places—what you call 'third places.' But it's the attitude of the people in a place that really matters," he contended.

Chad, who had come to the Northwest from New Jersey, believed that Americans here were freer of what he called "the national maladjustment" than anywhere else. "Sure you still get materialism here, but it's tempered with a sensitivity to the nonverbal energies that exist between people—the things that hang in the air unsaid that are the most powerful forces of all. Here people look you in the eyes when they talk. They nurture what they care about, they share experience openly, they transform judgmental habits into curiosity about human nature. People here are able to learn how to live all over again."

"Why here?" I asked him.

"It's the West Coast, of course," he answered. "The new world of the New World. It's the water and the mountains. And there's a cosmopolitan worldliness because we're so linked to British Columbia."

He looked at me expecting a question about the character of British Columbia. But I already knew. It was during my previous trips to British Columbia that this whole thesis about the importance of place had germinated. Instead I skipped to the next question: "Why not go to B.C. and stay there?"

"You mean, be an expatriate? A lot of people do that," he confirmed. "But I'm happy to be an American here in Bellingham and still be close enough to venture into that foreign world whenever I need a breath of different air."

I wished I had more time to spend in Bellingham. Unlike the Olympic Peninsula places, you really could get to Seattle quickly and easily from here, and Vancouver, B.C., was less than an hour and a border crossing in the other direction—a strong Cake Factor on the 10,000 Waves scale. There was a qualitative difference in the feel of Bellingham from the other Puget Sound places. The world was not on the make here; people did not seem to be breathing heavily over what they could take from the place. Thus I gave it a Fudge Factor of five. Because of the multiple downtowns, each within walking distance of its own constellation of neighborhoods, it got a four for Foot Factor.

Otherwise Bellingham was attractive as the one place in a region of overblown expectations where I was not primarily impressed with unanticipated negatives. It was largely location that did it—out of the line of fire in the Seattle–Olympic Peninsula connection, just beyond the pale of the southern California immigration, and so close to what Chad called the "different air" of British Columbia.

It was easy to see why the Puget Sound region had attracted so many Americans in the eighties. Seattle was the place that perhaps inspired the Cake Factor, offering big-city cultural excitement in a natural setting with a mild, though rainy, climate. And until the eighties the region apparently had been relatively unspoiled. But that had changed. Except for Bellingham, I came away from the Puget Sound region with a feeling that it was rapidly becoming the Long Island of the Northwest. The spirit of Seattle was too much Big Apple and the Olympic Peninsula was a pretty place to build bedrooms. The region had gotten too hot too quickly.

6

EXPATRIATE

One gray October day in Keene, a local Democratic activist tele-phoned and said she needed someone to pick up a governor from Arkansas who would shortly arrive at the airport to begin his quest for the presidency in the New Hampshire primary. Impressed by this educated, intelligent man from Arkansas who talked of engineering a renaissance of American community, I put the good place quest on hold and threw myself into his campaign.

We on the Clinton team in Keene became quite proud of ourselves —the week that he broke out of the pack, our local walk with him to the Keene Community Kitchen made photos in *Newsweek*. But then came Gennifer Flowers, the Little Rock draft board, and Rush Limbaugh. It looked as though America's tabloid obsessions would subvert this latest cause for hope.

So after the primary, I left for Vancouver, where I had business with my Canadian publisher. But that was just my excuse; I really wanted to use the time to consider seriously the expatriate alternative.

As I traveled westward across Canada by train, I experienced a phenomenon well known to Canadians. As one moves beyond the prairies, the climate gets warmer. The cause is the Japanese current, which strikes the North American coast north of the border. Westerly winds carry this warmth far inland, even over the Rockies, so that cities as far north as Calgary, Edmonton, and Jasper are milder than one might expect.

Thus, though much of Canada was written off by good place seekers because of climate, southern British Columbia in particular had emerged as one of the continent's prime good place regions. Coastal areas and low-lying inland valleys boasted year-round temperatures comparable to central and northern California. Snow was rare below the altitude of two thousand feet. Vancouver's climate was often compared to that of Seattle or Portland, but it was actually a little warmer and less rainy than either.

During the past few years I had come into Vancouver by bus, plane, train, ferry, and auto—from the south, east, north, and west. Except for one trip when I arrived on a socked-in rainy day (common in winter), I had always felt like Dorothy sighting the Emerald City from the yellow brick road, no matter what the approach. Driving in from the United States, you ride through the vast, flat Fraser delta farmlands, reminiscent of Iowa in a good rain year. To the north, sharply pointed, purple mountains rise in the distance. You tunnel under the Fraser River, come over a rise, and suddenly there it is, a compact city of modern spires intertwined with broad fingers of blue water reaching in from the west and backed by those previously purple mountains, now looming blue-green over even the tallest of the skyscrapers.

Arriving by train from the northern interior of B.C., you've just ridden down the hair-raising flanks of three-thousand-foot Fraser Canyon and then along the shores of a true fjord, Howe Sound, with vistas of glaciers on craggy peaks, herds of mountain sheep, and vast tracts of uninhabited wilderness. You begin to see little logging towns and pulp mills, then round a bend in the sound and the soaring curves of Lion's Gate Bridge lead the eye to a peninsula that is half forest and half city—big city—with towers outlined against blue sky. Here the mountains are at your back and the city stands tall with the ocean and Fraser delta behind it. The forest is Stanley Park, far and away North America's most spectacular urban green space. However approached, Vancouver always strikes the eye with its radically varied geography painted in two overwhelmingly dominant colors, green and blue. There is no city in North America where the works of nature and humans are so intermingled and balanced.

I stayed at the Sylvia Hotel, an old ivy-covered building located right on the waterfront of English Bay in the section of town known as West End. Spartan and cheap, the rooms had no air-conditioning, but with the balmy breezes blowing off the bay, where freighters lay at anchor, it wasn't needed. The windows had no screens. Despite all of the greenery, there were no bugs in Vancouver.

The Sylvia was a Vancouver institution, one of the city's designated heritage buildings, protected by statute from razing. Despite the simple accommodations, it was the destination of choice for writers and Vancouver cognoscenti because of its location in the West End and the sunset view of the bay from its comfortable old-world cocktail lounge.

I strolled along English Bay that first warm, breezy late March morning, munching a doughnut from a shop on nearby Denman Street. A youngish woman wearing Top-Siders, white jeans, and a green sweater that contrasted with her deep red ponytail was crawling around the rocks and driftwood at water's edge with a camera. I thought maybe she was a university student working on a photography project until she took a break and sat down cross-legged near enough for me to ask her if she was a photographer.

"I'd like to be," she answered with a voice too full of maturity and worldly tiredness for a college student. "What about you?" she asked, nodding toward my camera and notebook on the bench beside me. As we inspected each other's cameras, she quizzed me about what I was putting in my notebook and I queried her about life in Vancouver.

She protested that she wasn't a very representative Vancouverite, having recently washed up here with three of her five kids after a life of trouble; anyway, she wasn't even a native-born Canadian. Karen Dick was born in Rocky Mount, North Carolina, but at fourteen ran away from an abusive family and became a street kid. After nearly losing some fingers to frostbite as a neophyte in northern cities, she began hitchhiking her way west till she fetched up for the first time here in Vancouver.

This was a good place to be a street kid. "At least you didn't have to worry about freezing or starving to death," she said. Life was still hard—there were alcohol and drugs and petty theft and some other unsavory things she didn't want to tell me about. But Karen attributed her presence in Vancouver now to memories of her time here as a street kid.

"You really have the whole day to do nothing but hang out and talk to people who live here?" she asked me.

"That's it," I told her.

"I have till my kids get out of a day care program at four. I have nothing to do but take pictures."

So I followed her on her rounds of Stanley Park in search of good shots. First we walked the seawall promenade around the circumference of the park. The pavement was divided by a median line into pedestrian and bike lanes, and Karen had to keep yanking this undisciplined American out of the bike lane and harm's way. She showed me tennis courts, bowling lawns, stone park buildings with quaint eateries ranging from the beach hot dog stand to the elegant Teahouse Restaurant, magnificent gardens, the public zoo, the waterfront public pool filled with genuine English Bay saltwater, Third Beach, where she had seen whales and freighters beached, the view from below Lion's Gate Bridge, and the entrance to Burrard Inlet and the harbor. Throughout much of the walk, the path bounded vertical rock walls to the right, and at every turning there was some spectacular new vista: the distant gap of Howe Sound, the cloud-shrouded hump of Cypress Mountain, the tiered housing of West Vancouver, rising to dizzying heights up the mountainsides across the inlet, the spires and cable cars of North Vancouver and Grouse Mountain, the long, slow emergence from the harbor of a huge freighter bound for Hong Kong.

Circumnavigating Stanley Park took all morning, and during this time Karen told me more of her story. She had five children and had lived in two abusive common-law marriages. After escaping the second marriage, she wandered, homeless, with three of her kids. "I was right back to my street kid days, having to steal to feed my kids," she explained. She had enough schooling from her two stints at domestic living to work as a practical nurse and a social agency counselor, but she said she just wasn't able to settle in one place and make a life until she returned to Vancouver less than a year ago, "at the end of my rope. I guess I came here because of my memories of my first days here as a street kid, when it just wasn't as bad here as in every other place I'd been."

She went to a provincial welfare agency and asked for help, something she had never done before. She qualified and it saved everything. But welfare wasn't just a matter of getting a check; they didn't do things that way in Vancouver. The welfare people found her a decent place to stay, in an apartment slated for remodeling just a few blocks from the Sylvia, and the local Neighborhood House offered assistance ranging from scrounging up furniture and kitchen utensils to advising her on the opportunities and pitfalls for young kids growing up on these West End streets. Part of the deal was that she would work several days a week in maintenance and room cleaning for her landlord. The welfare people placed her kids in school and a comprehensive day-care program, which allowed Karen to work and pursue her study of photography. They provided a *Handbook for Newcomers to British Columbia*—"like an operating manual for life here"—containing addresses and phone numbers for virtually every community-based resource a person could possibly need. And finally, they placed Karen herself in an intensive program of counseling and group sessions to help her do nothing less than change the way she had learned to live from the day she ran away at age fourteen.

"For the first time in my life I've had the luxury of time to think without having to worry about the next crisis of the day, food or shelter, or protecting my kids from trouble," she said.

As I came to know more about Karen, I concluded for myself that she indeed had been saved here. Later that day occurred the first of two related incidents that demonstrated the positive effect of Karen's Vancouver experience. We were hungry after our long hike around Stanley Park and she suggested that we catch the little foot ferry that takes people across False Creek to the huge market at Granville Island for lunch. As we were meandering past the open-air food stalls, I spotted a twenty-dollar bill lying on the ground in front of a Chinese food vendor. When I picked it up, the Chinese woman behind the counter eyeballed me, so I gave it to her, telling her that some recent customer must have just dropped it and would be back shortly to claim it. As we walked on, Karen said, "She'll just stick it in her pocket, you know," and I felt a rush of foolishness. Of course she would, and here was my struggling friend, to whom twenty dollars would really mean something.

I forgot about the whole episode for a day as I went about other business, but the next afternoon there was a knock at my hotel room door. It was Karen. She had the twenty-dollar bill and insisted that I take it. I tried to give it back to her, of course, but she was adamant.

"You have to understand," she pleaded. "I can't let you give it back to me in any form. It's part of what I am struggling so hard to learn from my counseling. I spent so much of my life getting by with lying and stealing. I have to live absolutely honestly, more so than most people. It's like the alcoholic who can't even take a sip of a drink. I'll never make it if I don't."

I managed at least to convince her to tell me the whole story. She had gone back to the Chinese vendor after we had parted company for the day, determined to get the money for herself. She had made a scene with the woman behind the counter, calling on witnesses at neighboring counters whom she had carefully noted when the incident originally occurred. She made such a fuss that the woman, who first denied any knowledge of the money, relented and gave her the bill. But as soon as she had it in her hand, she knew she had to bring it back to me. I was grateful to Karen and Vancouver for providing me with this absolute reality check, affirming that human beings could be honest without any anticipated benefit. If Karen had gotten that bill back and spent it, I would never have known.

West End and downtown Vancouver were located on a peninsula between Burrard Inlet and English Bay, which narrowed into a smaller waterway known as False Creek. West of West End lay the huge preserve of forested Stanley Park, and to the east, at the connecting end of the peninsula, was downtown. West End had contended with Manhattan over the past few decades for the title of North America's most densely populated locale. Yet it didn't look or feel crowded at all.

The explanation lay in the fact that West End was almost entirely residential, and with the downtown immediately to the east and Stanley Park to the west, it was sandwiched between two huge sponges that absorbed people. It had one commercial street, Denman, which crossed the peninsula and functioned as a local downtown. And it had the English Bay waterfront, with its swimming beaches, broad, grassy lawns, gardens, and pedestrian and bikers' promenades leading west to Stanley Park and east up False Creek to other parts of the city. West End people moved about with ease and grace—there was none of the usual big-city dash and hassle.

I came to identify the Karen Dick episode with an emerging notion of a "spirit of Vancouver" that seemed somehow connected to the sane pace of life in this mild city. That same week I encountered it in

another form when I went to dinner at the home of two women I had
met on the train.

Dorothy and Barbara Stowe were wife and daughter of the deceased Irving Stowe, cofounder of the international environmental
organization Greenpeace. When I told them of my intentions regarding Vancouver that first evening back on the train, they insisted that
the birth of Greenpeace there was emblematic of the city and that I
had to visit them during my stay to find out why.

South of False Creek, between the University of British Columbia
and the eastern factory district lay the middle-class residential neighborhoods of Kitsilano, Shaughnessey, Dunbar, and Point Grey. They
were similar to the neighborhoods of Seattle, only better, because they
were more extensive, their exceedingly green lawns and well-
established trees were even more beautifully maintained, and trouble
didn't lie threatening at the fringes.

It surprised me that the house where Greenpeace was born could
be a simple split-level on a small lot in a very conventional block in
Point Grey. The living room could have been out of any of a million
suburban homes except for the pictures and mementos hanging on
the walls—artifacts from the Greenpeace saga. A deck off the kitchen
offered a teasing view through the tree branches of the mountains
beyond and the Stowes' city nestled at their base—the city of safety
Irving Stowe had chosen many years ago over all others in the world.

Dorothy began telling the family story over coffee, with Barbara
adding asides reflecting her childhood memories and occasionally re-
acting with surprise at unremembered details in her mother's narrative. The Stowes were originally Americans; Barbara and her brother
were born in Rhode Island, where Irving was a civil rights lawyer.
During the fifties they became Quakers, one family's response to the
fallout shelters, air raid drills, and nuclear madness of the cold war's
warmest years. But in 1961, when the government began development
of nuclear subs at nearby Groton, Connecticut, Irving and Dorothy
came to believe that keeping the pacifist faith was no longer possible
while residing in the United States. "We didn't want to pay taxes to a
country bent on developing the potential and the will to destroy human life on earth," she said.

As a civil rights lawyer Irving had a long history of committed
antiestablishment activism. But the fallout question provoked a soul-

searing dilemma: stay and fight the beast, or leave for conscience and safety. "It was us kids that did it," Barbara explained. "He would have stayed and fought. But he was terrified that we children would get irradiated." Few of us today remember how seriously people took that possibility back in those days. It wasn't until later in the evening that I would learn the terrible irony of Irving's premonition.

There was a feeling in those days that the southern hemisphere was safer, if not from all-out nuclear war, then at least from fallout resulting from testing. Thus Irving swept his family off to New Zealand to make a new life. The Stowes spent five and a half years there. But when the Vietnam War heated up, Irving's conscience stirred. He wanted to move his family back to some place of sanity in North America where they could fight the beast.

A friend suggested Vancouver, and everything clicked. New Zealand had just sent a token force to Vietnam, Americans were expatriating in droves to Canada, and Vancouver swept Stowe off his feet when he visited it. "It is a world-class city of enterprise and culture," he wrote to Dorothy in New Zealand, "set amidst a natural environment as beautiful as any I have ever seen, and, though only a short drive away, insulated from America by geography, politics and national boundaries as effectively as New Zealand."

In Vancouver the family became immersed in the environmental activism that was aborning here long before it became fashionable elsewhere. Irving wrote a column for the underground rag *Georgia Strait* in which he advocated a rapid transit system; the conversion of cars, particularly taxis and delivery vehicles, to propane; and the prohibition of oil tankers from the island-studded waters off the coast. (All three had become public policy by my time there, and the *Georgia Strait* had grown to become a prosperous alternative to the traditional media.)

It was three years of happy reunion with North America before the family's date with history. "It came one day when the phone rang," recalled Dorothy. Environmentalist acquaintances called to alert Irving to impending U.S. nuclear tests underwater at Amchitka, Alaska. Besides the principle of the thing, there was the double horror of possible water and airborne fallout—Vancouver was down current and downwind from Amchitka. The site was on an earthquake fault. A tidal wave might be generated that would threaten valuable waterfront real estate, and there would definitely be a massive slaughter of B.C.'s beloved sea otters, whose eardrums would be split open as they ranged near the Amchitka site.

Irving wrote a "stop the bomb" petition to the U.S. consulate and set himself up on a street corner in downtown Vancouver, gathering signatures. Simultaneously a group of students from the University of B.C. staged a lie-down protest at the border and succeeded in shutting it down for the first time since the War of 1812. One of them, a law student named Paul Cote, met with Irving and Sierra Club environmentalist Jim Bohlen in Irving's study at the house in Point Grey to found the Don't Make a Wave Committee. Though they didn't have the name right yet, Greenpeace was born.

After we had cleared the table and moved to the living room, where the seminal decisions in Greenpeace's early history had taken place, Barbara went to a file cabinet and brought me a copy of the original Don't Make a Wave Committee consitution. In Irving's lawyerly clauses it stated a simple goal: the raising of money to "foster public awareness of the possible environmental effects of the detonation of nuclear explosives" and "to support or conduct research in the area of environmental preservation."

Jim Bohlen's son designed the famous yellow-and-green button, Irving cranked out leaflets, and both families, along with Paul Cote and his friends, took to the Vancouver streets on weekends to hawk them from cardboard vending boxes hanging by strings from their necks. "There was one street corner on Granville," Barbara remembered, "where there were four corners of activists—we on one, a Vietnam protest on another, Hare Krishnas on a third, and black civil rights people on the fourth." She was fourteen at the time and now believed that the love and respect she had for her father's dedication had spared her many of the foolish traumas of adolescence. " 'If you're going to make the world a better place, you have to do your homework, Peaches!' he exhorted me, and he wasn't talking about grade-ten math."

But by Christmas the movement became frustrated. Less than a thousand dollars had been raised, the U.S. government seemed determined to go through with the tests, and the group's leaders felt disenchanted with the limited scope implied by the movement's name. Newcomers to the movement, many of them veterans of protests against America's war in Vietnam, infused the organization with a growing sense of a unified dual purpose—peace and protection of the environment.

One evening a week before Christmas, the Stowes, the Bohlens, and a group of young people sat in this living room wondering if a new name could encompass a return to the true spirit of Christmas, peace, ecology, and hope, all in one word. Someone mumbled something about how it was too bad that "Green Christmas" meant either lack of snow or the emphasis on making money out of the season. Someone else muttered, "Green Christmas, 'Greensleeves' . . ." A twenty-three-year-old student named Jim Darnell speculated, "What we really need is something like . . . ," and then he jumped up and shouted, "Greenpeace!" Bingo. The movement had a name.

The discovery of the name reenergized everything, because following on its heels came the clear vision that Greenpeace would charter a boat to sail to the Amchitka test site to, in the Quaker tradition, "bear witness." Irving and Jim Bohlen set off as delegates to the New Democratic party convention in Winnipeg in 1970 in the hope of raising the needed money. A boat was found, the *Phyllis McCormack,* which could be hired for eighteen thousand dollars.

Irving and Jim came back seventeen thousand dollars short, and the group reconvened in the Stowes' living room to ponder. Irving suggested a rock concert. The others groaned, as Quakers, but Irving persevered and sent out a flurry of letters. Joan Baez expressed sympathy but declined because of a previous engagement. Then Joni Mitchell answered yes, as did Phil Ochs and the locally popular band Chilliwack. The concert was on.

Local deejays, music critics, and UBC student leaders were recruited to spear the publicity effort and the Vancouver Coliseum was rented. Now the required last stop in North American concert tours, in 1970 Vancouver had never had a rock concert before. Soon the Stowe home was transformed into a hotbed of the new Canadian radicalism. Barbara wrote in an essay for school, "Phil Ochs came to our house raving and trailing a crowd of lefties far lefter than any of us (Trotskyites or Marxists or some such) and a smoke plume from his smelly Cuban cigar and went to work finishing off all of the liquor in the house."

Then two days before the concert Joni Mitchell called and asked if she could bring her boyfriend to play in the concert, somebody named James Taylor. Everyone in Barbara's very unhip family looked to her for name recognition; she thought he was maybe an obscure black blues singer. "Dad wanted to keep this Taylor guy a secret because nobody knew who he was, and if he was bad he might ruin the concert," she recalled. "But word leaked out, and at school the tallest, lankiest, hippest, jean-jacketed guy came up to me and asked, 'Is James Taylor really playing at your father's concert?' Then I heard 'Sweet Baby James' on the car radio. I was the happiest teenager in North America."

Thanks to Taylor and Mitchell, the concert was a sellout. "Mitchell's music was perfect," Barbara recalled. "Ochs gave a leftie speech, Taylor snarled 'Shut up' when the audience applauded him and they loved it, and my father addressed the crowd 'Brothers and sisters' and thanked them for helping to stop the madness." Greenpeace cleared just over seventeen thousand dollars, exactly the amount needed so that the voyage could proceed.

On September 15, 1971, the *Phyllis McCormack,* now renamed the *Greenpeace,* set sail from Vancouver. That first voyage the ship hit stormy weather and had to abort the mission before arriving at the test site, but the U.S. postponed the first nuclear test, and since Greenpeace now had money, it was able to acquire a second ship, rechristened the *Greenpeace Too.* The rescheduled blast occurred before *Greenpeace Too* could reach the island, but Greenpeace had generated even more far-reaching seismic rumblings. By the end of the year, the Atomic Energy Commission called off further tests, for "political and other reasons."

Irving worked for Greenpeace full-time until 1974, while Dorothy worked as a Vancouver social worker on cases very much like that of my friend Karen Dick. By then Greenpeace had offices in half a dozen cities around the world and a schism had developed that persists to this day. An increasingly influential enclave within the organization began to focus narrowly on the preservation of threatened wildlife— the "save the whales" movement—as opposed to the larger issue of saving the planet by uniting peace and ecological activism. Irving was not pleased with the new direction; even though he had told his family often that what had originally moved him most was the image of millions of sea otters with burst eardrums, it was human children who really mattered in the long run.

But the schism wasn't the reason for Irving's withdrawal from active participation in the movement. He was ill and died from pancreatic cancer six months later, in October of 1974. The doctors thought there might be some connection to the radiation treatments he had received for acne as a young man.

Ten years later, at age twenty-eight, Barbara was diagnosed with Hodgkin's disease. She endured chemotherapy for eight months, her long, dark hair falling out, her ballet dancer's body emaciated, her appetite for good food gone. Now, seven years later, at thirty-six, she showed no signs of that struggle. She was dancing again, but she had lost years in the prime of her life.

Dorothy believed that there was undocumented radiation around Groton in 1956. "Something was in the air and water," she said. "Irving was right, we just didn't get out quite soon enough."

Driving back over False Creek to the West End and the Sylvia that night, I believed that Dorothy's last statement was only partly true. There are other, nonphysical cancers that one can catch in modern America and it seemed to me that Irving Stowe had done an admirable job in sparing his family from those. I thought of my own young teen daughters back in New Hampshire and ruminated around the edges of a thought, that perhaps Irving Stowe had also given me something—just a seed yet, but it was planted. I called my daughters from the Sylvia the next day and told them some of the Stowe saga. And it was the first time that I myself used the words, "You've got to do your homework, Peaches."

I kicked around Vancouver rather aimlessly the next few days, strolled the paths along English Bay, and overheard more than once a comment about the extended period of clear, dry weather the city had been enjoying: "If it hasn't rained for a while people get twitchy and nervous like something isn't right with the world, eh?" On weekends during this and subsequent visits, I saw certain characters who were regular fixtures along the waterfront. There was the Parcheesi group, a dozen men and the occasional woman who had created a little bower out of a cane brake beside the water and beneath the seawall walkway. They were there every Sunday of every visit I ever made to Vancouver

—in their swimsuits, playing Parcheesi, and drinking beer and wine. There was also the slightly daft octogenarian who swam nude from his own little rocky point every afternoon, no matter what the month. He stripped in full view of the pedestrians and bikers on the walk, unmindful of exposing himself. When I asked him how the water was, he always answered that it was just fine.

A young couple set up shop selling hand-painted T-shirts every weekend. A water colorist was a regular, as were a zither player and an outrageous robotic mime. Groups of boys on Rollerblades played hockey with tennis balls and always there were the lovers, changing faces daily but in this romantic setting pursuing a ritual so singular in its form and gestures that they seemed like the same couple day after day. They walked in sunset light, almost painfully bright and golden in the unpolluted sky—more like a dawn on the prairie from whence so many Canadian immigrants to Vancouver had come.

I had to do a publicity phone interview for a radio station one morning and couldn't get a line out of the Sylvia. Ticket sales had just begun on a first-call, first-served basis for an upcoming U-2 concert, and B.C. Tel had crashed under the deluge. The owner of the hotel took me to his penthouse apartment in the neighboring building above the hotel's underground parking garage, where he had a special line that would still work.

When I finished my phone interview, he explained that he had built the apartment tower just a few years ago to help pay for the parking garage that the hotel so desperately needed. It was only seven stories high and sited on one of the most valuable urban properties in North America. I asked him why he hadn't built to the maximum allowed under Vancouver regulations. He smiled at me indulgently and commented, "That's a very American question. We found the level of wealth we were comfortable with some years ago. We just didn't need any more."

During my time in Vancouver, I didn't pay much attention to American headlines. The presidential primary campaign was still mired in desultory stories about Clinton's character. It was refreshing instead to immerse oneself in the novelty of the neighbors' news, so little of which we normally hear on our side of the border. One evening I went back to my hotel to catch the television news, more to watch the ads than anything else. I was intrigued with the ads of Japanese carmakers, whose Canadian pitch was different from their message to Americans. A Nissan ad showed its product in scenes that emphasized the difference between life in Canada and the United States. The voice-over said, "We want a Canada free from pollution, where people live without fear of crime, with sensible mass transit, energy conservation, and where people believe in taking care of one another." A Honda ad began, "At Honda we have a profound respect for the engineers of great roads and the builders of great communities."

But when I flipped on the TV this evening, there was no car ad running. Something terrible was on the screen. There were images of city blocks in flames, looters smashing storefront windows, and overhead helicopter shots of black men dragging white men from trucks and savaging them till they lay still in their own blood. It was Los Angeles. An all-white jury in the suburb of Simi Valley had that day acquitted the police officers recorded on videotape in the beating of Rodney King.

So much for my self-imposed embargo on American headlines. The King story and L.A. riots colored my view of everything I saw for the remainder of my swing through B.C. and then back into the northern tier of the United States that spring. Here was the ultimate in community dysfunction. Vancouverites couldn't help but feel the usual Canadian smugness at domestic trouble across the border. But then related racial disturbances occurred in Toronto, and the traditional Canadian vocabulary of multiculturalism was dusted off and read with newfound urgency.

I did another publicity interview with a talk show host named Philip Till for local radio station CKNW. Awkwardly I asked after the show if he was *the* Philip Till of Middle East radio news fame. He was, and we were pleased enough with each other's chatter that it was decided I would have lunch sometime at his house in North Vancouver.

He picked me up at the Sylvia on a day when it still hadn't rained and drove down Georgia Street through downtown to the east end of the city and the Second Narrows Bridge over Burrard Inlet to North Vancouver. I was amazed, as always, at how quickly and easily you could drive right through the heart of this big city. In East Vancouver he showed me bungalows along Wall Street that he guessed could be had for under $200,000. Just a few blocks away from downtown, they commanded a spectacular view of the inlet and mountains to the north. Philip was an unabashed community booster, and as we drove over the bridge with the Coast Range rising in the blue sky just ahead, filling our windshield, and the ships plying the water down below, he said, "After a rough day at the station, all I need to do is get on this bridge, and life is good."

As we wound through the curving streets of North Vancouver up the slope to his home, Philip explained how he had come to Vancouver. Born an Englishman, he was raised in Germany, where his dad introduced him to the news business. He returned to London with UPI at age fifteen and then began the world-hopping career that made him one of the premier foreign radio correspondents of our time. After living and working in Vienna, Brussels, Bonn, and London, he joined NBC in 1974 and was posted to Paris, where he met and married his wife, Michelle. When he became the foreign editor for NBC Radio his territory was Europe, Africa, and the Middle East. His coverage of the civil war in Beirut and the fall of the shah in Iran was what made him a name that I would recognize.

He had done it all, seen it all, and spent time in most of the world-class cities of the globe. Finally he wanted to ease up into a more domestic life someplace that was purely a good place to live. Sydney, Australia, was impressive and he tentatively accepted an off-air job there as foreign editor for the Australian Broadcasting Company.

A mutual acquaintance who knew Vancouver, which Till had never visited, suggested to CKNW management that Till just might be available to do their "World Tonight" combination news and talk show. It was a long shot considering Till's experience and resume, but CKNW phoned him in London and made an offer. "I had to get a map out to check where the hell Vancouver was," he chuckled. His friend insisted that it was a city of the first rank that he had somehow missed in his travels, so he agreed to accept a plane ticket from CKNW to check it out.

"As I flew in over Vancouver that first time and looked out the window," he said, "saw the view from the plane, the water, the mountains, and the impressive size of the city, I jumped up and announced to the whole cabin, 'This is the place.'"

The job offer, though a bit off the fast lane he was used to, was just about perfect—two and a half hours nightly of serious discussion of world news that would make Till an arbiter of global issues in one of the hottest corners of the Pacific Rim. He would spend his days doing what he liked best: prepping for his show by shortwave and telephone contact with his well-established sources worldwide. He concluded, "I was here just two days after a life of traveling the world and I have been here five years since with no intention of ever going anywhere else."

Philip's house was in a densely wooded neighborhood next to the school attended by his daughter. It was a contemporary design with a low-pitched roof and a large deck out back overlooking a swimming pool and a babbling brook. As we sat on his deck drinking nonalcoholic beer, he talked about his early days in Vancouver. "This is a very forgiving city, I discovered quickly," he said. Initially he knew nothing of the household names of British Columbia, not even the premier, and made frequent errors of nonrecognition in his talk show. "I did it over and over again. In most places it would have knocked me off the air."

We began to work our way through the talk show issues of life in Vancouver. Taxes: "They're very high. When you add it all up, you can figure about half of your income going to taxes. You have to get pretty good benefits to balance it off." Historically Canadians had never felt the visceral antipathy toward taxation so widespread in the United States. In B.C., as in most of the provinces, people believed that the purpose of government was for looking after one another. But the recently inaugurated 7 percent general sales tax had set off Canada's first rumblings of tax revolt.

The environment: Vancouver benefited from being downwind of nothing but five thousand miles of Pacific Ocean, and Vancouverites were rabid about any new local sources of pollution. This was a city whose buses were electric and whose taxis and delivery vehicles ran on propane fuel by law.

Medical care: Philip explained that Canadians could become quite exercised over the "bogus U.S. propaganda" about Canadian waiting lists and lack of specialty treatments. "I've lived in the U.K., where that's a real issue. In Canada, swift and excellent treatment is no problem." He took his British Columbia Care Card out of his wallet. "This is what you use when you go to the doctor or the hospital. You never pay a premium. You never see a bill."

Welfare and immigration: Because of the widespread acceptance of

the Canadian welfare state tradition, welfare became a hot-button issues only when linked to immigration. I told Philip the story of Karen
Dick and he thought few British Columbians would object to the
welfare assistance she received (though some might quibble at her
being able to live in West End). But he believed that Vancouver was
wrestling with what was perhaps the world's first foreign immigration
crisis where the issue was not the poverty of the newcomers but their
wealth. Because of common ties with the old British empire and an
aversion to the strong Japanese presence in West Coast U.S. cities,
Hong Kong capitalists fleeing the anticipated communist regime had
chosen Vancouver en masse as their new home and base of business
operations. There were advantages in this for Vancouver, to be sure.
The infusion of capital had fueled an economic juggernaut that made
Vancouver nearly immune to the continental recession.

But Vancouver was a particularly architecture-conscious city, with
heritage preservation codes enacted during the seventies and eighties
to prevent the remaking of designated neighborhoods in the mold of
so many placeless U.S. cities. The new Chinese could afford to buy the
unprotected bungalows of Kitsilano or Shaunessey for top dollar and
would tear them down to erect huge, ostentatious "monster houses,"
often in tawdry imitation of classical Greek architecture and completely at odds with the scale and style of the neighborhood.

Philip explained that there was another, related issue of class. "It
was one thing when lower-middle-class merchants of Chinatown kept
to themselves and their language. It was quite another when the richest family on the block, who drove their kids to private school in
Mercedes limousines, carried on the same way. We've now had a taste
of racial conflict as a result."

The L.A. riots: "A lot of people are gloating over an American
embarrassment and others are wringing their hands about when such
a thing will happen here. I don't buy either response. L.A. is L.A. just
like Beirut is Beirut—a world-class disaster waiting to happen. There
are lessons to be learned from it. But it's no indicator of the futures of
other places. The wonder is that it didn't happen there sooner."

As he drove me back to West End later that afternoon, Philip Till
explained the core of his belief that his quality of life was better in
Vancouver than it could be in the United States—or anywhere else in
the world, for that matter. It was a civil city, as unlike L.A. as a place

could get, set in the midst of natural grandeur. He earned less and paid more in taxes than he would in a U.S. city. "But here you learn that you can live with a degree less materialism because the public life and the environment are so rich. You get to the point where you're content not to have more. That's the Vancouver ethic."

The publishing company of Douglas and McIntyre, on Venables Street in East Vancouver, was the excuse for my frequent visits here during the past few years. In the Canadian publishing world, Toronto corresponded to New York and Vancouver to San Francisco. When you visit the offices of a publishing company in New York, you never see the machines that print and bind the books or the warehouses from which they are shipped. But at D and M, the entire publishing operation of this national trade publisher was located under one single-story roof. The arrangement was characteristic of Canadian microindustry, which flourished in a market one-tenth the size of its U.S. counterpart.

My editor there was Rob Sanders, a hearty, robust fellow of volcanic enthusiasms whom I came to see as a walking advertisement for the Vancouver way of life. He introduced me to the East Side of Vancouver, "Not so upscale as downtown, Kitsilano, or West End, but funky, ethnic, and progressive." We lunched several times at an Italian restaurant on Commercial Street, just a block away from the current offices of Greenpeace, where the pasta was rich and firm and the sauces like concentrated joy.

D and M had quite a backlist of books about British Columbia, and I asked Rob how Vancouver had evolved from the remote railway and shipping outpost of the nineteenth century to the world-class city it was today. He chided my Americanness in wondering why Canada's only Pacific seaport would become something grand and told me about a regional fantasy that was gaining popularity. Even in fairly respectable circles, people were talking about a new nation, Pacifica, that would become the best place to live in the world. Embracing the Northwest states of the United States (Washington, Oregon, and Idaho), Alberta, B.C., Yukon, and Alaska, Pacifica would unite American entrepreneurial aggressiveness with Canada's "kinder, gentler" form of government to become the leader of the Pacific Rim economic revolution.

Rob thought that things like the human scale of the skyline and the felicitous neighborhoods south of False Creek were examples of the positive influence of Vancouver's natural setting on all who built and lived here. "It's hard to do something ugly when all you have to do is raise your eyes to see glory," he said.

Be it noted here that Vancouver's skyline architecture wasn't particularly distinctive—some of it the worst of cheap modernist monoliths. But what was distinctive about Vancouver development was that at street level there was a sense of connectedness that was the result of thoughtful planning in the past twenty years. Developers had to apply to the city for permission to build, even when their projects clearly met designated zoning, with the burden of proof on the developer to show how the proposed design specifically related to its surroundings.

Thus there were no egotistical megastructures turning huge blank walls to their surroundings as had happened in so many modern American cities. As in Portland, there were copious windows along sidewalks. Entrances and plazas were strategically located so that you seldom emerged from one place without a prospect inviting you to enter another. New buildings adjacent to older heritage structures were scaled and lined to highlight, rather than dwarf, their neighbors.

Though Rob gave me a fine list of third places, I spent less time searching for them in Vancouver than I did elsewhere because they were everywhere; the city was a network of them, from the English Bay waterfront to the markets of Granville Island to West End's hip Denman Street to the historic, redeveloped Gastown, site of the original nineteenth-century settlement. I spent most of the remainder of my sojourn in Vancouver exploring neighborhoods. Though there were poor neighborhoods, especially in lower East Vancouver, I never did find anything like the vast tracts of hopelessness so emblematic of Chicago or L.A. or New York. I was delighted by the community centers, one in every sector of the city, where the local branch of the city library, a recreation center including swimming pools and gyms, classrooms, a day-care center, a nursery school, the welcome wagon, health and counseling services, and welfare offices were all housed under one roof—one-stop shopping for community amenities.

I found rents from $500 to more than $1,500 a month for places in which this middle-class American would be happy to live. Houses in the most attractive neighborhoods near the downtown or university

began at over $200,000, though there was the occasional low-ball price
of around $150,000. Houses in less favored but still generally safe and
decent areas could be had for under $100,000.

I returned to a West End apartment with my daughters that summer. It was the first city living they had ever experienced. They Roller-
bladed off to the Stanley Park tennis courts in the mornings and I
drove them to the Greenpeace offices in East Van for volunteer work
during the afternoons. There was a Chinese produce market just down
the street from Greenpeace where we bought vegetables and fresh
herbs for our kitchen. The kids found an alternative clothing store a
block in the other direction, where they bought the first blue-and-
green Doc Maartens to eventually grace the hallways of Keene High
School back in New Hampshire. And each of these afternoons ended
with the drive back to West End, all the way across the heart of the
city, during rush hour. It rarely took more than fifteen minutes.

We rode the cable car up Grouse Mountain and caught our breath
at the fantastic display of the city so far below us. We drove the forty-
five-minute excursion to Horseshoe Bay, up Howe Sound, and into
glaciered glory at Whistler and Blackcomb, where the skiing continued
right into summer. We rented a boat and sailed all over English Bay.
We biked and hiked the miles of paths in Stanley Park.

Karen Dick had gotten off welfare and moved with her kids out to
a small back-to-the-earth-type farm in Langley, twenty minutes outside the city. Rob Sanders took us to lunch in North Van and urged us
to move west—and north. One evening we ate dinner on Philip Till's
patio, after which he used his talk show skills to conduct a spirited
forum of generational communication with three teen daughters (one
his). And we enjoyed Shakespeare's *Twelfth Night* in Kitsilano under a
tent, its open end framing the magnificent northern vista of water and
mountains as set backdrop.

On the 10,000 Waves Scale, we rated Vancouver fives for all categories but Comfort because of the rain, which I had been so lucky to
miss, and Fudge, because of the squabble with the Hong Kong Chinese. Though certain features of the city may have been a matter of
geographical good luck, as Rob Sanders had said, it seemed to us no
accident that Greenpeace had been born here, that people like Karen
Dick credited the city with saving her life, and that a hardened
wanderer of the world like Philip Till had chosen this place above all

others in which to become a participant in community. Vancouver was indeed the new world of the New World. Like the wonderful species of life that Darwin found in Australia, Vancouver seemed to have evolved along its own separate path.

Finally it did rain. Vancouverites began sprouting the umbrellas that seemed an extension of their arms during the usually rainy winter months. But there were still just as many people out along English Bay and on the sidewalks of Robson Street. Rain did not drive Vancouverites indoors—too many of them had come from places of wind and snowdrifts, bugs and humidity, thunderstorms and tornadoes, to be daunted by warm showers. And when it rained in Vancouver, the greenery lit up from within to a neon hue almost lunatic in intensity.

Just at that age when a summer of separation from peers presented a really daunting prospect, my teen daughters had approached this trip with a lot of questions. "Why so long? Why so far?" In my own slightly less altruistic version of Irving Stowe's admonition to his teenage daughter, I told them, "If you want to find a good place to live, Peaches, you have to do your homework."

East of Vancouver, the warm Japanese-current weather crosses several mountain ranges that remove enough moisture to create a climatic miracle at the Okanagan Valley: a broad, two hundred–mile northerly valley with a year-round climate not much different from that of Napa, California. Here orchardists grow the oversize peaches, apples, and pears that people order from catalogs and send one another in pretty boxes for Christmas presents. Along the floor of the valley stretches the pristine blue water and white sandy beaches of the 150-mile Lake Okanagan. Canadians have come to call the place "Canada's California, the best place to live north of the border."

After that April visit to Vancouver, I rented a car and drove east on the Trans-Canada Highway to the Okanagan region. After the lush, verdant farmland of the Fraser Valley, the purple peaks of the Coast Range overwhelmed it, and I turned onto the Owl's Nest Highway. From here it was two hours of mythical driving—open road all to myself, mountains, hairpin turns, gulfs, sky, sun, deer, sheep, foxes, bear—deep green wilderness and wildlife enough for any die-hard Sierra Club member to be seduced into an Infiniti ad.

Things began to dry out beyond the little cowboy town of Princeton. I saw sagebrush and earth colors reminiscent of Santa Fe, then irrigated orchards and fruit stands, and finally, descending a grade, the gulf of the valley, with the long, blue lake seaming its curving floor.

Penticton, the first of the Okanagan towns one encounters on the route I took, was a carelessly developed resort town and I drove right through, considering bypassing the Okanagan entirely. Heading north along the west shore and through the cute little orchard and beach towns of Summerland and Peachland, I was surprised at the narrowness of the small ribbons of level developable land on either side of the lake beneath the steep, arid hillsides that gave the valley such a sense of oasis. If this place was as hot as Canadians said it was, it wouldn't take long for the bulldozers, bricklayers, and sign erectors to erase this thin green stripe, unless some severe growth controls were enacted quickly.

Then I crossed a bridge over a narrows in the lake and found myself suddenly in downtown Kelowna, where an expansive lakefront park suggested a very different regime from what I had seen in Penticton. The park was full of big old willows, flower gardens, grassy lawns, and clean white beaches at the shore. I noticed a number of teens hanging out there during what should have been school hours. The four main downtown streets were lined with thriving, tasteful shops set up in reclaimed early-century buildings—a pattern I had come to recognize as one of the hallmarks of renaissance towns. There were no empty storefronts, and lots of restaurants, bars, and coffeeshops—plenty of candidates for third places. Though it was only April, the air was summery and the sidewalks thronged with lightly tanned, handsome people.

Because of common language and democratic traditions, it should come as no surprise that the search for alternatives to the life that prevails in so many American communities might lead eventually to places in Canada besides remarkable Vancouver. Indeed, some of the characteristics of good places in America seemed endemic to our northern neighbor. Canadians' sense of community tends to focus locally rather than nationally. So while Canada continues to struggle with the search for a unifying national identity, its cities and towns and neighborhoods generally exhibit a communal solidarity that is lacking in most American places.

Canada has never embraced the myth of the rugged individualist

—an image Canadians see as nothing more than a licentious member of an anarchistic, unruly mob. As a result, communalism, environmentalism, and civility are refreshing norms in this country whose patriots strove for "peace, order, and good government" rather than "life, liberty, and the pursuit of happiness." Likewise, the Canadian model for assimilation of immigrants was never the melting pot. Instead Canadians revere the metaphor of the mosaic, a pattern of ethnic groups preserving their identity in local deviation without pressure to conform to a national demographic norm. This creates a much stronger sense of place in local Canadian settlements than is found in much of America.

As western American communities have profited by learning from the earlier mistakes of older, eastern places, Canadian communities have done the same thing with their counterparts in the United States. Whether by specific government policy (such as eschewing low-income project housing and adopting radical green space requirements) or by personally internalized values (such as the common practice among affluent Canadians of stepping off the income escalator and declaring, "This is enough"), Canadians have profited from observing some of our follies.

Canada's material standard of living might surprise many Americans. Though the United States may have a greater number of rich people, the average Canadian has a better material standard of living than does the average American, and the gap has accelerated in the past dozen years. A 1994 United Nations study proclaimed Canada to have the number-one quality of life of any country in the world. And finally, of course, there is the fact that Canada still has great wide-open spaces and a far lower population density than does the United States. As a result, Canadians have gathered into tight, intense communities where the howling wilderness is never far away.

In downtown Kelowna I found a bar and restaurant called Jonathan Livingston Segal's. The place was in a homely twenties-era building on a busy downtown corner near the lake. Inside, it was full of people at five o'clock and almost everyone was sitting, either at the bar or at the dozen tables of various sizes throughout the room. Few were standing the way they do in the "networking" bars I have come to loathe. A band was setting up in one corner of the room. Leaded glass windows and etched mirrors, paintings and window boxes, potted

plants and Tiffany lamps, brass, dark wood, and lots of beer logos
testified to the evolution of the decor; some of it clearly of long standing, some recently added—it certainly hadn't come off in one application from an interior decorator's easel.

Like many eating and drinking establishments in British Columbia, Segal's had the kind of liquor license that required you to order
food before you could be served even a beer. This made it easy to meet
people, because someone was always offering leftover fries or nachos
to a newcomer. Munchies and hors d'oeuvres here tended to become
communal fare, with each new patron advised to order whatever was
in short supply.

"Order some veggies," suggested a tall woman with a laughing,
husky voice who had turned to me as I bellied up to a space beside her
at the crowded bar. "Yer from the East, aren't ya?"

"How can you tell?" I asked her.

"Yer Top-Siders," she said. "That's a really eastern thing, eh?"

"You live here in Kelowna?"

"I wish," she laughed, and then shouted, "Portage!"

"Portage!" echoed a shorter woman sitting beside her, and then
there were several more echoes of "Portage!" from fellows around the
bar, raising their glasses in a mock toast.

"Nobody in Kelowna is from Kelowna," she explained. "Most are
like me. It's a place to run away to for a while when you can't stand
the cold and snow back home, eh?"

Shirley Kerwin and her friend Audrey Price, from Portage la Prairie, Manitoba, represented a segment of the local population that gave
the local census takers fits. Kelowna wasn't the usual tourist spot
where people planned tidy three- to seven-day vacations. People who
came here often stayed for extended periods—a month, three months
—and then many of them just never went home. "There's a tremendous transient population and a very blurry line between tourists and
residents that make our population figures pretty unreliable," a city
councilor would tell me later in my visit.

Shirley's friend Audrey, just celebrating her thirtieth birthday the
night I met her, had become the proprietor of a very successful
Ukrainian-Canadian restaurant back in Portage in her mid-twenties.
A married woman with responsibilities back home, she had never

planned the life she lived now. But her mother died several years back. "You can laugh if you want, I'm used to it," she chortled. "But I'm here because of my mother's ghost. She appeared to me in dreams and said just, 'Go to Kelowna.' "

Audrey professed not to be a superstitious person, but the dreams persisted enough to make an impression. She had been scheming a second restaurant in Winnipeg anyway. She visited Kelowna, loved the climate, and thought, "Why not?" Now she was a partner in the Zirka Hospitality Ukrainian-Canadian Restaurant on Bernard Street, and it was a roaring success. She made the three-day drive from Portage and back several times a year, with stays long enough in Kelowna that she had "two homes, two businesses, two worlds, two lives."

People like Audrey made Kelowna an experiment that challenged some old assumptions about the nature of community. Would a place where it was so easy to slip in and out of residence be a good place to live? Could communal values flourish in a place where there wasn't the traditional tightly knit fabric of familiar faces, or could such a fabric coexist with overlays of freshly changing faces?

I talked to the Ardises, a married couple who lived here year-round since immigrating five years ago from Vancouver. They had moved to Vancouver to get away from the prairie snow and then to Kelowna to get away from the Vancouver rain. They liked the idea that the town attracted so many transient residents from other places. "This valley is pretty isolated, eh?" said Bill Ardis. "Four and a half hours from Vancouver. But you don't feel isolated here because of all of the people coming and going from other parts of the world."

They also pointed out that behind the veneer of transience was a hard-core population that had been here forever and was still growing. "Kelowna is the last stop for Canadians in search of a good place to live. Nobody ever leaves for some better place elsewhere; it's the final resting place."

The little sidewalk coffee shop at my motel was another good third place. Though it had only half a dozen tiny tables, three indoors and three outside, people were continually stopping by to sit for a moment with pastry or coffee, to watch the passersby and the doings at the lakeside park across the street, and to talk with anyone else who sat down. It was a fine place to enjoy the balmy breezes coming off the lake. By the end of the week I would meet here a city councilor, an orchardist, quite a few young beachers escaping the sun for a few moments, a forest fire fighter, and fellows from the band at Segal's.

One morning, as I sat here with bandsman Ron Grace, I noticed again little knots of poorly dressed teens moving about the park during school hours. A couple of them wearing ratty cutoff jeans, broken-down sandals, and sixties-style headbands came into the shop and ordered coffee, carefully counting out change in dimes, nickels, and pennies from their pockets. They were the only ones who didn't smile and turn to those already seated for friendly small talk or an invitation to sit a spell.

"Who are they?" I asked Ron. I hadn't seen any poor neighborhoods during my drive around town the day before.

"Street kids," he answered. "Kelowna's supposed to be kind of a mecca for them these days." He had known street kids back in cold Saskatoon who dreamed of making it to Kelowna. Some had volunteered all manner of services to the band because they knew of its regular gigs here and hoped to hitch a ride.

I went for lunch to Audrey's Zirca Hospitality restaurant. With the exceptions of Montreal and Vancouver, Americans don't generally think of Canada as a place for cuisine. But the Canadian mosaic has produced ethnic enclaves where traditional old-world cooking is alive and well. Such was the case with Kelowna, new home to many East European families who had moved here from the prairies. A conservatively dressed family—father, mother, elderly uncle or grandfather, and three preteen kids—sat down at a table next to me and ordered without looking at the menu. Their conversation was about relatives and their doings. When the food came, they bowed their heads in unison just as the last dish was placed on the table and prayed silently. Then they began to eat, picking up right where they had left off. During a break in their talk the father looked over at me and we spoke. They were Ukrainian Mennonites, he told me, and had moved to Kelowna from Saskatchewan ten years ago. Yes, he thought Kelowna was a good place to live. He added that it had a grand future and would someday become one of Canada's great cities.

That was a sentiment I was not used to hearing in the good places I visited. Even the most aggressive progrowth people usually conceived of their community developing within more or less the same scale. The comment revealed an optimism and perhaps an innocence or simplicity reminiscent of the American fifties. But it was not a fluke, as I would confirm when I talked to city councilor John Weisbeck.

I met him at the sidewalk coffee shop in front of my motel one afternoon. Born and raised in Kelowna, Weisbeck was an affable, vigorous middle-aged man, a dentist by trade, who was proud of his city. His Russian father had fought for the czar and immigrated to the Okanagan to farm fruit in the 1930s. "Everybody who came to Canada emigrated from somewhere else where they fought a battle and lost," he laughed.

Five years ago Weisbeck had become concerned about environmental issues, joined the local Green party, and knocked off a former mayor to earn his seat on the council. He found that he liked politics and was now scheming to seek nomination for a seat in his riding by the federal Liberals, who he believed would come to power when the Conservative government fell in the next general election.

If Weisbeck was an environmentalist liberal, he didn't always talk like one. He explained with evident satisfaction that Kelowna, at a current population of around seventy-five thousand, was experiencing a growth rate of 6 percent a year, making it one of the fastest-growing places in North America. "There's a consensus here that we can double the population before we max out the valley," he contended. But the city had not done the water supply, traffic management, sewage and trash disposal, and economic studies usually considered necessary to come to such a conclusion.

"We're just not that far along. There's a consciousness about growth out there, but it hasn't caught on yet." He believed that the Okanagan Valley would follow the pattern of nearby Peachland, which simply slapped a total moratorium on growth when things got tight on its squeezed valley shelf.

But Weisbeck was still full of optimism for his town. Kelowna was surrounded by lots of open land, the largest sector of its economy was construction, and despite an unemployment figure of 15 percent, it was believed that the continental recession had not touched down here yet. "People chalk up the unemployment stats to the fact that we simply attract people faster than we can create new jobs for them," he said. "And those numbers are inflated by transients: pickers in between harvests, beachers who stay here for more than a vacation, and, of course, the street kids—you've probably seen them."

The boom had happened in just the past four years. "The Okanagan was pretty sleepy for generations and then suddenly the world discovered our sun, dry climate, fruitfulness, water, and winter skiing amenities," Weisbeck said. "It just happened. Nobody was even promoting it at first, though we do now." Culture had followed. The college earned university status, the Okanagan Symphony was founded, and several former summer stock theater companies had made Kelowna their year-round performing home, though culturally this was still no Santa Fe.

Talking to John Weisbeck, I began to see that here in Kelowna I was dealing with one of two very different possible mindsets. His optimism could have represented a dangerous naïveté about the growth monster staring them in the face. Or it might have indicated simply a refreshing absence of ideological thinking—a lack of knee-jerk association of certain images with assumed patterns of community development.

I asked him why, with socialism on the ropes in so many parts of the world, Canada's melding of it with democratic capitalism seemed to work so well. "To begin with," he answered, "Canada was founded by people with a deep respect for authority—the Tory Loyalists who fled your country's rebellion against the king. Second, people here believe in taking care of each other, whereas in your country it's every man for himself. But most important, we have the same Anglo-Saxon work ethic you Americans do. So socialism here doesn't beget sloth, incompetence, and dependency the way it has in so many other places that have tried it."

Weisbeck talked about the city's future and how the city would get there. "We're already eighty square miles—that's bigger than Vancouver. But we want to preserve what brings people here—the orchards and the way of life that goes with them and the open country not far from downtown. We have to preserve the ability to grow our own food." This was a sentiment that I had heard occasionally in various places, but it was a major theme in B.C., perhaps because here there was a realistic possibility of doing it. "And we can't continue the exurban sprawl, because traffic could ruin the valley. There's only one solution." He pointed toward the sky. "Kelowna has to grow up and not out. We need to encourage high-rise development and high-density infill in the heart of the city. Only then can we get the growth we want and preserve the green space and orchard land around us." And drinking coffee under the blue sky of a perfect Okanagan day, I began to think that with a fresh vision unclouded by ideology or "the things that we already know" about community development, these Kelownans might be able to build their big city and get away with it.

But there was still nature to contend with. As I strolled toward Segal's for supper one evening after an afternoon cooped up in my motel room with my word processor, the air was filled with a strong smell like burning creosote. At first I thought it was some noxious emission from the plywood mill, but then I noticed the traffic. Cars were lined up on Water Street heading toward the bridge over the lake and they were not moving. Though the sky was clear, I sensed a darkness through the trees of the lakeside park in the direction of Mount Boucherie across the lake. Crowds of people were headed toward the waterfront, so I followed.

Emerging from the trees of the park, I saw a black mushroom cloud towering over Mount Boucherie just across the water. Licks of violent flame were clearly visible on its slopes—a forest fire was burning out of control. A fellow watcher had a radio tuned to the Emergency Management Office, Canada's version of our civil defense broadcasts. Traffic across the bridge had been suspended so that fire and emergency vehicles could pass. It was the rush hour for commuters, many of whom worked in Kelowna but lived in the housing developments across the lake. Some of these neighborhoods lay at the base of Mount Boucherie, directly in the path of the conflagration unless there was a change in the wind. Residents stranded on the Kelowna side of the lake were advised to seek housing in the city for the night.

A small crowd of entranced gawkers like myself had lined up along the shore, but soon an impulse seemed to sweep the beach, and people began organizing into little groups that headed back to town to various volunteer marshalling areas. Younger men and a few women charged off to join the firefighting effort, while the rest set off to see what could be done to accommodate stranded residents of fire-threatened areas.

With darkness closing fast and nothing to be done by the shore of the lake, I headed back to Segal's, where the largest crowd of the week had gathered. The management was offering free bar tabs for the evening to those with a Westside address on their driver's license. Radios tuned to the emergency broadcast competed with the music of the band, which interrupted its playing periodically to announce urgent incoming phone messages: "John Smith, the house is OK, your wife and kids are at an EMO shelter in Westside," or "Sally Strudel, stay in Kelowna with your friends tonight. Mom and Dad have been evacuated and you can't get back till tomorrow."

By morning the fire was nearly under control. A change in the wind had blown it back against itself, and the firebreaks that crews had labored all night to build with bulldozers, chain saws, picks, and shovels had done their work. The mountain was ruined—a hundred hectares of trees gone—and some houses were scorched and smoke damaged. A hundred people had been evacuated. But no one was killed and no homes were lost. "God must really like Kelowna," said Kurt Swan, the newly hired emergency coordinator for the city of Kelowna and the Central Okanagan Regional District, "or He could have roasted a lot of houses tonight."

Other than the facts of the fire itself and the resulting damage, the stories under the four-inch headline FIRE! in the early edition of the *Daily Courier* focused on the spontaneous outpouring of volunteers throughout the night. "Hundreds jumped in to help in the face of disaster," began one. "The helpers outnumbered the victims by far." Besides those who offered their sweat to help forest service firefighters hack the firebreaks that eventually contained the blaze, there were scores of neighbors who helped threatened residents hose down their houses, dozens of volunteers who worked with radio communications, nearly a hundred residents who offered their homes to evacuees, women's service clubs that worked all night making sandwiches and brewing coffee, retirees who directed traffic, couriers who took supplies and messages to the front lines, blood donors at the Red Cross, and pencil pushers who helped to register and keep track of evacuated families.

Besides Segal's free bar tabs, other businesses found ways to help: the Overwaitea Grocery store donated platters of baked goods, sandwiches, and fruit, drugstores provided free pharmaceutical supplies, Smitty's Family Restaurant offered coffee and beverages, Glenmore

Kennels registered thirty pets into free boarding spaces, and the Salvation Army was flooded with new clothing given by several downtown department stores.

It had been the first day on the job for emergency coordinator Kurt Swan, a transplant from Los Angeles who had begun the day wondering how he would fight a forest fire in the midst of residential areas like those that Kelowna's growth was thrusting into fire-prone areas. "I left L.A. to get away from this. . . . It's a very dangerous situation, people carving houses into steep, dry, forested hills," he said. But, though people everywhere tend to come out to help in times of trouble, Kurt had never seen anything like the effort that poured out of Kelowna last night. And that gave him the answer to his question. Despite the careless siting of residences, this seemed like a fine place to coordinate emergency operations.

It was amazing to me how quickly Kelowna returned to normal. Though the fires would still burn, under control, for another week, it was business as usual the following afternoon. There was still something of a pioneer spirit here in rugged south-central B.C. that inured people to natural calamity and must have had something to do with the remarkable display of volunteerism I had witnessed.

I had heard expressions of concern about another aspect of Kelowna's growth that continued to trouble me: the proliferation of walled retirement communities. "The wrinkle cities," a welfare caseworker called them. "They don't belong. They put up a wall around their little patch of the sunshine and hide out there, never making any contribution to the city. It's a mentality of hostility.

"And you know the secret of the walled cities, don't you?" she asked. "It doesn't work. It kills them." She knew of people who had ripped up their roots from the prairies and died of loneliness in Kelowna's walled cities.

The caseworker asked if I had ever heard of the Elizabeth Fry Society. It was an organization started in England early in the century to look after the interests of women in prisons. For many years Kelowna had been the leader of the movement in North America. Today the society had broadened its scope to all forms of abuse of women. Here in Kelowna the big news had been the recent discovery of deeply hidden but severely scarring abuse by brothers and fathers of elderly women that had happened fifty or more years ago. "Remember

Freud's women with hysterical fantasies?" she said. "They weren't fantasies. And we would never have found out if it weren't for the walled cities."

"Why not?"

"Because elderly women in those places, their husband dies and then they have nothing but time and loneliness on their hands. And they start to remember."

That did it. I decided to confront the world of the walled cities I had been avoiding. I began by picking up a brochure for Canadian Adult Communities. "Enter a friendly new world where people just like you share a neighborly spirit, a pride in their home, and a new found freedom from the burden of home maintenance and security," it read. Glossy photos showed seniors in all-white groups of never more than two or three relaxing in manufactured settings of ponds and brickwork on boulder-strewn, chipped-bark-covered grounds. Testimonials from folks with Anglo-Saxon or Germanic names confirmed that grandchildren loved to visit, that it was so nice never having to worry about one's home when traveling, that everything one could want in a community was provided on-site, and that people were having more fun than they had had in years. I wasn't permitted to tour the Kelowna site—something about needing to go through the publicity director, who was away during my visit—but at Segal's I met one of the septuagenarians who lived there.

I was enjoying a surprisingly good Cajun-style seafood gumbo, not something I would have expected to find in western Canada, when two well-dressed elderly women came in from shopping and sat down to order lunch at the table beside me. They too were intrigued by the Cajun special, saw that I had ordered it, and asked me if it was good. We had a friendly chat; they were curious about where I was from and why I carried a notebook. Shortly after their food arrived, a telephone message called one of the women away for some urgent matter she had left undone. She insisted that her friend stay and enjoy her lunch. So I ended up joining the one left behind to continue our chat.

She wanted to hear what I had learned about Kelowna, and when I mentioned the business about abused women and the Fry Society, she blushed, considered for an awkward moment, and then looked me in the eye and told me straight out, "I'm one of the women you heard about."

Transplanted Americans, Jane Wittenhauer and her husband, Bob, had retired to Kelowna from back East five years previously after selling a printing business whose proceeds had enabled them to live just about anywhere they wanted. Their children had families and were dispersed. There just wasn't anything to keep them in the snow anymore. "The thought of moving to a retirement community in a dry, warm place was irresistible," she said.

But one year after the move, Bob had a heart attack. "He was gone when I found him sitting in his chair by the pool," she said. "The kids came for the funeral, and we buried him here in Kelowna. They talked about what a wonderful thing he had done before he died, getting me set up to live in a place like this where it would be so easy to carry on without him—no snow to shovel, no home or yard maintenance to worry about. And, of course, absolute security and safety."

But when her children returned to their lives, Jane began crying—day and night. She took to drinking gin straight from the bottle and chain-smoking cigarettes, and still the tears would not stop. She tried to take part in the retirement community's organized activities, but everyone else had a mate. "With Bob gone and nothing but time on my hands in that nice house with the flowers all watered and the swimming pool quietly swirling away, I began to think and think and think," she explained. "I was wallowing in self-pity and didn't know why. I just had this feeling that something terrible had been done to me, that it had always been done to me.

"It wasn't only that Bob had died and left me. That was just the last straw. I would occasionally come into town and watch those confident, young, tanned women go about their business—on their own. They would come in here and order a drink and lunch. Such silly things impressed me so much—they would argue with cops over parking tickets. They would buy the smartest clothes, and I could picture them going home and putting them on with such nonchalance —as if they actually had a right to wear such things. I hated them— their sureness, their freedom, their command."

Jane eventually went into therapy for incipient alcoholism and severe depression and discovered a long-repressed secret: that she had been sexually abused by her father and older brother when she was nine years old, in 1931.

"The rest of the story is an anticlimax," she said in Segal's on a sunny afternoon in 1992. "My therapist says my emotional progress is the fastest she's ever seen." Part of her therapy involved forced participation in community events outside the walls of the retirement village. "At first the therapist had to drag me kicking and screaming," she admitted. "'I'll never be one of those autonomous, confident women,' I kept telling her." But habit took hold and she began making friends, some of them much younger women, some of them men. She began to actually enjoy getting out and regretted that she had hidden from the world so long.

And then, on the night of the fire on Mount Boucherie, without any prompting from her therapist, Jane Wittenhauer drove to a volunteer center and made one hundred sandwiches.

I spent my last evening in Kelowna at Segal's, where everybody seemed to know everybody and by now many of them even knew me. Yes, everyone realized that Kelowna was going to be a big city, but no one could conceive that it might lose its small-town identity. Kelownans repeatedly cited the volunteer effort the night of the fire as proof. "People have always taken care of each other here," they said over and over again.

Americans I met farther down the road often asked me to characterize the look and feel of Kelowna, a place for which they had no frame of reference. The best I could do was to invoke the Steve Martin film *Roxanne*, which was filmed in nearby Nelson—not Aspen, Colorado, as is widely believed. Though I had witnessed firsthand that the firefighting capabilities of Kelowna were considerably better than those portrayed in Martin's film, the look of the film was right, and the bar where Martin performed his famous catalog of nose jokes was not unlike Segal's. When I told people this they were delighted and added Kelowna to their shortlist of good places. I gave Kelowna fours for Cheers and Comfort but only twos for Foot and Cake factors. Cultural sophistication was trying to get a foothold here but was yet engaged in an unequal race with people bringing only money and automobiles. The highlight of Kelowna was the Fudge Factor of five it earned for the community spirit I witnessed during the night of disaster.

But like a fire on the mountain, a growth boom beyond all imagining was coming to consume Kelowna. As my stay here came to an end, I had one lingering question: would Kelowna's blithe spirit mobilize in time to manage this conflagration as well as it did the flames on Mount Boucherie? If it could, there was a tremendous opportunity here to build a great city in a spectacular setting—maybe not another Vancouver, but perhaps a Calgary without the cold. I had seen enough to be convinced that it offered a dry alternative to Vancouver for Americans seeking that fresh air north of the border.

On the way back to my motel room after midnight, I stopped for a smoky dog at the street vendor located outside Iggy's, a heavy-metal hangout for youngsters of questionable drinking age. The place was just letting out, and as the rowdies flooded into the street, I headed off toward the quiet, moonlit lakefront to munch my dog.

"Sure smells good," I heard a husky young female voice say as I stepped into a shadow by the shore. And then a male voice, "Can you help us out, so we can get one, man?"

I was being panhandled by a trio of the homeless kids I had seen and heard about before—two earnest guys and the girl, a delicate, dark-haired waif whose only nondenim adornments were the bells she wore on her ankles. I remembered Karen Dick, and since the hot dog stand was just across the street, I went back over and bought three more.

The kids were honest panhandlers, grateful for the food, with never a hint of cynicism at my crude stratagem to see if they really wanted the money for something else, like drugs or alcohol. As thanks, they were willing, even eager, to talk to me.

Gerry, Franz, and Alexandra were all three just short of sixteen and had been street kids for several years—Gerry was fleeing alcoholic parents in Chicago, Franz was thrown out of his house in Winnipeg by his mother for doing drugs, and Alexandra was a refugee from abuse in an extended Russian family in New York. They all told the skeletal outlines of their tales with an automatic flatness of expression that spoke volumes. It was a ritual, they confirmed, an affirmation of identity and custom of introduction more important than handshakes and exchanges of names in the underground world of runaway kids. "I'm not Gerry," said Gerry. "I'm a kid who escaped Chicago, froze half to death in Winnipeg, and made it to Kelowna."

All three had that suffix to their epic catalog of identity: one who made it to Kelowna. "Why Kelowna?" I asked. "And how do kids so far away hear about it?"

"Word of mouth," answered Gerry with teenage blandness. "Kids on the street back East talk about it, especially in the winter. It's warm here, it's safe, like there aren't any gangs or mean cops. You can get apples right off the trees or pick 'em for money. And nobody hassles you."

"Yeah, people here take care of you, like if you get sick, or you need shoes," added Alexandra. "They even feed you."

7

A RIVER RUNS
THROUGH IT

One fine big-sky afternoon, a Russian, a Californian, and a Montanan were sitting on the Montanan's ranch porch drinking and plinking at cans with pistols. The Russian went to his Volvo and came back with a bottle of Stolichnaya. He poured a shot, tossed it back, threw the bottle in the air, and blasted it. "Thass alright," he said. "In Rossia, ve haf loss off wodka." The Californian went to his Lexus and came back with a bottle of Silver Oaks cabernet sauvignon. He poured a glass, quaffed it, threw the bottle in the air, potted it to pieces, and said, "It's cool, man, in California we have lots of wine." The Montanan went to his pickup and came back with a six-pack of Pabst. He yanked off one beer, chugged it, shot the Californian, and said, "That's OK, in Montana, we have lots of Californians."

For a year now I had been hearing Missoula pronounced the real Rocky Mountain good place to live, as opposed to fast-lane resort sites like Aspen and Jackson. And immigrating southern Californians, with their usual nose for sniffing out the best spots, had already found the place to an extent that provoked Californian jokes in the local bars.

Missoula was more than two hours away from a big city: five hundred miles separated it from Seattle, Salt Lake City, or Calgary, and twelve hundred from Minneapolis, the nearest city to the east. But testimony held that its very isolation had forced it to become its own place—that the curious history of western Montana, the course of the Northern Pacific Railroad, and the presence of a state university known more for turning out writers than engineers had combined to make Missoula perhaps the most cosmopolitan small unaffiliated city in America.

With a population of around forty thousand, Missoula was perched on a high valley shoulder where the Clark Fork River emerged from Hellgate Canyon. To the east and south rose treeless foothills with towering snowcapped peaks beyond, and to the west and north stretched a broad valley bounded by the Bitterroot Range, which Lewis and Clark had hoped in vain would be the last obstacle to their northwest passage. It was late April, but the region's relative proximity to the Pacific brought shorter winters to Missoula than places in the more easterly midcontinent Rockies and made for shorts and T-shirt weather already.

Even in the town center the mountains were never out of sight, and downtown Missoula, particularly the six-block core between the river and the old Northern Pacific rail line, buzzed with commercial good health. The main drag, Higgins Street, ran south from the old Northern Pacific Railroad station, now occupied by a brew pub and a restaurant, to a marquee theater and riverside park before bridging Clark Fork and entering an immaculate middle-class residential area bounded by the university. Many of the downtown establishments were housed in Victorian and art deco–era buildings that had clearly been reclaimed and spruced up in recent years. I was struck in partic-ular by the number and variety of restaurants and respectable bars in a downtown this small. The courthouse was set amid a Norman Rock-well block of lawns, gazebos, and towering trees where mothers strolled their infants and freshly dressed elderly men wearing straw hats sat on park benches and talked with animation and energy.

That was the dominant impression of downtown Missoula at mid-day: vigor. I had lunch at the pink-and-white art deco Uptown Diner, where patrons helped themselves from piles of the *New York Times,* the Seattle *Times,* the *New Yorker,* the *Atlantic, Esquire,* and the *Mis-soulian* at the diner-style counter. Everyone in the place seemed to have so much to talk about, and of course they all seemed to know one another. There were students from the university, professors, merchants, housewives, construction workers, secretaries, lawyers, and cops. The Uptown Diner was the first of several first-rate third places I found in Missoula, where I soon discovered that there were so many of them that I was unable to follow my usual practice of settling on one as my base of operations. Despite all of the vigor, however, there were countercurrents.

"If you want to live in Montana, you have to learn how to cook bark," said the thirty-year-old unemployed rail worker who had told the Californian joke as he leaned at the bar in the Iron Horse Brewpub on Higgins Street. "It's a hard state for a working man to make a living—you got the have-nots in the mountains and the haves in the east." His view was that the grain growers and cattlemen of eastern Montana enforced a regime of regressive taxation that hurt the workers and small businesses. "They don't want a sales tax on their grain and beef, so they hit us all with a flat income tax."

Another fellow joined in, "The state doesn't do shit to create jobs. We got an economy built on grain, cattle, mining, timber, and the railroad—not exactly growth industries. But those people run things in Helena and that's why we got hoboes out in the rail yards just like in the thirties. Goddamn Republicans."

For years Montana's image had been shaped largely by its presence in that solid block of Republican mountain states displayed on TV screens at presidential election time. For much of the nation, "big sky" was synonymous with the image of Ronald Reagan or John Wayne on horseback. But Missoula, Butte, Bozeman, and other mountain towns of the western half of the state were actually Democratic bastions, and from the left side of the party at that.

Despite their labor complaints, the drinkers at the Iron Horse claimed they would hang on in Missoula even if they had to clean toilets to do so. "It's the finest place to live in America," said the fellow who had told the joke. Besides the mountain wilderness at the edge of town, he wanted me to understand that places like Missoula had public schools second to none and cited a recent *USA Today* survey of the top one hundred high school students in the country. Twenty of them were from Montana.

"Why?" I asked.

"We spend money on our schools, but it ain't just that. Kids who have learned how to chop wood and ride have the discipline and toughness to be good students."

I asked about the state university to see if there was any anti-academic feeling among these Montana working men. "Without the university," said one, "there wouldn't be shit here in Missoula."

"And then there's Mayor Kemmis," said another. "There's a tradition in Missoula of mayors who are like philosopher-kings. You talk to Kemmis. He'll give you something to put in your notebook."

As I waited outside the Depot Restaurant and Bar the next afternoon to meet Dan Kemmis, I watched a long freight pull out on the Montana Link tracks. Cattle grazed placidly on a pasture above as three immaculate new engines belched and rasped past, followed by a mile of clanking and squealing coal and grain cars. These were the former tracks of robber baron Jay Cooke's great enterprise, the Northern Pacific, which failed in its competition with James Hill's Great Northern road. While Hill envisioned his thoroughfare connecting a rural empire, Cooke dreamed of cities. His eastern terminus, Duluth, which he presciently saw as an Atlantic port, was to be the Paris of the upper midcontinent. Places nourished by the railroad along its route, like Missoula, were to become oases of civilization in the wilderness.

Cooke's is a name of infamy in much of our history, with his manipulation of the stock market and politicians, his schemes for rail imperialism in Canada, and his part in precipitating one of our great national depressions. But his dream of cosmopolitan enclaves in the wilds took root in Missoula. There is a poem about Missoula by Robert Bly, well known to rail buffs. Its heart, I thought as I waited for Mayor Kemmis, was less about rail romance than about the delight of a comfortable arrival at a civilized place in the wilderness.

ON A TRAIN

There has been a light snow.
Dark car tracks move in and out of the darkness.
I stare at the train window marked with soft dust.
I have awakened at Missoula, Montana, utterly happy.

Mayor Kemmis arrived for our meeting on foot. The mayor of Missoula did not drive a car in town; he walked or took the bus, a gesture of leadership in a valley community threatened by auto exhaust pollution. Tall, thin, and white-haired, the mayor had a voice, personality, and physical height suggestive of firmness and health, but blue veins around his bespectacled eyes hinted at gentleness, even frailty. He sat down with me in the Depot lounge and sipped a glass of chardonnay during the hour we talked, despite the fact that he was to preside over a city council meeting later that evening.

Dan Kemmis had grown up on a farm in eastern Montana, spent eight years after college in New England, and returned to Missoula in his thirties to escape crowds and do graduate work in philosophy at the university. Since then he had served in the state legislature and in 1989 become mayor of Missoula.

Kemmis cut right to a troubling corollary of my project's thesis during the first few moments of our chat: if there was a migration of people with strong talents and initiative to a finite number of "good places" (and he agreed with me that there was), then what about the rest of the continent? "Will a kind of Darwinian natural selection concentrate the best and the brightest in certain localities and enervate the vast majority of American places?" he wondered. Of course, denizens of Manhattan had always believed that such a process defined the difference between city and heartland. But that neat delineation had broken down as the traumas of latter-day big cities began to cancel their traditional attractions. Kemmis saw trouble in a demographic separation of degrees of human talent that didn't fit the traditional pattern of city versus country. "You could get a kind of Balkanization of humanity," he said. He explored such ideas in a book he had just published, *Community and the Politics of Place.*

For the moment, though, he was happy that his small city had become one of the places attracting people of imagination, creativity, and energy. He advised me that I'd have to research some local history to understand how that had happened over the long term. But in the short run, it all began when the Southgate Mall was built and the downtown died overnight. City government, under former mayor John Toole, reacted in many of the right ways: drawing lines around the blighted area and going to the state for a special tax increment district so that increases in downtown property tax revenues could be reinvested exclusively in the downtown, setting up a redevelopment agency, building a parking garage, and planning for the development of a riverfront park. "But the real renaissance of our downtown was carried out by the new businesspeople who came in to replace those that had folded," Kemmis maintained. "Some were a new generation of locals but many were outsiders looking, like you, for a good place to live. They went into business here seeking adventure and they ended up discovering the secret to a successful downtown."

"And what is the secret?" I asked him.

"Fellowship, entertainment, and innovation. People will come downtown instead of to a mall to feel part of something, to socialize, to be entertained, and maybe to shop for things they can't find in the mall—usually things that are either locally produced or too esoteric to compete in a setting where shoppers are conditioned by mass advertising."

Missoula was the first small place I had visited, besides *Money* magazine's overrated Bremerton, that had not adopted the council–city manager form of government. Here the mayor was king, presiding with real power over his parliament, the city council. "A city needs a mayor who can act as a mobilizer and convener," Kemmis argued. "You can't do that with a mayor who is seen as a symbol and a city manager who is seen as a bureaucrat." He believed that council–city manager governments tended to err on the side of caution and timidity. In contrast, he cited the controversial building of a downtown parking garage on space that some would have preferred to see become a park. "So we named it Central Park—the name captures some of the essential playfulness of Missoula," he said. It also conveyed something of the confidence and personality of a strong mayor in a strong-mayor system.

Missoula was another good place under the siege of boom growth. "But it's unbalanced growth," Kemmis worried. "Developers want to build residential and commercial projects—a place to sleep and a place to shop—as if that's all there is to life." One of the mayor's most daunting ongoing tasks was to break the deadlock of the progrowth versus antigrowth debate, which he believed created an environment of conflict that enabled unscrupulous fast-buck developers to thrive. He was heartened that Missoula's business community, particularly the downtown merchants, had come to see that the bogus vocabulary of the traditional growth debate was of no benefit to them. But the world that was beating a path to Missoula's door wasn't necessarily a part of that consensus. "It's the great American question," he said. "Can a good place make a transition from boom growth to maintenance growth? Can we preserve what prompted the boom in the first place?"

Kemmis believed there were two radically different ways that people chose to live in a place like Missoula. He employed a mining term, "hi-graders," to describe those who came with the wrong attitude. "You pick the richest vein you can find and strip off the best, leaving to future generations the question of what to do with a diminished thing," he said. "These are people who see only the surface and miss the underlying civic culture that could sustain the good life as we know it in places like Missoula. They come in and buy into walled communities or low-density sprawl housing outside of town, shop at the mall, do a job or business that doesn't input into the heart of the community, drive around in cars, and complain about taxes."

Nonetheless, Kemmis was confident that Missoula received more than its share of people ready to take on the responsibilities of citizenship. "It's tremendously easy to get involved here and have an impact —easier I suspect than in your part of the country," he said. "In a room of twenty people, only one will be a native. A newcomer with bright ideas can quickly establish himself on the basis of his bright ideas alone."

As a result, Missoula had a particularly strong civic and cultural nucleus and the cosmopolitan flavor I had heard about before I ever came here. There was a joke around town—"Oh, you write for the New Yorker, you must live in Missoula"—because of the large number of contributing writers who had moved here in recent years. People involved in the visual arts, with a particularly strong need for urbanity, had discovered Missoula. Still, the mayor fretted, "But that's all vulnerable because of the hi-graders. True-living culture cannot tolerate what hi-grading does to the roots of community."

The other big issue on the mayor's plate was the curse of the valley: pollution. The combination of air currents funneling into a cul-de-sac valley and severe atmospheric temperature inversions created the irony of smog in big-sky country. Kemmis explained that the city had been making steady progress over the past thirty years: the infamous tepee burners in sawmills had been virtually eliminated, technological innovations had radically cut emissions from the pulp and plywood mills, and wood smoke had been cut through a combination of regulation and public consciousness raising. But all of the gains had been just about offset by increasing pollution from automobiles, despite the fact that the city had had a bus system since 1970 and, as home of the Bike Centennial, extensive bike paths and an established bicycling ethic as well.

With the downtown successfully revitalized, Mayor Kemmis was currently engaged in a major initiative to build consensus for an integrated solution to the other problems he had described. Echoing Kelowna's Councilor Weisbeck, he declared, "It begins with a vision that future residential and commercial growth will take place as infill development in the heart of town rather than out in the wide open spaces. I don't want to see the continued construction of 2 to 3 percent growth that simply expands out into the valley and increases the number of auto miles driven and openings for more Kmarts and Wal-Marts."

Kemmis was aware that his vision clashed sharply with the motivation of many of who came here: "The mountain living ethic, elbowroom, and big sky." But he hoped to create an alternative ethic that would be just as attractive in its own way: the advantages of an urban existence in close proximity to a mountain setting—cosmopolitan living at the edge of a wilderness. The key was to prevent further rural sprawl, to keep the edge of the wilderness close by.

The advantages of infill development with regard to auto use and pollution were obvious, but Kemmis saw other, more subtle, benefits. "If we can establish clearly that coming to Missoula for most people will mean living and working in town, we'll get more people interested in real citizenship—less of the hi-graders," he believed.

Kemmis indicated the approaching end of our conversation by asking if I would give him a ride, as the last bus that would get him home for dinner was due shortly. So we sat and chatted awhile longer about good places I had seen and then I drove the mayor of Missoula home. On the way to his modest house in the heart of one of those immaculate middle-class neighborhoods near the university and just twelve blocks from city hall, Kemmis explained that his real battle as mayor was to move the city to appreciate its true strengths, "where

Missoula is really rooted. And that is the miracle of civilization in the wilderness." He exhorted me to talk to some college students before I left town. Many of them held a particularly vital understanding of that truth, he believed, and those who stayed on here were the community's future. With that, he got out of the car, walked past the hedges of his trim bungalow, and arrived home for supper.

Missoula wasn't always the Athens of the West with a philosopher-king that I found in 1992, but throughout its rough-and-tumble history there were a series of oddities about the place that cumulated to make it what it had become. Canadian fur trappers penetrated the area shortly after Lewis and Clark were so warmly received here by the Flathead Indians, and in 1812 David Thompson of the North West Company gave the valley a name: Nemissoolatakoo, meaning, roughly, "the place of cold waters of surprise." By the 1850s, French Canadians were settling the area that became Frenchtown while Americans from the East established farms and whiskey trading posts in the valley near the junction of Clark Fork and Rattlesnake Creek. The construction of the Mullan Road opened the way for serious traders, such as Christopher Higgins and Francis Lyman Worden, who established a post at the mouth of the Hellgate and founded Missoula Mills in 1865.

Missoula's nickname, the Garden City, was not the creation of some modern chamber of commerce public relations committee. Travelers entering Missoula in the 1860s, having followed the Mullan Road across barren eastern plains and the rugged Continental Divide, were delighted to encounter the spectacular vegetable and flower garden surrounding the McWhirk brothers' log home. By word of mouth the notion spread that Missoula was a place of gardens in the mountains, and eventually a newspaper streamlined the phrase to the now long-established moniker.

One apocryphal explanation for Missoula's dissimilarity to the rest of the state has it that Missoula was never meant to be a part of Montana in the first place. When Congress created Montana Territory in 1864, it sent surveyors out to mark the border with neighboring Idaho Territory along the Continental Divide. But that same Bitterroot Range that so confounded Lewis and Clark now played havoc with the territorial surveyors. Lying several hundred miles to the west of and paralleling almost precisely the Continental Divide, the Bitterroots make up a very neatly defined ridge that the surveyors mistook for the main spine of the Rockies. As a result, they surveyed the wrong divide. Realizing their mistake late in the process, they finally went on to the Canadian border in a straight line that created the narrow panhandle of Idaho. But the errant survey, which eventually became enshrined as the state boundary, placed Missoula and its surrounding valleys firmly in Montana.

Missoula was different in other ways. Despite the presence of the French-Canadian trappers in Frenchtown, most of Montana's fur trade was conducted on the east side of the Continental Divide, where pelts could easily be shipped to the eastern states down the Missouri or to Canadian interests by way of the voyageurs' routes through Manitoba and the Great Lakes. Though the territory's earliest gold strikes occurred near here, Missoula never shared in the gold rushes that shaped Helena and Virginia City. The cattle trade and attendant cowboy life were even farther afield on the high plains far to the east. When the railroads eventually brought homesteaders to the prairie, few ever crossed the divide.

No furs, no gold, no beef, no wheat. What Missoula had were trees. Beginning with Higgins and Worden's mill, Missoula became and remains to this day the center of Montana's timber industry. When Jay Cooke's Northern Pacific Railroad came through the valley in 1883, the boom was on, and the Big Blackfoot Lumber Company built the largest sawmill in the world in nearby Bonner to supply the railroad's inexhaustible appetite for timber. The simultaneous opening of the Butte mines created further demand, and the mighty Anaconda Mining Company got into the lumber business on a massive scale. No Athens during these years, Missoula became a lumberjack's town of saloons and brothels catering to the voracious appetites of men who worked in the winter forests for months with no women, no whiskey, and no diversions.

But the same railroad that had created the demand for timber also brought to the valley businessmen who wanted Missoula to be a civilized place to raise their families. By the time of statehood in 1891, they had become a strong enough force in town that when Anaconda, Butte, Boulder, Bozeman, Helena, and Great Falls were vying to be the site of the future state capital, only Missoula bid instead for the future state university. The presence in town of a state university, so the reasoning went, would counter and civilize the roistering character of the logging industry. The upshot was a deal between Helena and Missoula under which Missoula supported Helena's claim to the capital and Helena backed Missoula's uncontested but unlikely dream of a state university.

In 1916 Missoula sent America's first woman to Congress. Five days after her arrival in the capitol, Jeannette Rankin voted against entry into World War I, stating, "The first time the first woman had the chance to say no against war, she should say it." She survived her apostasy well enough with the voters of Missoula that she was still around in 1941 to cast the sole vote against entry into World War II. Inheriting her passion for peace, Senator Mike Mansfield opposed the Vietnam War and inspired the university's Mansfield Center, which was years ahead of the rest of the country in establishing cultural and economic contacts with the nations of the Pacific Rim. And Missoula's Jeannette Rankin Peace Center predates the Vietnam War and the founding of other peace centers around the country by about two generations.

Nonetheless, Missoula was no bastion of enlightened liberalism for much of the twentieth century. The university in particular endured years of corporate and political hostility as its leaders fought to define a civilizing mission in the wilderness, and often lost. The adversary was frequently the Anaconda Mining Company, which could withdraw its financial support and pull strings in Helena to penalize the university for publishing criticism of company practices. When open labor unrest developed at the Butte mines, miners could count on support from university professors and students, and the university president in turn could count on more heat from Helena.

Far from the urbanity of the coasts, that heat frequently took the form of censorship, but the freethinking scholars and writers of the university fought back. And besides the stabilizing influence of the old timber industry, which eventually mellowed into a modern, sophisticated, community-sensitive business regime, what enabled the university and Missoula to win the war against ignorance was largely the intellectual and literary heritage established by H. G. Merriam, who came to Missoula as a young professor in 1919. He chaired the English department through tumultuous decades and founded the literary magazine *Frontier and Midland*, which launched careers for the likes of A. B. Guthrie, Wallace Stegner, and Dorothy Johnson. Succeeding

Merriam were Leslie Fiedler, Richard Hugo, and today's William Kittredge, who carried on Merriam's obsession with establishing a bastion of culture here in the northern Rockies. Throughout the tenures of these four giants, writers, thinkers, and practitioners of the visual arts flocked to Missoula. Now the university and the atmosphere it generated dominated the town, and Missoulians, to the least-educated unemployed rail worker, were grateful.

When I returned downtown after dropping off the mayor and began strolling around thinking about supper myself, I noticed something odd that became more apparent each day—the six o'clock silence of Missoula. In a town that had bustled with activity earlier, and would again in a few hours, the streets were absolutely deserted. This was different from any of the other good places I had visited, where part of the appeal was a continuing thrum of street life. In subsequent days I came to recognize that the downtown life of Missoula had a distinct rhythm with other, more subtle, lulls. There was the predictable rush of activity in the early morning as people headed for work, stopping at the diners and coffee shops for breakfast and the news of the day. Then a minor lull at midmorning, until noon approached and the downtown exploded with people—students, mothers shopping with children, businesspeople out to lunch, workers on break. The noontime crowds diminished only slightly following the lunch hour as the business set removed themselves from the mix, but by midafternoon they were replaced by public school teachers and professors from the university. Mothers and children became scarce in the late afternoon just as a few workers began strolling into the bars from their day's labor, but there wasn't the same intense level of after-work happy hours that I had seen elsewhere.

And then at six o'clock, everybody disappeared. Around seven, people began to trickle into the restaurants, usually in couples, married, and often holding hands. Then at nine things exploded again, as they had at noon, with people out on the town, big-city style. They didn't stay out quite as late as they might have in New York, but going out with people after eleven following, say, an evening of work at the word processor, was an entirely feasible proposition.

When I asked Missoulians about the six o'clock silence, they patiently explained, as if I were some alien unfamiliar with the biological necessities of earthlings, that it was suppertime. People had to eat.

Only a few young refugees from New York or L.A. responded to my question with understanding. They confirmed that Missoula's public life suffered from an exasperating inability to carry through continuously from happy hour till prime time. "People actually go home for early dinner," said one. Another pointed out with some ambivalence that Missoula was, after all, quite the family town, with more than the usual number of intact marriages. People who did go out to dinner made their public appearance after seven, with the kids fed and things at home squared away.

I walked over to the Iron Horse Brewpub one morning to talk with one of those thriving married couples, Jurgen Knoller and his wife, Tami. They were the proprietors of the Bayern Brewing Company and the Iron Horse respectively and had been recommended by Mayor Kemmis as good examples of that "best and brightest" selection of new businesspeople who had done so much to transform downtown Missoula.

They were finishing their chores in the brewery when I arrived. Tami, a robust young woman who looked as if she could handle a cow branding, puttered with glassware behind the bar while Jurgen, with a face right out of a tourist's fantasy of Alpen mountaineers, sat with me and sipped iced tea under a glass panel etched with the decree of Wilhelm IV and Ludwig X of Bavaria in 1516, "We wish no beer to be used and brewed unless it be made of barley, hops, and water alone." Like Brian Hunt of Willett's in Napa, the Knollers were purists.

"Is Missoula a good place to live?" I jumped right in.

"Oh, yeah," Jurgen affirmed. "Look. You can go over to the Top Hat later tonight and hear Bad to the Bone playing live in a setting where you can have a beer with them during breaks between sets. Two nights ago you could have seen Shakespeare down at the river park. Tomorrow noon you can stop in at the Uptown Diner and catch Bill Kittredge as he's doing a piece for the *New York Times Book Review*. And then in fifteen minutes, you could be casting for cutthroat trout on Rattlesnake Creek a million miles from civilization. I couldn't find a better place."

Jurgen had grown up in Bavaria near Garmisch, earned his M.A. in brewing at Munich, and become part of the German-based worldwide fraternity of brew masters. "There's continual long-distance networking going on among people looking for good opportunities to make real beer," he began. Friends of his had been traveling in America and stumbled across Missoula, where they found this beautiful empty railway building. "Americans in the West were going crazy over the brew pub boom but Missoula didn't have one yet. They said this was a hip town, as cosmopolitan as Montana can get, and with the mountains, something German about it. There was no redneck population. They thought it looked like a good place to brew beer."

After acquiring the railroad building, they invited Jurgen to come over for a year, see something of America, and set up the brewery. He found happiness here, met and married Tami, who was working in the restaurant, and together they bought out the bar (hers) and the brewery (his). Today, with sixteen outlets in Missoula and thirty-five elsewhere in the state, they had succeeded. They viewed the nearby Depot Restaurant and Bar as a partner in anchoring the north end of the downtown adventure, rather than as a competitor. "The Depot gets a pretty conservative upscale crowd. We get everyone else—lawyers, accountants, students, motorcyclists, rail people, granolas, and professors," Tami said. "People are proud to have a good brew pub in Missoula. Where else could a couple under thirty become pillars in the community the way we have?"

I was walking south on Higgins one day with thoughts of lunch at the Uptown Diner when I stumbled across Worden's Deli, about halfway between the Iron Horse and the center of downtown. Umbrella tables lined the sidewalk out front, and through the windows I caught glimpses of wine racks, people sitting on stools at high tables, and narrow aisles lined with merchandise of various sorts. But what really struck the eye was the heavy crush of customers streaming in and out the doors. At noon in a downtown generally bustling with activity, Worden's was a magnet of hyperactivity.

Worden's was a deli, a wine shop, a convenience store, a soda fountain, and a newsstand all rolled into one. Inside, a huge chalkboard listed a bewildering variety of specials, and half a dozen servers hustled to keep up with the stream of orders from customers lined up before a long, glassed deli case. Lunchers carried their orders to one of the tall tables and joined those already there for their repast. This communal eating arrangement led to a continuing recital of introductions and recognitions of acquaintances met here previously. Meanwhile, in the more remote parts of the place, folks shopped for wine, or aspirin or batteries or oatmeal, and another lineup stood at the soda fountain in the back corner. There was no speaker system playing pop hits or Muzak. The sound of the place was a loud hubbub of conversation and the ringing of cash registers.

I ordered a French-Canadian smoky pea soup and a corned beef and sat at a table with two women from Missoula's banking world and a man who was an electrician. The talk was about local economics— who was doing well and who wasn't, whether the local paper mill would get through another year of the recession without layoffs, the stabilizing cost of housing after the inflated eighties boom, and the shaky prospects for a new Wal-Mart construction proposal located on the outskirts of a town that had so successfully adopted the downtown ethic.

After lunch I indulged myself in a root beer float from the soda fountain and meandered outside to sit for a while in the sun at one of the sidewalk tables, where a ruddy, freckle-faced college-age woman sipped coffee and perused her notebook. Wendy Clark was no relation to the explorer who put this region on the map, but she had hiked much of his route through this part of the world. Originally from Wisconsin, she had chosen the University of Montana to study sociology because there was "no better place in the world for an outdoors person to go to college." Now, having earned her B.A., she was doing social work for a local agency while applying to law school. She feared that her interest in social justice would someday take her to places far from the mountains and so she was living the mountain experience during her time here in Missoula with fanaticism. We were shortly joined by her boyfriend, Benny Pirelli, who was a native Missoulian, and it wasn't long before he invited me to join them for a biking-fishing expedition on the Rattlesnake later in the week. He would get me a bike, a fly rod, and waders—all I had to do was get a two-day visitor's license. Done deal.

Wednesday a strange thing happened downtown just before noon. The usual late morning explosion of people all seemed to be headed in the same direction, toward the river and the bridge to the university, and in even larger numbers than I had seen before. I thought perhaps there was some kind of demonstration going on. But the mood of the crowd was wrong for that. It was festive. Men carried small children on their shoulders and women pushed strollers. Couples lugged small coolers and businesspeople and merchants carried brown-bag lunches. It was "Out to Lunch," I was told, a newly established Missoula tradition. A merchants association had established it as one way to ensure the continued vitality of the downtown, and it had become a huge success. The idea was to gather musicians, performers, and food vendors in Caras Park, the recently completed riverside green space along the Clark Fork, every Wednesday for the lunch hour.

People thronged the rolling grassy belt that stretched for a mile along the waterfront and under the Higgins Street Bridge. There was a large tent near the bridge where a dance performance was going on. Elsewhere folks congregated in little knots around musicians and other street acts and ate their lunches. A hot dog vendor was doing a land office business and there were several busy food stalls representing downtown restaurants and bakeries that must have had to scramble to avoid losing a day's lunch hour proceeds. Relocated Hmong and Tibetan refugees hawked vegetables from wicker baskets, and employees of various downtown merchants passed out handbills advertising current sales and specials at their stores. Here mingled black, white, Asian, Native American, young, old, affluent, and street people—while at this moment fifteen hundred miles away in L.A., residents were hunkered down in a sullen community of hatred.

I was told that the event was the brainchild of Pat Simmons, the one-woman staff of the Downtown Merchants Association. I went to see her in the association office that afternoon. The office walls were hung with colorful posters documenting more than a decade of association activism. Stacks of newspaper promotional inserts cluttered the corners and her "in" basket looked like the Leaning Tower of Pisa. Pat was a matronly woman who would never have guessed that someday she'd be a cog in the machinery of business and commerce. Her love had always been art, and for years before coming to this job she had worked in promotion and PR for the local arts council. "My husband says I stopped mothering artists and started mothering businesspeople," she offered as explanation for why she so loved the job.

The association had actually begun as a typical retailer's committee of the local chamber of commerce. "But I guess you could say that it was conflict, trouble, and controversy that made it what it is today," Pat laughed. In the mid-seventies, when Southgate Mall was on the drawing boards, the chamber officially supported it, in a knee-jerk chamber of commerce way. But many downtown merchants, who foresaw what it could do to their businesses, were so adamantly opposed that they did something unheard of in chambers of commerce where the first commandment is "Never do anything that divides the community": they split from the chamber to form their own Downtown Merchants Association.

When the mall opened in 1978, the downtown decline had already begun in anticipation; J. C. Penney and Montgomery Ward moved out and smaller businesses began following. Probably no more than a third of the remaining downtown merchants were members of the new association. But they tended to be the most activistic and farsighted, and they hit upon a strategy.

Membership in downtown associations is usually limited to actual merchants, but the activists of Missoula recognized that much of the business of the downtown was professional: lawyers, accountants, dentists, consultants. "These people weren't going to move to the mall and they had a stake in maintaining a healthy environment for their clients to pass through to get to their offices. When the association signed up the professionals, it really took off."

An innovative downtown association was one factor in successfully rejuvenating the city's core; the others I had already heard about from Mayor Kemmis: the activist intervention by local government under Mayor Toole (with Kemmis's help in the state legislature, Pat added) and the weeding out of laggard merchants prompted by the competition of the mall itself. "By the mid-eighties, people here were doing what was supposed to happen with the proceeds of the Reagan boom economy," she said. "They were embarking on great risky adventures in downtown investment. God knows the mall had left plenty of empty storefronts of opportunity."

Pat Simmons waxed positively rhapsodic in describing the new downtown entrepreneurs. They were relatively young people who wouldn't have gotten a chance at a downtown storefront if the mall hadn't driven out the older, more inflexible merchants. Many took spectacular risks with their livelihoods. Those who were most successful never stopped being curious about how to do things better. When she left the arts council, she had thought she would miss the artists' daring, creativity, and sensitivity. But the people she found herself working with now were like the young artists she had liked so much.

Some were children of Missoula whom she had known for their lifetimes, "like the couple who run Mammoth Bakery. I knew Kimmy when she was a kid. She liked to bake bread from the time she could walk. It became her dream, and when she got out of school, she married a man who also liked to bake. Now they are one of Missoula's success stories, but they never became hardheaded businesspeople, never quit being feeling and gentle. Their business has grown with the tastes and the times without abandoning her original mission."

Others were outsiders who came here looking for the good life and ended up making this a better place, like Hassam Merhi, who came all the way from Lebanon to set up the Greenleaf Cafe, or the young shoemaker at Hide and Soul, who came here to go to college and never left. Pat Simmons believed that the healthy mix of longtime Missoulians and newcomers was a formula for success: "The Missoulians strengthen our roots, the newcomers infuse us with their freshness and energy."

I pressed her on just what, specifically, the downtown association did to help these people along. She believed there was always a gap between what the city government could do and what individual entrepreneurs could do for themselves. The association tried to fill that gap. Its most important role was sponsoring events that brought action to the downtown. These ranged from special performances in Caras Park to regular affairs like New Year's First Night, downtownwide seasonal clearance sales, and the Wednesday Out to Lunch program. Through its dues, the association paid for publicity and the hiring of performers or other personnel necessary to pull off the event. It also paid Pat to provide administration and coordination.

Pat described the physical improvements program. She was quite proud of the hand-wrought iron flower baskets that had become a symbol of the downtown and that were provided and maintained by the association. The two tents used for events in Caras Park were another coup, and currently the association was sponsoring the construction of a carousel in the park by a local woodcarver.

"Everything seems to focus on Caras Park," I observed.

"It does," Pat affirmed. "We never realized back in the old days what a resource we had in that weedy, slimy, trash-cluttered river. It ran along the backside of everything and people just dumped their stuff into it—even broken supermarket carts." But in 1984, the mayor and members of the downtown association who had seen the remarkable riverfront projects of San Antonio and Portland initiated the waterfront cleanup, and then city hall constructed Caras Park. "We have a river park instead of your New England town square," Pat explained. "Everything happens there and its everyone's turf, as opposed to the neighborhood parks, which tend to belong to adjacent residents." Her fondest image of the success of the Out to Lunch program was seeing the richest man in town chatting with her favorite street person, a homeless Vietnam vet with a khaki overcoat and boom box. "That's what real community is all about."

I met Wendy Clark and Benny Pirelli in front of the Iron Horse at five-thirty one morning. A cold front had passed through during the night and a thick white haze like a lowering fog hovered over the rooftops of Missoula. On the street it wasn't that chilly; in fact, I felt stuffy and humid in the flannel shirt and jacket my young friends had advised me to wear. But I was witnessing a classic occurrence of the temperature inversions and resulting smog that were the curse of the valley. By the time we had ridden just a half mile and a few hundred vertical feet up Rattlesnake Road, I could see my breath as I panted to keep up with the youngsters on our mountain bikes. There was a touch of pulp smell in the air—not bad, but enough to be clearly recognizable.

Just when the uphill ride was becoming agonizing and I had finally caved in and shifted to the last gear, I saw Wendy and Benny, who were now a good two hundred yards ahead of me, pull off to the side of the road and begin to walk their bikes over the embankment. We had ridden above the valley smog and there was blue sky overhead, but the canyon was narrow here and the sun had not yet popped over the blackness of the southeast wall. I noted the lack of traffic noise on the road and the silence of Missoula, just a short bike ride down the canyon.

I followed the kids over a well-worn path to a large, slow-moving pool at the foot of a wide rapids. We wordlessly pulled on our waders, tied dry flies (mosquitoes) to our tippets, took up our stations, and began casting.

We didn't catch a lot of fish that morning, but it didn't matter; there were marvels to see, marvels that you just wouldn't see unless you were standing in this pool casting flies and waiting for them to drift past. Benny was a bit of a birder and counted a couple dozen species visiting the canyon this morning, from tiny groundling mountain sparrows skittering around in the bush above the bank to stately hawks turning in gyres on updrafts above the north face. Wendy spotted a family of marmots performing their morning ablutions along the shore above the rapids.

I was fascinated by the hatch of tiny yellow gossamer flies, unlike any of the artificials in Wendy's wallet, that were apparently the reason for our lack of success in catching fish. The larvae would drift up from the depths, flinching and twisting until they popped into their winged form near the surface and struggled to break through the water's surface tension. This was the moment that many of them became food for the fish who disdained our tied flies. Those that managed to break through the barrier and stand long enough on top to dry out their wings without disappearing in the snap of fishy jaws lifted toward the sun and sparkled like fireflies.

My companions became more talkative as the compulsion to actually catch fish weakened, and we finally ended up sitting on the bank watching the yellow flies hatch. Benny commented that there was something weird about us enjoying a moment like this while people in L.A. were fighting a civil war. "Racism," he said. "It's going to tear this country apart yet."

"It's deeper than that," countered Wendy, and Benny said, "Oh, here we go." Apparently Wendy had a sociological theory on the subject that Benny had heard before. But I hadn't, so I urged her to go on.

"It's a matter of dysfunctional lifestyles," she said. Wendy believed that the dysfunctional family concept that had gained such currency in recent years was just the tip of the iceberg. "There are lifestyles that are maladaptive, retrograde," she began. "They're harmless as long as they're idiosyncratic and individual. But when a society adopts them en masse as the model for how to live, you get trouble.

"I think our trouble all began back during the industrial revolution, when the Victorians began their retreat from the public world." I continued to watch the gossamer flies overhead and waited to see how she would relate this to racism.

"That was when society went back to the hearth, back to the family, back to the cave—thousands of years of social evolution undone with the purchase of a home in the country." Sociologist or no, this kid could turn a phrase, and I forgot about the flies as she went on. "Anybody who was not a member of the circle around your hearth was at best inconvenient, at worst a threat. It was originally the lifestyle of the aristocracy, the gentry. But with the advent of the suburban home, it became the way of life for the mass of humanity in the Western world."

The kid was onto something. I knew this lifestyle, had lived it, rebelled against it, and spent several years searching for places built around something else. Of course, this was the link between suburban living and racism, between the devaluation of public places and the rise of personal materialism. Racism didn't cause people to live in walled cities, it was the other way around. Materialism wasn't the root of all evil, it was the symptom of a lifestyle that gave people nothing else in which to take pleasure. Family life wasn't the solution to our problems, it was one of the causes—as a Republican presidential convention would make explicit a few months later when it used family values as a cover for an appeal to racial and outsider fear.

"As long as there are too many people whose humanity can only function in the private world around their hearth," Wendy concluded, "there will be racism, hatred, greed, chauvinism, and we will have a dysfunctional society."

A surprising amount of the literature of place delves into sociology and psychology. Maslow's classic hierarchy of human needs (food, water, warmth, security, social interaction, and self-actualization) is frequently cited as a road map for community evolution—a road map in which so many of our places seem stuck at the fourth turn. Rene Dubos is often invoked for his insistence on the human need for direct, sensory, communal experience—experience that is lacking in our individualistic, nuclear lifestyles and that is not adequately fulfilled by telecommunications or the video global village. In arguing the necessity of urban living, Christopher Alexander cites psychiatric studies by Herman Lantz showing a perfect inverse correlation between levels of mental illness and the number of personal human contacts habitually experienced daily by individuals over a lifetime. Alexander further cites a Viennese study showing that normal individuals expressed preferences for domestic settings providing some level of community, with a surprisingly high percentage preferring actual urban apartment living. But disturbed inmates in psychiatric institutions invariably preferred to live in large homes in the woods or other rural settings with abnormally large amounts of surrounding space.

Of course, this is not to suggest that everyone who chooses a solitary life in the country is a lunatic. But Wendy Clark had hit on the point: when the lifestyles of vast numbers of essentially social beings turned to large houses in the woods far from humanity, when the idiosyncratic became the model for the mainstream, something was amiss in the national psyche. Missoula was a prototype of a better way for most people to appreciate the space and solitude of the wilderness. What was so congenial about my outing on the river with Wendy and Benny was the anticipation of returning to the bustle and human good cheer of Missoula, just a short bike ride down the road.

Wendy still had cases to see that afternoon at the social agency and Benny had to get back to pursue his job hunt. The ride down into the valley was considerably easier than the ride up, which was a good thing, because as we descended through the smog, which never did burn off that day, the air became warm and muggy again. Wendy rode her bike right to work, in fishing clothes and all. Not bad. Four hours in a national wilderness just a bike ride away from a day at the office.

After the fishing outing with Wendy and Benny, I recognized the precious quality of life in a town at the edge of glory, as portrayed by Missoula author Norman MacLean in *A River Runs Through It*. That's what Mayor Kemmis was trying to preserve by channeling growth into urban infill so that the wilderness would never be far from the downtown. While I was in Missoula, Robert Redford was filming the movie of MacLean's book. If its viewers apprehended the secret of its spell, perhaps Kemmis's dream would catch on.

I had spent most of my time in Missoula deliberately avoiding my own kind—writers—even though their presence here in large numbers was certainly one of the reasons I thought this was a good place to live. I wanted to be sure that Missoula had some substance besides what appealed to me personally. With that firmly established on the last day of my visit, I met author and teacher of authors Bill Kittredge for lunch at the Uptown Diner.

The reigning head of the Missoula writing dynasty, Bill was a jovial, contented man with a longish shock of graying hair. He knew all of the waitresses in the place and ordered his lunch of bean soup and pork tenderloin sandwich without looking at the menu.

He had more than the usual peer-professional interest in my project because of its relation to one he was pursuing. "I'm fascinated by the idea of what makes a good place to live," he said. It started when he came to Missoula twenty-two years ago, prompted by a midlife crisis to leave the life of a cattle rancher in Oregon for the life of the intellect in Montana. He was struck by what a good place Missoula seemed to be and by some similarities it had with Thomas More's *Utopia*: "The population of close to fifty thousand, the ideal of urban living at the edge of natural grandeur, the presence of a university, the mixture of the best of small-town and city characteristics." He wondered about other people's visions of utopia today, their fantasies about how communities ought to be if we could ever get them right, and began collecting testimony through travel, interviews, and correspondence.

"What are you finding?" I asked.

"Utopia is different for people in different parts of the country, but overall, it looks an awful lot like Missoula," Bill answered.

The first criterion for utopia was an atmosphere of communalism; even people who called themselves conservatives wanted that, at least with their own kind in their own utopia. Bill thought Missoula was fortunate in this respect to have gone against the grain of individualist cowboy politics and gave me his view of how it had happened.

"It's Butte and the Anaconda Mines hassle that makes western Montana different, not just from eastern Montana, but from the rest of the West," he said, referring to the tradition of labor unrest that has prevailed in the region since the twenties. Martial law had been imposed twenty-one times, and in response, the miners took to the Wobblies and a politics utterly alien to the usual Wild West traditions of individualism and personal fulfillment. "You see, the miner's ethic is something radically different from the cowboy ethic. Miners go down in a mine together, cowboys are out on the range as individuals. Miners depend on each other for their survival, thus places with a miner's ethic have a lot of communalism and old-time liberalism. Add a progressive university and you've got Missoula."

The equation wouldn't have been completed by just any university. There were lots of places that had good colleges and universities that did not benefit from them as Missoula did from the University of Montana. Some were dominated by technology and fast-lane research-grant rats so wrapped up in their work that they contributed nothing to the community. Others with a more liberal arts bent cast a pall of suffocating academia, status consciousness, and political correctness over their host communities. At some, the ivied walls enforced a separation of town and gown more effective than an iron curtain. "The university here is radically different from most. First of all," Bill said with a chuckle, "the salaries are so lousy that no one comes here unless they're coming specifically for the place.

"It's easy to be a professor here and not get swallowed up by academia. There aren't a lot of committees and study groups—people know the importance of getting off campus and into the life of the real community." Bill's routine was to teach his classes, hold office hours here at the Uptown Diner, spend some hours writing at home, and then head for the hills.

He thought western Montana worked so well because it was still dominated by a strong middle class—a rare thing to find in America these days. "Much of the country is becoming a banana republic, everybody either rich or poor," he said. "Missoula is one of the last true middle-class towns. We have a complete, intact spectrum all the way from lower middle to affluent middle." Though there were a few street people, mostly burned-out Vietnam vets living on the fringes of the wilderness, there wasn't much real poverty in Missoula. "And besides builder Dennis Washington and a handful of celebrities who have a big-sky home here, [there's] not a whole lot of wealth, either."

That could change as Missoula's good-place status attracted more people with money; lower-middle-class working families were beginning to fear being pushed a rung down the ladder. But the influx of new people could also be another of Missoula's utopian blessings. "A lot of people come here who believe that a change of place can change a life entirely," Bill maintained. "I did that when I came here from Oregon. People with that attitude bring a revolutionary openness to a community—they contribute to a climate where anything seems possible."

Finally, there was the writers' community. At last count there were probably fifty writers working in the area. Kittredge knew of no other town in which a city cop, in this case Robert Sims Reid, had had five novels published. There was one month a few years ago when five books were published by different writers living on the same block on Wylie Street. James Welch, Bryan Di Salvatore, James Crumley, Beth Ferris, and dozens of others were longtime fixtures carrying on the tradition of Norman MacLean and Leslie Fiedler. "It's a good place to be a writer," Bill declared, "because there's an ethic: 'No one else's success diminishes my own.' " The writers of Missoula tended to live communally close to one another. Some were concentrated in certain neighborhoods, such as Wylie Street, and others settled into little satellite towns nearby, such as Livingston.

"This is a generous town, whether you're a struggling immigrant or a struggling writer. There's a healthy sense of humor and playfulness. We don't have walled communities yet, a lot of our businesspeople are former sixties hippies, and there are deadheads here of all ages." He thought Missoula would stay that way, despite its newfound popularity with good-place seekers. Nearby Bozeman was having its own boom in computer and high-tech industries, providing both an alternative to Missoula as well as some much-needed complementary regional industry and employment. Even those forest products industry and environmentalist adversaries had maintained a surprisingly congenial dialogue. Maybe it was the mountains, maybe it was the climate. Despite its relative mildness and the cosmopolitan nature of the town, this was still remote northern mountain country that could be counted on to have a braking influence on who came here and for what reasons.

As I drove to Whitefish, where I would catch a train bound for Minneapolis the next day, I thought Missoula deserved fours across the board on the 10,000 Waves scale, perhaps with a negative Fudge hedge for its isolation from big cities and the potential for winter severity. But there was also such a positive side to the setting. I caught my breath again and again at vistas of the Mission Range to the east. Only in Montana and Alberta did North American mountains have such a radical sweep upward to such staggering inclines and improbably ragged summits.

I stayed the night in Whitefish. Only about twenty square blocks, Whitefish was small and western-style cute, but make no mistake, this place was Rocky Mountain fast lane. Central Avenue was lined with pumped-up ski town bars, and I had no doubt that they were right in Missoula when they said this would be the next Aspen or Jackson Hole. After the complete experience of community in Missoula, just laying over in Whitefish was one-dimensional and exhausting. I boarded my train the next morning more convinced than ever that ski towns were one thing, real civilization in the wilderness quite another.

8

REFUGEE

Minneapolis was a tense city when I arrived. There had been race riots there shortly after the Rodney King verdict in L.A. and taxi drivers, waitresses, hotel porters, and people I spoke to on street corners were nervous—the whites, anyway. The blacks I encountered that first day wouldn't speak to me at all. With the dehumanizing backdrop of steely blue skyscrapers and the famous glass-enclosed second-story skyways that seemed so sensible in winter but otherwise sucked the prosperity out of life at street level, the cityscape that greeted me each morning as I emerged from my hotel conveyed anything but the legend that had brought me here. Stickers that read LOSE NO SLEEP OVER DEAD COPS—NONE! were ubiquitously posted on newspaper vending machines downtown, and the security guard at my hotel was escorting women to their cars in the parking lot at all hours of the day. For all I could see, I might as well have been in L.A. I chided myself for coming here and violating the good place values of climate, city size, and appealing topography, all for the sake of a myth presented in a TV show.

In 1991 the popular series "Thirtysomething" aired an episode in which the Philadelphia-based protagonists conspired with the president of a company in Minneapolis to overthrow their mean-spirited boss. They were motivated by the fact that the city's business culture presented a progressive, humane alternative to the grueling, cutthroat eighties-style regimes of both coasts. The episode contributed to a contemporary American legend that Minneapolis was a place where business wore a very human face, where free enterprise and classic liberalism went hand in hand, where maximizing profit was not the only bottom line.

I received my first introduction to the Twin Cities from members of Minnesota Public Radio's news staff, after doing an interview with them. MPR was funded better than the average public radio station, they explained, because of a historic tradition of contribution to public causes by the major players in the business community, especially the old business families, like the Pillsburys and the Daytons. The employees of MPR left no doubt that as far as they were concerned, the legend was real, and they had their studios to offer as proof. Besides the philanthropy of the founding families, there was also a long-standing habit of aggressive, even radical community outreach established by the local Lutheran and Catholic churches.

I was told I had to understand something about the "twinness" of the Twin Cities: it is "fraternal, but not congenital," in nature. The issue of the two cities' separateness was a very big deal, especially in St. Paul. In the 1870s there was a simultaneous migration of Irish and Scandinavian immigrants to Minnesota, and there were two sides to the Mississippi River. James Hill founded his Great Northern Railway empire in St. Paul on the east side of the river and attracted the Irish Catholic population that still dominates the area. Meanwhile, Scandinavian Lutherans founded a grain-milling industry and Minneapolis on the west bank.

The Irish were motivated by an urge to re-create Boston, and so St. Paul was America's most westerly eastern-style city. The Scandinavians were westward-looking pioneers, and so Minneapolis became America's first and most easterly western city. The difference showed in the street layouts and in the architecture—St. Paul appearing older, though it wasn't, with narrow, winding streets, while Minneapolis was laid out with wide sidewalks in the typical western city grid and developed a skyine that looked like it popped up out of the prairie overnight. St. Paul was quiet and inward looking. Minneapolis was a raucous, brawny, and enthusiastic participant in the global village.

But the two cities shared politics and an aggressive social agenda rooted in their two religious traditions that made them America's most successful site for the relocation of Cambodian and Hmong refugees and the headquarters for the American Refugee Committee.

The Hmong, refugees from the nasty mountain war in Laos, had contributed some curious chapters to local life, and MPR had spent a lot of time documenting their experience. When they first began arriving in the Twin Cities a decade ago, they experienced culture and climate shock. During those first years, their common practice of stripping the woodwork from their houses to build fires in the middle of the living room or kitchen floor resulted in a lot of burned-out homes.

But they brought with them another habit that had become local recreational custom. Residents of the Twin Cities had long regarded their fabulous network of small, pristine lakes as a primarily aesthetic resource. The identity of Minneapolis in particular was tightly bound up with the network of green spaces and connecting bicycle and pedestrian paths that made it possible to stroll or ride throughout the city, lake hopping, as it were, from park to park.

No one did much fishing in the lakes till the Hmong arrived and saw them as a source of food. At first, longtime residents looked askance at the Hmong lined up with their poles along the banks of the city lakes; the traditional Minnesota fisher had always associated fishing with getting away from the city to a distant wilderness lake. But the Hmong demonstrated that there were big fish in the lakes, and lots of them. Soon they were joined on those parkland banks with the steely spires of Minneapolis in the near background by Catholic and Lutheran fishers, and sport fishing in the city became so popular that the state had to stock the lakes to keep up.

The Hmong and Cambodians made other contributions to the cities, including the introduction of Thai cuisine, and among whites, I was told, there was little prejudice against them here. They were quiet, kept to themselves, struggled to maintain strong family values, and worked hard enough that few became permanent burdens on the welfare system.

But there was one segment of the Twin Cities' population that did not welcome them and their ways at all. Because of the reputation for liberalism, the Twin Cities had been for some time the object of a large immigration of unemployed African-Americans from places like Cleveland, Detroit, Akron, and Cincinnati. They resented the tight communities and aggressiveness of the new Asians. Even more they resented whites' praise of the newcomers—taking public comments about how quickly they got off welfare as an implied slur against blacks and Native Americans, who made up a disproportionate number of long-term welfare recipients.

This discord was one of the factors behind the racial troubles that had occurred shortly before my visit and left the city on edge. The spark had been a misreported shooting that happened just as the national news was broadcasting the Rodney King riots in L.A. The disturbance was nipped in the bud, though, through the efforts of two men who became heroes as a result. Deputy Chief of Police Dave Dobrotka went into black neighborhoods during the height of the conflict, and Spike Moss, the leader of a black community group, joined him in setting the record straight. The image of the white cop and the black activist jointly countering wild rumors in the streets day after day contrasted sharply with the breakdown of interracial communication that had happened in L.A. What could have turned into an explosive situation settled down quickly as a result of strikingly different action by leadership on both sides of the racial barrier. Though the city was still in the state of racial tension that I had already observed, there was a sense that for the moment, the Twin Cities had weathered the storm.

From an acquaintance back in New Hampshire I had the names and addresses of two people, both of whom were connected with the old families of the Twin Cities and held top jobs in the current business scene. Becky Roloff lived with her husband and children on the south side of the city in a residential neighborhood that was surprisingly modest, considering her career position as vice president for operations with the Sears financial service, IDS. Tim Marinen, a descendant of one of the oldest St. Paul families (140 years) and retired legal counsel for First Bank Systems, lived with his family in a similar neighborhood nearby. I had tea on Becky's living room couch one afternoon while she sat cross-legged in her stocking feet on the carpet. She could have been a character out of the "Thirtysomething" show that had brought me here in the first place, earnest and caring yet clearly an achiever in her business career.

She confirmed that the progressive nature of the Twin Cities went back to its wealthy founding families: the Pillsburys, the Hills, the Cargills (grain trading), the Daytons (Marshall Fields), the Crosbys (General Mills), and the McKnights (3M). "They knew early on that to get the culture they wanted for the city of their business, they would have to build it here," she said. "They established a tradition of private money going into public purposes that makes the Twin Cities what they are today." During the depression, the first families quantified their philanthropy with something that came to be known as the Five Percent Club, later actually institutionalized during the 1960s. If you aspired to be part of the peak of Twin Cities society, your business had to be part of it. Five percent of gross earnings were returned to the community in some sort of philanthropy—a corporate tithe. Different families had different pet projects: the Pillsburys' was education, the Daytons' was the downtown.

Becky was adamant that the legend that brought me here was a real, thriving thing. Besides the Five Percent Club, she said I would find the Twin Cities to be a giant web of grassroots philanthropic organizations. "But still it is a struggle," she said. "There's an underlying tension in all liberal efforts here because there are no successful models to learn from. We're the pioneers, always wondering when we're going to have to circle the wagons if things go terribly wrong."

Her own company, IDS, was currently wrestling with the meager successes of its attempts to bring black professionals into the company. Few had stayed, because for all of its good intentions, the city had never really made them feel as much a part of the community as had other cities with a less enlightened white populace but a better-established homegrown black culture. Becky was concerned that the community had not yet faced its greatest trials, that its liberalism was largely untested. "It's easy to be progressive when the local minority lives on a reservation," she said, referring to the fact that the Native Americans were the only minority presence that went back beyond a generation or so.

I asked her about middle-class flight from the city, recalling that a prime consideration in keeping Portland, Vancouver, and, to a lesser extent, Seattle, on my shortlist of good places was the presence of those extensive, secure middle-class neighborhoods close to the heart of town. "Middle-class flight here spans a very short distance," she answered. "Yes, people have left the true inner-city neighborhoods, but they moved to the neighborhoods surrounding the lake parks, just five minutes from downtown. People identify their neighborhood with the nearest lake." She felt that the decision by city founders generations ago to preserve the lakelands was a key to the livability of the city, not only for the green space it provided, but also because it established appealing residential patterns that kept middle-class members of the community living in the city.

Before I left to visit my other contact, Tim Marinen, Becky Roloff added that as a writer, I would find the Twin Cities agreeable. "It's a city of book readers," she said. And indeed, I was well aware that only New York itself, Seattle, and Boston surpassed Minneapolis as a profitable stop for a writer's PR tour.

It was gardening day at Tim Marinen's house, and as he ushered me into his living room, his wife was up to her elbows in the mulch and humus of the flower and vegetable gardens that adorned every nook and cranny of their small hillside corner lot. The Marinen children cheerfully misbehaved with the garden hose and came and went muddily into the house, despite frequent admonitions from their father. In nearly every other yard on the block, a similar scene was played, as Minnesotans reveled in the arrival of spring after the long, hard winter.

Tim, former legal counsel to First Bank, was a youthful forty-something who objected right off to my use of the word *myth* to describe the reputation of the Twin Cities' business community. "It's a fact of life here," he said and went on to describe the Five Percent Club that Becky Roloff had told me about earlier. He also told me about something called the August tradition, during which the churches recruited executives to paint houses for poor senior citizens. "Now that's a more personal commitment than just writing a check," he declared. "Every year, one thousand well-paid people descend on low-income houses all over both cities and spruce them up. I can take you for a ride and point to a dozen that I've done."

I asked him how the philanthropic tradition of the Twin Cities would respond to the current racial tension, and he said that people here reacted to challenge differently from people in other places. "Just as we use the fruits of business—money—to maintain the health of our city, we also use the methods of business," he said. Thus, during his own stint on the Urban Coalition, an affiliation of business and social service agencies, he had begun by working out the numbers. He discovered that the total minority population was only around 9 percent. "That's too low to support a real L.A.-style conflagration; there's just too much buffering, especially in a city where so many non-minorities are proactive with the minority communities. But we also discovered that we were experiencing a massive new immigration of minorities from all over—from Cambodia to inner Cleveland. The 9 percent wouldn't stand up long. The bottom line was that we had some time, but that we couldn't sit on our hands."

The Urban Coalition held the sociological equivalent of marketing focus groups with people on several sides of the racial barriers. "We found that there was, happily, little grassroots racial anger outside of a minuscule hard-core handful of disaffected, uneducated whites," he said. "But we also found that that could change as the numbers of minorities increased enough to achieve muscle and provoke backlash. Again, same bottom line, there was time for us to get our house in order, but we had better get to it."

Different arms of the Twin Cities philanthropic network were currently working on different aspects of the problem. So far the main response had been to shift funding away from some of the less people-oriented cost centers and toward neighborhood and grassroots agencies.

The Marinens had come to St. Paul from Ireland during the potato famine of 1848 and had been here ever since. From the start they seemed to share a congenital ability to achieve success in business that had provided members of every generation with the opportunity and temptation to leave for some other city with a more congenial climate. "But this is an awfully hard place to leave, and none ever did," he said and then described a report from 3M, where there had always been a large executive turnover as part of long-standing company operational habit. "They always struggle to get people to come here and then have a hard time getting them to willingly move on when they need them somewhere else."

With the Twin Cities' extreme climate, lack of mountains or ocean, and problematic sense of distance from the rest of the world, Tim thought what kept people here had to be the other people. "Sure, there's a diversity of things you can do, from fishing to dogsledding to good bars and dancing to opera and symphony," he said. "The Twin Cities is the smallest metro area by far to have big-league teams in football, baseball, basketball, and hockey. But the main thing is a collaborative style of living. That and the integration of nature and city living. The lakes and the river have a huge effect, I think, on how people behave—a kind of a tranquilizing effect. It's a city of thoughtfulness."

On Saturday night, acquaintances at MPR took me out for a night on the town. It was hot and steamy for early May as we drove to St. Paul and into what looked to me like a pretty rough neighborhood. But I had said I was in the mood for some down-and-dirty blues, so here we were, pushing and shoving our way into the crowded Blue Saloon, an upstairs bar with no air-conditioning and no emergency exit. But the band was hot, and word had gotten around. Here was the first place where I had seen blacks and whites mixing sociably. No question, social restraints as well as fire code regulations were being ignored here tonight, and I looked around wondering how one would get out of this windowless upstairs room with only two stairway entrances located perilously close to each other if there were a fire.

It wasn't long before we stepped outside onto the street for some fresh air and I heard what sounded like a muffler falling off a passing car, but then we saw rocks, big ones, bouncing off the wall behind us and landing at our feet. In the shadows of the softball field across the street, we could see maybe six or seven black kids of roughly junior high school age sprinting into the darkness. People from the Blue Saloon, a racially mixed group, picked up the rocks and concluded that the kids had been aiming at the blue fluorescent lights overhead, because the rocks had hit high and there were enough of us blues fans standing around that if we had been the targets, surely someone would have gotten hit.

The house man was out in no time, and soon a squad car arrived. But I couldn't help but note how calm the response of the Blue Saloon patrons had been and how rationally they had decided that the delinquents had not meant to hit anyone. A city of thoughtfulness.

I wanted to meet Virak "Rak" Khiev, a young Cambodian refugee who had written an impressive piece about his experience for *Newsweek*'s "My Turn" feature. I called the Blake School, mentioned in the article, and was given the telephone number of the family that was serving as his foster family—their address was in Kenwood, the most posh neighborhood in old Minneapolis.

Mary Ellis Harwood invited me to come to her house to meet Rak, as he was called, that very morning. Kenwood's Mount Curve Street was green with huge trees and freshly cut lawns. The houses were large, dignified turn-of-the-century monuments to domestic prosperity, set respectably back from the street without being hidden away. I expected a butler to greet me at the door, but it was Mary Ellis herself, an earnest woman in her forties who believed that if you were well off, you had a special duty to personally reach out to those less fortunate. She thought that sentiment was especially strong in Minneapolis.

Mary Ellis was quick to give credit to Rak's communications teacher, Barbara Mraz, who had sent his essay to *Newsweek*. And then there was the "saint, the angel," as Mary Ellis called her, Margot Rose, an unpaid freelance social worker who supported her philanthropic habit by working as a waitress. It was she who had personally rescued Rak from gang life and steered him toward the scholarship that got him into the Blake School.

Rak then appeared in the living room barefoot, wearing a black T-shirt, denim vest, jeans, and a red bandanna tied over his long black hair. He might have looked intimidating, but there was a gentle turn to his mouth and a genuine twinkle of friendliness and appreciation in his eye. He was not shy with adults and he reminded me instantly of certain students I had taught during my former career who were desperate for adult approbation and positively purred when they got it. Mary Ellis left for a tennis match and Rak and I sat on the front stoop of her home, drinking coffee and smoking cigarettes and watching the well-heeled neighbors walk their dogs.

Rak didn't know the year he was born. There was a war going on in Cambodia. He only knew it was during the time when people from the cities were force-marched into the countryside. His family was suspect not only because they were city people, but because they were artisans and his father was a college professor.

Rak laughed nervously when recalling those years, particularly the deaths of family members: His grandparents were tied to stakes and clubbed and burned to death. His little brother, suffering the pains of malnutrition, cried a lot; Khmer Rouge soldiers threw him in a hole, shoved a pile of dirt on top of him, and stomped on it till his cries ceased. There was a pretty lady who was raped by soldiers. When they demanded that she marry one of them and she refused, they raped her again and then buried her up to her belly so that the starved dogs came and ate her flesh till there was nothing left but raw, bloody bone.

Rak had seen the movie *The Killing Fields* and thought it was pretty realistic on the surface but just couldn't capture what it was to have been there. During those four years when Rak was separated from his family, he grew up surrounded by death. Daily he would stumble across rotting corpses in the paddies. He learned that the dead stopped bleeding quickly but that the real horror was when the bodies would dry and swell and crack, oozing a white mucus from the fissures for days.

In 1980, when the Vietnamese invaded and drove out the Khmer Rouge, they were welcomed as heroes by people like Rak and his family. But Cambodia was still a killing field as new scores were set-tled. Rak spent another year living on the streets in Kampuchon sepa-rated from his parents and subsisting on finding bullets and selling them to the Vietnamese soldiers, who never seemed to have enough of their own. Eventually the family was reunited at a United Nations refugee camp on the Thai border. An American woman who worked for Lutheran Social Services sponsored the family's immigration to America. "Then suddenly we were flying on a plane to Minneapolis," Rak recalled. He had never flown before and recalled staring in horror at the weird blue water in the airplane's toilet bowl and thinking, "This is all wrong. We're gonna die, we're all gonna die."

In Minneapolis the family was settled into a house on Portland Avenue, where a new struggle began, the one he always wrote about— he rarely wrote about Cambodia. In Cambodia he had always dreamed about living in America, about having good food, good clothes, a nice house, a car, and being rich. Now, at twelve or thirteen, he found another war. The family was shortly relocated to a home on Sixteenth Avenue in the heart of a Native American neighborhood, where he encountered racial prejudice, neighborhood violence, and a different kind of hatred.

"I became so angry. It wasn't supposed to be that way," he said. He got into fights nearly every day at school. Soon his anger and new image of toughness attracted the attention of gang members. He joined the gang, went back to that first Portland Avenue neighborhood, and took his first revenge. He wouldn't tell me the details of his personal actions in gang warfare, just the effects: "You'd do something, you know, to get revenge, and it would take away some of the anger for a while. Like taking aspirin to make a headache less bad for a while."

Home life didn't help. There was strife in the house over his father's romantic meanderings and over the growing gulf between Rak, who was becoming an American, and his parents, who never would. Rak quit school and drove with some gang members to California and then to Louisiana, where he hooked up with another gang, this one a multiracial group of Asians and blacks. "It was the first place where I had met black guys who would accept me," he said. "I made good friends there and it was high times." Rak learned to cook cocaine and make crack. Dealing drugs made good money, and he thought, "This is the life, this is how I want to die. We partied every day, drank, did drugs, had women and cars, ate oysters. I felt immortal." He nursed bad feelings about Minneapolis, hated his parents and the poor Cambodian slobs who lived there, neither Cambodian nor American, just hopeless refugees.

But it all came crashing down when he totaled his car with no license or insurance. Then a fight with a roommate over money was the final blow. "If I stayed, I would have to shoot his ass to get my money and settle the score," Rak recalled. "I had nowhere to go, the world was closing in." A black woman who had become a loyal friend said, "It's time to go back to school, kid."

He had one lifeline back to Minneapolis, Margot Rose, the unpaid social worker "angel" Mary Ellis had mentioned to me. Rak had corresponded with her occasionally throughout his odyssey. Now he wrote to her asking for help. She wrote back and promised to get him and another friend, Coonta, into school in Minneapolis. The two hitchhiked to Minneapolis and Margot kept her promise. "Coonta didn't like it here," Rak said. "Too quiet, so he got four kilos of coke and headed back to Louisiana, where he got busted and is now doing twenty years." But Rak wanted to see if school could help him to leave everything behind. "I read every book I could find, I got As and Bs."

It was a schizoid existence. He was still loosely involved with gang trouble on weekends and going to school and making friends with rich kids at Blake during the week. But besides Margot Rose and some black buddies in Louisiana, this was the first time he had ever dealt with people who seemed to really care, and they had a lot of money. He had no illusions about the fact that the caring was the result of affluent guilt. "But what's bad about that?" he wondered. "If having a lot of money makes some people care more about others, then it's a good thing for people to have a lot of money."

During his sophomore year at Blake, he began to make a reputation for his writing talent and attracted the attention of Mary Ellis Harwood, whose own kids attended Blake. At first she just gave him fifty dollars a month to help pay for a place to live, but by his senior year, she decided to take him into her own home. Now he was enrolled at the local St. John's University for next year and wanted to be a physicist or a writer or maybe both. He made no bones about wanting to be rich and successful. After college he wanted to travel the world, "to see everything before I die."

But I would learn from Mary Ellis and others that he wasn't yet in the clear. He suffered from severe posttraumatic shock, had violent and destructive nightmares, and still disappeared occasionally on weekends, sometimes returning scarred and violently hungover. I noticed as we sat there on Mary Ellis's stoop that he often paused and sighed deeply—a physical, not an emotional gasp—a symptom I had seen in some of my sixties college friends withdrawing from drug dependence. It was the oppressive exhaustion of being freshly straight.

The subject of his writing and of the video documentary he was currently working on was the life of refugees in America. "It depresses me the way immigrants and minorities here deal with life," he said. Hmong, Cambodians, Vietnamese, Laotians, blacks, and Native Americans all fought each other over stereotypes. Cambodians said Indians and blacks were lazy and depended too much on welfare. Indians and blacks said Cambodians were selfish and hostile. "They're all like ants in a cup," Rak reflected. "They can't see beyond the cup, can't climb out. If any of the other ants piss me off, I'll shoot their house, burn it down. There are some who will get out of the cup. Then they move out to the suburbs and try to forget the past and don't help those left behind. Not me."

Rak kept going back to his wonder at the various forms of hatred he had lived with all his life. It was the one component of his experience that he didn't internalize—anger, yes, but not hatred—and it seemed as if his success might have been the result of never quite understanding the emotion. He told me about a time when he was very young in Cambodia and he asked his mother why people were sick and dying all the time. She said it was because of the war. He asked her what war was. She explained that it was when human beings got so full of hatred that they killed one another. Young Rak understood fighting, as when children got into fights over toys, but he couldn't grasp the idea of fighting to the point where you actually made the other person dead. "Do they mean to really kill each other?" he asked his mother. She answered that yes, they meant to kill each other, just like when you step on bugs. Young Rak cried, "But they can't do that to people, Mother, they can't!"

Rak still loved his mother, but it was impossible for him to live with her. He loved the Harwoods too: "Mary Ellis was poor when she was young, her father got help and taught her that she owed it to others when they became rich." He was glad there were rich people in Minneapolis. "Poor people do drugs because it makes them feel good, and that's a bad thing, because drugs make the world worse. Rich people help out because it makes them feel good, and that's a good thing, because it makes the world a better place. In Cambodia I wanted to be rich just for myself. In America I want to be rich so I can do like Mary Ellis."

Most of all, though, he loved Margot Rose, the angel of St. Paul, who had saved him again and again, and who was not rich. Before I left, he said I should see her, that she could explain things he couldn't about how people cared for one another here in the Twin Cities. When I telephoned the number he gave me, Margot Rose answered and said she had been expecting my call. Rak had told her about me. She could pick me up at my hotel on Wednesday and I could join her for her day's tasks if I wanted.

I had a Monday evening and a Tuesday to kill before my appointment with Margot Rose, so around happy hour the first evening, I took a cab over to an area my MPR friends had shown me known as the warehouse district. This old section of town had been renovated under historical district status for primarily entertainment purposes— a twenty-square-block network of good, city third places. Nearby was the Target Center, the arena where Eric Clapton was scheduled to play that evening. The streets were mobbed with ticket holders awaiting the start of the concert, and I joined a group of them tanking up at a little hole in the wall called the Coyote Café.

I shared a table with a guy waiting for his date. We talked about Minneapolis and what I had learned about the city so far. When I mentioned the Five Percent Club, he laughed and said, "Well, you're on a lucky streak here." His date was a kindergarten teacher at the Wilder School, one of the inner-city schools funded by the philanthropy of the Pillsburys. Sure enough, when she arrived, Natasha Munter said she'd be delighted to show me around at her school the following morning.

From the outside, Wilder looked like any modern school building, but inside, I marveled at the wide carpeted corridors with curious bends in them as well as nooks and alcoves and places to sit. I was told they were designed to re-create the outside city streets and to provide gathering places, as well as spots to get away privately with a child for talk. All over the school I saw behavior modification posters with five slogans: LEARN MANNERS, SHOW RESPECT, TRY YOUR BEST, COOPERATE, MAKE IT RIGHT. The key slogan was that last one, a theme for the whole school.

Natasha Munter's kindergarten class was small, only a dozen children. It was well equipped with books, posters, games, computers, and video equipment and had that busy, cluttered, fertile look characteristic of a good elementary classroom. But there was order, too, which the casual eye might not have noticed. The room was subtly divided into four learning centers: life (anchored by a beautiful fish tank), the world (centered around a display of maps and travel photos), counting (with a collection of counting toys and a computer), and letters (with a little classroom library, big fuzzy letters, and another computer). The class size was made for ideally small clusters of three for group work.

The kids were well trained, spoke in turn, raised their hands, and didn't jostle each other when they later lined up at the door for library time. Like any good teacher, Natasha had seized on my visit to involve me in a minilesson about what a writer does and what you should learn in order to become one. One by one the kids took turns describing things they would like to write about and asking me questions like how many pencils it took to write a book, whether I ever had trouble staying inside the lines, and how I glued all of the pages together.

During library time, Natasha was free to show me around and tell me more about the school. Wilder had a mixture of differentiated and integrated classroom environments. "There are some areas of the school day where you want cooperative learning and others where you want opportunities for individual excellence," she explained.

The student population was drawn half from the local inner-city neighborhoods and half from families elsewhere who sent their children here to take advantage of the school's magnet attractions. The dominant minority was black, not Asian. The students not from the local neighborhood were almost always better motivated. But all groupings were a fifty-fifty mix of these two populations, regardless of whether the setting was grouped by ability or integrated. Thus, cooperative learning was the philosophy even in the top-level classes, where the less motivated kids were selected on the basis of aptitude rather than achievement testing. But they *were* selected, and Natasha hastened to point out that the cooperative learning aspect of the school was not dogmatic. This was not homogeneous grouping. Sharp, motivated kids were not held back by the expectation that they would do some of the teacher's work with less motivated students, as had happened in so many "progressive" schools where cooperative learning, homogeneous grouping, and a general lowering of academic standards all went hand in hand.

Natasha showed me the behavior mod room and introduced me to the full-time specialist who manned it. He explained that this was Wilder's substitute for traditional discipline methods. When students were sent here, the first thing they did was write about why they were here. Then he and the student talked it over until they worked out a contract for their return to the classroom. Students received tickets for timely meeting of behavioral goals as well as for spontaneous acts of responsibility, maturity, creativity, and caring. These could be redeemed for anything from greater freedom to special responsibilities and treats. Though all of the teachers had had enough behavior mod training to run the room themselves, they were expected to use their time teaching. Trouble quickly ended up here, where it belonged.

Natasha took me into the library learning center where her class was working. As a former teacher, I was impressed. Besides an extensive array of well-stocked bookshelves, the place featured half a dozen small rooms off to the side where students worked in small groups on special projects: one group was programming a mechanical robot to go through a maze painted on the floor, another was doing a video disc search, and another was drawing illustrations of historical scenes in their reading. They were relatively unsupervised, and all seemed to be on task.

While we waited for her class to finish, Natasha and I talked to the principal, who was surprisingly at ease about a stranger walking around his school with a notebook and camera. He told me that much of what I saw was the result of Wilder's partnership with Pillsbury. It was not only a matter of funding, which achieved levels that truly set the school apart, but also the personal involvement of Pillsbury executives, who participated in educational research and decision making as well as offering to come into the school to meet with teachers, do career-awareness work with students, and take the children on field trips into the community to show them the uses to which their education could be put.

But it wasn't just Pillsbury that made the school what it was. The city school system was independently strong, and Natasha related a recent episode to prove her point. Voters had recently passed a nonbinding referendum calling for smaller class sizes, but because of economic hard times, the city had been forced to cut the school budget. Thus, it would have been easy to ignore the referendum, citing financial circumstances, but the superintendent implemented the class size cuts anyway, paying for the extra hiring by cutting 80 percent of the top-level administration. The action just about closed down the administration building, and there were some inconveniences as a result, but the effect on the classroom and on a public delighted to see its wishes respected was salutary.

Wednesday morning, a Chevy badly in need of a paint job pulled up in front of the hotel where I was waiting and the woman driving gestured for me to get in. I leaned toward the window and did a double take, staring at her for an awkward moment. I had heard Margot Rose described as an angel, but I was quite unprepared for her to look so much like one. She was young, just thirty, had long, straight dusty blond hair, gemstone blue eyes, and facial features that belonged in a soap commercial. She was slender and wore a sweater, loose jeans, and sandals. She smiled at me warmly, diffusing my consternation as if she had dealt with it many a time, and said, "Let's go, Terry."

Throughout the day I noticed this endearing habit of frequently speaking the name of the person she was talking to. It was just one of the thousand and one ways that Margot Rose incorporated the concept of human outreach into her moment-by-moment existence. "People have names," she said. "Why not use them?"

Outreach—that was the word of the day with Margot Rose, and she believed it was a hallmark of the Twin Cities, though the more time I spent with her, the more convinced I became that she would find or create such a network wherever she went. As I had been told, Margot supported herself by waitressing and dedicated the rest of her life to unpaid social work, though she didn't like that term. She thought it was just a matter of being a good neighbor and human being.

We drove to the Asian projects in St. Paul. They were two-story units, similar in structure and layout to the low-rise projects found anywhere, except that they were freshly painted, with mowed lawns and flowering bushes. These places were well kept, and children played on tricycles, bikes, and roller skates. The adults I saw were sitting watching or playing with their kids in the grass in front of their homes. There was not one speck of graffiti or other habitat-marring expressions of grief or rage.

Margot first had to say good-bye and deliver a parting gift to a young mother and her high school–age daughter who were moving to another city for the mother's new job. The mother was friendly and well dressed and her daughter sparkled with teen energy. She handed me a camera and insisted that I take several shots of her and her daughter with Margot. Before we left I asked her if this had been a good place to live. "Oh, yes. A new life, it all began here," was all she said. The farewell to Margot was touching; all three women hugged and then brushed tear-dampened strands of hair out of their eyes to hold hands and look at one another one last time.

In the car, Margot said that despite experiences in Cambodia similar to Rak's, this was a family that would make it. I asked about the Cambodian families Rak talked about, who drank all day and lived in hopelessness. She answered that Rak's view was a bit distorted by his personal experience and that of the gang members he hung out with. "Sure, there are families like that, too many of them, and that's why we have so much work to do," she acknowledged. "But it's not the norm anymore. Many Cambodian families are living well in settings like what you just saw."

Our second stop was at another project very much like the first. This time Margot was visiting a family of women spanning three generations to deliver graduation pictures of the granddaughter, a friend of Rak's in school. They came out into the yard. The grandmother, bespectacled, traditionally robed, and absolutely hairless, peppered me with boasts about her granddaughter's success in school, where she was valedictorian. The granddaughter was embarrassed and whispered to me that I should forgive her grandmother's boldness, that she was a bodhisattva and therefore used to being indulged. The grandmother took exception to her granddaughter's having private words with me, and the granddaughter explained respectfully that she was only instructing me in the proper conduct before a bodhisattva. "Ah," said the grandmother, and everything was made right. The mother stood with Margot in the warm sunshine and beamed at her kin making such a fuss over her family's American success.

Back in the car, I said to Margot, "Looks like another success story."

"That family would make it anywhere, just given a fair chance," she said.

We made a few more stops for Margot to check in and see how things were going with some other families, and each time I saw the same appearance of domestic tranquility and stability. With her morning chores finished, Margot took me to lunch at St. Martin's Table, a Lutheran ecumenical neighborhood cooperative. The focus of this particular establishment was food and hunger causes. Paying customers and volunteers made it possible for the little restaurant to offer free meals to those in need. Besides working to feed the hungry in the city, the group worked on a Farmland Preservation Project, to keep productive farmland around the Twin Cities in the hands of people who would farm it.

As we ate our simple meal of vegetable tofu soup, excellent homemade bread, and garden salad, Margot ticked off the names of outreach agencies that were part of the network she worked through in the Twin Cities. Many of them were national or international headquarters: El Salvadoran Refugees Relief, the USSR Hunger Appeal, the

Santa Marta Project (for displaced persons still in El Salvador), the Ash Wednesday Project for Abandoned Children, Common Bread (combating local hunger), the North American Center for Victims of Torture, the Project for Pride in Living (housing rehab and reemployment), the People Center (budget veterinary and other domestic services), the Peace House for the Mentally Ill, the Catholic Worker Shelter for Abused Women and Children, the Teenage Medical Clinic, Refugee Resource Settlement (U.S. immigration had eighteen hundred applications in the last twenty-four hours before Cambodian immigration was shut down last year, and eight hundred of them were for the Twin Cities), Social Justice Center (part of an underground railroad for Central Americans making their way to Canada), Community Based Arts, and dozens of other co-ops. There was a subculture of outreach here. She insisted that it was dependent primarily on individual commitment to making the world a better place but had to concede that many of the resulting initiatives were tremendously dependent on corporate support.

It took some doing to convince Margot Rose to talk about herself. Promotion of a cult of any individual personality was definitely not part of the ethic, she insisted. And when she finally did begin to reminisce about her own experience, there were tantalizing omissions of detail that I simply could not get her to fill in. She did tell me that after college, she had a spiritual conversion experience that led to the life she lived now. She wouldn't tell precisely what the experience consisted of, just that it was cataclysmic, total, and truly spiritual, not just philosophical in nature. "I knew I had to go into the dark corridors and corners of the world and be a reflector of light," she said. She had chosen to become a Catholic because she wanted to emulate St. Francis, Dorothy Day, and Mother Teresa. "It was very deliberate," she said. "Catholics have a great tradition of presence at the sites of human trouble and they are great organizers."

I asked Margot what she had learned from her experience of the Twin Cities' outreach community. Most important, she felt, was tolerance, not just of diversity, but of real deviance; a respect for distinction and eccentricity; and a feeling for the local places and spaces that are the habitat of human beings. Margot never had the urge to be a missionary to another country. She believed we had problems enough of our own right here at home, which, as in the case of the Cambodians, were often connected to human misery elsewhere. She said that for her, missionary work abroad would have been another form of flight: "You have to stay engaged with the things you don't like at home."

But she reiterated that she did not consider herself a social worker: "What I do is simply to be a neighbor, a friend, a human being doing what people should be doing." She didn't elevate poverty for its own sake and had taken no Franciscan vow, but she did live on the edge, without a career, health insurance, or social security. "Living in the margins forces you to be constantly aware of the myth and distortion of American society," she believed. "You just can't stay in touch with the reality of troubled people unless you live there yourself."

We talked about Rak. What made him special, she thought, was his enormous promise. But he was not yet in the clear, despite the great strides he had made. "Rak is an ongoing group effort," she reminded me. "It takes eight support people to properly handle a case like his. And with all the kids needing that kind of support, there aren't enough people to answer the call. And soon I won't be here anymore either."

Five years was long enough for a ministry in any one place, Margot thought, and now she was planning a new life in Tacoma, Washington, where she had some Catholic Worker contacts. "There are some serious justice issues there," she explained. "It's not like Minneapolis–St. Paul, where you have this well-established network of caring. I want to link justice and compassion in a place in need of them. Another dark corner."

So Margot was leaving. That was part of the reason for this morning's visits. Her main task these last months had been to wean people from depending on her. "With some, it's easy—there are others already engaged who will carry on," she said pointedly. "Rak is one of the toughest. Mary Ellis and others are there, but he has special needs that I'm not sure we've fully taken care of yet. He desperately needs adult contact and approbation. He wants to be a writer." Then Margot Rose gave me a silent look, like the wave of a wand, and I knew what I was going to do.

Margot Rose got up at five-thirty the next morning to drive me to the station to catch my train back East. I didn't ask her to do it, in fact I urged her not to, saying I could just take a cab. "You're a visitor to my community and I want to be a good host for the Twin Cities," she explained. "Perhaps you'll be called on to do something for me or one of my neighbors someday." And again there was the look, and the sure knowledge that I was already being called.

Boarding the train, I thought of Dostoyevsky's Sonja and the ethical cosmology of *Crime and Punishment* that I used to lecture about as a teacher. For Sonja, "God does everything," holding her safely above the pit of despair and depravity so that she in turn can reach out to save others from falling. I used to draw a little cartoon on the chalkboard showing the hand of God holding Sonja, with her hands connected to others, who then connected to others in a web of compassion that defied the misery and hopelessness that lay in the pit below. There were others in Dostoyevsky's story who became part of the web through different ethical motivations, not always religious. But the key character had that spiritual link at the top of the cosmology.

Though Margot Rose never talked about God, she reiterated frequently that for her, everything was a spiritual matter, unlike the secular social responsibility motivating Mary Ellis Harwood and the CEOs of Pillsbury and 3M. While I visited the Twin Cities, there were Christians in other cities pouring blood on the steps of Planned Parenthood clinics and shooting doctors who performed abortions. But Minneapolis–St. Paul reaffirmed one's faith not only in the potential for good in responsible free enterprise, but also in responsible religion.

Was this enough to make the Twin Cities a good place to live, despite climate and the problems of poverty in an area that attracted so many "huddled masses yearning to be free"? It certainly was if you were a refugee like Rak or the harried minorities who were streaming here out of places like Cleveland or Detroit. But I came away from the Twin Cities convinced that they offered something for some of the rest of us as well. Even in the best of places I had visited, there were people who yearned for a spirituality that went deeper than the renaissance of companionship and public living upon which I had focused. While often turning away from traditional religion, they strained for a spiritual dimension in their existence, through star charts and crystals, wilderness pilgrimages and spiritual dancing, or encounter groups and Jungian therapy. In the Twin Cities they would find a spirituality of substance, of which even the secular philanthropists were truly a part. This was a place where large sectors of the community had adopted, intentionally or otherwise, the humanitarian teachings of the great religious masters. And it was infectious.

Rak Khiev came to visit me in New Hampshire the summer following my visit to Minneapolis. It was my own idea; nobody in Minneapolis–St. Paul directly asked me to invite him. But when I telephoned Mary Ellis Harwood, Margot Rose, and Rak himself to set it up, it was clear that my calls were expected, and it was amazing how quickly and smoothly arrangements were made.

Rak brought his writing notebooks and sat with me and other Keene area writers. "The kid's got it," the others agreed. There were powerful essays and poems about the refugee experience in America. There were fragments of an emerging autobiography that made *The Killing Fields* look tame. But most touching to all who saw them were the traditional Cambodian pastoral love poems Rak had written as a young boy, son of a university professor, while a holocaust began to explode around him.

Rak did enroll in St. John's University, where he began in earnest a study of writing and engineering. He took time off to return to Cambodia to teach English. The last time I talked to him, he still wanted to be rich, but he vowed never to forget his roots. He wanted to see the world, write about everything, and then somehow combine the vocations of writing and business—in the Twin Cities, where he would become a member of the Five Percent Club.

9

HOMECOMING

The woman in extravagant red and purple was cupping something in her hands as she sat on a ledge beneath the First Bank on Ithaca Commons, oblivious to my notebook scribbling just a few feet away and to the raw, clammy gusts that whipped down the mall this late October morning. The metal facade above her looked like a huge onion grater, and its nooks and crannies were home to swarms of sparrows, whose songs rang throughout the commons even during the noisiest of shopping hours. It was a dying bird the woman held in her hands, having seen it fall from its perch and sweep against the onion grater.

Ginny Miller, "Rukmini" in a former life on a nearby commune, worked for an organization called the Law Guardians, which operated out of a county courthouse to ensure that local children received humane and equal treatment in encounters with the law. Ginny wasn't an "animal rights person," though Ithaca was home to a vigorous chapter, but as an activist member of the spiritualist Dance for Universal Peace group and a general participant in Ithaca's greater alternative living community, it was natural for her to take this bird in hand and offer it compassion during its dying moments.

When the sparrow lay still, she carried it across the common to a

223

work site where a man was breaking up concrete that was to be replaced with slate tiles, part of a downtown beautification project. The man stopped his jackhammer, raised his safety goggles, and listened to Ginny explain that she wanted the bird buried under one of the tiles. "Sure," he said as if her request was something he heard every day.

Ginny had been on an errand from work when she found the bird and now had to return. But she agreed to meet me for lunch that afternoon, as long as it was a place where she could get vegetarian food.

I had found my way to Ithaca from Minneapolis after several brief explorations of other midwestern sites. Places like Sioux Falls, South Dakota; Mankato, Minnesota; Madison, Wisconsin; Traverse City, Michigan; Bloomington, Indiana; and Hannibal, Missouri, all eventually figured in the good place oral tradition. But the last migration initially tended to fixate on mountains and water the way the eighties' Sun Belt migration fixated on climate. There was also a prejudice that out there in the vast plains of Wal-Mart country, the cultural amenities that people sought in small cities might be hard to come by. That meant that the renaissance happened first in the West, then in the East, and arrived late to the Midwest. As this book goes to press, almost three years after I started my search, sites that didn't even register on the good place radar earlier in the project are popping up everywhere, especially in the Midwest.

I spent the next few months surveying the possibilities in the inland Northeast. Mired deeply in the recession, northeastern communities that didn't have Atlantic shoreline nearby were paralyzed. From New Jersey to New Hampshire and westward to Lake Erie, there was no money in public treasuries, less goodwill in taxpayers' hearts, and few private investors with enough vision and venture capital to initiate anything like the bold experiments in community renaissance that I had seen out West. Furthermore, the Northeast was home to many of those fundamentally dysfunctional places that people were fleeing for greater possibilities out West. But there were several small cities that emerged in good place testimony as exceptions to the Northeast pattern, and Ithaca was one of them.

Having grown up in central New York, I remembered all too well the reality of the climate: less than a hundred days of sunshine, more than a hundred inches of snow, and hills that reminded me of the hair on an angry German shepherd's back for so much of the year when the almost exclusively deciduous forest stood barren of foliage. But people were talking about Ithaca, and it wasn't just because of Cornell and Carl Sagan and Alex Haley. Ithaca had taken dramatic steps toward rethinking the nature of eastern community. It had established the nation's first mandatory recycling program. It had elected the nation's second socialist mayor and radically expanded the charge of local government to guarantee the well-being of its citizens. It had pioneered the redevelopment of the downtown as a pedestrian mall. Its location "high above Cayuga's waters" at the southern base of the wine-making Finger Lakes region offered an attractive alternative to mountains and ocean. And despite its horrible score for climate, it was by a significant margin the highest-ranked micropolis in the East by all of the conventional criteria in Thomas's *Life in America's Small Cities.*

"The secret to Ithaca besides Cornell is that it's 'centrally isolated,' " said Ginny as I forked into my beer sausages and sauerkraut lunch at Just a Taste on Aurora Street. "We're here in the heart of the Northeast but four or five hours from Boston, New York, Washington —anyplace that matters. So people who want to really get away from big-city living but who don't want to exile themselves to a small town or thousands of miles somewhere out West come here."

Ginny, who was born and raised in Toronto, had brought a Canadian expectation of community and a big-city lover's demands for culture when she moved to Ithaca fifteen years ago. But more than that, she was a seeker of a spiritual dimension to civic life that was rare east of the West Coast. It was Ithaca's reputation during the seventies as a mecca for experimenters in communal living that had brought her here and kept her here. She had lived on a commune, one of scores, way out in the country and strove to develop her spiritual nature. The spiritualism she spoke of wasn't necessarily a matter of religious conviction. "It was simply the search for alternatives to the purely materialistic life," she explained.

Ginny no longer lived on the commune, having found her spiritual waters in the network of fellowship that existed today in Ithaca itself. In addition to the people she worked with at the Law Guardians, she found like-minded souls in the "family" of a local food co-op, the Montessori school her twelve-year-old son attended, the close-knit local music scene, and, most important, the Dance for Universal Peace, a spiritual gathering that occupied every Sunday afternoon as fundamentally as did the churchgoing of traditional Christians.

"The community of Ithaca is a family, it really is," Ginny insisted. "See, people here don't stick to their private lives in private homes. There's a lot of public living—people spending the most important parts of their time when not working out and about in town. Most of the communes are gone, but Ithaca has the communal spirit in a conventional community at large." Ginny clearly had an ideological agenda, so after that first lunch, I set out to explore Ithaca on my own. Depending on what I found, maybe I would get back to her later in the visit.

The most promising feature of Ithaca at first glance was the presence of not one but two thriving downtowns: the central downtown surrounding the pedestrian mall of Ithaca Commons, and "Collegetown," a totally separate commercial culture centered along College Avenue on the hill adjacent to Cornell. Both were bustling with people this Friday of a Cornell homecoming weekend.

It was surprising to me that Ithaca was the first small city where I encountered a downtown pedestrian mall. The idea had been heavily promoted during the seventies by planners who saw the benefits to community of separating people from their automobiles. It was also touted as a way to preserve historic downtown facades and preempt the development of predatory regional malls on the outskirts of town.

But the innovation had had mixed success. Downtown merchants were generally put off at the prospect of routing cars away from their storefronts. I later visited eastern places where their fears had been realized and Main Streets had turned into empty, echoing chasms that felt more like historical parks than centers of commerce and community. Perhaps I didn't see downtown pedestrian malls out West because they were an invention born of an extremity that didn't exist in places where people still had a chance "to get it right this time." They turned out to be an eastern experiment, located primarily in places where radical measures were entertained only as a means to preserve endangered historical values. Ithaca was the first of several places I visited where I could see for myself what made them work or fail.

Ithaca Commons, one of the country's original pedestrian malls, appeared at first to be a clear success. Though there were quiet hours during the rhythm of the day when the place belonged primarily to the skateboarders and their groupies who always gravitate toward open, paved public spaces, the commons was otherwise swept by waves of pedestrians. After a few days, however, I began to see that much of the action of downtown Ithaca was not in the commons itself, but along the streets bordering it. Here were the popular restaurants (including the famous Moosewood, home of the cookbooks of the same name) and bars, diners and coffee shops, theaters and boutiques that made the downtown thrive. The places on the commons itself were not the prime draws, and I wondered whether this was because the location was detrimental or because the sharpest merchants had all hedged their bets by staying on the fringe of the great experiment.

Simeon's, a restaurant at the intersection of the commons and Aurora Street, seemed like a key location to get a perspective on the town. The place was done up with traditional brass rails and velvet hangers, blossom lamps and wooden fans hanging from a Victorian tin ceiling, and lots of dark wood. Owner Allan Cohen, a 1981 graduate of Cornell, sat with me at the bar and explained that it was the intellectual and educational timbre of the Ithaca community, fed by graduates of Cornell, that made it what it was. Two hundred members of his class had settled here. "I don't know if that figure holds up for other classes, but even if it's only half, how many small cities in America attract even a hundred new residents per year of Cornell graduate caliber?"

"What do they find for jobs?" I wanted to know.

"Everything," he said. "From construction workers and small contractors to teachers; from city employees to downtown merchants; lawyers, doctors, and other professionals. A lot get jobs with NCR or Emerson Electronics, and many start their own technical businesses based on the sciences they learned at Cornell. Ithaca is a town where you've got Cornell graduates sprinkled throughout the general populace in the whole range of occupations."

Allan also attributed Ithaca's unabashed liberalism to the residual Cornell community. "It shows in the fact that we have a thriving, accepted gay community—the smallest town in America to have its own ACT-UP chapter—and that we have become a magnet for homeless people. Other places buy homeless people one-way tickets to Ithaca. And Ithacans have decided to embrace that fact of life and build a community identity out of it rather than pursue the usual path of cynically fighting it and buying more bus tickets to someplace else farther down the road."

"How do you build a community identity out of an influx of people dependent on welfare?" I asked.

"You get colorful eccentricity," he said. "It helps distinguish the city from Anyplace, USA. But more important, it breeds a culture of cooperative enterprise—a sense that we're all in this together. A businessman like me finds ways to assist the city and people in it who are needy, and the city in turn finds ways to help me as a businessman."

I spent much of homecoming weekend in the gathering places of Collegetown. Outside, the temperature dropped and blustery winds howling off the lake blew in the season's first flakes. Inside places like Ruloff's, which looked like a venerable college library with a restaurant and bar in it, the ivy cheer was heightened by the World Series and early snow. But in the Cornell people I met, I noticed a vague inability to tell me much of significance about the life of the people in the town below, and I decided it was time to get another perspective on the city.

Before you could talk to the mayor in Ithaca, you had to pass muster with Theresa Alt, assistant to the mayor and keeper of the gate, keys, Rolodexes, file cabinets, and appointment book in his outer office. Theresa filled me in on the history of Mayor Ben Nichols's ascendancy in local politics. In the fifties and sixties Ithaca was a thoroughly Republican town, like so many places in upstate New York. The horse races that mattered in those days were usually between the conservative and Rockefeller liberal wings of the Republican party. Democrats, never mind Socialists, were irrelevant.

But the beginnings of a slow, linear change occurred with the election of the mainstream Democrat regime in the seventies. It was this administration that became famous for building the pedestrian commons in the heart of downtown and was followed by the liberal Democrat John Gutenberger.

Gutenberger presided over what some might call a true city political machine and was thought to be ensconced so securely in city hall that nothing would ever shake him. But it took money to finance his liberal causes, so in order to expand the tax base, Gutenberger became an aggressive prodevelopment advocate at a time when growth control was coming to be a deep concern of voters. A small local Green movement focused on growth and environmental issues became the core of a revolt against Gutenberger, and Ben Nichols ran as a Democratic-Socialist at the head of that movement in 1989. Now, a year into his second term, Nichols was aggressively pursuing his leftist agenda to make Ithaca a city of compassion—a haven for those with human needs not met elsewhere.

Finally the mayor arrived. He was older than I had expected, heavyset, and he paused so long before answering my questions that it was almost as if he were going into a Zen trance to find responses. His desk was buried under a deep layer of papers, and his office was generally more cluttered and casual than that of any city official I had ever visited. File cabinets and cardboard boxes labeled with felt marker on masking tape seemed to give equal prominence to categories like "Budget FY 93" and "Wood St. Neighbors Petition."

In response to my question about how Ithaca had become a bastion of green socialism during the Reagan-Bush years, he said after closing his eyes a moment, "It's more cosmopolitan than similar communities elsewhere. It's dominated by people from the academic world and educated refugees from other, less enlightened, places. It also draws more people from abroad than any similar-sized community you can think of."

"But that would have been true thirty years ago during the Republican years," I countered.

"Yes, but even then Ithaca Republicans were doing things that Republicans elsewhere don't do. Take our public transit system. It was originally a small private business that failed. A Republican city government took it on and expanded it. You still don't see today many cities the size of Ithaca—Socialist, Democrat, or Republican—with a publicly funded system like ours."

It was Nichols's belief that Ithaca's unique academic ethos had always provided a culture in which liberalism would eventually flourish and triumph. "In the right kind of open intellectual climate," he believed, "it is natural evolution for each generation to become more liberal than those before it." He listed the issues that had become activistic causes in Ithaca long before they did in the nation as a whole: child abuse, battered women, sexual abuse, displaced home-

makers, homelessness, homosexual equality, AIDS awareness, cooperative markets, employee day care and maternity leave, mandatory
recycling, opposition to American policy in Latin America and more
recently in Iraq. "We're generally five to ten years ahead of the national curve, and this was going on long before I came to office," he
concluded.

When I asked about his own role in all of this, he explained that it
began when he returned from service in World War II. "Both parties
were like clubs; people tended to inherit their positions in government." Fresh from the horrors of war to defend democracy, he was
offended by the status quo and joined others in a personal crusade to
change it, challenging first Republican incumbents and later Democratic incumbents who had become complacent and lazy. During the
transition years the touchstone issues were questions like, Should the
city build public housing? Should there be a government role in
downtown development? Should the city mandate environmentally
sound waste disposal?

"Today those issues are just routine nitty-gritty," Nichols maintained, "no longer ideological. Now the leading edge issues are things
like, Should we be sponsoring public day care or interventionist youth
support services? Should we be promoting Ithaca as a refuge for the
homeless to a degree that actually attracts them from other places that
want to get rid of them? Can we make housing a public amenity and
do real rent control?"

Despite his successes, the mayor had his worries. He presided over
a community with some troubling structural divisions. First, of
course, there was Collegetown versus downtown. Townies and gown-
ies, though not in outright conflict, were nevertheless separated into
two distinct communities that did not tend to mingle. There was also
money versus nonmoney and yuppie versus hippie. These fractures
concerned the mayor far more than any ideologial opposition to his
program. It was his hope that the aggressive community activism of
his government might help close these divisions. He believed that such
change was already happening and was probably just a question of
time, but he was not a young man. "In the right kind of ethical
climate, people evolve to a global stage of development," he went on.
"As they do that, the community they share comes together. But there
are still too many people, even here, who stay withdrawn into their

private lives. I'd like to be around to see the process carried to fulfillment."

It took me aback when, a few days later, I met people who were
harsh critics of Mayor Nichols and the greens. Steve MacGruder, an
African-American businessman with a vintage clothing shop in the
Dewitt Downtown Mall just across the street from the commons,
offered me a minority perspective on the city. Steve was a hulking
fellow in his early thirties who had come to Ithaca eight years ago with
a shaved head and safety pins in his lips. He had evolved into a
Republican because, he said, "The black businessman today doesn't
want the liberal white politician's handouts nor his condescension. He
wants to make his own money and be one of those running the
show." Steve's change of politics also reflected the simple matter that
in order to fundamentally oppose the Democratic-Socialist status quo,
the Republican party was the only game in town.

He pointed out that he respected Ithaca on many levels—for its
quiet energy, its activist philanthropy, the fact that there was money
here to be made. He was amused and entertained by some of the
activist causes. A woman who once came into his store shortly after he
opened was outraged by the transplant of the baboon heart to Baby
Faye. "How do you think the baboon's mother felt?" she ranted and
raved.

"You could get a support group for hangnails in this town," Steve
chortled. "But despite the silliness of some of it, it's a good instinct.
Everybody here does some kind of pro bono work."

"What is Ithaca all about?" Steve asked himself rhetorically after
taking care of a customer who left delighted with the 1920s vest she
had just purchased. "There are people on the Fortune 500 walking up
and down the commons. Ithaca has a level of sophistication that's
world class, cultured, a lot of people with double addresses like
'Ithaca-Rio' or 'Ithaca-Paris.' You hear a lot of foreign languages here.
But there are drugs, some organized crime, and the community is
polarized racially. There are no African-Americans in local government. So it's not perfect."

To the contrary, Steve thought there were undercurrents of resentment masked by Ithaca's appearance of liberal solidarity. He knew of
people living in the West End who drank Black Label beer in quarts to
save pennies because they couldn't afford to eat or shop downtown—

people who loved Ithaca for the same reasons as everyone else but couldn't find decent jobs and were effectively locked out. "There are layers and layers of groups, class levels. You'll find some of them at the State Diner or Moonshadow Tavern rather than at Simeon's or Plums, and most have probably never even been to Ruloff's up in Collegetown," he said.

When I asked Steve about his opposition to the green regime of Nichols, he shook his head and said, "They're typical white liberals full of personal ambition. They're unyielding and fearful of real black autonomy." He believed that while Ithaca had highly visible gay, spiritual, and animal rights communities, the black community was invisible because the city was not fully integrated, and the greens seemed content to keep it that way. "How can the local government take the leadership role in minority issues when there are no elected or appointed black leaders in city hall? Look, when the civil war broke out in L.A., people of color in government posts all over the country went into the black communities, knocking on doors, saying everything was OK. But here there are no black leaders to do that. The races don't mix much. What the hell is going to happen here when we have trouble like that?"

"So that's why you're a Republican?"

"That's right."

"And one of these days a coalition of people like you and business, blue-collar, and monied interests is going to take down Nichols the same way they took down Gutenberger?"

"You got it."

In the days following my talk with Steve MacGruder, I spent a lot of time patronizing the establishments that I had learned represented the various factions of Ithaca. At Ruloff's in Collegetown, the Cornell academics seemed cheerfully oblivious to the presence of deep schisms in the community below and showed a vague intellectual support for Nichols and his program. At Simeon's and Plums, near the commons, where the patrons were a mix of downtown business, professional, and Ithaca College people, I found attitudes that coincided almost exactly with the views of Nichols: Ithaca had troubling schisms, but the liberal program of the greens was the town's best hope to close them.

But at Moonshadow and the State Diner, I found confirmation of the differences I had heard about. Here the patrons were blue-collar people, teachers, reporters, clerical workers, and the unemployed. The greens had some partisans here too, but more common was the attitude of a fellow who worked at the Ithaca *Times*. "They're ineffectual and incompetent," he said. "I agree with most of their program but don't like their condescending style. They don't realize that no-growth policies hurt people like us."

It was the most curious thing. In recent years, American communities with deep divisions tended to cleave along ideological lines. I thought of Santa Fe and my own town of Keene, where the people who mistrusted one another and withdrew into their own exclusive enclaves did so out of deep philosophical and political differences. But in Ithaca I found a profound solidarity of relatively liberal ideological thinking among all groups. What divided people in Ithaca was class.

I felt a need to get back to Ginny Miller, the woman with the bird who had insisted so strongly that the alternative community in Ithaca bridged all divisions. She agreed to let me shadow her through a weekend so I could see for myself the communal network she moved in.

Saturday morning we drove ten miles north to run errands in Trumansburg, a town of immaculate gingerbread Victorian houses and home to the Rongovian Embassy, a funky bar that hosted all of the best local musical talent. Returning I began to see, despite the barren season, why locals went on so about the beauty of Ithaca's setting, which frankly hadn't impressed me so far. As the road rose along the west hill of Cayuga, the expanse of water opened out, nearly infinite to the north and anchored by the spires of Cornell and the city blocks of Ithaca far below to the south. At Taughannock Gorge Park, a yawning chasm half a mile across had been carved out of the hill by the tiniest creek—as if some behemoth, enraged by the dense monotony of the leafless forest, had devoured a chunk of it to leave a vast gulf of light and air.

Back in Ithaca, Ginny visited the farmer's market down by the waterfront, a bookstore on the commons, the Greenstar Cooperative Market, and, later that evening, the Haunt, a nightspot with live Grateful Dead–style music.

In all of these stops, Ginny ran into friends and acquaintances. The talk was of other friends, the various community activities they were engaged in, and today's headlines concerning killer tornadoes that had rampaged through the South. "Say what you will about Ithaca's climate," said one of Ginny's friends, "we don't have to deal with that shit here."

What struck me was the truth of what Ginny had promised. Though they all adopted the dress and lifestyle that people would describe as "granola," I met during this day representatives of all of Ithaca's class divisions: Cornell academics, a lawyer and a doctor, a city official, teachers, downtown merchants, blue-collar working folks, farmers, homesteaders, and members of communes. They came from a variety of racial and national backgrounds and all seemed to be supporters of Mayor Nichols and his belief in the power of liberal activism to bridge the community's differences. They also held an even stronger belief in the power of their grassroots and spiritual activism to do the same. "The goal of spiritual activism," Ginny said to me, "is to bring together the whole community."

I was particularly intrigued by the Greenstar Cooperative Market. No struggling co-op operating out of the back room of a church, Greenstar occupied a building that was once a regular supermarket. Its shelves were stocked as fully as any supermarket and it operated like one, complete with shopping baskets and checkout counters. Subscribers bought shares in the company and could count on prices 75 to 50 percent of retail. Those who worked in the co-op received an additional 20 percent off. All earnings above operating costs went to Greenstar for Hunger, an allied agency that distributed food to the poor.

The bulletin board at Greenstar was a monument to communal democracy. All decisions about additions or deletions of product lines were subject to a referendum of shareholders and all such transactions were recorded on the bulletin board. I noted that a proposal to add pet food to the product line had recently lost by a vote of 292 to 293. A hand-scribbled note from the managers admonished dog lovers who hadn't bothered to vote. Another item involved adding aseptically packaged soy milk. It too had lost by just one vote, 277 to 278. Another note reminded subscribers, "Yes, your vote counts at Greenstar!"

There was also a comment board, where subscribers' complaints and suggestions all received handwritten responses from the manag-

ers. These involved such requests as an effective fan for the bathroom
to high chairs for the eating area to complaints about items in the
frozen deli case. But the most interesting item read, "Female workers
on 'Moontime' should not be allowed to handle food." The response
from the managers stated, "Greenstar needs to be careful not to im-
pose narrow worldviews or quasi-religious practices on a diverse community of individuals."

On Sunday, Ginny invited me to stop by the Montessori school
where she participated in the Dance for Universal Peace. The school
was located atop a southerly hill beyond Ithaca College, but it was
raining miserably when I drove out, so I saw none of the spectacular
view I was sure could be had from there. The dance had been going on
for an hour when I entered the lobby dripping and was offered cookies and cider by a woman tending the children. From the school's
darkened gymnasium issued some of the sweetest sounds I had ever
heard. It was the dancers slowly chanting in extremely musical mul-
tipart harmony with understated acoustic guitar accompaniment.
Through the glass doors I could see them, maybe a hundred of them,
arranged in a rotating circle, holding hands. Ginny was in the center
with the guitar player, performing a gracefully expressive contemporary dance. The only lighting was candles placed in the corners of the
room.

For this I was just too much of an outsider, so I spent the remaining half hour of the dance in the lobby, listening. During that time,
my New England reserve, my writer's detachment, my stranger's solitude all melted away as the rain pattered down on the roof and
splashed in the puddles outside the lobby windows. When the dance
came to a close, the dancers embraced one another and then gathered
in little knots of quiet conversation in the darkened gym, often holding hands or just touching, before emerging into the lobby for noisier
conversation. Some of them talked to me, and again I found that
eclectic mix of people from a variety of Ithacan walks of life.

Ginny was one of the last to emerge, and over more cider and
cookies, she told me about the group. Part of an international organization based in Fairfax, California, that recognized or honored all
religious traditions with spiritual folk dancing, they performed sacred
music from all over the world—the chant that had so moved me was
actually Hebrew—and recruited talented musicians to anchor the mu-

sic and guarantee the harmony. Trained dancers such as Ginny did the same for the movement. "Every dance includes a radical variety of chants from different religious traditions," she said. "By becoming swept up in all of them, we recognize our oneness with people and creeds different from us and from each other. The goal is to find peace for ourselves and with others. The dance makes a concrete manifestation of how we're trying to be better people in a better world."

I began the following week in a quandary. What was the real truth of Ithaca? The fundamentally fractured community in which Ginny's world was a fringe tolerated for its color, or a microcosm of the divided world at large in which Ginny's people were really performing the miraculous unifying function they believed they were? I wanted to witness someone from the green persuasion actively involved with people struggling in the darker corners of Ithaca. Ginny arranged for me to meet with a woman named Marjorie Olds, who was a superior court judge in the county where the Law Guardians did much of their work. "Marjorie treats aggressive yuppie lawyers like misbehaving children," Ginny said. "She's a great equalizer here in Ithaca."

Marjorie Olds stepped out of a small anteroom in superior court to meet me one morning. Not at all the motherly figure I had expected, she was a few years younger than I. She whispered that in the anteroom she was meeting with a particularly troubled case and invited me to come in and observe her work for myself.

The room in which so many life-shaking decisions were articulated to people in family court was a twenty-by-twelve-foot cubicle with a small conference table and chairs in the center. At one end of the table sat a young woman, poorly dressed in a threadbare canvas coat and sneakers whose holes were not a fashion statement. Her brown hair, pulled back with a large paperclip, needed washing. But it was the face that stopped me. Drooped into a visage of pain such as I had never seen, it was a face that had been crying and was going to go on crying for a long time—a hopeless maw of absolute loss, for which nothing could ever compensate.

The judge spoke to the girl in almost a whisper. "So do you understand what the court has had to do?"

The girl nodded and convulsed with a sob so deep it moved her chair.

"And do you understand why the court had to do what it did?"

The girl shook her head angrily and then stared straight ahead, her eyes red and wet. Judge Olds, now showing a deep complexion of the pain herself, answered, "We have to do what's best for the child, even if it's hard for you."

Then she urged the girl to stand up. "Can you take the bus or do you want us to get you a taxi? We can do that." The girl, disconsolate to the end, would not answer, did not want to leave, and finally had to be gently helped to a taxi by an officer of the court.

When she was gone, I sat in her seat in the anteroom and talked with Judge Olds. The girl was homeless, mentally retarded, and constitutionally unable to care for herself. Twenty years old, she was one of those who fifteen years ago would have been cared for in an institutional setting. But as a result of the deinstitutionalizing program promoted by a coalition of tax-cutting Reagan Republicans and "politically correct" liberals who believed that persons like her were better off integrated into communities, she had been "dumped by the system" onto the streets of Ithaca.

Unable to make responsible decisions for herself, she had become pregnant and had a baby whom she loved dearly. But she had shown a bad habit of losing track of the baby's whereabouts. Most recently she had left the baby in a shopping cart in a supermarket. The court, which meant Judge Olds, had just this day taken the baby away from her once and for all. Judge Olds assured me that this was almost a routine case, but that didn't erase the tension in her eyes and her fear that the girl might commit suicide before the day was done.

"Who picks up the ball for her when she walks out that door?" I asked.

Judge Olds explained that the girl was enrolled in HOMES, one of Ithaca's answers to the question of street people—a structured residential environment for the otherwise homeless and maladapted. "The cab driver I called works with them," she said. "He'll get her there. Her counselor will pick up while she's so vulnerable." Beyond that, the judge showed an amazing ability to put this case behind her, although she still carried the pain in her face and her gestures throughout our talk.

Born on the middle day of the twentieth century, June 16, 1950, Marjorie Olds came of age in the sixties as a hippie high-school dropout in Washington, D.C. By the time she regained her footing and

realized it would take an education and a career to harness her idealism, she had developed a habit of being just naive enough that she
didn't know she couldn't do the things she wanted to do. Thus she
applied to Johns Hopkins University and was accepted, unaware till
the day she commenced classes that Hopkins was one of the last all-
male colleges and that she was number one—the first woman to break
that barrier.

When she came to Ithaca, she knew little of Cornell and so was
unintimidated by the reputation of its law school. She graduated with
peers headed for Wall Street while all she wanted to do was work for
social justice in Ithaca. Soon, as the city's first female prosecutor, she
became a specialist in sex crimes, domestic violence, and child abuse
and founder of the Law Guardians. "During the eighties there was a
tremendous increase in the number of kids who had nothing to lose
because they had no hope," she went on. "Government said during
the Reagan years that it was a time of shrinking resources, so social
agencies had to do something like triage, spending their efforts only
on the most promising cases. We went after the ones that didn't get
through triage."

Judge Olds's success with the Law Guardians delighted Mayor
Nichols, who appointed her Ithaca's first female judge in one of his
first acts upon election. Judge Olds loved Ithaca. The ideals she'd
grown up with in the sixties were alive here. She liked living downtown, shopping at the Greenstar co-op, dallying in the coffee shops
and restaurants, and getting around on her beat–up old bicycle. She
considered it refreshing to be able to join a gay couple for dinner
without raising any eyebrows. And she and her husband pursued their
love for distressed children by serving as foster parents—ten times
over at last count.

She believed that so many people were so devoted to Ithaca because "if there is a chance for real community anywhere in America, it
would happen here, despite the fact that we are not immune to the
forces of unrest and unhappiness." It was those forces, basic facts of
life in contemporary American society, that in her view were the root
of the divisions I had observed in Ithaca. "The antidote is a community of work," she said, "where all become compatriots in improving
the quality of life for everyone."

Drinking coffee at the bar of Simeon's my last afternoon in Ithaca,

I met a man in his seventies who was a legend in the community of communes. I had heard of Sought Corliss from Ginny Miller. He came into town once or twice a week from the commune where he served as patriarch some twenty miles out in the sticks, the same commune where Ginny had once lived in her early days in Ithaca. He wore a heavy bush jacket and a hunter's cap over his bald head. Behind his thick, black-rimmed glasses twinkled the eyes of a man who had not forgotten, or perhaps recently rediscovered, his reckless youth. I asked him to tell me about the communes of the sixties and seventies and what they had to do with the life of Ithaca today.

"Oh, this was the place all right, unless you wanted to go to California," he said. "People came here from all over to do the commune thing. Thanks to Cornell and the rich hippies, it really cooked here. It took a lot of money, you know."

Sought deserted his life as a married Manhattan businessman commuting from Long Island to come to Ithaca. "I was a totally unhappy atheist till I met those kids chanting and singing about the life of the commune they were setting up here," he recalled. "They were down there recruiting, see? Now most of them are in-town yuppies with spouses and kids and dogs, and I'm still out on the commune with a new generation of young ones."

His group had started out as the "Yea God Family," founded by an avatar from India named Sia Baba. The one constant of commune life had been change and upheaval. The disciple of Sia Baba who led the Yea God group heard voices and dropped the Indian spiritual trip for a born-again-Christian philosophy, expecting his three-hundred-member group to follow. They didn't, and the group split up. "Some went for a Zen thing, some went into Zoroastrianism, some became spiritual agrarians, a few started a cult of the drug ecstasy," Sought explained. "People went all different directions, and that's what seeded more of the communes. Each new phase was like a different movie—that's what we always said, 'The movies keep changing.' "

The Zen Buddhist commune still existed, as did the agrarians at the Dawes Hill Commune. There was the Tupper Road Commune, with a large gay men's group and a lesbian women's group, though Sought had recently heard that it might be splitting up. There was also the art commune and a number of in-town communes, group houses where people led a communal urban existence.

The one permanent fixture on the piece of land that once hosted the Yea God Family, now called the Beech Hill Pond Community, was Sought Corliss himself. Today two dozen people lived on the site and owned shares of its deed as a legitimate New York State corporation. "It's mainly an aesthetic life choice today," he said. "People still call it a commune, but everyone is doing his own thing now. We try to run it democratically. I'm the old reprobate, the SOB who makes the young ones deal with the facts of life." The commune was centered around a heart-shaped pond. There was no electricity, and all heating was done with propane and firewood. There was no mail delivery, no road maintenance or snowplowing, no fire protection. But the place was still tied to Ithaca for the necessities of life and contentment. Residents had long since given up any hope of self-sufficiency, the local growing season being what it was. They spent many an hour driving to and from Ithaca for cultural and social satisfaction.

And Sought Corliss had given up any expectation that members of his communal family would stay on for the long term. "It's young ones, and the faces keep changing. Fact is, the back-to-the-land commune life now is just a way station for most. Ithaca's pretty attractive —the whole city is like a commune. For years I was so into our group that I had blinders on, not seeing other parts of life, and it's only been the past few years that I've explored the mainstream aspects of Ithaca myself.

"Ithaca's a soft city," he went on. "No skinheads or rednecks or brutal cops or shit like that. Thanks to Cornell, you can get tremendous intellectual stimulation. The commune movement was once a statement that you couldn't live in an American city and be humane— that you had to flee to your own world, 'Wooden Ships' and all that. But here people can have their cake and eat it too."

"Seems like the sixties never ended in Ithaca," I said.

"Wrong," he countered. "No, Ithaca looks more like the sixties today than it did in the sixties."

"Will you ever move into the city?" I asked him.

He answered by way of a story. There was a time when he had left the commune to work for a year for the Peace Corps in Samoa. He had gone for a walk in the woods near the commune before departing. In previous walks, he had always just seen the white tails of deer fleeing as he approached. But on this day he walked into a clearing and realized that he was standing in the midst of a herd of a dozen, maybe two dozen deer, who placidly stood there chewing and looking at him. "It was like they knew I was leaving and they allowed me to say good-bye," he thought. "There are people doing wonderful things in Ithaca. But I don't know if there's a place in town for a person who experiences miracles like that. Someone has to stay on the mountain and listen for the voice of God."

For me, Ithaca was a strange homecoming. Nothing in my memory of growing up in Rockefeller Republican central New York had prepared me for what I found there. No place I had been ever evinced such a broad-based commitment to community idealism.

Ithaca might have rated close to five for Cheers on the 10,000 Waves scale—there certainly was a lifestyle built around its third places, and if you were part of the green movement, like Ginny Miller, the whole city was one great third place. But people at the Moonshadow on the commons did not mix with those at Ruloff's in Collegetown. Folks at the State Diner didn't visit Simeon's. There were public figures here who really did not like one another. Yet I found no one who disagreed radically with the basic philosophical goals of Ithaca's liberal mainstream. It was the strangest thing, that a community of such apparent ideological solidarity could be so divided socially and culturally.

Maybe I had it all backward. Maybe the point of Ithaca was what the greens said it was—that class and social tensions were a natural fact of life in American society and that only a solidarity of ideological idealism could bind those divisions. Maybe Ithaca was a place where the power of intellect lifted people to a level of tolerance transcending social division. Certainly Ithaca rated a five for Someplace. I never found another place quite like it, though my next stop was its perfect reverse image.

10

GREEN CHRISTMAS

BURLINGTON, VERMONT

Between Ithaca and Burlington, the headlines had the Clinton victory in the presidential election and people being shot in their cars on Florida's Interstate 295. In an effort to do the right thing, the federal government had initiated a civil rights case against the police officers who had savaged Rodney King, inadvertently setting up a scenario under which the L.A. riots might happen again. It was Christmas week, and I approached Burlington full of hope for making America a better place to live while the air echoed with reminders of how far most places had to go.

Burlington was the other American city that had made headlines by electing a socialist city government under Bernie Sanders, who had now been sent to Congress via the recent election. Sanders's successor, Mayor Peter Clavell, called his administration Progressive but he was the clear inheritor of Sanders's socialist mantle.

As late in the season as it was, it hadn't yet snowed here in northern Vermont, where snow is worth its weight in hundred-dollar bills. Stowe and Sugarbush were emptying the Green Mountain creeks to make snow for the skiers and had produced an environmentalist backlash typical of the new age in Vermont.

The old New England was nonexistent in both Vermont and my own New Hampshire. Both states had long since been overrun by folks from the "flatlands" who had migrated to New England to escape the perils of megalopolis and had changed fundamentally the character of their adopted homes. But the two states had fared very differently in this regard. Because of its stronger antitax tradition, New Hampshire attracted many flatlanders who were concerned primarily about conserving their money. As a result, what was preserved and exploited of the old Yankee tradition in New Hampshire was often the worst of it —the small-minded, petty, penny-pinching, antisocial mentality that made New Hampshire the most politically retrograde state north of Alabama.

Vermont got flatlanders intent on finding a good place to live, and so the state's politics had become radically different from those of its neighbor. The pieces of Yankee tradition that did survive there involved the values associated with the traditional New England village green and streaks of common sense, tolerance, and true libertarianism that had become so rare elsewhere in New England that they were no longer counted as New England virtues.

Burlington was the queen city of Vermont—indeed, at thirty-nine thousand in population, its only real city. When I was in college down the road in the late sixties, Burlington wasn't much. People came to town in those days to buy things or see a movie they didn't have out in East Overshoe. As a small city in a state with a dominant rural ethic, it was an appendix, a utility room in the house of state. The real Vermont was, by definition, anyplace but Burlington.

This hadn't always been the case. Railroad barons of the late nineteenth century recognized that with its strategic location at the junction of three natural rail corridors on the shore of an inland sea, Burlington would become a transportation nexus for rail and barge traffic linking Boston and New York with Canada. Here would rise a sophisticated metropolis, a center of education for the state, and a cosmopolitan gateway to Canada in a stunning natural setting. So they bought up the waterfront, laid out the downtown grid, and built much of the downtown's Victorian architecture, anticipating a grand future that went south with the failing New England mill economy in the early twentieth century. When the rail industry also began to decline, only the University of Vermont (UVM) and the city's role as general store for the surrounding rural area kept Burlington on the map at all.

In recent years, Burlington finally came to realize its ancient mission when several factors, including the expansion of UVM, the arrival of IBM and GE, and the exodus from megalopolis, created a demand for urban values in this corner of Vermont. The newcomers rediscovered the marvelous architecture of the Church Street storefronts, the pedestrian compactness of the downtown grid, and perhaps most important, the city's geographical setting, which had been too easy to overlook during the years of Burlington's neglect.

Located on a hillside crowned by the University of Vermont and sloping down to Lake Champlain, Burlington occupied a physical site that no eastern city could match. Across the lake to the west, and visible from virtually every street in the city, were the summits of the Adirondack Mountains of New York. To the east loomed the highest peaks of the Green Mountains, including Mount Mansfield, home of Stowe, the East's premier ski resort, and Camel's Hump, a rocky pyramid of verticality not at all like the modest "rolling hills" image many people have of these mountains.

Once a saltwater sea, Lake Champlain is a very big lake—much bigger than Cayuga—125 miles long and 10 miles across at its widest point, which is precisely at Burlington. Driving around Burlington and the surrounding environs, I felt a sense of "big-sky" country I experienced nowhere else in the East. With mountains on two sides and the expanse of the lake, Burlington offered an eastern approximation of the feel of the great Northwest cities, Seattle in particular. And as Seattle had world-class Vancouver just an hour's drive across the border, Burlington had Montreal about the same distance north. The difference, of course, was that Burlington was a small city.

Besides setting, the next thing I noted was a dichotomy of exurban sprawl on the outskirts and a particularly vital and novel downtown configuration. It was as if people couldn't decide which way to live in Burlington, as commuters from the surrounding country or as truly urban residents downtown.

Burlington's downtown seemed to have the best of several worlds and a future to boot. There was a traditional Main Street—with cars and parking spaces, restaurants, a grassy park in front of the city hall, and a marquee theater—linking an underdeveloped waterfront to the university at the top of the hill. But midway between these points, at the city hall, was the intersection of Church Street, which had developed as a second "main street," with attractive Victorian and early-twentieth-century architecture and a high density of establishments. Church Street had been turned into a downtown pedestrian mall, so Burlington had been able to have it both ways—a traditional auto-based Main Street and a pedestrian mall.

I spent my first few days in Burlington cruising Church Street. Although it was predictably crazed this last week before Christmas, I was assured by shoppers I talked to that this pedestrian mall was always busy. There were no lulls in the action, no waves. People were continually strolling and bustling about the bricked street. Open-air vendors of hot dogs, jewelry, woolen goods, watercolor canvases, and bagels did a brisk business from 9:00 A.M. till 9:00 P.M. even with the temperature below freezing. The doors to the stores, restaurants, and shops on Church Street were swinging and cash registers were ringing.

There were a lot of likely-looking third places on Church Street and people seemed to have a good habit of frequenting them. But one in particular stood out, Leunig's Old World Cafe, located on the corner of Church and College. I had noticed outside speakers on this corner playing Gregorian chants and had thought it was a nice touch by the city. But it turned out that the music was piped from inside Leunig's, where the regime was strictly classical. The music drew me in.

The place lived up to its name, with a corner bar dominated by a huge authentic cappuccino machine and just a handful of tables scattered in a rather small room. Overhead, a large crystal chandelier and a 1930s vintage wooden fan hung from a white painted tin ceiling. In the center of the room, separating the smoking and nonsmoking tables, a standing street clock ticked off bar time. Behind the bar, Greek statuary subordinated the rows of spirits bottles, and on the bar itself sat a large glass vase containing an elaborate flower arrangement of roses and gardenias. Counterpoint to the otherwise classical theme was the sign over the door to the lavatories, PISSOIR, and a two-foot-tall plaster cupid on the bar which dispensed the house wine from its penis.

Behind the bar, a heavy man with a shock of graying hair and magnificent handlebar mustache chatted with half a dozen regulars in for the lunch hour. A tall stack of newspapers on the corner of the bar —*New York Times, Wall Street Journal,* Boston *Globe,* and Burlington *Free Press*—was the key to how Leunig's worked. People came in and read as they sipped their cappuccino or munched their lunch and then talked about the news at the bar. Others with more solitary intentions, ranging from studying college students to homemakers paying bills to shoppers and cops taking a break, settled in with a paper at one of the tables. But in Leunig's, people stayed awhile, and sooner or later most of them joined the current political discussion going on at the bar. Bob Conlon, the day bartender, arrived as early as five-thirty in the morning to read all of the day's papers and so be prepared to preside over the discussions that began with regulars in for "Bob's Breakfast Club" at seven o'clock.

I had never seen an American café that so fulfilled the formula described by Ray Oldenburg in *The Great Good Place.* There was a man standing at the end of the bar talking to a foot patrol cop about a street person who had been hassling shoppers. The man was Dennis Morriseau, owner of Leunig's. Soon he sat next to me and, after brief introductions, suggested that Oldenburg's was a book I ought to read. He had read it and patterned his place after Oldenburg's precepts.

Dennis was a vigorous, handsome fellow in his forties with a repu-tation for expressing strong opinions. "The only good things that ever happened in this country came out of bars," he began. "They sure as hell didn't come out of churches." Dennis had made a long transition from sixties radical to nineties libertarian conservative. He had pro-tested the Vietnam War with Al Lowenstein in front of the White House and later become one of the original founders of the Liberty Union party, the socialist group that launched Bernie Sanders. But after he'd been back in Vermont awhile, he began to listen to Republi-can friends who kept saying, "It's a phase, you'll get over it." He did. Now he was an outspoken opponent of the programs of Progressive Mayor Clavell, although he still considered him a personal friend. "That's the way it is in Burlington," he explained. "There are plenty of people here to disagree with, the whole Birkenstock do-the-right-thing crowd. But people can be misguided and still be good people that you care about and like to talk to."

Dennis had opened Leunig's in the late seventies before the city turned Church Street into a pedestrian mall. At that time the place, with its perfect location, was an abandoned A & W outlet that nobody wanted. "People thought the downtown had no future," he said. "We bought this place for a song and fitted it out for peanuts. Most everything you see in here we got from salvage—the clock, the statues, the cupid." The marble for the bar came from slabs found in a farmer's field that Dennis cut himself with an expendable Skil saw.

Meanwhile, the city countered the perceived threat from malls scheduled for construction on the booming outskirts with its plan for the pedestrian mall. It had actually been discussed for some twenty years by progressive businesspeople, who tested the idea by temporarily closing the street to auto traffic—infuriating the rural Vermonters who had come into town to do their shopping chores. Then there was a series of false starts. The first plan, by architect Bill Treux, called for excavating down to the footings of the buildings and setting up retail in basement levels, something like Montreal's Ville Marie. Support for the idea collapsed at the last moment, and in the subsequent scramble, another design team came along with a minimal plan for bricking the street and creating a formal layout of tall trees with benches, European style. "That's the plan we should have built," Dennis believed. "But the business community had gotten hooked on glitz, so they called in Cal Lynch Associates, who had done Poughkeepsie."

Lynch's people proposed laying the brick in wave patterns to remind people of Lake Champlain and incorporating hunks of rock to invoke the rural mountain heritage. Storefronts would be sheltered by glass canopies that looked light and airy on the drawing boards. "But they turned out like bridges built to withstand a direct nuclear hit," Dennis said. "We got rid of the wave patterns but the rocks remained, and the only way to get your place clear of that god-awful canopy is to have it declared a historic building."

Although he had quibbles with details of the plan, Dennis couldn't fault its role in Burlington's recent success story. "What really powers this town is IBM coming here thirty years ago and then staying here, and GE, and the medical center at the University, and now recently Burton Snowboards and Bombardier [a Canadian manufacturer of railway cars]. You don't get that kind of continuing corporate attention unless you've made the city itself pretty attractive," he declared. Dennis thought that Burlington had discovered the formula for creat-

ing a truly cosmopolitan environment in a small city and that it would
continue to attract and retain business while other places struggled
with the recession. He believed it would take a full-blown depression
to defeat the area now.

Not that there weren't, in his view, people whose misguided leadership threatened to inhibit Burlington's future. The city had another
largely undeveloped asset in its waterfront. Dennis was well aware of
the miracles that places like San Antonio, Portland, and Vancouver
had performed with waterfronts. "We've got a waterfront with potential that rivals those places," he argued, "and look what the greens
have done with it—they've made it a green desert."

Burlington's waterfront had been the object of conflict for years.
When a legal settlement finally awarded the city control of seventy-six
acres after a long struggle with the railroads, a new controversy commenced among local interests with different visions of the land's future. Some wanted the city to auction it off to private developers to let
"market forces" shape its future. Others envisaged various schemes of
public-private partnership in developing a waterfront with both public and profit values. But the most activist faction was one that wanted
it protected from private exploitation entirely and kept open to public
values exclusively. "So we got a half-assed mini–commercial area and
a boathouse and Siberia on the water," Dennis said with disgust.

I asked him what kind of plan he would have preferred, and again
it seemed as if he had been reading the same things I had. "You've got
to have waterfront commercial areas that become an extension of the
downtown," he answered. "And you've got to create thriving adjacent
residential neighborhoods so that there are bodies with money in their
pockets walking around there on foot." But the Progressives in city
hall and their green supporters out on the hustings saw Dennis's vision as nothing but the most overintensive, exploitative option of all.

I left Leunig's to hike down to the water and see for myself what
all the fuss was about. Separating the downtown from the lakefront
was a bit of the usual former railroad and warehouse dereliction.
From the water, a vast lawn stretched northward to a distant woods—
Dennis's "Siberia." The only attractive feature about it, besides the
fact that it hadn't been despoiled, was a magnificent bike path that ran
the length of the waterfront. Immediately below College Avenue, a
floating "lake house" anchored the center of the little harbor inside

the breakwater. It looked like a private club but turned out to be a public amenity provided by the city. With a restaurant and spaces inside for children's activities, it was said to be a focal point of social gatherings on warm summer nights and during ice-skating season. At the moment, though, the ice had not formed yet and it looked deserted.

South of the lake house were the public piers and the dock for the ferry to New York. And finally, at the southern end of the property, I came upon what looked like a mini downtown, like Main Street in a town of two thousand people. Burlington's chamber of commerce was located here, as were a sporting goods store, a couple of little restaurants, and other specialty stores. I had to concur with Dennis Morriseau that this was hardly enough to energize a waterfront.

Still, Burlington hadn't done anything to ruin it yet—the wonderful potential was there. Nothing blocked Burlingtoners' view of clouds scudding over the Adirondacks across the lake and the islands with their stately pines to the north and south. A pedestrian could approach the water at virtually any point along the entire shoreline. Children could sit in the grass and watch the ferry or the tug-drawn barges tracing their wakes on the gray slate of the winter lake.

"I think it's super what they're not doing with the waterfront," said Mark Johnson as we sat at Leunig's bar one evening. Mark was the young owner of a local radio station who had carried on a long "dialogue" with the proprietor of his favorite local watering hole. "You have to understand, Dennis is seen as the point man for the far-conservative business wing of Burlington politics. Though he runs the best public house in town, he does not represent the mainstream."

Mark was glad that schemes to build six-story condos by the water had been defeated by a two-thirds referendum vote. He liked being able to walk three blocks from downtown into the waterfront green space and feel a true sense of being out in the open in the heart of a city. He also liked the rhythms of community activity there—the festival weekends, when it seemed as if the whole city converged by the water; the ice-skating evenings, when the boathouse served as warming hut and social center; the summertime concerts. But the times between these events, when the waterfront was a quiet refuge from the hustle and noise of city life, were just as valuable, he believed.

It was Mark who first told me about "Westward Ho!" when he

returned to the theme of the politics of Leunig's proprietor. "If you want to really get a rise out of Dennis sometime, ask him about Westward Ho!" As in Ithaca, Burlington's "kinder, gentler" Progressive government and its amenable open public spaces had attracted more than one city's share of homeless people; I had noticed a number of them on Church Street the past few days. In the early days of the influx, the city provided homeless shelters with little or no attempt at regulating the potentially disruptive conduct of street people, many of whom were alcoholics or drug addicts or severly emotionally disturbed. "This enraged Dennis," Mark explained. "It was his view that homeless people were allowed to do things that would get anybody else arrested, just because they were homeless." There were several whom Church Street merchants considered a real danger, including one drunk who had taken the windows out of a lot of downtown establishments and threatened to physically assault shoppers.

"Dennis decided to take a free enterprise shot at solving the problem. So he collected money from downtown merchants to buy one-way bus tickets for some of these guys to places out West," Mark explained. "He pitched the plan not as charity but as an investment in downtown improvement and called it 'Westward Ho!' " Mark, then a reporter for the *Free Press,* got the story and really ran with it. The liberal public was outraged. The *Free Press* sold a lot of papers.

"What made it such a good story was that Dennis was so true to his ideology," Mark continued. " 'Westward Ho' was formally incorporated under state statute and thus left a paper trail to every contributor as well as to Dennis as prime organizer. What a stink. He wouldn't speak to me for a year."

Only one miscreant ever actually got on a bus—the window smasher, who was now reportedly smashing windows somewhere in Oregon. "But you could say that Dennis eventually won the war," Mark added. Despite the public outcry over the tactics of Westward Ho! the issue of public conduct by recipients of the city's welfare efforts got on the political agenda. And even the Progressives bought into the idea that homeless people should be held accountable for their conduct the same as anyone else.

When I later asked Dennis about Westward Ho! he insisted that the scheme had actually begun with a social worker's suggestion that the window smasher repeatedly expressed a desire to go to Oregon.

"We just wanted to help him realize his dream," he said facetiously. When I asked him about forming a corporation and leaving a paper trail, he explained that the intent was to manage liability issues and to make donations tax-exempt. But he wasn't sure he'd do it that way again.

"The unfortunate thing is that the issue obscured a lot of other, perhaps more responsible, activist things we did that really turned city policy around," Dennis contended. The corporation collected fourteen affidavits from women assaulted by one street person and got the state attorney to prosecute. In another case, it prepared a suit against Howard Mental Health for inadequate supervision of dangerously disturbed individuals. The threat of the suit alone forced Howard to institute new procedures. Dennis had been active in pushing the city to institute the foot patrol police, who now strictly enforced public drunkenness and disorderly conduct laws. Street drunks were rounded up and sent to detox. Harassment of other citizens was not tolerated. And the homeless shelters themselves established rules for behavior and personal care followed up by aggressive caseworker supervision.

Henceforth I couldn't walk Church Street without being conscious of the presence of the street people and, even more so, the cops. I realized that I had never seen a downtown before where police were such a ubiquitous visual presence. They were physically big and wore spiffy dark blue SWAT squad–style uniforms, black combat boots, and billed caps; and with their buckles and radios and clearly displayed pistols and nightsticks, they presented an image that I thought many of the local Birkenstockers would surely call Gestapo.

One morning I watched two of them apprehend an elderly drunk, firmly take away his bottle, and gently guide him to a patrol car, which whisked him off to the detox unit. When a deranged woman danced barefoot on the cold bricks one day, two foot cops watched her from a distance until she began taking off her clothes. Then they were quickly beside her, advising first in friendly terms of the cold and then in more authoritarian tones of the ordinance concerning public nudity. She thanked them for their concern and continued her dance, fully clothed.

Despite the dominance of city politics by what Dennis called the liberal do-the-right-thing crowd, I never heard anyone in Burlington voice the old left-wing rhetoric about aggressive cops. Even college students, particularly the women, seemed to accept their presence as a welcome guarantee of personal security.

One night I stepped into the stairwell of a parking garage after a late evening of shooting pool with a few of those college students and wished for a moment that this hadn't been one of the few places where there was not a cop in sight. Some of the lightbulbs in the stairway were out and it was gloomy in there. As the steel door slammed shut behind me, I saw them, four figures sprawled in the shadows on the floor in a circle, of which I was the center. Two of them held quart bottles of Old Milwaukee in their hands and all eight bleary eyes were on me.

"Got any extra cigarettes?" said one with neither menace nor friendliness in his voice. I fumbled for my pack and passed out four. "Thanks. He's OK," said the man who had asked for cigarettes. "Drink?" and he held up his quart toward me. I declined but pulled out a fifth cigarette for myself and sat down on the step nearest the quickest exit from the circle.

The man who had spoken called himself Dumpster Don and introduced the others as Tom, Dick, and Harry. They were all drunk, but Don was intelligent and as articulate as anyone at the billiards bar at this hour. Tom was absolutely incoherent, slobbering and uttering only guttural sounds, like a suffering animal. He was dying of AIDS, the others said. Dick was not much better off, alternating between catatonic hypnotic glazes and outbursts of drunken anger and hubris. Even in the dark I could see huge swollen bruises along the veins of his bare arms. Harry was coherent, like Don, and the two of them seemed to be buddies.

"Ever hear of something called Westward Ho!?" I asked.

"Aw shit, you work for Dennis?" Don groaned. "He still doin' that shit? Don't give me no fucking bus ticket. I'm a happy citizen of Burlington." And he raised his bottle to giggles all around.

After I explained my real purpose in Burlington, Dick rallied from one of his stupors and began shouting, "Writer, my ass. I could be a writer, I could be anything I want, I'll be mayor of this town soon so watch what you say . . ." He rambled on until Don shouted him down. "You wanna be a star, be a star. You wanta tell the truth, tell the truth. The man's here for the truth."

Don was a veteran of Korea and Vietnam. When he returned from

Vietnam to his hometown of Woburn, Massachusetts, his life fell apart "because nobody knew anybody anymore." He became a drunk who fetched up here in Burlington and got a job working as a dishwasher for Dennis Morriseau. "I got nothing against Dennis, he was OK to work for. But Westward Ho! was a piece of shit," he said. "It's like someone trying to bring the niggers back to Africa where they came from. You can't do people like that."

When I mentioned the window smasher who had been bused off to Oregon, they all giggled again. "He came back, but they don't know it," laughed Harry. "He lays low and he don't smash windows no more, but he's here."

But Don interjected, "Guys like that make life tough for the rest of us good old drunks." Don had been sleeping out in the open for twenty years, even during the time he had a job with Dennis. "Everybody's got his own spot for the winter," he confided. "There's a lot of people sleeping on the streets trying to make a meal by day and get a buzz at night. You go to the shelters and get thrown out of the fucking Salvation Army for not following the rules and decide it's easier on the street till it gets cold and you go back to the shelters again. You choose the life you lead. We're just plain old drunks."

Harry lifted his quart to Don and said, "But some are better drunks than others. If there's a person I ever met closer to a perfect Santa Claus, it's Dumpster Don. He's my friend. He's everybody's friend." Don got his nickname because, as a dumpster diver for twenty years, he had established a reputation for charity. "He always found whatever he needed and then he kept on looking and found stuff for everybody else," Harry continued. "He done donated more stuff to charity—TVs, stereos, blankets, furniture, bicycles, things the kids throw out. There's guys that owe more to him than to any fucking social worker."

Don was embarrassed. "Shut the fuck up, will you?"

But Harry pressed on. "He knows all the camp spots and helps others find 'em. He even made friends with a couple of the cops and showed them his spots so they could send guys there who were really hurting. He's a beam, man, like a light—just shinin' in the dark. We all just follow the beam."

There was emotion in his voice as he spoke this. The group fell silent and I got up to leave. As I went up the steps, Don called out after me, "You write in your book, a man can find real friends here in Burlington, even a dumpster-divin' drunk like me. You write that. That's the truth about Burlington. Isn't that what makes a good place to live?"

If Dennis Morriseau represented the right side of the entrepreneurial world in Burlington, Jerry Greenfield, the Jerry of Ben and Jerry's ice cream, staked out the left. We sat in the corner window of Leunig's one morning and over cups of cappuccino he told me the story that had become legend among people interested in making a lot of money while doing the right thing. Jerry was a large man of my generation with longish thinning hair and a careless mien that didn't quite fit his expensive country catalog clothes. He looked like a man who might be more at ease in secondhand Salvation Army duds.

It all began with a friendship. He and Ben had been friends since seventh grade growing up on Long Island. After college, the two brainstormed for something they could do together to make a living and have some fun. Ice cream seemed like fun, and people surely would buy it, so they took a correspondence course from Penn State in ice-cream making. When it came time to look for a warm city in which to set up shop, they found that others, particularly Baskin Robbins, had gotten there ahead of them. Besides a climate that seemed appropriate for ice-cream sales, they wanted a rural setting and the presence of a college. Ben had spent some time in the Adirondacks and suggested Burlington, which had no ice-cream parlors. Jerry fell in love with its juxtaposition of a vital downtown with the lake and mountains.

"So much for the warm climate," Jerry shrugged. "People thought we were crazy." They found an abandoned gas station on College Avenue about a block from Leunig's, fixed it up, and opened in May of 1978 with one five-gallon rock salt ice-cream maker and an old player piano. "We made it a funky place with a community bulletin board where people would come in and hang out. We took an oath that if we were still in business a year down the road, we would set aside a day and give away free ice cream. We never dreamed it would become what it has."

The first year was hard. When the temperature went down to zero for days at a time that winter, people stopped walking in. So Ben and Jerry started delivering to local restaurants out of an old VW

Squareback wagon. "We weren't trying to expand," he said, "just survive." It was the same motivation that prompted them to sell pint containers to mom-and-pop groceries around the state. When they eventually began to contemplate serious expansion, mainly to hold their ground against copycat competitors, they made their first radical business decision.

"We didn't want to go to a venture capitalist for money. We wanted the community to be involved in the craziness with us," he explained. So they issued an in-state stock offering, Vermont's first ever. The minimum purchase was set at $126 so that anyone could afford to buy. "Even so, we were a huge risk," Jerry said. "But eventually one out of every one hundred families in this city bought in. We've tried to remain very appreciative."

"What would I have now if I had bought in at the minimum $126 nine years ago?" I asked.

"About two thousand dollars," he answered. "I guess a lot of our investors are appreciative today too."

From the start, Ben and Jerry had exercised their urge to be a focal point in the community by giving away ice cream for public festivals, showing free outdoor movies on the wall of a neighboring building, and maintaining the most thorough bulletin board in town. But once they began to realize that they seemed destined for success, they grew philosophical. "We asked ourselves, What does a business do? It makes money. So we concluded that in order to be socially responsible, we had to give away money." They established their own version of Minneapolis's corporate tithe, 7.5 percent, through the Ben and Jerry's Foundation.

"Soon we were overwhelmed with requests for money, far more than we could accommodate. So we took the question a step further: What else can a business that generates money and a product do to contribute to a better world?" That's when they came up with the two ideas so closely associated with them today: the products with a message and the program of selectively doing business with other businesses operating under a similar socially responsible philosophy. It started with the famous Peace Pop. "Here we had a product and packaging that could remind millions of people at moments when they are in a positive frame of mind about an important global issue," Jerry said. With Rain Forest Crunch, they put substance behind their message by using nuts harvested by organic methods that protected a sustainable rain forest. With the Chocolate Fudge Brownie, they imported ingredients from a New York cooperative that dedicated profits to helping the homeless. And then there was the matter of simply investing their money with institutions providing novel and innovative approaches to community nurturing across the country. One of Jerry's current favorites was the South Shore Bank of Chicago, which had done so much to funnel loans to inner-city neighborhoods struggling toward renaissance.

"It's been an evolution, and we're still learning," Jerry told me that day in Leunig's. "All along the key has been to show that you can have a business that gives back to the community, whether it be local, national, or global."

I asked him if he thought Burlington provided particularly fertile ground for such an enterprise. "If you mean something about the economic climate here," he answered, "I don't think our success was ever based on the economics of the city, but on the values of the community of people here that supported us. Progressive business comes to a place where there's a vibrant sense of community values. Values first. The economics follow."

I had to suspend my sojourn in Burlington for the Christmas holiday with my family. When I returned a few weeks later, the temperature was in the single digits, but it still hadn't snowed. The downtown was active, however—perhaps at slower pace, but the quality was the same. Nothing kept these Burlingtoners from getting out and about their downtown on foot, not cold, not a lack of the manna of snow, not the traditional postholiday lull.

For Christmas, my teenage daughter had been delighted to find in her packages a CD entitled *A Picture of Nectar* from the emerging alternative rock band Phish. Nectar, it turned out, was Nectar Rorris, owner of Nectar's Place in Burlington, where Phish had gotten their start. After Ben and Jerry's, Ithaca's Moosewood Cafe, Minneapolis's appearance on "Thirtysomething," Missoula's *A River Runs Through It,* Vancouver's Greenpeace, and Napa's Silver Oaks Winery, it no longer surprised me to find names that had become part of the popular iconography associated with sites touted as good places to live. The New Agers liked to talk about locations with physical nodes of creative energy. It seemed more likely to me that it was a matter of natural selection; people with creative instincts naturally gravitated toward places with certain qualities of community.

Nectar's Place, on Main Street, had two large rooms. On one side it was a classic cafeteria-style diner specializing in huge, cheap mounds of meat and potatoes and an offering for late-night seekers of fries with gravy. On the other it was a circular bar with an area where local musicians performed every night of the year while listeners lounged in scattered hard-back chairs. When I visited, an obscure group of earnest hopefuls played a song entitled "It's Been a Whole Lot Easier Since Phish Left Town."

Nectar Rorris was a short, mustachioed, balding man who had come to Burlington from Greece by way of ten years in Chicago. Working with an uncle, he had opened up Burlington's first fifteen-cent hamburger joint in the sixties. He had worked for a stint at a Holiday Inn but declared, "I was never a suit-and-tie kind of guy. I just wanted to make a business of my own and I knew from how it was in Greece that to do that you had to make friendships." He started out cultivating contacts with other young Burlingtoners, but he found that as he got older, the age of those he related to best remained the same.

In 1975 the place that would become Nectar's was what he called "a hi-hat place. They had a doorman in a tuxedo who came out and took your order. The place had a niche but it was losing ground. I had a different idea." So he took an option and set up the cafeteria-diner format with the idea of running volume at five dollars a plate rather than the sparse clientele the old place got at twenty dollars. "I thought I would have a small piano bar, quiet, cozy. But the young crowd followed me in here, hungry for their kind of music. Give the people what they want, I say. So I started doing the bands—no cover, and I didn't pay them much. But it gave them a place to play and be heard. It made me and my place popular. I liked that."

When the state raised the drinking age from eighteen to twenty-one, many of the nightclubs in town went under, but not Nectar's. "People knew I had made a commitment to the musicians," Nectar believed. "We needed each other. I gave 'em guaranteed dates, helped them buy instruments with credit on future performances in here. They paid me back by generating an audience while other places went empty."

Nectar Rorris became a pillar in the downtown community, sponsoring a basketball team and the Special Olympics, supporting the New Year's Eve celebration First Night and the fund drive to save the Flynn marquee theater. And then there was Phish. "They were just a bunch of UVM music majors when they started coming in here," Nectar explained. "They didn't have much material and couldn't do much more than one set. People thought they were outrageous; we'd stick their little set in between some heavy metal guys who could go all evening long, and people would come in just for that half hour. We ended up giving them whole evenings, where they mostly practiced and experimented with new ideas. When something didn't work out, they would just stop and try something else. It was spontaneous music, I mean they just fooled around with nobody telling what they could or couldn't do—and got some of their best music out of it. Songs like 'Bouncing Around the Room' happened that way."

Eventually the band got a manager who knew what he was doing, and with a little help from local radio stations, Phish was on its way up and out of Burlington. "But they came back after they were famous to play at the Flynn and support the fund drive. They stopped in here to say hello. And they put a picture of me on their album cover. They're good boys. They don't forget their roots."

Nectar thought the key to Burlington was youth, and he didn't mean just the students of UVM. "We got a lot of young doctors at the medical center and a lot of young professionals at IBM. Burlington has a lot to offer if you are ready to do it, and people with a young spirit are coming here and making contributions. There's a lot of air to breathe here." And echoing precisely Philip Till's sentiments driving over the Lion's Gate Bridge every morning in Vancouver, Nectar Rorris said, "When I drive into town from my home in South Burlington every morning, I look out at that lake and the Adirondacks and think, What a feeling! It's a place where I'll never get old."

I asked him what he would do to perpetuate Burlington's advantages if he were mayor. "We need to develop the waterfront," he answered. "It needs a mix of commercial business and open space, no more of this arguing about it being all one or the other." Second, he thought Burlington needed to build on what it had begun with the pedestrian mall on Church Street. "People are coming back to cities because they want to be able to park their car and walk. They're getting sick of driving cars everywhere. In Chicago I had to get in my car to buy a newspaper. Here I walk." Nectar wanted to see the city's bus system expanded and perhaps a trolley connecting the waterfront to the heart of downtown.

Public safety was his third point. "Nothing works in a city if people don't feel safe. We do OK, but we have our problems with drugs, alcohol, and wise guys."

"What about the street people?" I asked.

"They're just like anybody else, they come to Vermont to find peace of mind too. You have to do something to give them what they came here for and then expect something in return," he explained. "Most of them just need a break, and everybody has to work, so there it is."

"You mean government should make jobs for them?"

"No, no. We don't live in that kind of country; we don't go to a government store and stand in line to get a loaf of bread. No, it's my responsibility, I have to make jobs for them, and Dennis Morriseau and all the other businessmen downtown."

Government's limited role, in Nectar's eyes, was to provide space, parking, transportation alternatives, safety, lines of communication between segments of the community, and promotion of life in the downtown. "You know, the mayor who did all that and put Burlington on the map was a Socialist, Bernie Sanders," Nectar remonstrated. "He promoted the arts and the jazz festival, and the reggae festival, First Night, and a lot of other stuff that brought new business into town. And on the other side, guys like Dennis Morriseau make a lot of conservative noise but do their own contribution to the community. You shouldn't pay too much attention to all the political talk. They do that just for sport."

One morning in Leunig's, all discussion turned to the local headlines: CITY PASSES BENEFITS PLAN FOR DOMESTIC PARTNERS. The city had extended health benefits, previously available only to marital partners and children of employees, to cover all domestic partners, including gay partners, live-in lovers, and potentially anyone else who happened to reside full-time in the same house as a city employee. Dennis's archconservative morning bartender, Bob Conlon, was in humorous high dudgeon against this latest move by Mayor Clavell's Progressives in city hall. "Come live with me and be my lover, and I will all your medical bills cover," he sang out with gales of laughter. "What a great pick-up line—'Come on home with me, if you get pregnant, you're covered.'"

This was the kind of issue that exercised the differences in Burlingtoners' politics. The legislation had begun as a move to offer fair and equal treatment to gay couples but had expanded as a result of the difficulty in legally defining the key point of qualification, which now was simply long-term cohabitation and declaration of personal commitment. "It's the most foolish thing they've come up with yet, but if you oppose it, you'll be labeled a homophobe," explained Bob. "But there's a silver lining here. This could be the hook that finally yanks the Progressives down."

Armed now with an issue that would put me on a level playing field with any mayor bent on droning the usual promotional spiel for visiting journalists, I went to the city hall, just a block down Church Street from Leunig's, to talk with Mayor Clavell that afternoon.

Unlike the tiny, disorderly, side street building out of which Ben Nichols ran Ithaca, Burlington's city hall was an edifice, an imposing building with large, airy hallways, an auditorium, and warrens of brightly lit, efficiently organized offices. Mayor Clavell himself had a corner office worthy of a CEO. He was a soft-spoken, pleasant, balding man with a ready smile and a reserve of equanimity. He was nothing of the firebrand that Bernie Sanders had been and viewed his role in the historical political evolution of Burlington as one who cemented liberal gains and managed an orderly extension of the Progressive program. I couldn't help but personally warm to him as he began by candidly acknowledging that Sanders and the Progressives' ascension to power had been largely a fluke.

Sanders had been elected by only ten votes in 1981 when longtime Democratic incumbent Gordon Paquette had dismissed him as a fringe challenger. "The old guard was caught off guard," Clavell explained. "And there was a Republican and other minor candidates who siphoned off votes. Bernie stirred up passion among a unique coalition of low-income people, students, young professionals, disenfranchised elderly, renters, gays, and a small core of traditional leftward thinkers." The Progressive movement Clavell inherited now seemed so well established largely because Burlington had boomed economically under Sanders, a development his ideological opponents couldn't have foreseen and were at a loss to explain.

Clavell believed that perhaps the boldest move of the entire Sanders tenure was entering into the complicated process of litigation, legislation, confrontation, and negotiation that led to the city acquiring control of the prime waterfront acreage from the railroad. "Bernie really touched a nerve when he announced that the waterfront was not for sale—'We may not own it but it's ours,' " Clavell believed. "But we had no idea what a fight we would then have among ourselves over what we were going to do with it."

After an uprising by their own green supporters against the Progressives' plan for mixed commercial and green space development, the north forty acres was set aside as an urban reserve, a land bank for future generations. With a mischievous laugh, Clavell said, "Essentially we decided, 'We've had so much fun arguing over the future of the Burlington waterfront that we're going to save a chunk for our children to argue about.' " There were still a few additional improvements on the boards: a science center, some public housing, and some expansion of the existing commercial center toward the center of the property. But the thrust would be preservation of the current fragile and rather minimal public consensus on the waterfront. And again Clavell flashed that playful grin of a man with too much candor to keep a straight face while playing politics.

Besides establishing a cease-fire on the waterfront issue, I asked him what else he would point to as accomplishments of his tenure. He launched into issues about which he clearly felt some passion. "Our homeless policy is one of the hallmarks of the Progressive administration," he said. "Our aim is to decommodify housing. We believe housing is a basic right, not just another commodity for sale." His administration had established a "tenure ladder" under which the homeless could move from life on the streets to emergency shelter, to single-room occupancy, to home ownership. The city had entered into partnership with the nonprofit housing sector, funding the program through philanthropy and a significant increase in property taxes approved directly by the voters.

At the same time, the city moved to create the aggressive foot patrol police presence that, in a sense, rewarded the voters' generosity with increased public safety. "We knew we would become a draw for homeless from other places, so we took an aggressive proactive stance to instill an attitude that beneficiaries of the city's policy are responsible for their conduct just like any other citizen, and if you abuse it, you will deal with the consequences."

Then Clavell turned to what he called "health discrimination," and finally we had come around to the headlines of that morning's paper. "The old policy was discriminatory and violated the language of our existing personnel policy, which states that all employees are to be treated equally regardless of sexual orientation or marital status," he explained. "We concluded that failure to extend health insurance to loving, caring, long-term domestic partners who didn't happen to be traditional marital spouses was unfair." Clavell's people looked at corporate giants like Levi's, Hewlett-Packard, Lotus, and others that had long-established domestic partners coverage and found that the increased cost was only in a range of 1 to 2 percent.

And then he broke into that smile and asked me with a twinkle in his eye, "So you've been out on the street today. How are we doin'?"

"Not so well," I told him. It was nearly unanimous at Bob's Breakfast Club in Leunig's that this might precipitate the fall of Clavell's regime. And I had watched a TV reporter surveying people at the corner of Church and College streets where the response was ten to one against the scheme. Clavell laughed sincerely when I related Bob Conlon's jokes.

I observed that it was a strange time to broach such a controversial program, with an election just a few months away and the opposition desperate for an issue. Clavell replied, "That's part of our philosophy. We don't dodge difficult issues just because an election is imminent. In fact, I think it eventually helps guarantee our success. Burlington is full of people disdainful of politics as usual. Some may disagree with a specific initative like this, but they may end up caring more about our integrity when they walk into the voting booth."

You couldn't go into a bar or coffee shop during the next few days without overhearing spirited debate on the domestic partners issue, whether you were in Leunig's, the "yuppie Cheers bar" Sweetwaters, the blue-collar Oasis, or even the relatively apolitical Nectar's. I even overheard street people speculating about it on the benches along Church Street. I had never seen a city in which people from all walks of life were so current and voluble about local politics. And yet the discussions were consistently without rancor. There were barbs attached to some of the humor, to be sure, but little of the angry ill will so common in American politics during the eighties.

Perhaps goodwill came easy in Burlington because the city was relatively free of the economic pain that afflicted much of the country during the recession. This issue made the other red-letter headline of the week. While papers all over America were announcing IBM's plans to close down local plants, the Burlington *Free Press* printed the same story with a very different lead, because 550 of the jobs displaced by closings in other places were being transferred to the Burlington plant.

And yet I finally found someone who didn't participate in the general feel-good spirit so prevalent in town. Alison Sibley sat beside me at the bar at Nectar's and said, "Oh, oh. You're not from around here, are you?" When I answered that I wasn't, she said, "Are you gonna move here and be one more person making it hard for us real Vermonters?"

Alison was a twenty-nine-year-old employee of the phone company whose family had maintained a farm in nearby Waitsfield for four generations. Though Woody Jackson's famous cow had promoted the image of Vermont as a dairy state, the fact was that it had been a generation since most dairying families could make ends meet on the produce of the farm alone. Farmers and their families needed second jobs in places like Burlington.

"It's hard to hold on," Alison said as she carefully counted out the change from her purse to pay for her pint. "The Burlington yuppies and the skiers run the cost of everything up so much, not to mention taxes. And the jobs you can find get shittier and shittier. You can be an accountant or you can flip burgers at McDonald's. There's not much in between."

She saw little chance for advancement at her job in the billing department of the phone company. "I'd have to go back to school, but my rent takes so much of my paycheck that I can't afford it. I'll just have to win megabucks or marry rich."

Alison believed that her family, so far, had been one of the lucky ones. They had managed to hold on to their land, and she could rattle off an epic catalog of families she knew that hadn't. A few whose land had the right location had hit the jackpot when they sold out to developers or ski resorts. But many saw their debts mount up faster than their land value appreciated. They were the sad ones, those who sold out and had little to show for it.

"What becomes of them?" I asked.

"They move away to someplace where they can get work and write letters full of hurt about missing Vermont. Or they stay here and change bedsheets at ski resorts. A few sit on the benches on Church Street and sleep at the Salvation Army."

Alison's family faced a brighter future but one still marked with distress. "Our land is valuable. One of these days there's going to be a bitch of a decision."

"What would your vote be?"

"Don't sell. I'd wait tables in here for Nectar before I'd let Daddy sell the farm."

"Why?"

"For the same reason that all these yuppies are coming here. This is a great place to live, and if you can afford it, it keeps getting better. But goddamn it, this is *my place*. I belong here."

Alison's passion echoed through my journeys all the way back to Santa Fe. It wasn't just the yuppies and new people and writers who were so powerfully drawn to the good places. There were always those of lesser means as well, often natives, who would struggle and scrape and scrap, doing whatever it took to hang on. There was pain in change and there was a question of fairness about who had to bear it.

But I was beginning to see a historical necessity in this. I never found a good place where the population was primarily those who had always been there. It's the story of America itself—the infusion of fresh blood, diverse people, new energy and thinking that draws a place out of the shackles of tradition and sets it on a course toward renaissance. Nobody articulated the fact more clearly than Alison Sibley herself when I asked her if she missed the old Burlington. "It was pretty dead," she said. "You couldn't have anything like Nectar's. People were pretty closed minded and they weren't so outgoing, like you just traded gossip about people with your family and a few old friends."

When I left Nectar's that night, it had begun to snow—big, fluffy flakes drifting down from a breezeless sky. In the morning there was a foot and a half on the ground and still it came down. Burlington was well equipped for snow. The kids went to school, traffic moved (slowly) through the streets. If anything there were more people than usual out on Church Street. Preschoolers played king of the mountain on the huge piles of snow that the city trucks had dumped strategically all up and down the pedestrian mall while their mothers held cups of coffee in their mittened hands and beamed with good cheer. People spoke heartily to strangers, with smiles on their faces and ruddy cheeks. It was Christmas all over again.

In the chamber of commerce office down on the waterfront, phones were ringing off the hooks, and in city hall the controversy over domestic partners was momentarily forgotten as officials shifted gears and scurried to their faxes to help Burlington do what it did best: turn winter into money and joy. Word spread throughout the coffee shops and bars: Stowe had gotten nearly three feet of fresh powder. Sugarbush had picked up only a little less. This, on top of the machine-made base that had nearly drained northern Vermont's winter creeks dry, would guarantee skiing as good as anything out West for months to come. And the forecast called for still more, with no end in sight.

I went skiing at Stowe with a friend from the conservative side of Burlington's body politic. We drove out I-89, which rolled east through the Winooski River valley, a yawning gap in the chain of the highest of the Green Mountains. To the right, the pyramid peak of Camel's Hump now spiked the lowering snow clouds, and the miles of evergreens all down its sides were dressed out in winter's best garb. After the turnoff on Vermont 100, we negotiated the stream of traffic through the village of Stowe, with its quaint pencil-thin church steeple, and headed for the slopes.

The much-maligned ski resorts of New England had changed a lot in the past twenty years. Gone were the days of narrow trails twisting over stumps, ice, and rocks. Resort managers had embarked on ambitious campaigns of tree cutting to widen slopes, and the snow-making machines that were the bane of Vermont environmentalists had put the rocks well under a reliable layer of hard pack. Places like Stowe, with its twenty-three-hundred-foot vertical drop and five-mile-long lifts, had always ranked with most western sites in terms of sheer size. Now when it snowed as it had today, only the most cussed western skier could complain that this wasn't real skiing.

We rode the high-speed chairlift to the nose of Mount Mansfield, Vermont's highest peak, and found what we were looking for: a steep slope of light, fluffy, untracked powder. Kicking up our own little blizzards, we whooped and howled down the run and marveled at the huge burden of snow layered across the mountain pines.

Of course, people like Alison Sibley, not to mention Dumpster Don and his friends, didn't go skiing at Stowe, as I was reminded that evening by a man who managed the most fascinating city project I had encountered anywhere in America. I was in Leunig's, nursing the sore muscles of the day's outing with cups of hot spiced wine at the bar. Outside, the snowflakes still drifted down and people arrived on cross-country skis. Andy Lee came in the door wearing piles of snow and not looking too happy about it. A tall, gangly fellow in his late thirties, he was one of the first people I had met who wasn't warmed by the snowfall. "A good place to live?" he said when he sat down beside me and I introduced myself. "Someplace like Burlington where it doesn't snow. Work is going to be a bitch out at the farm tomorrow."

At first I thought he might be from another farming family, like Alison, but Andy Lee was the director of something called the Intervale Foundation. Operating under the auspices of the Gardner Supply Company and with considerable support from the city government, Intervale was a community subscription farm operating right in the heart of Burlington. The city owned the land and the foundation hired a professional farmer and his staff to run it. Citizens wanting cheap, healthfully grown produce bought shares and contributed twelve hours of work a year. There was also a composting plant and an electric power–generating plant fueled by wood chips.

Andy explained that the concept of community-supported agriculture originated in Switzerland in 1985 in response to the growing insolvency of family farms. "You have a group of people who want food who acquire land and hire a farmer, or you have a farmer with the land who wants to associate himself with a guaranteed local market," he said. "Either way, you eliminate the costs of marketing and transportation and disperse operating costs throughout a cooperative community of people."

The idea came to Burlington in 1990, when Andy was hired by Gardner Supply, and he believed he was now in the forefront of the movement that would eventually save farming in America. "We already know that in order to make a traditional profit these days, American farms have to be huge conglomerates. The small family farm is fast dying and the conglomerates are poisoning the earth, producing less nutritious food, and people have lost the connection to the earth as a result of their remoteness from the source of their food. The community farm offers hope for an alternative—cheaper, fresher, healthier food and the opportunity to personally connect with its source." There were seven such farms now in Vermont and others in every state in the country. A national organization, Community Supported Agriculture of North America, worked to promote the concept from coast to coast.

The city's involvement in Burlington was crucial. It brought in grants to get the project started, bought the land from Gardner, and leased it to Intervale for a dollar a year. The mayor, a subscription member, lent his name to all promotional efforts. Now 130 families were full-time subscribers and more than 20,000 Burlington residents supplemented their groceries with food from the farm by way of cooperatives and direct sales through markets. "And this is just the beginning," Andy believed.

I met Andy the next morning for a drive out to Intervale. It occupied the white area I had seen on Burlington maps, the floodplain of the Winooski River in between the hills of downtown Burlington and neighbor city Winooski, but the vast, flat agricultural kingdom was hidden by the hills from the urban parts of both cities. You could reside in Burlington for months, maybe years, and never know this quiet preserve existed just a dozen blocks from Church Street.

We made our first stop at the McNeil Power Plant, where wood chips from low-quality Northeast timber were turned into the low-cost electricity pumped into the grid supplying Burlington. A huge grinding machine created additional fuel from wood scraps—pallets, Christmas trees, stumps, uncontaminated construction debris. State-of-the-art scrubbers removed pollutants from stack emissions that were as white as the snow on the slopes of Stowe. Currently operating at only 40 percent of capacity, the plant had already enabled the city to avoid buying power from the controversial Hydro Quebec. And Andy was already scheming ways to use residual hot water from the plant to heat huge greenhouses that would defy the climate. And considering the unused capacity of the plant, he thought it was quite possible that Burlington would one day be energy independent.

We drove down a tree-lined lane past the power plant and out into the farm itself. Enormous expanses of eye-numbing whiteness stretched in both directions. "The fields are all in a floodplain, which was protected under the Hatch Act from development. So it was easy for the politicians to say, 'Gee, maybe we ought to just use this land for agriculture.' They never dreamed it would be a moneymaker," Andy explained and launched into a barrage of figures. "Each acre can employ one person and bring in ten thousand dollars of income. We're aiming for a million dollars a year by 2000. With four hundred acres, we've got the potential to do four million eventually. There's no reason why Burlington can't grow at least 25 percent of its own vegetables."

Besides the mass production of market produce, Intervale had a number of special projects. Andy showed me a building out of which the Burlington Youth Employment Project operated. The idea was for youthful offenders to work off their debt to society here on the farm. But Burlington being the place that it was, there weren't enough of them to make the scheme work. So now the outfit also brought in mentally disturbed and other street people learning to hold a job and make the transition to self-sufficiency. The building also housed an intern training program whose purpose was to make a permanent job available for people interested in growing vegetables for a living without making the personal investment in a farmstead. Each student was assigned a nearby plot, which served as a learning laboratory. There were compost fields steaming in the snow where organic refuse and the sludge from Burlington's sewage treatment plant were turned into rich fertilizer sold for lawns and ornamental gardens. There were plots that citizens could lease at marginal cost to do their own gardening independent of the cooperative.

Andy took me into the Intervale headquarters located in a small building at the edge of the farm. Inside were clean, brightly lit offices outfitted with computers, drafting boards, and maps and staffed by people dressed more as office workers and lab technicians than farmers. In the reception area, a tall glass contrivance was actually a self-contained biospheric aquarium. Plants generated food for the fish, and the waste of the fish was turned into food for the plants by snails and a few microorganisms. The only input was sunlight, a few minerals and nutrients, and electricity to run the water-circulation pumps. The output was fish, since they multiplied and the system had limited capacity. The fish were edible. The thing was a food machine.

Andy showed me blueprints of some of his plans for the future: stables for horses (while raising livestock for food wasted land, catering to Burlington's horsey set was a clear moneymaking proposition), a cannery, and the greenhouses he hoped would further improve the economics of raising vegetables in a cold climate. I was impressed throughout the visit by the emphasis placed on economics. "That's the whole point," Andy enthused as he drove me back into town. "I may be in this because I believe in raising wholesome, affordable food that doesn't waste the land and making it readily available to ordinary people. I may be in it because I believe in a psychic element involved in a community growing its own food. It's a healing alternative to our unhealthy way of life. But I know that to make it work, to make it become the norm instead of something out there on the fringe —I have to make it a system that is not only economically viable, but economically superior to agricultural business as usual."

In a few days the excitement of the snow died down and Burlington settled comfortably into its usual role as queen of winter delights. Ice-skating had begun down at the boathouse on the waterfront and the town was filling up with flatlanders spending their money in between trips to the slopes. Politics reemerged as the talk about town, and players were beginning to make their moves in response to the domestic partners issue and the imminence of an election that suddenly seemed less a foregone conclusion than it had when I first arrived. There was endless speculation about whether a Republican might be able to wedge his unlikely way into office as Bernie Sanders had a decade ago and whether a mainstream Democrat would emerge to challenge.

A Republican, Peter Brownell, announced a press conference to declare his candidacy. Mayor Clavell preempted him by holding one of his own just an hour and a half earlier.

The mayor's press conference took place in the city hall auditorium and was attended by the full complement of local press, radio, and television newspeople along with about a dozen of Clavell's earnest, affluent do-the-right-thing shock troops in their L. L. Bean catalog clothes. Clavell spoke briefly of his upcoming trip to attend the inauguration of the Clinton administration in Washington. After years of declining federal assistance to cities under the Reagan and Bush administrations, Clavell now saw hope for a new partnership between Progressive local government and a revitalized national Democratic leadership. "Burlington's vision and prescience has been vindicated," he declaimed. "While national voters throughout the eighties looked to conservative leaders, Burlingtoners looked to independent Progressives. Today Burlington is a model of a good place to live and national voters have finally rejected the conservative way."

During the question-and-answer session, reporters questioned him about his first declared opponent, Republican Peter Brownell— "He gives voters a clear choice, a Progressive independent against a conservative Republican"; and about the likely Republican theme that Burlington was acquiring a reputation under the Progressives of being tough on business—"More of the same tired old conservative rhetoric." Clavell was clearly running against conservativism.

But Peter Brownell was no conservative, not on any scale by which we measure that species in New Hampshire, anyway. I joined the scramble of the media people to attend his press conference across town just a few minutes after the mayor's. Festooned in red, white, and blue, the Republican room was quite a change in culture. The audience looked as if they were taking time out from bridge at the country club, with their short coiffed hair, tailored wool jackets and skirts, and dark suits with red ties. One woman was even wearing furs with the heads still attached.

Brownell announced two campaign themes: first, to initiate a serious debate about growth in the sheer size of local government, and second, to work with business for a better climate in which to attract and keep jobs. He ended by saying, "I have spoken cordially with the mayor. We are both committed to running a clean, issues-oriented campaign. We have both taken a pledge that there will be no negative campaigning."

During questioning, reporters asked if he would attack the mayor's handling of the waterfront—"I don't fault the mayor for anything he's done concerning the waterfront. I think we can talk about the question of leaving the north forty to the future"; if he was a conservative, as Clavell had labeled him—"No, don't pigeonhole me like that. I am a moderate Republican and Burlington is a city of moderates"; if he thought the mayor's domestic partners initiative was an affront to traditional values—"No, I see it as a question of cost and timing, not morality"; if he had concerns about the mayor's handling of the economy—"I'm not going to fault the mayor for the successes he's had. But we will talk about the growing perception that the city is not friendly to new business"; and whether he also intended to seek the regular Democratic party's endorsement—"That's a possibility. I would welcome discussions with my Democratic friends."

This was no declaration of war to "throw the rascals out." This was a love-in. Afterward I mixed with some of the reporters and expressed my incredulity that we had just witnessed a display of American politics. "It's Burlington politics," said Natalie Borrock, the anchorwoman from WMUR television. "It's been that way ever since Bernie Sanders turned out not to be so bad. Maybe he burned out our passion for divisiveness. Maybe Burlington has gotten fat and complacent. Sure makes it tough to get a screaming lead for the six o'clock news."

As I packed up my bags back at my hotel, which looked out over the waterfront and Lake Champlain, I watched cross-country skiers down on the bike path. I couldn't tell from this distance whether they knew one another as they stopped and exchanged pleasantries with others heading in the opposite direction, but I imagined that they didn't. That's what Burlington was all about, people heading in opposite directions who stopped and shared goodwill.

Peter Brownell was eventually elected by a landslide and many credited the domestic partners issue for the demise of the Progressives.* But nothing much changed in the town's social tenor. For all their disagreement over ideology, politicians of all persuasions in Burlington continued to put the highest priority on community. The hard-core conservatives at Leunig's insisted that Brownell was really a liberal and continued railing at the establishment agenda while buying drinks for its authors seated at their side. With its politically diverse and fractious character, I had never seen a city of such civility anywhere in America. It was the absolute mirror image of Ithaca, where

---

* Two years later, Progressive Peter Clavell regained the mayor's chair in an election against Republican Brownell and a mainstream Democrat, while the Gingrich revolution was happening nationally.

everybody toed the same party line but different groups hardly spoke to one another. Burlington rated as high a five for Cheers as anyplace I had ever been. It had a confident quirkiness as a place uniting an unlikely pair of attributes, individualism and tolerance, which also rated it a five for Someplace. Perhaps the grand eastern setting helped too.

People didn't hunker down in ideological enclaves to share their prejudices exclusively with their own kind in Burlington. Instead they debated their differences publicly and spiritedly with ideological opponents and discovered diverse friendships in the process. If Americans were ever going to return to living together in their cities, that's one thing they would have to learn to do.

11

SERENDIPITY AND
STRAWBERRY BANKE

PORTSMOUTH, NEW HAMPSHIRE

John Vaughan had a problem on his hands. As program chairman for the Portsmouth Chamber of Commerce, it was his headache when the speaker he had scheduled for the annual meeting canceled at the last minute. This was the meeting that everyone attended, the politicians, merchants, property owners, and professionals who formed the core of Portsmouth's civic life. They weren't going to be happy with a local stand-in getting up and mouthing the usual chamber of commerce platitudes. Vaughan was desperate.

His sister Dorothy was a bit of a gadfly about historical preservation. While the mainstream leaders talked about getting their share of federal urban renewal moneys to clear away the decaying remnants of a city three centuries old and replace them with new, up-to-date structures, Dorothy Vaughan had a different vision. Hers would be a city of historic buildings, streets, byways, and neighborhoods refurbished—a city that celebrated its glorious past by making it the infrastructure of its future.

John Vaughan considered asking her to fill in, but hesitated. His audience was interested in making money, not in museum stewardship, and Dorothy was not eager to get up before a tough audience and speak. But as the hour of the program approached, he ran out of options and ended up virtually dragging her to the hall. Dorothy Vaughan took the stage before the Portsmouth Chamber of Commerce that seminal day in 1958 and spoke for forty-five minutes. When she was finished, the hall rose to its feet in enthusiastic applause. The movers and shakers of Portsmouth crowded around her at the podium with congratulations and expressions of thanks. "Where should we start?" "How soon could we start?" "What's to be done?"

What Dorothy Vaughan had said during her talk was that historical preservation and renovation could be an engine of prosperity. A city of spruced-up historicity would attract people with money in their bank accounts searching for a good place to live, and it would further attract people with money in their pockets looking for a good place to visit. People parted happily with their money when in the presence of history—look at Colonial Williamsburg, Santa Fe, and the tourist venues of Europe. Historical preservation wasn't just an intelligent and tasteful thing to do; it could be the touchstone of a community's economic renaissance.

The business community of Portsmouth caught fire with the idea, expecting to accomplish it overnight. Despite its long history as the site of New Hampshire's first colonists, the state's only seaport, and the urban center for the nearby seacoast, Portsmouth was not a happy town in 1958. Its economy was based almost entirely on the nearby military installations at Pease Air Force Base and the Portsmouth Naval Shipyard. That it still possessed so much of its historic infrastructure was due more to neglect than foresight. Old houses, dilapidated downtown buildings, and rough streets offered cheap opportunities to cater to the needs of soldiers and sailors in town on R and R. Downtown near the port was a brawling red-light district off-limits to the daughters and wives of merchants who had looked to urban renewal to clean up the front yard of the place where their families lived. Now they looked to Dorothy Vaughan's preservation scheme to do it more quickly and profitably.

It began with Strawberry Banke. South of the downtown, along the waterfront, was the site of an English plantation founded in 1630 and named for the profusion of wild strawberries the early colonists found growing there. Overlaying part of the old site was an early-nineteenth-century immigrant neighborhood known as Puddle Dock. Here still stood a mix of early colonial, federal, and early Victorian structures that Vaughan proposed to make the centerpiece of Portsmouth's historical revival when Strawberry Banke Inc. was formed shortly after her speech. Whereas Williamsburg was entirely a reconstruction and Massachusetts's Sturbridge Village was cobbled out of buildings transported from places all over New England, Strawberry Banke became a renovated historic neighborhood of original buildings mostly on their original sites. Newer buildings were moved away and the entire ten-block area was set aside as a museum.

There were obstacles. The state of New Hampshire, responsible for administering federal urban renewal grants, required that such moneys be tied to projects that tore down something old and replaced it with something new. Vaughan and the earnest merchants of Portsmouth marched off to Concord and got those rules changed. There was grumbling from displaced residents of Puddle Dock, which nearly forty years later still constitituted a hot issue. But Strawberry Banke opened in 1965 and profoundly shaped the Portsmouth that has emerged since.

Strawberry Banke established a new urban ethic. Owners of private and commercial properties throughout the city followed its lead and began renovating and gentrifying. The bed and breakfast phenomenon swept Portsmouth as owners of magnificent old houses discovered that tourists enjoyed sleeping in a place as authentic as the museum they came to see. Homeowners got on the bandwagon, priding themselves in sprucing up their little piece of the historical tableau. Restaurateurs discovered that visitors liked to eat in old buildings that appeared to be a commercial extension of the museum down the street.

The core of old Portsmouth came to be one of America's best-preserved historic cities. Tourists flocked. Affluent homeseekers invested. The rough stuff downtown abated. Money flowed in. "I guess you could call the legend 'Blind, dumb luck,' " said Ray Brighton, senior local historian, as we sat in the grand hall of the Atheneum, a private library located on a corner of the downtown Market Square, founded by contemporaries of George Washington. "If John Vaughan's speaker had shown up, if a waterfront industry had ever come in and torn down Puddle Dock, if we weren't located less than an hour from Boston and Portland, if a lot of things—none of this might have happened."

But when Ray spoke of luck, he was referring only to the preservation of Portsmouth's historical treasures. Concerning the common local wisdom that tourism had made Portsmouth a thriving town, he was less sanguine. When I commented on what seemed to me a healthy flux of people out on Market Square and along the downtown streets, he looked out the window, made a face, and said, "What people? There's nobody out there, just a few tourists." In his eighties, he was old enough to remember the days preceding the age when getting bodies into the downtown had become an issue. "Tourism can't replace what the malls killed off," he said. "The department stores, the haberdasheries, the hardware stores. That's what brings real people into the downtown and we don't have them anymore. Now it's just boutiques and restaurants."

But there was a great mystery about Portsmouth that most other people I talked to explained with tourism. In the past twenty years the city had absorbed blows that would have killed many a community. Major industries, such as Data General, had departed. The federal government had closed down Pease Air Force Base. The tonnage handled by the port had steadily declined. And now the feds were scaling back the Portsmouth Naval Shipyard.

Yet during the same time, the median household income of the greater metro region had soared to forty-one thousand dollars, and the percentage of people living below the poverty line was one of the lowest in the state. With a population of only twenty-six thousand, Portsmouth supported eighty-four restaurants (fifty-one of them in the downtown) and had established a reputation as the culinary capital of the seacoast north of Boston. With the exception of the recently departed department store Newberry's, there were no significant empty storefronts downtown. And to my eye, the streets thronged with people at all hours.

That most Portsmouth residents credited the tourist industry for all of this seemed ironic after I visited several other places that had bet the ranch on tourism: Fredericksburg, Virginia, Newburyport, Massachusetts, Beaufort, South Carolina. It was a siren call that tempted many a place not more firmly grounded economically. Even in Santa Fe, tourism had become as much a curse as blessing. Too often a primarily tourist economy distorted the community life, destroyed the downtown as a focal point for locals, and subjected a place to boom-and-bust cycles. But that hadn't happened in Portsmouth.

Ray Brighton argued simply that tourism wasn't as significant here as others maintained. In his mind, the foundation of Portsmouth's economy was and always had been the naval shipyard; the air force base and tourism were merely icing on the cake. "Pease never produced anything. It was strictly military employment. And the dollars earned there were spent at the commissary, not in Portsmouth," he argued. "But the shipyard employs civilians who reside and spend their money in Portsmouth. It supports good schools, good police and fire departments. We'll see how well tourism carries us through if the shipyard closes." He wasn't optimistic.

Ray gave me a tour of the Atheneum. Founded by Nathaniel Adams in 1817, it was owned today by three hundred proprietors and was better off financially than at any time in its history. It housed priceless collections of eighteenth-century paintings, letters authored by the founding fathers, one of the country's most valuable collections of model sailing vessels, a roomful of mementos of the signing here of the Treaty of Portsmouth, ending the Russo-Japanese War, and of course, a library of historically significant rare and first editions. When we had finished and stepped out of the silent rooms into the busy contemporary bustle of Market Square, Ray Brighton said, "It still shocks me how quiet it is downtown these days."

Nothing would have startled me more at the start of these journeys than the suggestion that I would end up finding a renaissance town anyplace in my own state of New Hampshire. In addition to our reputation for political buffoonery (epitomized by Governor Meldrim Thompson's threat to send troops against neighbor Maine back in the seventies), our tardiness in endorsing Martin Luther King Day, and the stubborn refusal to establish broad-based taxation (New Hampshire had neither a sales nor an income tax), which left us with stratospheric property taxes and an inability to pay for public amenities taken for granted in other states, New Hampshire had some serious problems.

There was a myth in New Hampshire that we enjoyed something called "home rule" because of our tradition of town meetings in which all residents could vote directly on issues of policy, taxation, and expenditures. But because of a deeply ingrained mistrust of government power, we were also an "enabling legislation state." That meant that communities, no matter how democratically run, were forbidden to do anything but what was "enabled" by specific state legislation. Other states with true home rule operated under an opposite philosophy: communities were allowed to do anything but what was forbidden by specific state legislation or under the state constitution. Any teenager knows that you have more freedom when you are allowed to do anything but what is categorically forbidden than when you are forbidden to do anything but what is categorically allowed. The enabling legislation philosophy of New Hampshire inevitably hampered communities' efforts at progressive action. Portsmouth could never have founded Strawberry Banke if Dorothy Vaughan and her colleagues had not been successful at changing state regulations.

New Hampshire also maintained a tradition of ponderously large legislative bodies, even beyond the town meeting setting. The state legislature, at 420 members, was the largest parliamentary body in the world. The Keene City Council on which I served, at fifteen members, was the one of the largest city councils I found anywhere in America. Most were nine, seven, or occasionally five members, and I had frequently been asked how we in New Hampshire ever got anything done. The fact was, we didn't. People in New Hampshire thought they liked it that way. A smaller council, I was often told by my native neighbors, might do something rash. It was another example of how the fundamental suspicion of government in this state paralyzed the kind of attempts at community renaissance that I had seen elsewhere.

New Hampshire had little of the socially engaged rural gentry that I would later find in Virginia, where the land had long been the basis of someone's prosperity. Here the old families had owned the mills, and rarely was anyone's wealth based on the region's rocky, unproductive land. When the mill economy went south, so did the fortunes and often the families themselves. Those who hung on became either landed poor or the moneyed landless who preserved their wealth through investment in newer kinds of manufacturing plants rather than through productive use of the land.

Either way, their offspring didn't have the same combination of incentives to stay home. Each succeeding generation found fewer of the old families involved in local society, culture, and economy, and those who did remain played far less vital and influential roles than they might have if there were strong family prosperity and land behind them. Instead the local movers and shakers were often either immigrants from the flatlands seeking a tax-free environment for their money or local boys of modest provincial roots who had shouldered their way past the families they had grown up envying.

The Portsmouth region did not feel like New Hampshire. The seacoast north of Boston was a magnificent gradual transition from the broad golden beaches of Cape Cod and Massachusetts Bay to the rocky wave-blasted shores of Maine. New Hampshire's little piece of coast was the essence of the transition. Here were broad beaches and granite points. Here were lowland marshes and towering escarpments. Here was the cause of the most radical grassroots movement ever spawned in this conservative state: opposition to Governor John Sununu's Seabrook Nuclear Power Plant, sited on the shore in the Seabrook marshes. Here, too, was milder weather than the rest of the region enjoyed.

I had visited Portsmouth in each of the four seasons, since it was so close to home, and each time I drove from inland Keene to the seacoast, I noted a moderation of climate. In the spring and fall, I was able to wear shorts in Portsmouth at times when it would have been unthinkable back in Keene. In the winter, snow was occasional enough to be special, and the weeks of bone-chilling cold so well known to inland New Englanders rarely happened here. Fogs, drizzle, and windy nor'easter snows could blow in off the Atlantic, but not with the same frequency as was common a hundred miles north in Maine. More often than not, Portsmouth seemed to be on the friendly side of nasty stuff that happened farther north or inland. It may seem strange to cite weather as an advantage in New England, but Portsmouth, with its January average temperature of forty-six degrees and July average of seventy-two degrees, had the best climate of any place I had visited since Kelowna.

For a year I had searched the seacoast north of Boston for a renaissance town to write about. Rockport, Massachusetts, on Cape Ann, was appealing, but it was too small and tourist oriented. Newburyport, Massachusetts, was larger and was a fine place, but it too was boutiqued to the hilt. Portland, Maine, was clearly the center of a good life, yet I kept coming back to centrally located Portsmouth, which was close to all of these places, and Ray Brighton's complaint notwithstanding, its downtown was the best of the lot.

Downtown Portsmouth was a particularly pedestrian-friendly place: compact, with ample sidewalks and narrow, curving streets. This wasn't the result of any recent planner's enlightenment. It was just the way things used to be, and here they had never changed. The mix of architecture from different eras presented a cityscape of almost European-caliber historical continuity like few places on this continent.

To the north of the downtown center, I liked the grubby view of the port, with its tugboats and real-world piles of scrap metal and salt (the main commodities of the port these days) offering a gritty counterpoint to any tendency to see the place as a sanitized tourist stop. The new Seacoast Repertory Theater was housed in the Bow Street Inn development along the waterfront, and to the south I found the open grass of Prescott Park running for blocks along the Piscataqua River. There was an outdoor stage here and flower gardens. In the summer, people flocked to performances on the stage and strolled through the gardens; in the winter, the expanse was populated with snow sculptures.

During one autumn visit, I met a brother and sister at the Rusty Hammer who introduced themselves as just "the lobsterman's children." Now in their forties, they had been raised on an island in the Piscataqua River, where their father ran a lobster boat. Each was divorced and the sole parent of teenage children. The brother now worked at the naval shipyard; the sister was a waitress. Life's squalls had brought them close to each other. They were philosophical about how the town was a still a good place to live, despite the tourist "invasion."

"I can drop my daughter off at her field hockey game and stick around to watch with a dozen people I've known since junior high," said the lobsterman's daughter. "Or I can stop in here for a drink with another dozen people I've known since junior high." They believed that Portsmouth's unique brand of tourism actually contributed to making the downtown a better place for locals. As the lobsterman's son explained, "I don't make my living from tourism, I work in the shipyard. I work hard. But the tourism business makes this town a place where I can get something with the money I earn. There's a life here after you leave the yard."

I often took my lunches in Portsmouth at a place called the Stockpot, which had great chowder in a town of great chowders and strategically placed windows overlooking the harbor. The manager sat with me one day and explained that in his view, Portsmouth did run on tourism, if you accepted a broad definition of the term. Certainly a lot of the people who spent money here were from Boston or farther afield. But most of the downtown clientele who didn't live in Portsmouth were regular visitors from a constellation of nearby places: affluent Rye and Hampton; blue-collar Dover and Kittery, Maine; artsy Wells and Ogunquit, Maine; middle-class Rochester. Other regular day or evening trippers came from even farther: Nashua and Manchester; Newburyport, Massachusetts; and Portland, Maine. And then there were the college students from the University of New Hampshire, fifteen minutes west in Durham. Portsmouth enjoyed the economic advantages of a college town without the disadvantages of having fifteen thousand twenty-year-olds living right in town.

"It works the other way, too," he said. "There are lots of people living in Portsmouth and working in one of these places fifteen to forty-five minutes away." There were industries employing more than a thousand people each in nearby Rochester, Hampton, Somersworth, Newington, Dover, and Seabrook. "Location is the key to this town. It's a hub. And five minutes from here, you can be out at the shore."

Third places on every street in downtown Portsmouth catered to the various walks of regional community life. The tourists tended to sprinkle themselves sparsely throughout almost all of them, so they didn't dominate any. Unlike downtown Santa Fe, downtown Portsmouth was still very much a locals scene. I met Monika Aring, founder of a community renaissance group called Pro-Portsmouth, at the Cafe Brioche one sunny morning when it was warm enough to sip coffee at an outside table on the corner of Market Square.

Monika Aring had been the leader of a second wave of community activism in Portsmouth after John and Dorothy Vaughan's generation. When Monika arrived in Portsmouth from Germany with her husband in 1976, the city was stagnant. Though Strawberry Banke had been a roaring success, the ethic of historical preservation was well established, and tourism was beginning to pump dollars into the local economy, Monika was disturbed by the lack of a thriving life for locals in the downtown. "In Europe, people live in their town centers when they're not working; the town center is everyone's living room," she said. She had found Portsmouth appealing because it had a physical look reminiscent of European towns, but that wasn't enough.

It all began when she went to the city council to advocate application for federal funds to fix up the sidewalks, which were in a sad state of disrepair. "I was shocked at the mental model I found of what people thought the town life should be," she recalled. "They wanted a place to park cars, they thought we needed a big Zayre store. They didn't see the need for street beauty to complement the historical beauty of the preserved architecture."

Monika spoke to the council about making Market Square the city's living room, about how it was people and not cars that would make it strong. There was polite silence. But then she started getting telephone calls from people who had heard about her little speech, and someone found some Humanities Council money to fund a study, "Options and Alternatives for a New Market Square." Soon she had established the organization called Pro-Portsmouth, which engaged the community in an eighteen-month dialogue about the purpose of a downtown. There were town meetings in the church on the square, older residents told oral histories, artists did projects, the people from Boston's Faneuil Hall came and made a presentation. There were musical performances, bake sales, and street guerrilla theater interpreting various opinions about the future of the downtown. "By the time we were done, old Ray Brighton himself had pink cheeks," she recalled. "We were celebrating all of the things that made Portsmouth Portsmouth."

It all culminated with the first Market Square Day, a downtown festival that closed off the streets to cars. The event was not without obstacles. "The chamber of commerce didn't believe it would ever work, they thought we were wasting money. Some of the old-time merchants objected to closing the street to traffic, thought it would hurt business." But Monika credited two merchants in particular, Arnold Fishbine and Sam Jarvis, with changing the stance of their peers in the chamber, and since 1978, Market Square Day has been held every year. The tawdrier shops disappeared. The wire services picked up the story of a town rejuvenating itself and suddenly there was a wave of new entrepreneurs to fill the vacant storefronts. But most important, Pro-Portsmouth got locals back into the habit of living in their downtown. I met half a dozen downtown merchants who affirmed that Monika Aring deserved much of the credit for the fact that here, local people more than held their own in the downtown with the tourists.

Now Monika had withdrawn from active participation in Pro-Portsmouth. A third generation had taken up the baton, just as she had taken it from the Strawberry Banke people. "Life goes on, my husband's family just got their land out of government holding back in Estonia. We may be moving there," she sighed. "I guess I was a carpetbagger, came to Portsmouth to make it more like my old home in Europe, and now I may go back there. But we helped change Portsmouth. Today the people here who resent outsiders are a distinct minority."

A new regime had come to city hall after the former city manager was caught with his hand in the till, and with it came new issues for digestion on the public plate. One of the new faces in city hall was an old graduate school buddy of mine, Welfare Director Keith Bates. I went to visit him and his wife, Susan, at their home on Lincoln Street one Sunday afternoon when Susan and the kids were busily repainting the entryway. I sat with Keith in his living room, surrounded by his world-class record collection.

The issues in Portsmouth today involved a classic struggle between left and right, he thought, which was the first thing about my visit here that reminded me that I was still in New Hampshire, where political and ideological polarization was what public affairs were all about. The conservative side consisted primarily of longtime residents and taxpayers who saw new people coming into Portsmouth and getting ahead of them. They were working or retired people who believed that they did not benefit from the general renaissance of the city. I had looked for this type of activist backlash against new people in other places I had visited because I knew it was so common in New Hampshire. But except for the old Spanish families in Santa Fe and some of the old Vermont farming families in Burlington, I had not found it.

One of the boons of the renaissance process in most of the places I visited was that it was inclusive; few felt left out, though there were certainly those who had to struggle to hang on.

The difference here was just what the insurgents' group said it was: taxes. In a state with no sales or income tax, as much as 95 percent of the financial support for schools and infrastructure fell on the local property tax. Retirees and others on fixed incomes in New Hampshire fell further and further behind as the property tax increased to finance the things a progressive community did that required public money. It was difficult to feel sympathetic, though, because those same crusty Hampshire folk hit hardest by the state's draconian tax structure formed the core of support for state politicians elected year after year on their pledge to oppose any broad-based state taxation.

I asked Keith why I had seen so few street people during my meanderings downtown. Portsmouth had the smallest visible homeless population of any place I had been. "Well, New Hampshire's not exactly a good welfare stop," he answered. "So we don't draw them from other sites the way some places do." But even my own Keene had far more street people than Portsmouth did—possibly as a result of Keene's isolation, we decided, whereas Portsmouth was a short hitch-hike from half a dozen small cities as well as Boston and Portland. Most of the welfare cases Keith dealt with were the usual locals down on their luck; he saw little evidence from his office that the economics of Portsmouth were driving people into poverty. But the availability of low-income housing was an issue that might be related to the way Portsmouth was developing. Keith invited me to visit him at city hall the following day, where I would meet people who could tell me more about it.

The city hall was located in a former hospital on a southerly hill overlooking the city. Compared to what we had in Keene, a city of about the same size, it was a grand edifice. Portsmouth had an Office of Community Development, and the planning director supervised a staff of six professional planners, each specializing in a different aspect of the community. Keith introduced me to planner Cathy Menici, whose specialty was demographics and housing. She explained that because of Portsmouth's proximity to Dover and Rochester, it was part of a Metropolitan Survey Area that made it an "entitlement community," a recipient of half a million dollars in federal Community

Development Block Grant funds per year. More blind, dumb luck. Her figures showed a steady population growth rate of about 7 percent each census period (.7 percent per year), despite the departures and closings of significant employers. To her, there was no mystery in this. "It's just a desirable place to live and there's always employment somewhere within a commuting drive."

The affordable housing issue went back as far as Puddle Dock. Ever since Dorothy Vaughan, Portsmouth housing had been subject to steady gentrification. As older homes were restored, their values increased. As time went on, restoration efforts focused on homes at ever-lower levels of value. Memories were long and bitter in families that had been moved out of the South End and Puddle Dock to make way for Prescott Park and Strawberry Banke. In the seventies, the low-income housing of the North End was razed in Portsmouth's one misguided escapade with demolition-style urban renewal. I thought the Sheraton Hotel built on the site made it one of the least attractive quadrants of the city.

But Cathy didn't believe affordable housing was getting squeezed out by new money any longer, and she had been involved in what she thought would be the turning point case. Portsmouth's largest remaining stock of low-income housing was in a development called Mariner's Village, built in the 1940s as mass housing for servicemen. For years, Mariner's Village had housed more than seven hundred families with incomes well below the region's median. It was located on a pleasant site with rolling topography, old trees, and views. In 1985, Portsmouth Coastal Development Partners (PCDP) bought the entire property for $11 million with plans to turn it into upscale condos. What the developers had not foreseen, though, was that the residents of Mariner's Village had developed a fierce neighborhood pride and cohesion. They formed SOHO (Save Our Homes) and fought PCDP every inch of the way in the face of rent increases, evictions, and what the neighbors considered general harassment by the developers.

The city got involved, requiring the developer to put $2.5 million into a housing assistance trust in return for the increased density zoning he wanted for his new condos. PCDP redeveloped part of the property as Spinnaker Point, made two payments totaling $800,000 to the trust fund, and installed a chain-link fence separating the new condos from the old housing. Then the developer declared bankruptcy, and the city was left with a mess on its hands.

Meanwhile, SOHO continued its activism, led by resident Linda Panori, who was elected to the city council, and the city sought a deal that could give a developer an investment worth making while preserving the majority of Mariner's Village as renovated low-income housing. "We spelled out exactly what we wanted and told developers to take it or leave it," Cathy explained. "They kept trying to deal, as if we had staked out a negotiable bargaining position. When it became clear that we meant business, we stopped hearing from most of them. But there was one that we had never taken very seriously who kept calling and asking for increasingly slighter concessions. I kept saying no concessions, and each time I could hear his calculator running as he punched in numbers. Finally, I was in a meeting when I got a call from him. I just knew it, 'Oh my God, he's going to do it!' " As a result of the deal struck that day, the remaining affordable housing in Mariner's Village would be upgraded to the level of Spinnaker Point without increases in rent.

After so many years of frustration, SOHO still had some reservations about the future of housing in Portsmouth, but the resolution of the Mariner's Village fiasco had established a precedent for the future. Existing affordable housing would be protected, with guarantees of affordability even if gentrified. Now developers were eyeing another neighborhood in Atlantic Heights and were poised to test the city's commitment.

Mariner's Village activist and current city council member Linda Panori wrote an editorial for the local paper that captured the neighborhood cohesiveness and pride that won the original dispute:

> We [in Mariner's Village] are someone's grandparents, parents, sons, daughters, and grandchildren. We are employed by the city, the schools, the state, the navy yard, Liberty Mutual, K-Mart, the offices around town, the restaurants downtown. Some of us are retired. Some of us are starting our lives over. . . . If you talk to a resident you will hear wonderful stories, of block parties, barbeques, dances, children's play groups. There were bad times too when neighbors helped each other—no questions asked. . . . Are we so different because

we don't own our homes? Are we so different because we don't have the best of everything? Are we so different because we are elderly, disabled, Black, Caucasian, Oriental or single moms all living in one big wonderful neighborhood? Why is it that when I mention the Village, I get "Tsk, Tsk, we should help those people" or "Why should I spend my tax dollars on those people?" One extreme or the other—with the emphasis placed on "those people". . . . Dream with me for a moment. Picture in your mind a beautiful neighborhood full of life again, a beautiful neighborhood that provides rental as well as owner- ship opportunities for Portsmouth families to live and grow, with no racial, gender or financial fences.

Because this was New Hampshire, a state whose cussedness would question even the strongest certitudes in other places, Portsmouth was a good place to explore some negatives sometimes associated with the renaissance process. Gentrification and the affordable housing crunch was one of them. William Whyte has argued against the notion that gentrification necessarily entailed the loss of affordable homes. It was pernicious, he believed, to hold that deliberate neglect of the quality of people's homes constituted a legitimate affordable housing policy. Portsmouth had proven him right. Gentrification was at odds with preserving affordable housing only when government would not or could not intervene to assure both housing improvements and af- fordability. If government could perform such a role in a New Hamp- shire town, it could do it anywhere.

Another quibble I encountered concerned the fear that projects and communities whose aesthetic was based on historical renovation for commercial purposes ended up having a uniform boutiquish look throughout the country, nearly as placeless as those built around Mc- Donald's, shopping malls, and multicinema theaters. There were some who therefore despised Boston's Faneuil Hall or Baltimore's water- front and were revolted by my observation that these kinds of projects were becoming the key to the renaissance of small cities all across America.

I would concede that it is certainly possible to take a historical property and renovate it for an inappropriate commercial use, and that may even have been the case with Faneuil Hall. I have certainly seen downtowns—in Santa Fe, in Fredericksburg, Virginia, in Dodge City, Kansas—whose historical preservation was so skewed toward tourism that the T-shirt emporiums alone constituted just the kind of homogenizing formula the naysayers feared.

But where the effect of redeveloped historical buildings and street-scapes was to restore a community infrastructure and aesthetic that worked in some time past and could now work again to move people to live more publicly and communally, these were places where the naysayers' quibbles simply missed the point. If the venture attracted tourism into the bargain, or even if its point had been tourism in the first place, as in Portsmouth, what was wrong with generating a little prosperity while restoring the values of community life?

City Councilor Jay Smith owned and operated a bar in Portsmouth called the Press Room. I talked to him one evening in his place while a folk guitarist played and a half dozen crewmen from a recently docked merchant ship sipped Courvoisier and flirted with single women at the bar. "There are some places where the system is accessible and others where the prize is worth winning," he declared. "Here in Portsmouth you have both."

Smith came to Portsmouth from Ohio during the time people called "the renaissance" in the 1970s, when the beast was beginning to stir. Though the downtown was still rough, there was the Theater by the Sea right next to the tugboats. Smith believed that once Dorothy Vaughan had set the stage with her historical preservation movement, it was actually the restaurants of Portsmouth that carried the show.

"It began with the Blue Strawberry," he said. "Here in the middle of tugs and bums and rough stuff, you had a nationally recognized five-star restaurant. They offered a three-hour meal and you ate whatever they felt like serving you. It was a radical thing that put downtown Portsmouth on the map." Then two investors put serious money into the Harbor Sandwich Shop and Dolphin Striker on the roughest corner of the waterfront. "That turned a lot of heads," Jay said. "And suddenly, in less than five years, the restaurant culture of this town just exploded."

It got to the point of craziness in the eighties when people were lined up to pay 120 percent of asking price for a good downtown location. There were setbacks, but for every place that failed, two more opened up. "We've sobered up now," Smith maintained. "There's business to take care of—social justice issues, affordable housing, and healing the rift between ideological factions. There are hard-core conservatives here who viscerally hate me because I get elected and I'm a liberal. That bothers me more than any of the specific things we disagree about."

Smith used an analogy to present his view of how Portsmouth had philosophically matured and would continue to grow. "It's like an icicle. Some people come here and go, some stay. Those that stay become part of the structure for other newcomers to build on. The icicle grows in beauty and substance. That's how a creative community develops."

A year after my first visits to Portsmouth, I was invited to speak at a forum sponsored by that third wave of historical preservationist activism that Monika Aring had told me about. Portsmouth Advocates was an organization spearheaded by folks like New Hampshire state legislator Martha Fuller Clark and Portsmouth advertising executive Malcolm Boyd. Its purpose was to continue the periodic renewal of Portsmouth's commitment to historical preservation. "We can't rely on momentum from past movements," Malcolm explained during the conference. "You have to consciously revive the movement under changed circumstances every few years."

Besides holding forums to highlight the issue, Portsmouth Advocates publicly recognized businesses and developers that had made contributions to the Portsmouth architectural and historical profile. Their goal was to promote an ethic of development that continued the pioneering work of Strawberry Banke. And now Martha Fuller Clark had gone statewide as head of an organization called Inherit New Hampshire, whose purpose was to promote historical preservation across the state. She had recently hired as executive director Jane Sheffield, a young, energetic former Main Street Program director, who spoke passionately about economic revival through heritage tourism. Gray heads throughout New Hampshire rose from their torpor and listened. Jane Sheffield had attracted the attention of the National Trusts's Main Street Center, which was in the process of establishing New England's first Main Street Center Headquarters in Concord. These women of Portsmouth seemed determined to change the habits of this state in which I had so little faith.

I spent my last evening of my last trip to Portsmouth enjoying the bars and the subtle differences in clientele that were a sociologist's delight. The Portsmouth Brewery was the upscale, yuppie place, but not exclusively so. There were colorful, well-beloved characters who were regulars and who were not affluent. Above the brewery on the social pyramid were some of the elegant hideaways, like the Dolphin Striker Restaurant. Jay Smith's Press Room attracted music-hip professionals and sailors. The Rusty Hammer was the bastion of longtime locals on the borderline between blue and white collar. Rosa's was the place for folks who liked to dance to live music without demeaning themselves at one of the flesh and testosterone emporiums on the outskirts.

A five for Cheers in New Hampshire? Who would have thought it! With the seacoast and the inland waterways so close to Boston and a respectable theater and music scene right in Portsmouth itself, Portsmouth rated a strong four for Cake. The extensive old neighborhoods surrounding the downtown and the firmly established historical identity also merited four ratings for Foot and Someplace factors.

On the other hand, I was tempted to apply a negative Fudge Factor for the presence of I-95 just outside of town and the advance of rural sprawl between Portsmouth and most of its neighbors. And there were concerns about the possible closing of the shipyard and ways in which the vagaries of New Hampshire politics might blight the city's blooming. The tax issue alone could yet cause Portsmouth to stumble.

But the lesson of Portsmouth was that with a little luck, renaissance towns could blossom in states where the soil was not very fertile. Furthermore, Portsmouth showed that the common quick fix of tourism, so rabidly embraced by many desperate chambers of commerce and so ardently opposed by many thoughtful thinkers and planners, could, under the right circumstances, actually succeed in sparking and maintaining a community renaissance. It was fitting. Leave it to New Hampshire to reject what worked elsewhere and to succeed with what so often failed.

12

A JEFFERSONIAN
CIVICS LESSON

CHARLOTTESVILLE, VIRGINIA

It was late winter in New England, a nasty one, but you could still count on it being warm down South. You didn't have to go all the way to the Caribbean, just far enough to get the numbing cold out of your bones and to shed a few layers of clothing.

Charlottesville, Virginia, had long figured in New Englanders' fantasies of good places to live. Though we knew it occasionally snowed there, it was significantly warmer than New Hampshire while still offering the delight of seasonal change. But more than that was a kind of historical, cultural, and psychological affinity between Virginia and New England. Virginia was the other place whose patriots shared the credit for founding the nation. It was the other place where the land and the towns and the families traced their lineage back to colonial days and still preserved the character of that history.

I had driven from New Hampshire to Charlottesville twice before in the summer, past the weltering oil refineries of the New Jersey meadowlands and the cars crawling like ants along the Pulaski Skyway into the murk of Golgotha, past the sprawl of commercial clutter that so obliterated the sense of place between Newark and Philadelphia, and, perhaps worst, past the empty office complexes despoiling the Maryland and northern Virginia countryside around Washington. But

I remembered that southwest of Fredericksburg, Megalopolis suddenly ceased to exist, as if one had crossed a border into another country and the decree of some benevolent despot ordered the invasion stopped at a line drawn in the soil.

I had spent much of my time those summer trips exploring the central Virginia countryside surrounding Charlottesville and marveling at the good, uncrowded roads, the rolling green fields and deciduous forests, the charming horse and dairy farms with their white-painted fences, and the little villages tucked in the dells. This time I came to Charlottesville by train, and the effect of entering that Virginian middle kingdom was heightened when the snow cover of a late winter storm ended at precisely that same line beyond which Megalopolis seemed forbidden. Now the horse farms and dairies were not quite so green and the budded trees didn't yet wear the lushness of summer, but winter had already lost its tenuous hold on the land. And, scan as I might, I could not find images of rural ugliness, even along the likely setting of the railroad tracks.

The urban neighborhood around the Charlottesville train station where I detrained in the late afternoon was another matter. The station itself was an old, multiple-gabled brick building with wonderful potential, but because of location and community neglect, it was not appealing. Situated along the run-down midpoint of the West Main corridor, it should have been a focus of community pride, since there was no other city in America of Charlottesville's size that still had four passenger trains a day, complete with sleepers and dining cars, that ran directly to places as far away as Philadelphia and New York, Atlanta and New Orleans, Cincinnati and Chicago.

After picking up my rental car and checking in at my hotel, I headed back to a likely spot I had noticed across the street from the train station—the Blue Ridge Brewing Company—and was delighted to find that it was indeed a true brew pub of the kind I had appreciated so much in the Northwest. In fact, its Hawksbill Lager was the first draft I had tasted anywhere that really rivaled Brian Hunt's brews at Willett's in Napa, California.

A good blues-rock band began playing at about ten o'clock and the place filled up quickly. The social tone was loose, friendlier than in similar places in the Northeast but more gentrified than out West. Attire ranged from trendy denim to high-fashion suits and glamorous dresses. When I asked about the clientele, a woman said, "It's just us townies, Jefferson's illegitimate children."

At around eleven o'clock, something started happening out in the street and people moved toward the windows to check it out. A procession of maybe fifty to seventy-five people, most of them black, was marching, carrying signs—FIFEVILLE NOT CRACKVILLE—and chanting slogans—"What do we want: clean town; when do we want it: now." The group was accompanied by a police cruiser and two more cops on horseback. A few of the patrons of the Blue Ridge went out and raised fists and joined the chant, but most remained inside, expressing detached support.

I asked the fellow behind the bar what it was all about and he explained that it was a neighborhood group trying to get crack dealers out of town. I asked if Charlottesville had a drug problem and he said, gesturing toward the street, "Not when they get through." There had been a sharp rise in crack dealing in some neighborhoods during the past five years, he explained. But then these groups formed and launched a movement. "Guys in city hall are still scratching their heads while those folks are out there winning the battle."

I asked why more of his customers didn't go out to join the marchers. "Actually, there's a segment of our clientele that is already out there," he said. "But otherwise, a lot of our people here tonight come in from the county. Maybe they don't think it's their problem."

I spent the next day driving and walking around Charlottesville to get a feel for the lay of the town. It was a community of contrasts, more so than other good places I had visited. The university anchored the west end of town, with its classical lawns and Georgian architecture, its old dormitories where students could still burn wood in their fireplaces. North of the university section lay the wealthy neighborhoods of beautiful old homes and curving streets. But just beyond that sprawled the strip development of U.S. Route 13, as raunchy as any I'd seen.

The east end of town had two focal points, side by side: the historical blocks dating from the days of Jefferson surrounding Jackson Park and Court Square and the turn-of-the-century downtown, now preserved as a pedestrian mall. North of this was a thriving middle-class neighborhood of older homes, but east and south there were projects and the remnants of poorer neighborhoods. At the west corner of the downtown mall loomed the modernistic Omni Hotel and in front of that a particularly unfriendly traffic intersection.

The geography of Charlottesville was like a barbell, with two centers of substance, aesthetics, and prosperity connected by the rather dismal West Main corridor I had first seen when I arrived at the train station. Besides the poorly maintained railroad property and adjacent neighborhoods that didn't appear to be doing so well, the street itself and the walkways along it were not inviting, despite the presence of the Blue Ridge. Apparently local attention had focused on the university and the old downtown at the two ends, and yet any visitor could have told the city leaders that as the link, West Main was the real heart of town. Why didn't they do more with it?

The downtown pedestrian mall wasn't anything like those in Ithaca or Burlington. Because there had been a median in the old Main Street, it was shaded by big old trees. Restaurants and bars had tables set up under umbrellas out in the center of the common, where you could sit with your lunch or drinks and watch the passersby. But at three-thirty in the afternoon there wasn't much to watch—not enough, it seemed to me, to make the downtown truly viable. There were a significant number of empty storefronts and aggressive panhandlers, and though there were bursts of clientele in the morning, at lunchtime, and after work, Charlottesville's downtown pedestrian mall seemed only a marginal success.

I did see a few little knots of elderly black men who philosophically occupied mall benches for large chunks of the day, and after school hours there were skateboarders and rappers. A Japanese woman set up a tape deck and danced in the street. And later a group of conga players occupied a corner and made the echoing mall bounce with their music. The mall had evolved its own colorful little culture, but there just weren't enough paying customers.

Back at the Blue Ridge, I found the fellow behind the bar who had told me about the antidrug march last night. It was quiet in the bar now as the waitresses rushed about dressing up the tables in preparation for the dinner hour, so he had time to talk to me. His name was Jesse Hayden and he was one of the owners. Born and raised in Charlottesville, he and a little group who had grown up together went out West after college and founded the San Francisco Brewing Company as part of the eighties West Coast brew pub movement. Five years ago they returned to Charlottesville to duplicate the feat with Virginia's first brew pub, after Anheuser-Busch convinced the state legislature to rescind hoary laws prohibiting on-site brewing in bars in order to make Busch Gardens in Williamsburg work.

I asked him why generation after generation of the old families stayed and he explained that the big old families ran farms—plantations once upon a time. His father's family raised peaches and his mother's raised horses. Though the land had made crop transitions in different historical periods, it had always remained productive enough that people could afford to hold on to it and stay well-to-do—nobody became land poor. Though the land was surpassed in the sixties by other local industries as the mainstay of the economy, it still provided a strong base for the families who lived on it. Most of the equestrian farms, for instance, were leased out to guys who ran several farms, or combinations of pieces of farms, and who did a thriving business. The lease money more than covered the taxes and upkeep. "So there was always both land to be passed on and enough moldy money around that the offspring could afford to stay," he said. "There was just no incentive to leave." What Jesse described was in sharp contrast to the situation back in New England.

I asked him why he thought outsiders found Charlottesville to be a good place to live. "It's a place of strong identity and tradition that is also friendly and open to newcomers," he said. "You've got the same background up in New England but you don't have the same reputation for friendliness." He also thought it had a lot to do with preserving the old southern charm without being Deep South. "People think they can come to Virginia and have the best of the southern tradition without the worst of it."

There was also the beautifully preserved surrounding land, of course, the Blue Ridge Mountains, Monticello, and the rich local history. "There's a sense that being a Virginian means something noble, distinct, and romantic," he went on. "Virginia is for lovers, you know, Jefferson himself started that publicity campaign." And the capital of the world was less than two hours away, an advantage that was at the same time threatening. "Too close for comfort," Jesse shuddered. "It may swallow us yet. But because it's there, you can live a rural life here totally free of any sense of isolation or provincialism."

But Jesse confirmed my observation that the downtown mall

wasn't working that well. "A lot of people don't go there," he said. "Except for the north side, there are real war-zone neighborhoods surrounding the downtown. We do better here than we would there, even though the neighborhoods around here aren't so good either, because much of our clientele comes in from out in the county and they just feel more comfortable pulling up at the curb right out in the front than having to walk from a parking garage downtown." He believed that the Blue Ridge and another little restaurant next door had become, more than any place on the pedestrian mall downtown, the gathering places for people whose homes were out in the county but for whom the social life of Charlottesville was a daily requirement. That was the lifestyle of not only the young gentry but also a few immigrant celebrities and the top management of the thriving new industrial plants of the region, Sperry, Comdial, and GE.

On my way back to the hotel that evening, there were crowds of people streaming between nightspots on West Main, and I saw some kind of disturbance amid a knot of mostly black people across the street. A woman was screaming at a teenager; I couldn't hear what she was saying, but as I approached, another woman came along, apparently in defense of the teen. More harsh words were exchanged until suddenly the second woman swung a mean fist that smacked the first full in the face and sent her sprawling and bawling to the pavement.

Instantly two police cruisers materialized out of nowhere, a crowd gathered, and everyone seemed to know the participants in the squabble. The majority of the crowd seemed to be supportive of the woman who had been upbraiding the teen and was still lying on the ground moaning. But a few gathered in little separate groups and muttered things like, "Gets what she deserved."

Notebook in hand, I questioned a few people from both camps. They took me for a local newspaper reporter and contended with one another to present the proper view of what had gone down. First, members of the smaller, more furtive faction expounded that the injured woman was a troublemaker sticking her nose into other people's business. The aggressor was the kid's aunt, coming to his defense against a meddling neighbor. Then a few members of the larger faction stepped up and said that the injured woman had caught the kid, who was from a family on her block in Fifeville, selling crack. The aggressor was "responding with the old values, my kin right or wrong," explained one man. "But the woman got smacked did the right thing, that's how we gonna get this scum outa Charlottesville."

More shoving and shouting commenced, and for a moment I feared that I was going to be at the epicenter of a second episode. But just as I determined to call for the cops, a chant started up among the majority faction, "What do we want: clean town. When do we want it: now!" At this show of strength, the sullen members of the smaller faction withdrew and slunk off, leaving me in the protective and inquisitive company of my rescuers. They were disappointed that I wasn't a reporter from the paper and lost interest quickly, but not before dropping a few names I should look up if I wanted to learn more about how Charlottesville was going to whip the crack dealers.

I visited the city manager, Cole Hendrix, at city hall the next morning. Most city managers I knew kept a very low profile, preferring to work as much as possible within the invisible warrens of city government. As unelected officials with tremendous power over the life of a city, but whose tenure often depended on a one- or two-vote majority any given night in city council, they tended to be extremely cautious about the public exercise of that power. But in Charlottesville I had already seen parking signs unlike those anywhere else: NO PARKING, PER ORDER OF THE CITY MANAGER. The excellent city manager I worked with in Keene would never have dared put out a sign like that.

So it surprised me a bit to find in Cole Hendrix a modest, cautious, middle-aged man who fit absolutely the usual cut of city managers. He eyed me warily across his mammoth desk and answered my questions in a circumspect manner. But there was one thing he was not shy about, and that was the downtown pedestrian mall—his baby, his vision made concrete.

He had come to Charlottesville in 1971 from Kansas City impressed by the cosmopolitan nature of this old university town, the beauty of the Blue Ridge Mountains, the proximity to Washington. But what really hooked him was a task that needed doing: the historic downtown was dying, and here was a community with enough sophistication to consider the radical measures he believed were needed to save small-city centers. At that date, converting Main Street to a pedestrian mall was still a new and relatively untried experiment in

America. But the idea had already been broached in Charlottesville, and Hendrix, excited to be part of a pioneering thing, threw himself into the effort.

"We were careful to do it by the book," Hendrix said. "I gave talks to the downtown merchants, a skeptical bunch at that point. We brought in the best landscape designer, Lawrence Halperin, to draw up a plan and make presentations. We allowed a lengthy public comment period during which we took a lot of flak. Merchants had the usual concerns about parking and doing business without cars driving by." A compromise emerged. The city, which didn't have the funds to do the whole thing right away anyway, would do just five blocks on a trial basis. "The attitude changed overnight as soon as construction began," Hendrix recalled. "Finally something was happening downtown." It was finished in 1976. Downtown property owners paid 40 percent of the cost, the city the remaining 60 percent.

"Still, there were two unfinished pieces of the puzzle. We had to find ways to fill the downtown up with people now that they couldn't drive their cars through." So the city built the first parking garage at one end. And then it entered into a partnership to build the Omni Hotel on a patch of vacant fields and shanties at the other end. "Besides those things, the key to the success of the downtown mall has been the restaurants with their outdoor seating on the mall itself—" he began to say, but I had to interrupt him.

"How successful is it really?" and I mentioned the empty storefronts I had seen and the lack of a continual stream of pedestrian traffic.

He paused and regrouped. "Well, we are in a recession. And it's still tough to get people away from their cars. We're looking at another parking garage on the other side. And some of our merchants haven't really adapted yet. These aren't long-term vacancies you're looking at. A lot of places come and go, but I think the bottom line is that downtown property values have increased." And quickly he turned the conversation to the clear success of a city project at the other end of West Main, the renovation of the little college-associated commercial area known as the Corner. "Check it out. It's beautiful and it's continually full of people."

Of course it was—twenty thousand UVA students lived just across the street. "Why hasn't the city done more to connect the two nodes by redeveloping the West Main corridor connecting them?" I asked.

He acknowledged that this was an unmet need so far. There were problems with the railroad owning a significant chunk of the real estate and being none too eager to do anything with it. And there was the university to contend with, which had its own tentative plan to expand the residential college down West Main. But no one had taken a real lead, and meanwhile, the neighborhoods along West Main had problems.

"Like crack?" I asked.

"Yeah, we got it. The phenomenon here is eighteen-, nineteen-, twenty-year-olds from those poorer neighborhoods buying crack on the street in D.C. and bringing it in on the train or bus and selling it locally at a double profit. It's market economics." Hendrix hastened to point out that it was no longer strictly a black problem, that college kids and affluent whites out on Rugby Road had gotten into the action as well.

Cole Hendrix seemed fatalistic. There didn't seem to be much the city could do. "We move it around with our police action, like a balloon thing, squeeze it here and it pops up there," he said with a shrug. He never even mentioned the grassroots neighborhood movement I had seen marching in the street the night before.

He concluded our interview by turning the conversation back to the positive. "There are pieces of the old southern culture that exist here, the good pieces. We have a cosmopolitan feeling that makes race relations friendly. And the history here makes this a richer community than the golf course communities you've probably seen all over the country. For the life of me, I can't see why people pull up all their roots and move to places like that." He went on to talk about how Charlottesville had been spared the influx of people searching for gated communities. It was as if he had been prepped on issues I had been much concerned about in earlier visits to places like Santa Fe, Kelowna, and Missoula. But in Charlottesville I was more interested in something else.

I found it at the Blue Ridge a few nights later. Two women in their thirties were sitting at the bar talking about the antidrug march. Virginia Coffey and Mary Mudge were next-door neighbors in Fifeville, one of the troubled neighborhoods along West Main. Virginia and her husband, Steve Taylor, were teachers with three children who still had time to be activists in the grassroots movement to drive out the crack dealers and otherwise improve their neighborhood. "We live there because we choose to," she said, "not because we have to. We wanted a downtown residence where we were close to everything and where we felt part of a community. But we've discovered that we have to fight to hold the politicians and police accountable for helping us to save our neighborhood."

Mary Mudge was a recent transplant from northern Virginia. She was single, striving to preserve her perfect 4.0 at the university, and wavering between a career in medicine and a personal dream of farming the land in some mountainous place. Virginia pointed to Mary as proof that the old neighborhood could still attract young, vital people.

I went to visit them the following morning for coffee. Nalle Street in the heart of Fifeville was just a couple of blocks across the railroad tracks from West Main. I could see immediately that any politician who dismissed this as just another troubled neighborhood ought to have his or her head examined. Most of the twenties- and thirties-vintage houses were freshly painted. Some were surrounded by well-kept shrubbery and little lawns. Children of both races played at streetside while mothers looked on from porches or gardens.

But there were holes in this picture. Three or four houses looked completely out of place, with broken windows, open doorways, and littered grounds. In contrast, there was one house in particular that was extremely trim and surrounded by a springtime bloom of myriad flowers with an extensive vegetable garden at the side and out back. This was Mary Mudge's house.

Next door there was the sound of squealing children, and when I knocked, one of them greeted me and led me into the kitchen, where Virginia's husband, Steve, was pickling vegetables. He poured me a cup of coffee and we chatted about teaching until Virginia came charging through the front door, just back from grocery shopping. After the groceries were stacked away, she sat down with us and told the story of the antidrug marches.

It began with a visit by comedian and antidrug crusader Dick Gregory back in July of the previous summer. "His message was that it's your neighborhood," Virginia recalled. "You need to take responsibility and do something yourself to save it." But *how?* everyone had asked him. His answer was that it was a matter of market economics, and I remembered Cole Hendrix's use of the same term to describe how the problem came about. "We can't do anything about the supply or the demand," said Virginia, "but we can make marketing difficult and eventually unfeasible. We do that by making it difficult for dealers to find a place to set up shop and sell and by making it difficult for customers to buy."

Residents of Fifeville started holding neighborhood meetings right after Gregory's visit. They didn't want to just push the problem into other neighborhoods. So they began with the antidrug marches, right through the most troubled areas as well as better neighborhoods a few blocks away, where people felt concerned about what was happening down the street. This helped to attract more residents to activism as well as to put the enemy on notice that the drug business was going to become more difficult everywhere in Charlottesville. "Numbers are terribly important," Virginia emphasized. "We don't carry Uzis or shotguns. It takes a lot of people to intimidate guys who might. We get hundreds out now."

But the really effective tactic was to apply pressure at the point of sale. When a dealer set up shop on a corner or in a house, a telephone tree alerted dozens of neighbors, who would congregate, chanting, taking pictures, and otherwise intimidating would-be customers. Video cameras were set up across the street from well-known crack houses. Off-duty cops were privately hired to sit in uniform at curbside and challenge all who came and went. "These tactics worked pretty well with the mobile, street corner guys," Virginia said. "But the ones who could operate out of apartments that they rented were another matter. You couldn't monitor them twenty-four hours a day."

That's when the group—it now had a name, the Fifeville Neighborhood Organization—started going after problem landlords. "Some were absentee landlords who didn't give a damn, some just had a casual idea of what is a good tenant and well-maintained property, some were slum landlords who would actually argue that everybody needs a place to live and that substandard places were all they could afford, some bought property as an investment and then just got lazy about maintaining it, and some properties were just stuck in inheritance trust funds and not maintained by anybody. Our thrust was to make all property owners take care of their property as if they lived there. We expected landlords to be serious about the management of *their* property in *our* neighborhood."

Virginia got a printout from the city assessing department of all neighborhood properties and highlighted places where the owners' addresses differed from the street address. Then a letter was sent to each one listing five escalating steps that neighbors would take regarding problem properties: landlords would be called and put on notice, their houses would be reported to the city, names would be brought before the city council, property would be reported to the fire chief for seizure, and finally, grand jury proceedings would be initiated against the landlord for maintaining a public nuisance. The neighbors and their lawyers found an old Virginia law, Code S48-3, dating back to 1919, that was still on the books and provided for just such a procedure.

"What an uproar we caused," she said, throwing up her hands in delight. "The headlines read, FIFEVILLE RESIDENTS THREATENING LAND-LORDS. But the law was there, and once we showed that we could go through the process a few times, landlords began to respond, some by hiring lawyers and harassing us, but others by calling us up and seriously talking about the problem."

Some people were concerned that Virginia's efforts amounted to neighborhood gentrification that would make housing unaffordable. "You bet we want to gentrify the neighborhoods—that's the whole point. But we also work to reassure the elderly in particular that having well-maintained, attractive properties doesn't mean they will be forced out of their homes."

City hall had not yet been very helpful, and Virginia just rolled her eyes and said, "There it is," when I related the city manager's comments about the problem. But contacts with individual police officers had been very productive, and a number of community groups, most of them with black leaders, had come forward with many innovative programs. They had established a midnight basketball program in the downtown recreation center. A group called Reading Partners went into public housing projects, pairing up with kids and reading aloud with them. Small libraries had been set up, again at the initiative of neighborhood groups, in each of the projects. Other organizations, including the traditional service clubs, had begun providing volunteers to assist landlords in renovating their houses. And a number of young, respected black professionals, sports figures, teachers, and clergy had made personal commitments to work individually with youngsters to offer solid role models.

"The problem now," Virginia said, "is that we need an umbrella organization to coordinate all of these efforts. So far that task has fallen to the Fifeville Neighborhood Organization. I don't want that responsibility. There's the danger that we'll burn out." Throughout our talk there were children scuttling into the kitchen making demands on Mother. Steve ran interference but also had planning to do for school. Twice the phone rang with people needing to talk about this or that in connection with the next antidrug march. I could see why Virginia was concerned about burnout.

What a shame that ordinary people had to struggle so hard to make their communities good places to live. The forces bent on sucking the life out of a community to make a few bucks always had vaster resources, time, and energy at their disposal, be they crack dealers, industrial polluters, or unscrupulous mall developers. Then, when aroused ordinary citizens like Virginia took action, they were all too often regarded by the pols at city hall as gadflies. But Virginia was hopeful. "We are winning, and city hall takes us seriously now." She showed me a publication called *The Winnable War,* about successful grassroots antidrug campaigns in communities all across the country. "We're going to add a chapter to this," she declared. And she invited me to come along on Friday night's antidrug march just to see what a broad spectrum of the community was now involved.

I made a pilgrimage out to Jefferson's Monticello the next morning. Monticello was one of the purest preservations of American history I had ever seen. There was no commercial Busch Gardens nearby as there was at Williamsburg, no souvenir vendors, no multimedia interpretations; even the parking lots were located out of sight. And Monticello was smaller than one might expect, thus providing a human scale that one could appreciate. It was possible to imagine actually living in this house. The guided tour interpreted the house as an expression of a life of integrated functions. Most impressive were the library, where Jefferson read, studied, wrote, designed, and invented, but also where he played with his children; and the gardens out back, where a fertile mind could ponder amid a setting of ordered natural beauty.

Down in the valley I could see the city and university that Jefferson himself had laid out and the azure line of the Blue Ridge beyond. Jefferson believed that the blessings of American liberty and bounty would be secured by an agrarian society of landowners, clustered around small magnet communities like Charlottesville, who would make government and civic action an essential part of their existence. There would be no need for professional politicians, lobbyists, and power brokers, because the people themselves would serve in government, their legitimacy derived from their connections to the land and their community service.

He never foresaw the industrial revolution or the implications of large numbers of people living and working full-time in cities. Nonetheless, his core tenet had flourished throughout our history in the tradition of grassroots movements. It had become a countercurrent, almost subversive to the directions of mainstream government since his time. It was happening today in Fifeville.

It occurred to me as I watched cars crawl into Charlottesville from the country that the other, historically discredited part of Jefferson's vision lived on here as well in altered form. One of the things that made Charlottesville a good place to live was the presence of the prosperous landowners in the surrounding countryside. They prevented the despoliation of the region by fast-buck developers and infused money and sophistication into Charlottesville itself. But they were largely disconnected from the grassroots works of the neighbors of Fifeville. If only Charlottesville could connect the two living parts of Jefferson's vision—the civic prose and the rural poetry—here might be a place where American life would exist in fragments no longer.

Fifeville was named after an old Charlottesville family who still had their antebellum home on the remaining 5-plus acres of the 350 they once had owned. I went for a walk through Fifeville one morning with the current head of the family, Francis Fife, a retired banker. He showed me the old boundary lines where neighborhoods like Nalle Street had been carved off of the original estate as his ancestors were forced by wars, depressions, and changing times to sell off pieces of the property bit by bit, much of it to the railroad. The Fife homestead, built by one of Jefferson's builders in 1820 and home to Francis's sister-in-law today, was a large, gracious brick house, utterly out of character with the Fifeville neighborhoods nearby. For generations it had marked the boundary between urban Charlottesville and the rural county.

"That's the story of Virginia places like Charlottesville," he told me as we strolled past a park where small boys played a rough-and-tumble game of basketball, "the absolute separation of cities and counties into alien domains. We had to move a pigpen once because the boundary of the city ran across our property. Pigpens were allowed in the county, but not in the city."

The problem was that the counties attracted money and landed gentry while the cities shouldered the burden of social responsibilities. "What we need is a merger," he said. "Tax some of that rural money to help maintain Charlottesville as the pleasant little focal point that the county people appreciate so much. They're largely cosmopolitan people despite their attraction to rural properties. They wouldn't buy those farms out there if the amenities of Charlottesville and the university weren't right nearby."

I asked if the new people moving into the county were bad neighbors, like Missoula mayor Kemmis's hi-graders. "No, not generally," he answered. "Some of them are genuinely ignorant that there are poor people here who have been around for generations. And some of these folks are highly responsible, kicking in their resources in a variety of public endeavors. But there are those that aren't. So far, involvement by the gentry in the affairs of the town they need so much is mainly an ad hoc volunteer affair."

The issue that was best guaranteed to stir the county gentry was unrestrained growth. While conceding that the gentry's generally anti-growth activism (and preemptive purchasing of threatened properties) had certainly preserved the quality of the countryside, Fife was concerned that when it came to importing new jobs for Charlottesville, the gentry's knee-jerk opposition was harmful. The city had already lost one prospective new employer because of anticipated resistance to the project.

But Francis Fife's real passion was low-income housing. As vice president of the Charlottesville Housing Improvement Association, he raised funds to restore declining properties and to subsidize renters of modest means. He was well aware of the efforts of the Fifeville group and had worked to establish liaisons between his semiofficial group and grassroots people working toward the same end. "Public housing has had a controversial history in Charlottesville," he explained. "In the fifties, when the concept was first broached, there were a lot of folks who just didn't believe in it on philosophical grounds. The individual was responsible for making sure he had a roof over his family's heads. Then it got worse when our first projects focused on longtime black neighborhoods and business districts."

An area known as Vinegar Hill was targeted for urban renewal by white planners who had little understanding of the importance of the little businesses there to the black community. "It was wiped out," he said. "Many in the black community felt that they had lost their center and their territory, despite the fact that the effort was intended to provide them with better housing. Some had to move off Vinegar Hill, which they regarded as their ancestral home." Ironically, it was these early efforts to provide housing that had caused Charlottesville's only memorable racial conflict. As recently as the seventies there were disturbances over what happened at Vinegar Hill, and resentment lingered even today.

Otherwise Fife believed that people in Charlottesville had always had a reservoir of tolerance and sophistication on racial issues. The city was one of the first ordered to desegregate schools in the sixties. "We had a mayor," he recalled, "Judge Michie, who went on the radio and said that there would be no difficulty over the order. Thanks to his leadership, we had none of the trouble so common in other southern cities."

It was part of what made Charlottesville a good place to live in Fife's eyes and he urged that I follow up on Virginia's invitation to join an antidrug march to see it for myself. "Don't take my word for it," he concluded. He also suggested two black leaders I ought to see, former mayor Alvin Edwards, of Fife's generation, and Charles Alexander, a young man leading the charge to provide black youth with an alternative model to the allure of the drug culture.

Late Friday afternoon, something was finally happening in the pedestrian mall downtown. There was a bandstand set up at the west entrance and Fat Ammons's Band played loud dancing blues. The pavement was crowded with people, those closest to the music gyrating enthusiastically, foaming cups of beer in hand. I asked a man what was going on and he said, "Friday After Five, stranger. Don't you just love it? The whole city turns out every week."

There were people of all ages, black, white, singles, couples, families, some attired in business suits and dresses, others shirtless or in tank tops and ripped blue-jean shorts. The relaxed-looking cops on duty smiled and chatted amiably with citizens. Merchants did the same in their doorways. Children whooped about, frequently hitting up their parents for snack or soda money. People moved from group to group and I saw little evidence of clans or cliques. Everybody danced with everybody, even kids with their parents and saleswomen with the cops.

Viewed from the rise of the Omni Hotel at the west end of the mall, the scene was a tableau of communal felicity, despite Jesse Hayden's grumblings that it unfairly deprived the Blue Ridge of much of its TGIF clientele. "Still," he said, "it does get people out. We get 'em later in the evening."

He was right. Friday After Five in Charlottesville heralded one of the most spirited Friday nights I had seen in any place I had visited. There were crowds in the streets, in the mall, and in all of the bars and restaurants all evening long, almost as if the general population had somehow increased for the weekend. Charlottesville was a pretty quiet, genteel place during the week. But on Friday night, it loved to party.

So it surprised me when I went to the staging area at nine-thirty for that night's antidrug march to find an equally strong and spirited turnout for an event of much more serious purpose there. Nearly a hundred people had gathered in the parking lot of a gas station with their signs and flashlights and bullhorns. The majority of the marchers were black, but there was a significant white presence as well. I even noted a few of the genteel county folks I had met at the Blue Ridge. Virginia Coffey hustled about pep-talking, networking, and giving instructions. I watched her approach a burly black cop and ask him, "You cruising tonight?" When he nodded, she listed a number of addresses where trouble might be possible. Francis Fife collared me and took me about, introducing me to people, and then he pointed out a young black man who was mounting the trunk of a car and carrying a bullhorn. "That's Charles Alexander. He'll set 'em on fire."

Alexander stood on the roof of the car and asked for attention. People quieted immediately. "We are all leaders here, right?" he began and the crowd cheered, "Yes!"

"I am not a leader, you are. I'm just a doer. And here's what we been doing since our last march. Gonna be a mass march next month with national speakers. We gonna galvanize the students of Charlottesville, from K to Ph.D. at UVA.

"Now, you know, you got problems with landlords you let us know. Network to your neighbors who are unable to march. Everybody's included. We got city government people coming to our next march. We're expanding, always expanding.

"We're letting the drug people know that we aren't gonna take it no more. Who got the power?"

"We got the power!" shouted the crowd.

"Who got the power?"

"We got the power!"

"We've made a difference since last summer. Who's the talk of the town?"

"We the talk of the town!"

"Who's gonna soon be the talk of the state?"

"We gonna be the talk of the state!"

"We're on a mission to reclaim our children, our homes, and our neighborhoods. And who's gonna stop us?"

"Nobody gonna stop us!"

"Everybody's welcome. Even drug users and dealers who want to change. Some are ready to come over already. You know why? 'Cause who got the power?"

"We got the power!"

Then he gave marching instructions. Everyone was to stay close together in twos. Every child should hold the hand of an adult. And again it was more chants:

"Eenie meeny miny moe, drug dealers have got to go"; "Drug dealer ride, but baby you can't hide"; "How you call yourself a brother when you're out there killin' your very own mother"; "Drug dealer, drug dealer hear what I say, you're killin' more brothers than the KKK."

And so it went till the crowd was ready to move. Then, with two patrol cars, lights flashing, leading and trailing the marchers, followed by two more cops on horseback, the throng turned into a line two abreast and headed out.

For an hour and a half we wound through the urban neighborhoods of Charlottesville carrying the signs and chanting the slogans. On most streets, I saw faces in the windows of nearly every house, sometimes raising clenched fists, often merely staring with something like awe. At some corners, groups of neighbors and their kids greeted us with their own signs and slogans as we passed by. Many joined the march so that it swelled to close to 150 by the time we were done. But at other houses, furtive, sullen faces glanced out and disappeared. We stopped at some of these and chanted our loudest and most intimidating antidealer slogans. A bottle flew out of the darkness and crashed near us once, sending the horseback cops off at a canter in the direction from which the missile had come.

Otherwise there were no confrontations, and by the time we made our final pass down West Main past the Blue Ridge and Southern Culture, the group hummed with an electricity of invincibility. At the end of the march, people were chanted out and dispersed quickly and quietly to their homes. I went to the Blue Ridge with Virginia and a small group of her neighbors for a postmortem. There the campaign continued.

"A community is like an ecosystem or a chain, it's as strong as its weakest link," she was saying as we quenched our thirst at the bar and curious patrons gathered around us.

One of the young country squires who frequented the place inquired, "You're talking about Fifeville?"

"Maybe," answered one of Virginia's cohorts. "Or maybe we're talking about the people who don't see the relevance of the problem to their own case." There was nothing confrontational in this statement —the man was just earnest. He went on, "You can't ignore the weak links in the system and think that those at the top can survive." And then he leaned over to the squire and whispered, "Join us next time. You lose Fifeville and you lose the Blue Ridge."

After participating in the march, I began to get phone calls. First was the Reverend Alvin Edwards, former mayor and an activist in the antidrug crusade who preceded even Virginia. He stopped by the coffee shop in my hotel for a chat Saturday afternoon. A black man of modest height and build, Rev. Edwards conveyed a sense of hard-earned wisdom and soft-spoken toughness. Perhaps it was the gray peppered through his thinning hair. Perhaps it was the firmness of his talk; he spoke like a man who was accustomed to having people heed him.

He believed I had witnessed firsthand at the march the key reason for Charlottesville's being a truly good place to live. "Charlottesville is the closest thing to a meritocracy I've ever seen," he began. "Who are the most highly respected people in town right now? The organizers of the drug marches, that's who, even though they come from the wrong side of the tracks and some have pretty modest educations. I had lived here only nine years when I was elected mayor. Where else could a black man of only nine years' standing get elected mayor?"

I asked if the aristocracy out in the county had any connection to the phenomenon he was talking about. "Yes, they do. What do you think Charlottesville would be without those people? Just another college town. They set a tone, a model of sophistication for people to strive for. And some of them are really involved, like John Kluge, who distributes his wealth to people and organizations in town doing good works. It was Henry Silver, another wealthy man out in the county, who brought Dick Gregory here in the first place to institute the antidrug movement. I don't buy this argument that the county is somehow estranged from the city."

He believed there was a silver lining in the town's drug problem. "You already had a town where people cared about their families, their neighborhoods," he said. "What the drug trade has done is to bring people from disparate walks of life together to care about the community as a whole."

He thought the biggest difficulty now was a national cultural and legal permissiveness that often tied the hands of communities and neighborhoods wanting to deal aggressively with a crime problem. "A generation ago, black families used to watch out for one another. If you misbehaved down the street in front of a neighbor's house, you got a whupping there and another when you got home. Now the laws and cultural mores prevent that. It hurts the black family because neighbors were always a key part of our extended families. Now you can't spank a child, can't touch a child who's not your own."

He advocated a return to a "happy medium of discipline" in schools, communities, religion, and politics. "The laws are too often on the side of the criminal, and the druggies know them better than we do," the reverend complained. I pointed out that many of the laws he complained about had been instituted during the civil rights movement to correct racial abuses, and we had a little debate in which I took positions advocated by the NAACP while he staked out the ground once occupied by Spiro Agnew. The reverend was adamant that protecting civil rights and maintaining tough law enforcement were not mutually exclusive options. "If cops are abusive, don't throw out the case if the defendants are guilty. Discipline the cops. But don't tie their hands so it's next to impossible for them not to screw up. Don't assume that all cops are going to operate like the LAPD."

"How do you prevent Rodney King episodes?" I asked.

"Regular and vigilant police review," he said. "You don't think that was an isolated case. Regular police review would have turned up practices like that long ago. The trouble out there was that nobody was paying attention. Nobody punished racist police action and nobody rewarded successful work."

"As in a meritocracy."

"Precisely. The law needs to be made more user friendly, with the user being residents who want to use the law to guarantee safe neighborhoods—to feel comfortable sitting out on their porch, to stop worrying about having to keep the kids in the backyard. That would do a lot to combat the cynicism that people feel about law enforcement. Law enforcement shouldn't be just a police problem. It's our problem. If government doesn't do its job, it's because people haven't held them accountable. You've got to hold people accountable for their actions, from the kid who chooses to deal drugs on up to the city councilor who decides to look away from a serious community-problem."

Rev. Edwards's passion for aggressive direct action had gotten him into hot water with his church on one occasion, when he volunteered to go undercover for the police department and make drug buys. "How could that work?" I asked, incredulous. "You're too well known."

"You don't know the South," he answered with a chuckle. "People assume that preachers slip and slide. Dealers who knew me sold to me with a grin and a wink."

He had also personally gone on the ensuing drug busts and received threatening phone calls as a result. "My church wants me to quit that. But I had to do it. God is not an extremist. But he holds me accountable too."

I also got a telephone call that weekend from Charles Alexander, the man who had led the drug march. We met for coffee on Sunday during the hour Rev. Edwards was preaching a sermon at his church entitled "Weathering a Storm." Charles ("Alex-Zan," people called him) was a big, athletic man who spoke a muscular vernacular of street smarts further toughened by rigorous education. I noticed that in our conversation he had dropped the slangy "we gonna" syntax of his pep talk the night of the drug march.

Alex-Zan was a motivational consultant hired by schools, corporations, civic organizations, churches, and a few well-heeled families to help individuals make the most of themselves. On his own time, he ran Club RAPP (responsibility, attitude, potential, and persistence), a daily gathering of nine- to twelve-year-olds in the Fifeville Park, in which he worked to instill strong character, self-confidence, a sense of direction, values, and respect for self and others. "I'm a lucky man," he said, "because my profession is totally integrated with the rest of my life. I'm very conscious that what I want out of life is to serve as a role model. Everything I do works to that end."

He also was the publisher of central Virginia's only minority resource guide, listing all black businesses, clubs, fraternities, sororities, employment organizations, and public assistance opportunities. "It's not just whites who are coming to Charlottesville these days. We get a lot of new black residents funneled through UVA, the GE regional plant, and State Farm. The black economic base may not be quite as good here as it is in North Carolina, places like Durham or Charlotte, but it's coming on. The key is information and control. That's what the resource guide is for."

Control of their own economic base was what blacks didn't have back in the dark days of the Vinegar Hill episode. Alex-Zan confirmed that a deep resentment lingered among blacks of his generation who could remember their tired, old daddies throwing up their hands when the city moved them out of establishments that had been started by their granddaddies. "They were too old to start over," he said, "so they just gave up. Who decided that it was better to tear down their shops? White men in city hall. That's what we mean by control."

He disagreed with Rev. Edwards concerning the relationship between the city and county. In his mind, there *was* a schism and there was a crying need to educate those affluent white gentry to understand that if Fifeville went down, much of what they cared about in Charlottesville would go down. Furthermore, the drug problem was out there as well; it was just hidden behind heavy oak doors rather than displayed openly on street corners. He agreed with Edwards that law enforcement had to be tougher with the dealer on the street, though he was nervous about some of Edwards's proposed revisions to laws protecting civil rights. But even though he actively supported the theory of making it hard to do business, he believed that the ultimate solution was motivational.

"Why does a young man decide to become a dealer, or even a user? I don't buy the market economics thing. I don't buy the idea that someone wakes up one morning and decides, Hey, I can make some bucks selling drugs. It's just not that easy. You have to spend some time being a kind of apprentice. So that means spending some time in the drug culture long before you decide to become a dealer yourself. That's where you have to attack it.

"Our whole society speaks a message of the quick fix—find a need and fill it. So we think that's how it is with people getting into the drug trade and then we fool ourselves some more thinking that's the key also to beating the drug trade. Wrong, wrong, wrong. You've got to look at the individual and ask not why does he decide to sell drugs, but why does he decide to let himself be drawn to the drug milieu long before he makes that other decision."

"Why does he?"

"Because we allow the drug culture to be the hottest thing going in the limited world of an inner-city youth. Because we allow the so-called successful drug dealer to be biggest man on the block. He can afford the jewelry and the cars and all the stuff that society says is the mark of success.

"I can't change the shit that the kids see on TV. But I can teach them to look at it critically. I can help them to feel the rush of power taking over their own lives. And I can show them that me, Alex-Zan, I'm the biggest man on the block.

"I take a brown paper bag into the schools filled with all of the meanest, nastiest drugs and paraphernalia. I set it on a table and say, 'This package won't do anything to you unless you make a move with it. You got more power than it does as long as you don't touch it. And if you do touch it, then don't tell me you became a drug scumbag because you wanted fancy shoes or because your mamma was poor and you wanted to become a big man. No, you become a drug scumbag because you gave up the power when you decided to touch that brown bag.' "

Charles Alexander viewed the drug trade as just a symptom of a much larger societal problem that he felt a personal responsibility to combat here in his town of Charlottesville. Mass materialism, the distorted images of success conveyed by the mass media, unequal economic opportunity, remote and irrelevant government, and the lack of the right kind of role models—all of these had combined to disempower the individual. In his view, it was simple: people made bad choices because they didn't know they had the power to make better ones.

I spent a few more days enjoying the delights of Charlottesville: a drive out Skyline Drive along the rim of the Blue Ridge Mountains, some long afternoons hanging out with members of Charlottesville's burgeoning alternative lifestyle crowd on the veranda of the Kafkafe sipping tea, and walks on the campus talking politics with some of UVA's delightfully informed and articulate students. It was possible to live graciously in or near Charlottesville and ignore the rumblings in Fifeville. But most people didn't choose to do that. The threat of drugs and Fifeville's response had fostered a grassroots ethic of participatory democracy that reached throughout all segments of the community. The Fifeville movement happened because many people wanted to live close to the heart of town and preserve the tranquility of their homes. It was only a matter of time before even the politicians and bureaucrats in city hall began to catch up with their constituents and see that the key to the heart of Charlottesville was not more parking garages, but the in-town neighborhoods, no matter how humble.

You can look southeast from almost any spot in Charlottesville and see Monticello up there on the hill. Every time I did, I thought of Jefferson's vision of Americans empowered by their roots in their land

and their homes, and by their participatory form of government. I thought he might well frown if he were to look down on what has become of the nation as a whole. But I thought he might be cheered looking closer to home, to the town whose streets he laid out with a quill pen and straightedge in the library of Monticello.

13

BE HERE NOW

ASHEVILLE, NORTH CAROLINA

"I just wanta be a pretty little princess," the girl quipped as she did a faltering little dance, half grace, half awkwardness, clutching her bowler hat to her breast, rolling her big brown eyes skyward and stroking her unshaven calf with the back of her hand. She was a high school student, dressed in rock logo T-shirt, torn blue-jean shorts, and black Mary Janes, playing at being a typical girl with two of her buddies on the back porch of Malaprop's Bookstore and Café in Asheville, North Carolina. But she wasn't a typical girl; she was a young lesbian just discovering her true colors, still tentatively trying out her personal possibilities.

"I'm gonna tell Caroline you said you wanted to be a pretty little princess," teased one of her mates as the first girl tucked her hair up under the bowler and tried a different pose.

"How about Charlie Chaplin?" she said. "Suppose Caroline would like this look?" And she took a big draft of her milkshake, deliberately leaving a froth on her upper lip, which she wiggled in a Chaplinesque parody.

Established and run by a lesbian couple who had come to Asheville from Atlanta, Malaprop's was, among other things, a haven for adolescent lesbians whose parents didn't know and who found this back porch of a place frequented by adult lesbians, heterosexual feminists, New Agers, writers, artists, and other colorful square pegs to be a stage where they could play at their newfound identities, secure from conventional censure.

Upstairs, the place was a bookstore, a good one with a broad spectrum of titles but with particularly well-stocked sections of feminist, gay, New Age, and alternative lifestyle literature. Every renaissance town I had ever visited had at least one bookstore with this theme; it was a hallmark. But Malaprop's also had the café downstairs where you could quaff a beer or a cappuccino, slurp yogurt shakes, or spread cream cheese on a bagel. People came in here and read all day. At the bottom of the steps near the back door, the wall was hung with the largest community bulletin board I had ever seen. You could spend hours exploring the notices tacked up there: HARLEY-DAVIDSON FOR SALE, CHEAP BECAUSE OF BAD KARMA; DIVORCED 30 YR. OLD WOMAN SEEKING PREVIOUSLY HETEROSEXUAL FEMALE ROOMMATE WILLING TO EXPLORE THE OTHER SIDE; GUITARIST NEEDS DRUG-FREE JAM-MATES; SUPPORT GROUP FOR MEN SHEDDING SEXISM; and announcements of concerts, benefits, poetry slams, lectures, and so on.

The back porch, opening off of the café into a dirt parking lot, was a place of absolute freedom. You could smoke here in an otherwise nonsmoking establishment, drink a beer with a high school kid slugging soda pop, read poetry aloud, sketch nudes, quote Shakespeare, or be a teenager coming to grips with something you couldn't anywhere else.

I hadn't expected to find this in Asheville. Recently spotlighted as a good place by *Outside* magazine and located in the heart of the Smoky Mountains, Asheville would be a place of outfitters, bicyclers, and rock climbers, I had thought. You could see mountains by looking in any direction from virtually any street. The air was cool and clean, even with summer approaching. Memories were rich with images of the Civil War and the lore of the mountain people. The Foxfire Books had been done here. But mountain places had a way of drawing to their rocky dells folks living outside of the mainstream, even here in the hillbilly, moonshiner South.

From my first impressions, it wasn't readily apparent that Asheville would turn out to be one of the renaissance towns I sought. Old mills on the outskirts of town lay rusting, abandoned. Asheville's oversize downtown grid presented more empty storefronts than any good place candidate I had ever seen. It was impossible to identify its focal point and there seemed to be a paucity of third places. The streets were too quiet, even at noon and in the after-work hour.

Asheville's downtown had several nodes of activity. There was Haywood Road, where Malaprop's and a popular conventional bar and restaurant called Chickadees and Rye were located. A couple of blocks to the west, cobblestoned Wall Street had obviously been the object of recent renovation, with quaint little boutiques and restaurants. Then, two blocks to the east, there was an antique shop row on Lexington Street and a traditional beer, pool, and music bar called Gatsby's. Two blocks south of this area, the main drag, Patton Avenue, intersected with Biltmore Avenue at Pack Square, where buildings in a stunning range of architectural styles from I. M. Pei Bauhaus to Gothic to art deco faced one another across an obelisk-dominated commons. Here, afternoon luncheoners relaxed languidly at the outdoor plaza tables of the Cafe on the Square. Three blocks east of Pack Square at the beflowered City/County Plaza, two contrasting buildings, one done in the most outrageous pink art deco style and the other a sedate block of neoclassic convention, formed the seats of city and county government, respectively.

Between these nodes, empty storefronts broke up any sense of continuity. But within each node, meticulously restored early-twentieth-century buildings displayed marvelously eclectic and whimsical architecture constructed of lavishly colorful materials: red granite, blue slate, yellow- and even green-tinted marble. "There's a thing here about architecture," said Chris Hardwick, owner of the radical bar Be Here Now, just a few doors down Biltmore Avenue from the Café on the Square. "But it's not my thing, so I can't tell you much about it."

I had found Chris, a hale fortyish entrepreneur who had never left his music-loving twenties roots, counting tickets in his messy office. Be Here Now was a nonsmoking bar with a huge inner hall for concerts and dancing. It was midafternoon, and Chris's hired hand kept interrupting us to inquire how the seats should be set up for tonight's entertainment. Chris was fussy about making sure that the seating would create the impression of a full house, since he expected a relatively small turnout for this particular folk performance. "But tomorrow night we have Chris Smither and Saturday we got Guitar Gabriel. It will be packed those nights, then the chairs have got to be arranged to make it seem like there's more space," he explained.

Chris was another of those new migrants who had found his place after a deliberate search. He came to Asheville with a school bus and a pocket full of money from a successful bicycle business in Columbia, South Carolina. There was magic in the mountains around Asheville and the Black Mountain Music Festival was held here. "I was a little discouraged by the nightlife at first," he said. "But I could tell at the street festivals that this town was already loaded down with good people, and more were coming." So he decided to make his living here, addressing the nightlife problem personally. Be Here Now had been in business just five months at the time of my visit and was already a roaring success.

Asheville's renaissance was a relatively recent phenomenon; this was no Charlottesville or Napa, with their long standing as good places for at least a generation or two of seekers. "You musta seen the empty storefronts," Chris commented. "The town is a half cup filling rapidly, but it hasn't been at it all that long." Yet he thought Asheville had already become a town of transplants, "people who have already done time in some troubled cultural mecca like New York and come here because culture is on the rise with a clean quality of life already so well established."

There was opportunity here for people like him. It wasn't easy, because you had to accept a cut in earnings no matter where you came from. But the quality of opportunity more than compensated. "We're on a small-is-beautiful wavelength," he said. "I'm here to look out my front door and see mountains reaching into clean air, a river in my front yard, and to hang out listening to national-caliber music with like-minded people who dropped out of the big-city corporate scene."

Chris believed that Asheville was ripe for change. "The city fathers once had this vision—the city would become either a retirement community or a haven for polluting, rust-belt industry," he said. The new people here had a different vision, of tourism, entertainment, and culture. "That's green dollars—and why not? We got the mountains and a tradition of homegrown American music."

I asked Chris if I would encounter the occasional coolness I had

faced elsewhere from people not happy to see me publicize their perfect place. "This is a book, right? Not a TV show," he answered. "No
problem, you'll bring people here who read. Go for it."

At Chris's recommendation, I bought some fruit and vegetables at
the French Broad Food Co-op down the street to supplement my
restaurant-based diet during my stay in Asheville. Located in an abandoned grocery store and named after a local river, the co-op was
another manifestation of the impact of new people, and it reminded
me of Ithaca. Here was aisle after aisle of real food, most of it fresh
and produced locally. The place was conspicuously clean and cheerful,
with poster photos of the producers alongside many of the offerings
and people chatting in all of the aisles. Everyone seemed to know
everyone else.

The woman at the checkout counter commented on my Yankee
accent, wondering if I was yet another transplant. "Happens all the
tahm," she drawled. "Ah see a fresh face with an accent in here gittin'
their groceries and next thing ah see 'em agin drinkin' a beer at a bar
askin' about apartments to rent."

The co-op had been founded in 1975, but in the old days its
operations were limited to supplying a small group of devotees with
whole and organic foods. Now, just in the past five years, the world
had changed, Asheville was bursting with people demanding this kind
of food, and the co-op had learned to compete with the conventional
stores that had begun carrying lines of organic foods. Gone were the
purist days of recycling all jars and containers. A few purists grumbled
at the new packaged foods, but most were happy to see an organic
food co-op come to be one of the biggest and most successful grocery
stores in town.

At Chickadees and Rye the next afternoon, I sat beside a fellow at
the bar who was wearing wire-rim glasses and a look remarkably like
Harrison Ford's in his first Indiana Jones film. When he spoke, it was
with the richest, lowest-pitched southern accent I had ever heard.
Patrick Padgett was an erudite man in his early thirties who had seen
the world, loved his town, and so was heartened by the movements
toward change that were occurring here.

"We Padgetts are southern liberals with roots in the hill country,"
he said in deep, mellifluous tones that would land him a part in the

movies for sure if his current schemes didn't work out. His ancestors had been newspaper publishers in the mountain town of Haysville till his father moved to Asheville to practice as an architect. Patrick studied to follow in his father's footsteps but was now trying his fortune importing modern English guttering for the renovation industry that was booming in Asheville and other places that had discovered they had beautiful old buildings that could be put to good use. He was well versed in the literature of place and community and also liked to drink beer, play pool, and talk for hours. We were destined to become friends.

He quickly cleared up some of my first questions about Asheville. The downtown had such spotty renovation and multiple nodes of renaissance activity because the downtown was simply quite large for a town of approximately sixty-two thousand and because Asheville's renaissance was still very young and moving slowly.

Yes, Asheville did have a thing about architecture. The Vanderbilts, whose Asheville home of Biltmore was a major tourist draw, had imported world-class architects after the turn of the century when they decided to make the city their seat of residence. The tradition had taken hold as part of the community identity and stuck right through the horrendous depression years, and it was now born again as creative developers discovered the marvels hidden behind plastic and plaster facades erected during the fifties.

He traced the town's tolerance of idiosyncracy back to the region's bootleggers and moonshiners. "They were deviants and outlaws beloved by the culture that grew up around them," he intoned in that delicious voice that made everything he said seem profound. "When the marijuana culture began here in the seventies, it was the same old thing. There are landing strips back in the hills all over the place. Now nonconformists of all stripes seem to have inherited that protective mantle. Ashevillians just never developed the judgmental habits of so many places in the South."

After our supper together at the bar, Patrick took me on a tour of his city, showing me the frame house, renovated by his father, where Thomas Wolfe had lived and written *Look Homeward Angel;* the domed art deco First Baptist Church; the neo-Gothic Jackson tower with its gargoyles; the Tudor cottage, once a filling station, now home of the organic restaurant Stone Soup; the Romanesque Drhumor Building; the Spanish Baroque Church of St. Lawrence; Asheville's own Flatiron building; the neo-Georgian Battery Park Hotel. Never had I seen such an eclectic collection of architectural styles in one downtown.

We then drove south of town and out to Biltmore Forest. Developed on the grounds of the Vanderbilts' famous estate, Biltmore Forest was one of the most affluent addresses in America. Scores upon scores of homes valued in seven figures were tucked into the tall trees along the winding roads. Though it existed as a separate entity, with byways patrolled by its own security apparatus, this was no "gated community." Residents of most gated communities couldn't afford to live here, for one thing, and there were no gates or security checkpoints at the entrances. The wealth of Biltmore Forest was not in retreat from the community of Asheville but rather represented its apogee. Patrick himself aspired to live here. "And thus you see the limits of my liberalism," he mused self-deprecatingly.

"Who lives here? What is this money?" I wanted to know as we cruised slowly and suspiciously along the forest roads in Patrick's gutter installation pickup.

"Some of it is remnants of old Asheville money from the Vanderbilt days," Patrick answered. "Asheville was a summer community for many in the twenties, and now the next generation lives here in retirement. Some comes from the medical establishment here. Some is new money. There are some very wealthy doctors here and aspiring millionaires of every type."

"But Asheville doesn't have a wealth-generating economy; where does the new money come from?"

"Atlanta, Columbia, Charlotte, the North Carolina research triangle. A lot of wealth has been made in those places and then it gets retired here because people don't want to live there. Asheville is a residential crossroads of the Southeast."

Later that evening he took me to Gatsby's downtown, where we played pool and drank beer with people who couldn't dream of living in Biltmore Forest. Gatsby's was the closest thing to a true third place that I ever found in Asheville, besides those like Malaprop's and Be Here Now that specialized in the new people's scene. There were new people in Gatsby's, too, but mostly the feel was good ol' boy, blues, and bluegrass, without any of the violent redneck culture one might have expected.

I had speculated in Charlottesville that the downtown there was so free of the redneck culture because it was pedestrianized, and rednecks cannot survive far from their automobiles. But in Asheville I reflected on the fact that the redneck phenomenon was generally absent from renaissance downtowns wherever I went, pedestrianized or not. Instead the tough guys were drawn to the auto-friendly places in malls on the outskirts. This was quite a change from a few decades back, when their presence downtown had been one of the things making small cities hostile places for newcomers. I imagined that there were still plenty of benighted places where a fear of redneck violence haunted downtown streetcorners on warm evenings. But the absence of this once-common American syndrome, as much as the presence of gays and New Agers, had become a hallmark of renaissance towns everywhere.

The best pool player in Gatsby's that night was a young, ratty, tattooed fellow with long, dirty blond hair who looked like Axl Rose. But whenever he opened his mouth to speak, out came those sonorous southern-accented tones. He was kind, thoughtful, and courteous. Even here in a pool hall, civility and manners were the southern habits most on display. Patrick thought it was a key to Asheville's identity: the city presented the best of the southern tradition.

More than any other place I had visited, Asheville was what it was because of a recurring pattern in its history. The town had learned to appreciate newcomers and their effect on its life. Isolated in a high valley, Asheville was first settled and incorporated in 1797 as a small trading center for trappers and other pioneer settlers who lived in the surrounding mountains. According to early visitors, it was a hard place to get to and not very accommodating once you were there. They didn't expect it would stay on the map very long.

But after the federal government designated the settlement a postal distribution center in 1806, it was "discovered" by outsiders, well-to-do South Carolinians attracted by its moderate mountain climate. With the construction of a luxury hotel and a turnpike linking Asheville to South Carolina and Tennessee, locals had their first taste of the cosmopolitan sophistication that an influx of new people could bring to a rude pioneer town. Like no other pioneer town in the entire

Appalachian chain, Asheville prospered during the antebellum years as a mountain home for people who demanded certain amenities of civilization.

The Civil War ended all of that, devastating the town economically while leaving it physically unscathed. With little help from Reconstruction, Asheville became a crude, poverty-stricken but pristine monument to a bygone era. The town began to experience its second resurrection when the railroad arrived in 1880. Given access by the rails, the outside world again discovered something here—the high, clean, dry mountain air—and during the late nineteenth century, Asheville became a mecca for respiratory illness sanitoriums. First-rate doctors came to take the cure themselves and discovered that they could live in these gorgeous mountains and minister to the needs of patients who paid their bills on time.

George Vanderbilt's mother came to Asheville for the cure in 1887. When he stopped by to visit her, he said, "God, I want to build here." But Vanderbilt had greater ambitions than simply to build America's greatest mansion in a pretty mountain town. He had a prescience about architecture and community building, perhaps as a result of European travels, and his vision challenged the poverty of spirit so often expressed by the places Americans built around themselves. To make Asheville a worthy setting for Biltmore, he initiated the parade of great architects who left their mark on Asheville. The cult of the Vanderbilts further attracted art, music, and a cosmopolitan style and diversity. Industries besides tourism and sanitoriums eventually sprang up, including tobacco, cotton, and furniture factories, wagon makers, tanneries, warehouses, and literary clubs. Longtime Ashevillians prospered from the invasion of trendy newcomers and welcomed them with warm southern courtesy.

By the 1920s, Asheville was a boom town crawling with world-class talent. Ashevillians who predated the Vanderbilts rode the wave pumped up by the moneyed outsiders and adapted their mountain pride to the facts of life. Asheville had been a hard place before the arrival of the new people and everyone knew it.

But the crash of 1929 pulled the rug out from under everything once again. The wealthy, many of them no longer so wealthy, left en masse; the city, as a result of the grand construction schemes undertaken in the twenties, entered the depression with the highest per capita debt in the country. All across America, city governments declared bankruptcy, further contributing to the depth of the national depression. But Ashevillians' stubborn mountain pride led them to choose a different path—ironically, one that made Asheville what it is today. They created a sinking fund to pay off every cent of the debt no matter how long it took, and the debt wasn't retired until 1977. For forty years Asheville lay in an economic cocoon—a long sleep.

Since there was no money for redevelopment of any sort, Asheville never underwent any drastic reconstruction, even during the fifties and sixties, when communities elsewhere that had long since regained their prosperity were busy tearing down old buildings and erecting plastic and neon, Bauhaus glass boxes, and the institutional architecture of urban renewal. In the seventies, with the debt finally paid off and prosperity returning, people began tearing off the cheap facades that had been erected over the years and discovered treasure—the tremendous stock of beautiful vintage buildings of the teens and twenties. The downtown was designated a historical area, and developers and government officials alike wanted to rush into revitalizing it with a bang. But voters with a long memory nixed ambitious plans for a public-private partnership in a radical renaissance program.

Instead, the third wave of outsiders appeared in the eighties, attracted by the same factors of geography and climate that had rescued Asheville from stagnation twice before. If the lifestyles of this latest crop of new people were exotic and alien, it mattered little to longtime Ashevillians, who recognized the pattern of newcomers able to do for Asheville what it was unable to do for itself. The third renaissance would be slow and cautious, but it was happening here now. No one I met in my time in Asheville had any doubt about it.

There was something grand and monumental about the seats of county and city government in Asheville that suggested a much more ambitious history than those in many of the places I had visited. Located at the east end of Pack Square, the government complex fronted on great lawns, fountains, and manicured gardens. The two buildings themselves offered a jarring visual contrast. The county seat was a tall, blockish, sedate gray pseudoclassic building. City hall, on the other hand, was an eye-catching art deco wonder like no other edifice I had ever seen. It was circular, stacked in levels, and topped by the most outrageous pink-and-purple tiles with an octagonal dome on top. Frankly it looked like a great decorated cake.

City Manager Doug Bean invited me into his spacious office, poured me some coffee, and sat with me at a conference table. He was a confident middle-aged man, seemingly accustomed to talking to people from the media with a frankness and casual sureness that I found refreshing after some of the mayors and city managers I had dealt with. Perhaps this was because the city manager form of government was more firmly established here than in other places. In 1931 Asheville was one of the early bastions of the movement in response to the corruption of elected commissioners who ran the city into huge debt during the booming twenties.

Bean started right off with the legend of the two government buildings. World-class architect Douglas Ellington had been one of those attracted by the blandishments of the Vanderbilts and brought to Asheville his vision of a small mountain city whose identity would be forever linked to the distinctly American art deco architecture he planned to erect. He was commissioned to design the two seats of city and county government and produced blueprints for two buildings in the style of the current city hall. But the two governments were jealously separate entities, and while the city endorsed his plan, the more conservative county rejected it and commissioned the stodgy neoclassic design of the present county building. Neither governing body would budge toward conciliation or compromise. "The result was what you see today, a clashing architecture that says a lot about the conflicted local political culture then and now."

Bean affirmed that the depression debt and its consequences had shaped absolutely the character of Asheville today. "When the Asheville Mall was built on the east side in 1979, it seemed like it would all collapse again," he said. "The stores that were still here moved out to the mall. People questioned whether there was any future for the downtown, no matter how beautiful its buildings." That was why, in Doug Bean's view, the community had since pursued the go-slow approach. Bean was well aware of the problem of empty storefronts separating the nodes of new activity but believed there was now a momentum that would fill them in, largely through private initiative.

After Ithaca and Burlington and Charlottesville, I asked him whether any thought had been given to pedestrianizing a part of the downtown. "We were lucky to come late to the process of guiding a downtown renaissance," he answered. "We missed the downtown mall mania, and it was fortunate. Downtown malls end up competing with suburban malls, usually, and losing. It's still an auto-based culture, whether we like it or not. That's why we have focused on small, strategically located parking garages rather than the behemoths that downtown pedestrian malls require."

With the basic shape and identity of the downtown established, city government had shifted the thrust of its activism. "We've changed our efforts here in city hall now to marketing and promotion." And indeed, I had witnessed slick ads on CNN promoting Asheville as a good place to visit, live, and invest. Separate teams worked full-time in city hall publicizing tourism, relocation, and industrial development opportunities, while private organizations downtown did the same thing out of street-front offices, all of it coordinated by city hall.

Remembering some of Chris Hardwick's comments, I questioned Bean about concerns that these efforts might attract action that was inappropriate or harmful to the city. "We have some fortuitous safe-guards," he answered. "Concerning tourism, we don't have the beach culture and we don't have theme parks. People come here for the mountains, the conventions, the retreats, the health spas, Biltmore. This type of tourism is a plus, and it often leads to people settling here for the right reasons."

He thought the nature of the terrain, allowing primarily small industrial sites, didn't lend itself to the kind of large-scale industry that could harm the quality of the environment and also provided a guarantee against the exurban and rural sprawl that had come to characterize so much of the South, particularly North Carolina. He cited ITT Tevis as a clean, attractive industry that had recently set up shop here. Electronics industries had come. And the city was still a mecca of medical facilities, as specialists from all over the country simply wanted to live here. "The same is true of a dozen corporate and regional headquarters whose top officers locate here because they want to live here personally."

"In Biltmore Forest?"

"Absolutely."

Doug Bean ended our discussion by explaining that when times were hard, Ashevillians were willing to let government take an activist role in charting the shape of the city, but in times of normalcy, people wanted traditional market forces to have their way. Asheville was currently experiencing a lucky stroke in that a significant vector of that market force consisted of new people like Chris Hardwick and the proprietors of Malaprop's, whose directions were largely in harmony with the goals of liberal believers in community proprietorship.

I went with Patrick Padgett to hear Guitar Gabriel at Be Here Now on Saturday night. It was dark inside and it took a few minutes for the eyes to adjust well enough to see that there was a huge crowd, many seated around wooden tables but most dancing or just swaying and stomping out in the huge inner hall before the bandstand. There was another singular sensation. Not since San Luis Obispo had I walked into a crowded bar free of smoke. I liked the way you could really smell the beer and the perfume and the clean sweat of the dancers.

We sat with a group of news photographers who were in Asheville for a national convention. They were from places all over the country, and the singular topic of conversation was what a wonderful place Asheville seemed to be. There was something about the mildness of life here, the warmth and manners of the people, the thrashing of every outsider's preconceptions about the reception he or she would receive in a small southern mountain city. I described the Axl Rose pool player I had met at Gatsby's who looked so rough and spoke with courtesy and honey. "Right!" they all cried. They had all met the same fellow in one guise or another.

As the band played on, I heard several vows among the news photographers about returning to Asheville, possibly to find work and make a new life—maybe even to open a deli or a coffee shop in one of the many empty storefronts downtown. Here it was, Doug Bean's prescription for how Asheville would continue to be populated and enriched by visitors who thought they were here just for a convention or a retreat.

On a Sunday afternoon, I drove out to the Blue Ridge Parkway and Great Smoky Mountains National Park. Even at the highest elevations, the dogwood and honeysuckle were in springtime bloom now in late April. The Smokies were big, steep, thickly forested eastern mountains comprising an area nearly the size of all of New England, yet what struck this northern mountain person was how warm and habitable they felt. Indeed, until I entered the park itself, I saw homes tucked into the crannies and hollows at every turn. These mountains were full of people and scores of new homes. But they weren't stacked in developments. Rare were the Colorado-style atrocities with slabs of glass and redwood angles perched out in the open and thus spoiling some otherwise scenic prospect. These mountain homes were isolated and scattered, and usually built into the forest and landscape with something like good environmental taste, so that you had to look hard to see them.

This sense of balance came up quickly in my conversation with Leni Sitnick about her reasons for having come to Asheville eighteen years earlier. Born a New York Jew, she and her husband had started a family amid the old art deco neighborhoods of Miami Beach. But they felt they could no longer endure the crime and concrete and so embarked on a five-year good place search of mountain settings from the Laurentians to California.

I met Leni on the back porch of Malaprop's one afternoon as the kids were beginning to gather after school. She said that when her family first came to Asheville, work was scarce and the community renaissance had not yet begun. "There were no decent restaurants or bookstores, it was just the mountains, the spirituality we sensed in the air, and the peace that kept us here, for a while."

But the necessity of jobs sent them off to Manchester, New Hampshire, for a five-year stint before their eventual return eight years ago. It was in New Hampshire's nasty politics that Leni learned the ropes of grassroots activism. When she and her family returned to Asheville to newly available jobs eight years ago, she hardly recognized the place. "Such a gathering of energy and special people had converged here in our absence," she enthused. "It was cosmopolitan, diverse, packed with people passionate about political and social justice." There were artists and musicians, gays and lesbians, Asians, Greeks, Jews, "rainbow children." "Such a flowering. And it was so nice to get away from the black flies and the long, long New Hampshire winters.

"We've been so grateful since our return. God bent down and kissed the earth here. There's a comfort and softness, the mountains are mild and sweet. The seasons change but they're all a delight. The people are staunchly independent with an old-fashioned ethicalness that is so refreshing."

Nonetheless, it was her task, she believed, to be an activist here, as she had been in New Hampshire. The difference? In Asheville, idealism and spirituality were winning. "America is a place of failed communities," she concluded. "The cities, the suburbs, the farm towns. But there are certain places where the survivors are gathering. That's what's happening here in Asheville. It's our last best hope."

As I finished my talk with Leni Sitnick, I noticed another woman sitting on a step, sipping a cappuccino with a reporter's notebook like mine on her lap. She caught my eye and smiled knowingly.

Meanwhile, the kids came and went on the back porch of Malaprop's with their book bags, milkshakes, and bubble gum. There were some young gay men here today too, and they fit right in with the banter and experimental playfulness of the young lesbians. When Leni was gone, I sat for a while watching them and listening to some of the most gorgeous electronic music I had ever heard coming over Malaprop's speaker system. I asked one of the kids about it. She said it was a group called This Mortal Coil. I said it reminded me of standing behind a waterfall, and her eyes gleamed. "Yeah, that's good, that's what it does sound like," she said. "Makes you peaceful, doesn't it?" There was a pause. I recognized from my teaching days the look of gratefulness at adult attention and approbation. And then the spell passed as two of the boys burst through the door roughhousing and the girls jumped onto their backs, one of them shouting, "We'll have no displays of macho behavior here today!"

I looked to see what the woman with the notebook thought of all of this, but she was gone. I saw her again, just pulling away from the curb of Haywood Street when I emerged from Malaprop's. She saw me, stopped, and called out through her open window, "Do I know you?"

She was Sally Coxe, a freelance writer who had worked recently for *National Geographic,* just about to leave Asheville that moment to return to her work in Washington, D.C. I had already noted a Coxe Street and a Coxe Building here in Asheville. "I'm in the D.C. phone book," she said. And then she was gone.

City councilor and mayoral candidate Gene Ellison lived with his beautiful wife and young son on a quiet residential street in the Montrose neighborhood just across the bypass north of downtown Asheville. When I pulled into his driveway one sunny morning, he was showing his son how to slam-dunk a tiny basketball through a four-foot-high toy hoop. When the boy would fall on the ground, Ellison would exhort him urgently, "Get up quick, brush yourself off," and the game would continue without a tear. His wife was expecting a baby at any moment, so Ellison, a lawyer by trade, had set aside his practice for a few days. He was a big, athletic, handsome black man in his thirties, ready to take his place in a new generation of power.

Born and raised in Asheville's Hillcrest public housing, Ellison got into college at Virginia Union playing basketball. "I grew up in what is considered a dangerous place to live," he said. "I always had an interest in working with people to make things better, to influence change."

From a black man's perspective, Asheville had not always been the place it was today. It was a thoroughly segregated city in the sixties, and integration did not come peacefully. People on both sides would stage violent marches downtown, smashing windows and looking for fights. Kids fought at school daily. The last riot was in 1972, several years after the schools were integrated.

"You can't stop those of us who do want to live together just because you don't," he declared. "We'll never be rid of black radicals and white racists; it's OK for them to speak their minds, but they are now the minority, and we have to keep them that way."

He stressed that he didn't see himself as a councilor or mayoral candidate for blacks, but for Asheville. "We have a lot of problems that have nothing to do with race, and we have to get on with it. We're still feeling the impact of the long-term depression debt, with major infrastructure problems and a downtown just struggling to come alive."

The key to finishing the downtown, and indeed to guaranteeing Asheville's quality of life, was residential development. "That's what's going to fill in the empty spaces downtown," Ellison said. "These days, more and more people are looking for a place to live where everything they need is nearby, where they can walk to perform most of their daily routines. That's the false promise held out by the gated developments that have become so big in other places. Here people will live downtown. We have to sell that concept. It's the missing piece."

It had been a struggle for Ellison and his allies on the council to bring along other segments of the community. Business interests out-side of the downtown were opposed to spending public monies there; taxpayers who lived in other parts of the city and had no intention of moving downtown complained, as did that philosophically opposed faction Doug Bean had told me about who distrusted anything but the invisible hand of the market. "But people have come around as they have seen the benefits of our investments downtown and as we have put greater emphasis on public-private cooperative ventures rather than simply government," Ellison maintained.

Ellison had been one of those most avid about establishing the aggressive promotional efforts the city was recently known for. "We're not interested in being Charlotte or Atlanta. We don't need the fast lane here. But we do need jobs, quality jobs that make it possible for our people to stay here and thrive on the new excitement that's going on."

"By that do you mean the influx of new people and what they have brought here?" I asked.

He did, though he felt there were strains in the new demographics that would be eased if there were a bigger economic pie for everyone. "The new people are going through growing pains, learning to respect the rights of the longtime natives just as the natives have had to do with them. There's some pushing and shoving going on. I tell people we need to use our diversity as a strength instead of a weakness. In the past we made ourselves feel bigger by making others feel smaller. We can't do that anymore; everybody has to respect everybody else's right to be who they are."

I asked him if his success and conciliatory stance caused him prob-lems with radicals in the black community. "I'm the only politician in town who can feel comfortable in any neighborhood or community setting, from the country club to Hillcrest," he answered. "I've worked hard to become that kind of person. But yes, I can't avoid dealing with the angry black radical faction not interested in harmony. But I also can't let the fact that others don't want to take risks and initiative hold me back from doing the right thing in a world of change."

I wanted to talk to old Ashevillians and learn more about their view of what was happening to Asheville. Kent Newell was an officer of the local historical society, and he met me for coffee one day at the

Mediterranean, a hole-in-the-wall diner that the new people hadn't yet discovered. The place was a classic locals' greasy spoon with booths, a long lunch counter, stacks of newspapers, and minimal decoration. Instead of piped-in music, the background sound was the sizzle of bacon, sausage, and burgers on the huge grill behind the counter.

As I waited for Kent, reading in the paper the horrific details about the religious cult standoff in Waco, Texas, a young man in the next booth was earnestly talking to a pretty young woman about religion. "The churches have always had the gospel message all wrong; you just have to read them with the clear light of your own mind," he was saying. " 'Cast not your pearls before swine.' What does that really mean?" he asked rhetorically. He didn't wait for the woman to answer. "If you got gifts, a talent, money, or"—and here he paused and grasped her hands—"a natural beauty like yours, don't waste it on swine. Don't waste it on the unworthy." And he reached up and stroked her cheek.

"Gawd, ah hate it when they do that," said the matronly waitress who had just brought me my coffee and had been observing the same scene. I pointed conspiratorially to the Waco article I had been reading, and she laughed and said, "Aw, let me take that paper, honey, and plunk it down where it might do some good." And sure enough, she took the page, folded it to the article, and shortly let it drop on the table where the religious discussion had now proceeded on to the issue of who may cast the first stone.

Kent Newell came in and sat down with a flourish of energy that was refreshing to see in an older gentleman. He was sorry he was late but there was always just so much to do in Asheville these days. "Don't leave out the retirees," he said after we had talked for a few minutes about the invasion of Asheville by new people. "They're an important part of the phenomenon you're interested in. They're progressive, activist. They're people who know how to get things done."

I had to admit that I did tend to overlook the impact of retirees, believing that all too often they simply retreated into gated communities, playing golf, hiding out from the world, and contributing nothing to the life of a place. But Kent Newell insisted that Asheville's retirement community wasn't like that at all. "We get a different breed here," he insisted. "People who retire here do so because they know our history. There was a golden age here and they come here to be part of its revival."

Kent went on to tell the now-familiar story of the depression, Asheville's long sleep while the debt was paid off, and the beginnings of its recent revival. "And now it's happening all over again—with the physical environment of the twenties so well preserved and nearly intact—like an architectural cryogenics. That's what attracts monied, activist retirees today, the chance to make a second start on the twentieth century and get it right this time."

Thus, Kent's retirees tended to be environmentalists and preservationists. They were people who believed in the downtown and wanted to live there instead of in some suburban tract. They wanted to bring back the modern equivalent of streetcars and to get away from the automobile.

Kent thought there was conflict in Asheville between longtime residents and the new demographics, including the moneyed activist retirees. "A lot of the locals are still licking the wounds of the depression saga and all they care about is jobs, jobs, jobs," he said. "They'd rather see a new industrial park or another commercial strip than what they're getting in the downtown. They do look askance at some of the lifestyles coming in, and I can sympathize. To a degree, the new people, they're all mildly hysterical. And this still is a southern town." But that long-established mountain independence and moonshiner tolerance tended to attenuate any inflammatory counterresponse from the natives, and the result was that natives, instead of being an embittered, opposing force outside the renaissance process, were engaged and playing a conservative role within it.

There was an emerging vision, Kent believed, pursued by men like retired Texas developer Don Martell and *Southern Living* magazine executive Roger McGuire, who were putting their money and their activist efforts into promoting residential development downtown. "Asheville's population is today about what it was in the twenties," Newell explained. "But it's dispersed outward from the core of the city. Back then it was concentrated in the downtown and nearby streetcar suburbs. What these guys see is that as Asheville attracts more people and grows, the place to put the people is in the empty spaces downtown, not only for the residential values people are redis-covering in downtown living, but also to prevent sprawl."

I almost forgot, as I was talking to Kent Newell, that he was sup-posed to represent a native rather than new people's viewpoint. "Will I find anyone who will voice a strong contrary vision to what I keep hearing?" I asked.

"Probably not," he said. "Remember, even those with a more conservative stance are part of the process here. They like growth, and what's happening here is growth, even if it's not of the magnitude and kind that some might prefer. So they're not going to gainsay it."

I found Downtown Development Director Leslie Anderson in her office on Haywood Street, just half a block down from Malaprop's and across the street from Chickadees and Rye. A few doors down, workers were hauling Sheetrock into a building under renovation, and pas-sersby stopped to chat with their foreman.

While we talked in one office, a workshop on promoting down-town investment was going on in the next room. Leslie's view of Asheville history began in the late seventies, after the depression debt had been paid off. "So here they had a city ready for a fresh start," she said, "and wham, they ran up against the same things that were belea-guering cities elsewhere that *hadn't* lived through a forty-year depres-sion—the malls coming in on the outskirts, the auto culture taking people away from center city, the closing up of all the traditional downtown department stores."

Revitalization efforts began in 1980 when the city went to the voters with a bond issue to do a fourteen-square-block urban renewal project. It was defeated two to one. "So much for grand, sweeping gestures," said Leslie. But meanwhile, private developers on Lexington Street had shown the way. With minimal help from the city, they had turned their corner of the downtown into a row of antique shops with people living in loft apartments above. In light of their success, the city shifted to limited-scale efforts on certain blocks in public-private partnership.

Like officials of downtown associations everywhere, Leslie concen-trated first on establishing festival events to bring people into the downtown to feel some excitement. There was "Belles Cheres" in Au-gust and "Light Up Your Holidays" from Thanksgiving to Christmas, times when the community suspended its routines and took to the streets to party. Additionally there were attractions ranging from the Ringling Brothers Circus to the Asheville Symphony to teen street dances virtually every week of the year.

The thrust of her efforts the past few years had been to make matches between properties and developers or tenants. "It's much like what a mall director does," she explained. "We have a vision of what we want where in our downtown, and when we make a match that fits it, then we run interference with the red tape that might otherwise stifle getting it done." She showed me an impressive collection of publications promoting the downtown and offering vital information to prospective buyers, developers, and tenants. The next phase would be to get people to live downtown. "I always thought that that would come later," she said. "There's a higher return on investment for retail and office space." But people like Don Martell had already taken a lead in that direction and the director of downtown development was only too happy to follow.

"He came in out of Texas," she said, "and started buying old buildings. People thought he wanted to put in offices, but then it turned out his first project was condos—'Just an experiment to test the market,' he called it. Well, now he's into it on a large scale. You want to see?" And with that she was on her feet leading me out onto Haywood Street and down to the construction site I had noticed on my way in. Inside, there was Sheetrock dust and extension cords everywhere as she led me up the stairs to the second level. There we met Don Martell's partner and supervisor of construction, who showed us around.

Besides the lifestyle offered by the downtown location (and the affordable rent), the advantage of these places, he enthused, was going to be light, light, and more light. "They made window openings taller back in the twenties," he said. And with modern glazing, skylights, and eggshell-painted walls, these downtown apartments were awash with light. Off the back, the designers had cleverly conceived of stacked open-air balconies so that every apartment had one. I asked Leslie what guarantees residents would have that their views of the mountains across the low rooftops of the city would remain unblocked. "That's an issue before city council right now, the skyline ordinance," she answered. "We'll get it right."

Back on the sidewalk out front, she elaborated. "What our down-town has going for it is its human scale. We have to preserve that if we want it to be residential. There's a physical and psychological ambi-ence here right now that would be lost if we got a lot of high-rise development." The city's role was to own and maintain "everybody's front yard." That meant an investment in what she called "space ame-nities": street furniture, period lighting fixtures, trees, landscaping, trash cans, and so on. The record had shown so far that for every dollar invested by the city in these and other items of infrastructure, eight dollars were invested on the private side. "I have to remind the taxpaying community of that fact every day if we're to keep it going."

Returning to Malaprop's a few days later, I found Pickett Huffines, one of the partners who owned the place, lingering over a cup of coffee on the back porch. I explained that I was about to end my visit to Asheville and offered her a shot at having the last word. "Ah, the guy with the notebook, I've been hearing about you. Sit down and fire away," she said.

Pickett was a stocky, middle-aged woman with a ready laugh and a sparkle in her eye who seemed to feel no need to wear her identity as a badge. She looked like any of my daughters' friends' perfectly conven-tional heterosexual moms. But neither was she shy about who she was: "We're just two girls who wanted to open up a mom-and-mom's place for books."

Originally from Yemassee, South Carolina, and Greenwich, Con-necticut, she and her Hungarian-born partner arrived in Asheville after taking a year's "sabbatical from life," backpacking around South America. "We came here and it looked terrible," she said, "an already stagnant downtown taking its first hit from suburban malls. But they weren't responding by putting in a downtown mall like so many of the other places we looked at. We didn't want that, we wanted a real, old-time downtown that was making a fresh start and deserved a focal point like a good bookstore. And we thought we detected streaks of tolerance in some of the people we met here, so we found this place and stayed.

"We wanted a general bookstore with a feminist theme—no books on war, football, how to hurt and kill Bambi. But the main thing was to satisfy people who can't be without books, who aren't going to settle for a B. Dalton or Waldenbooks."

She and her partner never envisioned that their place would become a counterculture hangout, except insofar as an establishment that caters to readers is singular by its very nature. The downstairs café and the back porch were intended as places where readers could either gather or be solitary, and many perfectly orthodox men and women who loved books were regulars. But it pleased her that nonconformists, particularly the teenagers, felt so at ease in her place. "It's become the cool spot," she said. "Like a family room away from home where they can be weird if they have to."

Pickett also owned the Downtown Books and News, where a cross-section of Asheville came in to get their papers—from bankers after the *New York Times* to tattooed kids picking up *High Times*. "We just love to bring people together who are really different and smash 'em up together," she said, laughing. "What has been so good about Asheville is that this is a place where you can do that."

So I was surprised when I asked her if she had ever encountered any hostility from the community and she answered, "Oh, shit, yes. Are you kidding?" The first year Malaprop's was open, preachers blasted them with vitriolic diatribes from their pulpits every Sunday. People smeared feces on the front doors, petitions were circulated, and the KKK made a special trip down Haywood Road during one of its marches just for Malaprop's benefit. I was brought up short by these revelations; they seemed to contradict so profoundly the theme of Asheville everyone had been describing.

"Relax. We expected all that," Pickett reassured me. "I'm from Yemassee orginally, remember." The important thing was that the hostility abated so quickly. "This is the South, but weirdness can be accepted as long as it's seen as an eccentricity. Southerners have respect for having a few bats in your belfry."

In this place with a history of new people coming in and then some of them leaving, it was the fact that Pickett and her partner stuck it out that won over the town. "If you stay, see it through, people will say, 'OK, you're eccentric, but you're our eccentrics.' But you had to do well at what you said you were going to do. If we hadn't done well in the marketplace, they would have run us out of town."

Asheville had changed during the time Malaprop's had been in business. The deluge of new people had shortly followed, and those walking in Pickett's footsteps didn't have to go through the same bitter initiation. Hostility like that had become unthinkable in just a few short years. "Oh, the KKK still marches every year and everybody, black, white, straight, gay, whatever, lines up on the streets quietly holding hands as they go by. The only trouble in this town besides greedy real estate people are the occasional drunk rednecks, and they tend to stay out by the malls. It's worked out pretty well for a couple of girls who just wanted to do a bookstore. The town keeps giving us money and we feel like we've contributed to making it a freer, happier place. We won't let it get too staid."

It turned out that Pickett Huffines didn't have the last word. As I had suspected all along, there was yet another world in Asheville besides the new people of downtown, the hill people in mountain homes, the wealth of Biltmore Forest, and the black community in Montrose where Gene Ellison lived, and I finally found it during a second visit to Asheville in August. Sally Coxe, the D.C. writer I had met so fleetingly at Malaprop's, arranged for me to attend a gathering of her friends, descendants of the old Asheville families.

The party was held at the North Asheville home of Benn Fasse on a sunny, cool Sunday afternoon that showed just what twenty-two hundred feet of elevation in the Smoky Mountains could do for summertime life in a small southern city. The house, a 1930s brick Tudor just off Lakeshore Drive, sat on the side of a hill with a view across Beaver Dam Valley toward Elk Mountain. When I arrived, there were already half a dozen couples my age or younger engaged, along with the children of some of them, in a furious war of water guns and soakers under the towering oaks in the backyard. A healthy outlet for good old southern aggression, someone said to me as I awkwardly maneuvered my notebook to avoid its getting soaked. Combatants were fortified with hot dogs and chips, beer and soda, and Jell-O shooters made with vodka. It was all traditional, I was told. The group convened monthly to celebrate various birthdays, and the August gathering always featured the soakers and kids and Jell-O shooters.

Besides Sally Coxe, who protested that she was only distantly related to Colonel Coxe, here were young MacKenzies, Kimberlys, Fowlers, Edneys, Fasses, and others, all families who could trace their residence in Asheville at least to the last century. They said it was the search for paradise that had brought many of their ancestors to Asheville in the first place. Now most of them were clustered here in North

Asheville, which had been the last undeveloped area close to down-town during the fifties and sixties when racial troubles forced many of them to move out of older neighborhoods.

When the water wars settled down, I sat with Jay Bartlett and Mark MacKenzie, watching the shadows of mountains spread across Beaver Dam Valley in the late afternoon sun. Both big fellows in their late thirties, they explained that everyone here could make more money in business somewhere else but chose to be here now because life was richer here. "These are the oldest mountains on the continent, and we're not so far removed from nature not to be affected by that," said Jay. I told him he sounded just like some of the new people I had talked to and he agreed and said the influx of outsiders was tremen-dously important in maintaining the energy of Asheville. "But make sure you get it right," he urged. "The new people didn't bring this ambience here. It was already here. It's why they come, and why people like us always come back." Mark added that nearly everyone in the group had drifted away for a time, usually to make more money. "But how much do you need to survive? What's really important? I wouldn't trade these friends on this ground for all the fast-track glitter of the world."

Benn Fasse, the widowed mother of one of the partyers, who of-fered her home for these gatherings, took me on a tour of her house later in the evening. She had purchased the house, currently assessed at $375,000, for $35,000 during the migration of old Asheville families to North Asheville in 1962. Now it was filled with the memories, creations, and collections of a family with a variety of talents. At the back, what was once a porch was now a library with huge glass win-dows preserving the view of the valley and Elk Mountain. "We always read out here," she explained, "and stacks of books would always end up wet when it rained." Besides volumes ranging from Samuel John-son to John Grisham, the room was dominated by a dark, Dutch masters–style painting of a lion done by her brother and a porcelain ram's head that was her own work. Benn Fasse had a fascination with porcelain. We wandered past a square oak staircase into the high-ceilinged living room that was her museum. Elaborate crystal deco-rated lamps lit the porcelain figures, and the walls were festooned with Benn's collection of gilt-framed antique paintings.

But there was humor in the house, too. In the entry, guests were greeted by a five-foot-tall heavy bronze seminude figure of a native woman holding a spray of palms with tiny lights at the tips. The figure had been retrieved from a cathouse, and everyone called her the broad in the hall. Since this was a house where children ran free, there was more concern for their safety than for the breakage of items in Benn's collection. Thus the lights had been added to the tips of the spray to blunt their sharp points.

Downstairs there was a warren of rooms and utilities for visiting family. Some of the partyers were down there now, attending to children with soaked clothes. When Benn spoke of family, she clearly intended it to mean an extended family of her daughter's friends and their families.

I had toyed during my previous visit to Asheville with the idea of following the tourists through Biltmore. But that was a house and a life that was decadent and dead. The home of Benn Fasse, resonant with the good cheer of three generations of settled Ashevilleians, was something else—a living monument to a life of rootedness.

Benn thought there was a simple and traditional answer to why her guests enjoyed life so richly in Asheville. "You've spent two years looking at places people are moving into because they're good places to live. Our young people didn't have to do that. It was here for them all along. They're somebody here, they belong and have an identity. They have roots."

After the party, I was concerned about what my hosts would think of my focusing so much on the new people and alternative-lifestyle types of Malaprop's. I asked Sally Coxe about it when I talked to her later. "Asheville needs them and it needs someone to acknowledge their importance. No one wants to go back to the dead years. It'll be just fine," she assured me.

Asheville's current renaissance was perhaps the youngest one I had seen, even more recent than Burlington's, and the town was moving more slowly than most of the other places I had visited. With the empty storefronts and the lack of a well-established network of third places, one without an eye for mountains or architecture could drive through here and not spot it as one of the good places. But there were people who were glad they had found Napa or Missoula or Burlington at an earlier stage of their ripening. That's what I left Asheville believing it offered, a chance to get in on the ground floor, as it had several

times before during its history. That there were long-established residents who would cheer your making the effort rated it a five for Fudge
Factor, to go along with fives for Someplace and Cake. You could
make Asheville's weaknesses your work here, as had Chris Hardwick,
by buying one of the empty buildings that still could be had cheaply,
fitting out the upper floors with modern apartments and setting up a
Leunig's-style pub and café (quiet classical music only) on the ground
floor below.

Asheville, like Burlington and Portsmouth, represented a uniquely
eastern phenomenon—of old places that, ironically, got their start on
a new day later than did young places out West that were founded
with that expectation. I was soon to find another one awaiting me at
the other end of North Carolina that was older and even younger.

14

WE CALL
THIS PLACE HOME

There was a World War II battleship, the *North Carolina*, berthed in an inlet of the Cape Fear River in Wilmington. Across the waterway, the Hilton hotel was crawling with veterans of service from another battleship, the *Arkansas*, here for a reunion. Arriving after ten in the evening, I set out down Front Street, just one block in from the water-front, and after five or six blocks came across a traditional dive bar called the Barbary Coast. I probably wouldn't have gone in but for the red neon sign in a porthole window that flashed THIS IS IT.

Inside, a large dog was lying on the bar. Behind it a huge, graffiti-marked Confederate flag covered the wall and a half torso of a manne-quin was thrust through a hole in the ceiling. The place was dusty, dirty even, but it was full of people ranging from fake-ID younguns in cut-off jeans and halter tops to over-the-hill geezers in flannel and dungarees. A hard-looking man sitting beside me at the bar turned and said, "Ah hear a Yankee accent. Where y'all from?"

"New Hampshire," I answered.

"Where'd they fight? They were commandos or special forces or somethin', weren't they?"

I was confused. I didn't know there had been units organized by state in Vietnam. But it wasn't Vietnam he was talking about, of course, it was the Civil War.

He bought me a beer and shook my hand with genuine goodwill. We talked about Civil War battles, blunders, and the great tragedy of it all, I from my reading of history, he from direct oral tradition. I had seen this elsewhere in the South. Deeply rooted provincial southerners seemed to have little animosity toward a Yank these days. Though the passion of it all still formed the core of their identity and conversation, they tended to regard Yanks not as enemies but as compatriots in a great tragic human drama. And that feeling of camaraderie would last as long as you didn't tell them it wasn't that way up North.

Angie the bartender asked me my purpose in visiting Wilmington and how I had heard about it. My Asheville acquaintances had directed me to this place at the other end of the state, and when I told her so, she winked and said, "Yep, I came here from Asheville and so did about a dozen of my friends. It's a pretty well-kept secret outside of the state, but Wilmington is the best place to live in the Southeast."

"What's so great about Wilmington?"

"Oh, wait'll you see. Great nightlife. All the good bands play here. The beaches just a few minutes away. You can live downtown and be close to everything that's happening. They make movies here, you know."

In the morning I woke to the sterility of my hotel room, the view of the battleship across the river, and the hungover, bleary eyes of the *Arkansas* veterans in the elevator. Yesterday's two-hour drive from the train station at Fayetteville hadn't been encouraging. Much of that heat-wave country near the rail line consists of some of the most depressed, benighted southern redneck towns imaginable whose landmarks were billboards like the one that read JUST SAY NO TO ABORTION, DRUGS, HEAVY METAL, ALCOHOL, AND HOMOSEXUALS or the graffiti on a brick wall advising PRESIDENT CLINTON, RESIGN WHILE YOU'RE STILL ALIVE. But I had to admit that the last thirty miles before Wilmington had presented a different aspect of green lowland farms, fertile marshes, and placid waterways like scenes in the movie *The Prince of Tides*. I decided I'd give Wilmington a day and make a decision by suppertime.

Behind the hotel, a riverside boardwalk ran for blocks in each direction, and as I strolled outside and looked over at the battleship, I noticed things I hadn't in the dark last night. Here was an early-twentieth-century downtown of a city of fewer than fifty-six thousand people fronting directly on a river whose opposite shore, except for the battleship, was entirely virgin marsh, creeks, and timberland. Tugs and pleasure boats plied the water and a pretty stern-wheeler sat moored at the dock near the hotel. To the south ran brick-surfaced Water Street, with the steps of the federal courthouse just a paper airplane's throw from the water. Ice-cream vendors worked the board-walk and a horse-drawn surrey clopped down the street. People were out and many had deep summer beach tans. Wilmington was beauti-ful, far more attractive than my first impressions of Asheville or Char-lottesville.

I found air-conditioned lodgings on an interior Charleston-style courtyard for an inexpensive weekly rate in the Livery at St. Thomas Court. It was June and so it was hot in Wilmington, in the nineties most of the days of my visit. Soon I learned to drink a lot of tea and fruit juice and move slowly and deliberately, counting a day well spent if just two or three tasks were done well with smooth, graceful move-ments in between.

Downtown Wilmington was plainly and simply a marvel of every-thing I had learned to look for. There were true third places on nearly every block along Water and Front streets—the Cape Fear Coffee Shop, Caffe Phoenix, Riverboat Landing, Crooks by the River, Stenamen's, Paddy's Hollow, Water Street Market and Deli. So many people were out and frequenting these places at all hours of the hot day that it was clear that many were downtown residents, not subur-banites in town with their cars in a parking garage.

The city center was tightly localized around the riverside intersec-tion of Market and Water streets, extending three blocks north to the Coast Lines Inn project, a redevelopment of old rail terminal facilities into an inn, museum, and convention center, and four blocks south to Chandler's Wharf, a redevelopment of old port facilities into restau-rants and shops. There were no empty spaces between nodes, as in Asheville, though there was the occasional vacant individual building or storefront. This too was a downtown in the process of becoming, but it was more compact, it seemed as if things were happening faster here, and it was more finished. Trucks loaded with Sheetrock rolled up

and down Front Street and restoration scaffolding covered several of
the unoccupied buildings, like the old Masonic Temple, a Gothic wonder of rose granite, marble, and stained-glass windows.

The Cotton Exchange, near the north end of Front Street, was a
renovated warren of stone passages and landings in the old cotton
warehouses. Shops, studios, and Paddy's Hollow—an upscale restaurant and bar and a fine third place candidate—filled the interior.
Wandering through and relishing the feel of brick and heavy old tim-
bers underfoot, the vines and mosses growing in stony corners, the
smell of food cooking at Paddy's, and the sounds of people laughing
as they lounged on benches in the cool interior spaces, I wondered,
What is so satisfying about this space? It wasn't that it was quaint and
cute and old. To dismiss the renewal of old American buildings as a
nostalgic, boutiquish fad for tourists was to be guilty of criminally
missing the point.

Whether it was Fairhaven in Bellingham, Church Street in Burlington, or Market Square in Portsmouth, Americans were discovering
what Europeans have known for centuries. We learn which built environments work best by leaving them standing for a few lifetimes or a
few centuries. The widespread preference for older ones was not mere
nostalgia but an instinctive recognition that constructed spaces don't
feel truly comfortable until we have lived in them for a while, like
clothing that doesn't feel right till it's been worn several times. Their
age fosters a feeling of connectedness to a community's past and its
identity.

All across the country, but especially in the East, these renovations
of old American buildings and spaces were making their communities
feel a little more like Europe in that most positive sense that had
always drawn American tourists over there. Not that we were imitating
European environments. On the contrary, what was happening was
the rediscovery of our own authentic American streetscape—a fundamental missing piece in the puzzle of our civilization. After two centuries of tearing down and covering up, Americans in the good places
were finally learning that you couldn't have a sense of place without a
sense of permanence and continuity that overarched the lifetime of
one generation.

Down by the river, public access to the waterfront boardwalk
offered that same link between the place, the present, and the past

that simply made people feel comfortable. The tides came and went and the sun set behind the marshes on the opposite shore just as they always had. Ships and barges moved past so close you could call out to the crew leaning at the rail smoking. Except for the Hilton and a recklessly placed parking garage, all of the structures along Water Street were older buildings that had been around for generations, many of them only recently rediscovered and fixed up for commercial use.

The Barbary Coast, great dive that it was, did not become my third place base of operations in Wilmington. Just two blocks from my lodgings, I found the source of the live music I had been hearing as I hiked around this part of town late that second hot afternoon. Blues musicians were set up on the waterfront loading dock of an old L-shaped warehouse. Within the L was a huge open bricked court-yard, where listeners lounged with their beer or iced tea at wooden benches and tables. Across the patio from the loading dock stage, the pilothouse of a salvaged tugboat served as a huge refrigerator for kegs, and more patrons lounged on its deck. In the other leg of the L was the bar, with an indoor performance area furnished by someone who liked the combination of old Persian rugs and antique American furniture. The interior on this side was open to a long porch with rockers and tables where regulars sat and held court looking out over the patio.

The Ice House was a dangerously good third place. It was all too easy to waste away the whole day and evening sitting on that porch watching the comings and goings on the patio and the ships and barges moving up and down the river beyond. The place and some of its regulars were straight out of a Jimmy Buffet song—seductive women, hustlers who could get you into big trouble with a nod and a wink, and alcoholics wasting away in Margaritaville.

"The Ice House is the unofficial headquarters of the arts and entertainment community," said Brad Thomas, a wiry bespectacled fellow in his thirties who seemed to know everybody in the bar.

"What arts and entertainment community?" I asked.

"Shit, man, you did come down in the last shower, didn't you," he said. "De Laurentis came here in '82, built a lot. Carolco bought him out a few years later. Telemedia is here. *Firestarter, King Kong II, Mountains of the Moon, Super Mario Brothers, Sleeping with the Enemy,* dozens of others, they were all made here. And then the music people followed—Charlie Daniels and Bobbi Billings and Dave Pike. Arts and entertainment, the real thing."

Brad was a refugee from L.A. drawn to Wilmington by the opportunities in filmmaking. He had worked as a script supervisor and stand-in for a variety of related functions in the business. "You'll find Wilmington is today a place dominated by outsiders like me," he maintained. "The southerners here are not xenophobic about outsiders taking over their town because many of them got richer. We've even got a mayor from Rochester, New York."

Like Asheville, Wilmington had been transformed in just a few years by an invasion of newcomers. But Wilmington didn't have the boom-and-bust history of glamorous outsiders coming and going that Asheville had. Instead it was a southern city with a thoroughly conventional history and a twentieth-century decline into a seedy port and military red-light district. The mothballed battleship was located here in 1962 and De Laurentis set up shop twenty years later. Word got out in L.A. and New York about this little eastern place in the sun near the beach where you could work in film or music and get sane. People from Atlanta, Charlotte, or the research triangle who had some money in their pockets and preferred water over the mountains of Asheville came here and bought downtown buildings. The University of North Carolina at Wilmington expanded, and the feds finally finished the last extension of I-40, making Wilmington its eastern terminus. As Brad put it, "It's all happened in less than ten years, most of it in just the past two or three—pretty scary, huh?"

We sat and watched people come and go as the sun lowered across the river. "It's going to set right behind the battleship," I said to Brad as we leaned back in our chairs on the Ice House porch.

"That's just one of my problems with it," he snapped. A petition had been circulated anonymously a few months back suggesting that Wilmington would be better off without the SS *North Carolina*. A lot of people thought it just didn't fit the new Wilmington. "But say so publicly and you better watch your back. People think it's what brings tourism here."

In the morning I walked down to the Water Street Market, where Brad had arranged for me to talk to the owner, Harper Peterson, a downtown entrepreneur and irreverent president of the Downtown Wilmington Association (DWA). "This isn't a good place to live," he joked when I called him. "Go somewhere else."

Like nearly everyone I would meet in Wilmington, Harper Peterson was from somewhere else—in his case, Long Island. He was a handsome fellow with a mustache, about my age, who had migrated to nearby Wrightsville Beach as a hell-raising party animal twenty years ago. Today he was notorious as the author of a proposed noise ordinance that was anathema to the arts and music people at the Ice House. And yet they were the ones who had recommended that I talk to him. Shades of Burlington.

"Yeah, ten years ago I could give a shit, turn up the volume and party all night. Let the old codgers all move out," he said as we sat down with coffee and bagels at one of the tables in front of the market, the sun already high on the river before us and a blessed breeze rippling the water. Now he was a prominent businessman and community leader living downtown with his wife and five kids. "Living in Wilmington these days does that to you, you start to care."

Harper confirmed that what I was seeing in Wilmington today had happened incredibly fast. "The downtown, especially the waterfront, was still blighted just three or four years ago. Decent women wouldn't walk down this street. But the film people were already well established and we had little pockets of the kind of development that you now see everywhere, the Cotton Exchange, Chandler's Wharf. It was ripe. Then I-40 opened and people in the Raleigh-Durham area discovered our beaches as a quality destination and suddenly I had all kinds of company who also liked to play with old buildings."

Besides the Water Street Market, Harper had also renovated two old buildings on Market Street for commercial use as well as an old warehouse on Water Street for the new Wilmington City Market, host to the local farmer's market and various artists and craftspeople. Harper believed that what made it so easy to be labeled a visionary was other people's inability to see past the present moment. "People thought I was crazy when I opened this place a year ago—called it 'Harper's Folly.' Nobody would hang out down by the waterfront. It didn't look like this then. But the boardwalk was here, the little pavilion was here, and nobody used it because there weren't any commercial establishments nearby. Location, location, location—everybody knows that's what it's all about, but they can't see it until at least one business exploits it."

He gave me some other pieces of the Wilmington puzzle to work on. A coordinated effort had been launched to develop the downtown according to a grand consensus vision, so I should talk to a man named Bob Murphery of the Downtown Area Redevelopment Effort (DARE) to learn more about it. Designating the entire downtown a historic preservation district had been the key tool in the process. Long-term natives, though more conservative than Wilmington's new movers and shakers, welcomed the changes that were happening because they brought prosperity and banished Wilmington's old reputation as a rough and dangerous port of call. Harper anticipated a few new problems: the verdant land across the river was owned by an old-guard family who would probably sell it for development one day, and the booming beach economy at nearby Wrightsville and Carolina Beach was threatening to go the way of Florida's. But Wilmington, with its historic designation and river location fifteen miles inland, was firmly enough established as its own place that he hoped it would be spared the worst of what Americans typically did to the communities along their shores.

While DARE worked on blueprints for the grand scheme, Harper's DWA focused on simple things like parking, trash, police presence, and noise. "A lot of people are pretty unhappy with me about the proposed noise ordinance, and I recognize the vital importance of entertainment to making this downtown what we want it to be," Harper said. "But they have to understand the equally crucial necessity of downtown residence. You've got to have people living in the downtown. It isn't enough to build parking garages for people to commute in from the suburbs. And people won't live downtown unless we have some kind of a handle on the levels of noise."

Long before North Carolina, I had been convinced of the importance of residential areas *near* the downtown. But in this state, famous for exurban sprawl stretching from Raleigh to Charlotte, there were two cities that took the reasoning a step further, right into the heart of the downtown itself. Why not? Wilmington crime statistics now showed the downtown to be the safest part of the city. Few suburban locations offered backyard amenities anything like Wilmington's riverfront. Downtown auto traffic didn't even approach the madness of the mall boulevards. If only downtown living could be kept quiet enough. Harper's noise ordinance seemed to make some sense.

With Harper's help, I was able to visit a few people living in renovated downtown buildings. These homes were nothing like the usual image of grimy upper-floor downtown apartments. They were open, airy dwellings full of light, much like the place I had seen under renovation in Asheville. The architects had made creative use of split levels, lofts, skylights, and all of the odd corners and angles attendant to the effort to put living spaces into old buildings originally built for commercial purposes. The interiors were finished with rich, substantial materials—hardwoods, tiles, stained glass, brass, wrought iron, fabric wallcoverings—extravagances whose cost was manageable when the builder didn't have the expense of putting up the entire building from scratch. Balconies and interior courtyards provided intimacy with the outdoors, even in the heart of downtown. The residents I visited, a single woman in her thirties who worked in a downtown office and a retired couple, believed they had found the next place to heaven.

I spent the rest of the day in my rental car exploring the territory between Wilmington and the shore. Stretching east and south of Wilmington, New Hanover County was a vast wasteland of malls and strip boulevards dotted with conventional suburban housing tracts. A large gated community called Landmark had sprung up along the road to Wrightsville Beach. Here was the monster that the town visionaries would have to keep at bay if they wanted to preserve Wilmington's mellow downtown living alternative to the usual regime of places in the sun by the shore.

Wrightsville Beach itself was subtly different from other densely developed offshore barrier islands along the East Coast in that it was almost entirely residential, a neighborhood of tasteful contemporary beach houses by the sea where residents gathered in little knots of conviviality on street corners, at entrances to the beach, and out along the surf line. Like a suburb to Wilmington, with sand instead of lawns and an ocean in the backyard instead of a pool, this quiet beachside community had little commercial clutter and only a couple of hotels. As usual, the dunes had been largely sacrificed, but the beach was broad and hard and the sand was fine and clean.

Farther down the coast of Cape Fear, Carolina Beach and Kure Beach looked more like the usual beach culture, complete with T-shirt shops, amusement parks, and a boardwalk adolescent hangout scene. I passed these beaches quickly, took the car ferry across the mouth of the Cape Fear River to Southport, and boarded the foot ferry for Bald Head Island, where Harper Peterson had assured me I would find a shore development like none I had ever seen before.

The southernmost of the string of offshore islands, Bald Head Island constituted the tip of Cape Fear itself, from which pirates had once lured ships to their destruction with false lights from the tops of dunes. In 1983, the Mitchell family from Texas acquired the undefiled island with the intention of developing a true alternative to the beach communities that had spoiled so many other offshore islands. There would be no automobiles; only 2 percent of the two thousand developed acres would actually be altered in any way, with the ten thousand remaining acres deeded to the North Carolina Conservancy; and all development would be shaped by the existing natural land forms, vegetation, and ecology. At the ferry landing, the most striking feature was simply the lack of parking lots. In place of the enormous spaces typically consumed by cars, there were simply bicycle racks and a row of electric golf carts lined up like taxis outside an airport terminal.

I rented a bicycle, picked up a guide brochure, and headed off for the afternoon. For much of my ride I saw no houses, no shops, no marks of the human hand whatsoever. Instead I pedaled through live oak, dogwood, and palm forest echoing with the songs of birds, along tidal creeks and salt marshes where I could look down and see fish in the water, and out into a nearly unblemished world of dunes and tall grasses. When I did come upon residential clusters, the homes, ranging in cost from $190,000 to $1 million, were tucked so neatly into an otherwise undisturbed landscape that it was easy to miss them. Only the dune houses stuck out as an alteration of the island's natural profile.

A twenty-eight-hole championship golf course snaked its way through the island, but when I came within view of it, its contours and water were so consistent with what I had been seeing that I hardly noticed it, except for the openness and sunny fairway grass. This was in keeping with the island's master plan. I talked to a golfer who insisted that this also added to the richness of the game. That was the way the old courses in Scotland were laid out before the days of bulldozers, he told me, when the natural topography provided the challenge of the game.

I left Bald Head Island reminded in some ways of the highly acclaimed Seaside development in Florida, where world-class architects and planners were following the principles of good place design to carve out a new shore town from the scrub coast of the northern gulf. But the natural landscape of Bald Head Island was far more spectacular, and Bald Head had something Seaside would forever lack unless it grew spectacularly itself: a real renaissance town of fifty-six thousand just ten miles up the river.

One afternoon, as I emerged from the court of my Wilmington lodgings, I found an elderly man followed by a group of tourists peering through the wrought iron gate at the street. Wearing a straw hat, a kerchief, hiking shorts, and knee socks and carrying a gnarled old walking stick with a brass tip, he excused himself and his followers for poking into my private abode and introduced himself as Bob Jenkins, conductor of the Wilmington Historic Downtown Walking Tour. "Did you know that you live in a cathouse, sir?" he asked me, pointing his walking stick at my nose. "Well, that's what it always was until recently."

Bob Jenkins was a one-man institution in Wilmington, and I had been told that I could not claim to know the city until I had spent some time with him. The next morning I walked down to the river pavilion in front of Water Street Market as his tour group was gathering. "We are not used to tourism," Bob Jenkins began with a bark, bringing his audience firmly under his spell. "It's a new thing of just the past five years. My family goes back to 1609 and these thirteen waterfront blocks were laid out in 1734. Until the aftermath of the War of Northern Aggression this port was a seafaring and railroad crossroads of the world. Then during the most recent century we lost all that and became isolated down here on the wrong side of the river in this remote corner of North Carolina. Didn't even get a bridge until 1926. Then they finished I-40 five years ago and now the world has discovered us. So you see, we are not used to tourism."

Bob was a showman in the tradition of the great southern storytellers. During his little introduction his voice soared to a shout at

"War of Northern Aggression" and diminished to a whisper at the second "we are not used to tourism," where he paused with a deep bow and a wink. He brandished the walking stick like a conductor's baton and kept the twelve of us sitting before him on the boardwalk bench rapt for the next hour.

The French explored the river in 1524 and there was a shortlived Spanish colony a few years after that. Jenkins had once met a ninety-two-year-old woman from Charleston, South Carolina, who whupped him on the butt for claiming that the first Charleston was located here, but it was a fact that in 1616, English colonists from Massachusetts Bay settled here, naming the place Charleston. In 1667, a ferocious Indian uprising drove them out and farther south to found the Charleston of South Carolina we know today. Bob elaborated, "The cause of the uprising was long a mystery until recent anthropological discoveries suggested that those fine, upright Puritans from Massachusetts—you know they came here to worship as they chose and God help you if you chose to worship other than as they did—those godly, Christy men from Massachusetts were selling the Indian women and children into slavery in the Caribbean."

In 1700, England desperately needed pine products—the tar and pitch as much as the lumber—when it was discovered that the Wilmington port sat amid the continent's largest stand of yellowleaf pines. Throughout the eighteenth century and well into the nineteenth, the town enjoyed its salad days as a port with a local product demanded by a global empire.

Railroads arrived in Wilmington before the Civil War, carrying cotton directly from the plantations for transshipment to the world. "When the Last Great Unpleasantness broke out—I use the euphemism out of respect for the sensibilities of you Yankees here with me today," Bob quipped, "—Wilmington was a port for blockade runners." But it was miraculously spared destruction during Sherman's final march, thus leaving a considerable amount of antebellum property intact today.

Bob skipped a lot of Wilmington's history between the Civil War and World War II, but at the local library I was able to learn that these years were marked by continuation of the cotton transshipment trade, hurricane disasters, and particularly nasty racial riots, and that the twenties saw a beach culture boom similar to that of today. The depression didn't bring the same financial hangover to Wilmington that it had to Asheville, since the town hadn't been gilded by the Vanderbilt glitter.

Bob resumed his telling of Wilmington history at World War II, when the port became a major shipbuilder for the Atlantic convoys carrying the arsenal of democracy. The city's population exploded from twenty-two thousand to ninety thousand during the first year of the war as the shipyard turned out Liberty freighters at the rate of one every five months. For decades the well-to-do families of Wilmington had maintained a tradition of moving to the beach for the summer. The women and children would escape the miasmas and vapors, while the daddies stayed in town during the week to attend to business. But during the war these families stayed at the beach for the duration to offer up housing for the workers at the shipyard.

These were the years Wilmington became a red-light district. After the war it was the bars and brothels and their patrons that stayed on in the downtown. Many of the old families never came back. The cotton trade was gone, the railroads moved out, and surviving Wilmington businesspeople realized they had erred horribly in putting all of their eggs in the military basket.

In 1955 Wilmington's Committee of One Hundred vowed that such urban deterioration would never again happen in their city. Their first initiatives followed the destructive urban renewal model. "People were moving to the suburbs," Bob Jenkins explained. "You had to tear things down, make downtown modern and auto-oriented to get them back, they thought." That's when the ill-conceived and soon-to-be-demolished waterfront parking garage had been built. Prime old buildings began to face the wrecking ball.

Then in the 1960s a local businessman named Hugh Morton heard that the battleship *North Carolina* was going to be scrapped. He mounted a campaign in which schoolchildren collected enough nickels and pennies to have the boat brought here. Though the ship dated only from the 1940s, the arrival of the *North Carolina* helped spark a renewed interest in historical preservation. In 1965 the Cape Fear Historical Society convinced the city council to abandon the urban renewal campaign, and a historical preservation ordinance was passed. Two hundred historically significant buildings had already been torn down, but wealthy old families stepped in to buy out grandfathered properties scheduled for demolition. In 1965 the destruction was stopped, dead in the water.

There was one block on Front Street that private initiatives saved and sold off cheaply to people who would either start a business or establish a downtown residence. "Suddenly we had an artsy crowd, theater people from God knows where, gays, girls that wouldn't shave their legs, guys with ponytails—and all of them young," Bob whispered with a wink. They bought the properties for as little as five hundred dollars, started quirky little businesses, and lived upstairs. There was a rule that they had to paint or otherwise fix up the front of the place. People said, "Isn't it wonderful what these strange young people are doing for our downtown."

Bob himself bought a twenty-one-room mansion with eight fireplaces on the edge of the downtown during these years for thirty-five hundred dollars. "Downtown Wilmington was still pretty rough; decent people left for the suburbs at dark and the rowdies came in and the hookers came out. Across the street from my house the johns baby-sat for the prostitutes' little ones as they waited their turn. I slept on the floor with a shotgun beside my head that first winter."

In 1977 Bob was the first to invest in the rehabilitation of an old downtown building on Market Street for combined commercial and residential purposes. The Cotton Exchange project soon followed, and then in 1982 the movie people came to town. With the waterfront revival a few years later, the citizens of Wilmington, many of them now newcomers, suddenly began to reclaim their downtown from the drunks, streetwalkers, and bingeing soldiers on R and R from Camp Lejeune. "And look at where we're sitting today," he concluded with a flourish of outstretched arms toward the sunny boardwalk where young families with small children strolled, licking ice-cream cones.

I would see Bob Jenkins with his little groups of tourists every day of my visit to Wilmington, pointing with his stick at a building or gesturing from a street corner. "We are not used to tourism," he had said, yet more than anyone else in town, he had hitched his star to it. Bob was a native who delighted in the rediscovery of his town by the world at large, but he would never talk or dress like the movie and music people who had invaded. Instead he acted as a human institution of continuity with the past and guarantor of local identity in the present.

Film writer and producer Francine De Courcey, on the other hand, consciously represented the new wave that had swept over Wilmington since Dino De Laurentis built the first stages for the film version of Stephen King's *Firestarter* in 1983. At Brad Thomas's suggestion, I met her for lunch at the Caffe Phoenix on Front Street, the preferred lunching ground for Wilmington's film set.

The Caffe Phoenix was a restaurant with a theatrical design. Two ground-floor dining areas, one smoking, one non, were separated by a tiny circular bar and an area of empty floor in front of the entrance. Upstairs, balconies with more tables lined the back and the side walls. The effect was to guarantee that from every table in the place, one had a clear view of the front door and that stagelike entry space. Likewise, everyone entering and pausing in the entry space could instantly sweep the room and know exactly who was here. I tried sitting at several different spots as I waited for my lunch partner and realized that every table in the room also had an unobstructed sight line to every other table. This was a place in which to see and be seen.

Francine De Courcey spotted me with my notebook as she came in and sat down in a bustle of energy and presence. Currently working for Telemedia on *Inkwell*, a film about coming of age in a black American family, she had spent the past few days hustling extras for a huge beach scene. "It's not all glamor," she said. "I just concluded delicate negotiations with Harper Peterson to contribute potato salad and watermelons to feed them."

She had come to Wilmington from New York eight years ago purely because of the then-fledgling film industry. "The word was out about this sane alternative to working in New York and L.A. It was a ground-floor opportunity, and if it failed, I could always retire to the beach." She found a downtown apartment reminiscent of a New York loft for about a fifth of the money and got a job on the set of the film *Track 22* down at the old Coast Lines rail yards.

She liked the size of Wilmington, the ease with which she could network and feel connected here, and the feeling of impending revival. The town was big enough to have things like Riverfest, the Azalea Festival, the performance theater of Thalian Hall, and of course all of the action attending the film industry presence. "There's a natural selection that goes on with the film and entertainment people who come here," she said. "They're people who can no longer brook the bullshit of New York or L.A. Many have families and were seeking values besides 'get it done and don't count the bodies.' They value living in a place of neighbors. So we get the best of a creative lot."

I asked her where the film people lived, and she explained that the casts, who would be here for only one film, usually stayed at the Hilton or in rented places out at Shell Island or Carolina Beach. A few well-known actors had fallen in love with the town and stayed on, like Dennis Hopper, who was renovating the downtown Masonic Temple building as an acting school, and Nick Nolte, who built a house out near the beach. But the crew people were permanent residents. Some lived at the beach, in the suburbs, or the older neighborhoods in town, but many lived right downtown in places like those I had visited earlier.

It would be hard to overestimate the film industry's impact on Wilmington, beginning with a total of $490 million pumped into the local economy. Dozens of related businesses had sprung up: casting agents, lighting and grip outfits, car rentals, sushi bars, and opportunities for every construction trade imaginable. "Film interjected a level of sophistication to this town really fast," Francine said. "Wilmington's learning curve just shot off the chart." Fortunately, the longtime natives, folks like Bob Jenkins, had a southern reserve, a capacity to absorb shock, that kept them from being overwhelmed by it all, Francine thought. And of course, they remembered the time before the film people, back in Wilmington's red-light days, when these streets had seen too much of the real trouble that was now only make believe.

Dino De Laurentis was originally drawn to the area because he wanted to film Stephen King's *Firestarter* at Orton Plantation. He soon discovered other advantages: North Carolina's right-to-work legislation; immediate, enthusiastic support from government officials hungry for investment and positioned to court it; uncrowded, unfamiliar, and film-friendly settings in the Cape Fear region; and Wilmington's early-twentieth-century streetscapes. He bought an office on Twenty-third Street, enough land to erect stages, and a huge back lot to create the one thing Wilmington didn't have: the big-city street set used in movies like *King Kong II*. As he imported people he had worked with from Italy, Canada, and L.A., the film world soon recognized that the man was serious about establishing a permanent presence here. "Film people had long known the agonizing experience of shooting one film in an idyllic place like this and then having to move on for their next project," Francine explained. "But here you could stay on and do film after film."

In the winter of 1986 De Laurentis declared bankruptcy, and people who had settled here feared that the idyll was at an end. But within two years, Carolco came along and set up shop in De Laurentis's former properties. This time the "film neighbors," as Francine liked to call the nascent film community, decided not to rely on the vicissitudes of one big filmmaker's fate. "We realized that whether it was with De Laurentis or Carolco or whomever, Wilmington had gathered a permanent presence of all of the professions and skills, the crew base, needed to make movies." There were currently five hundred to seven hundred people employed as full-time film professionals and an additional two thousand employed through related skills as carpenters, electricians, and so forth.

A newly formed nonprofit Cape Fear Filmmakers' Association began to aggressively promote the area and its professionals as a permanent, long-term filmmaking center. Now, though Carolco was still the biggest Wilmington-based operation, other motion picture companies had made individual movies here, and Telemedia was leasing part of the old De Laurentis facility to make TV shows. "Wilmington has become a shopping center for film production," Francine said.

Francine felt that it didn't matter that Carolco was currently a little shaky. Wilmington had gone beyond being simply an industry center to establishing itself as a true filmmaking community that had staying power. It was the binding energy of shared experiences, like the long, hot summer making *Super Mario Brothers* out in the dust of the Ideal Cement Factory, with everyone clad in suffocating black leather and the toilets going out daily, or the spontaneous fund-raisers for a crewman whose house burned and for a woman in a medical crisis. During the filming of *Sleeping with the Enemy,* the entire community converged on the Ice House for a concert benefiting victims of domestic violence.

And then, of course, there was the accidental shooting death of Brandon Lee during filming of *The Crow* and the ensuing tabloid orgy. "This was insanity, like what we all fled L.A. to get away from," said Francine. "But here it made us pull even closer together."

At the time of my visit, three films and the TV show *Matlock* were being done in Wilmington. I visited the *Matlock* production when shooting was taking place at Slater's, a singles bar in a mall out near Wrightsville Beach.

I caught up with actress Jill Novik, also currently featured in the show *Sisters*, while she took a cigarette break that afternoon, and she told me more about Wilmington's unique film community. She liked Hollywood, of course, or she wouldn't be in the business, but Wilmington was a good place to work and let your hair down. Everyone, cast, crew, and extras alike, hung out together at the beach or in the bars and pool halls. When we went back inside, the sound crew was cranking up the music to be used in a dance scene. Half of the people in the room stopped work and broke out dancing, including the director. "See? This is it," Jill said. When the grips called out for milkshakes after a particularly grueling set change later in the afternoon, it was Jill Novik, one of the leading actors, who took orders and hustled out to oblige.

Later that evening I met up with *Matlock* actors Kurt Deutsch, Jeri Lynn Ryan, and Jill Novik and several of the crew and extras for pool in Stenamen's. They all had to be back on set at six-thirty in the morning, but that didn't keep them from carrying on like any other twenty-something gang out on the town. In Wilmington you didn't get hustled for autographs, and flashbulbs didn't go off in your face every time you stepped through a doorway, Kurt explained. There also wasn't the pressure to be continually on form for the good of your career. He was flying out to New York in the morning to work on a different project, and he savored this evening's last moments of sanity before facing the beast.

I found Ice House owner Jim Bass one Sunday afternoon sitting in his tobacco-stained shirt on the porch of his place with another recent retiree to the warmth of Wilmington. A blues band led by a female vocalist was cooing the song "Summertime," the breeze was brisk off the river, and Jim's friend was shaking his head at the good luck that had led him to settle in Wilmington.

Jim, a wiry, bearded, pipe-smoking son-of-a-gun in his seventies whom Francine De Courcey had cast as an extra in half a dozen movies because he was so picturesque, had come here himself only four years ago. In a previous life he had been an industrial consultant in California with degrees from Notre Dame, Rutgers, University of Athens, and half a dozen other places. He had his midlife crisis, separated from his wife, left his career, and hit the road in 1969. He sailed in the Faeroe Islands, fixed up a 170-foot barkentine and sailed to New York for the Tall Ships Festival, worked in codfishing boats in Sweden and Iceland, sojourned in Nepal, where he designed a complex to observe elephants in the wild, lived in D.C. and slept with the homeless in LaFayette Park. He walked across the United States from San Francisco to Key West, picking up beer cans, living off the recycling proceeds and writing a book about it called *Traveling America on Your Can*, and generally drifted with the winds of adventure till he sailed up the Cape Fear River in 1989, exactly twenty years into his second life. He was on his way to Venezuela at the time, with the idea that his social security checks would stretch farther there. He had friends in Wilmington and thought he'd stop off for about a month.

"Well, it didn't work out that way," he said as he leaned back in his chair and relit his pipe in a furious cloud of smoke. When he first arrived here his boat was moored south of downtown at the Masonborough Boat Yard, and each day he would walk into town, picking up enough beer cans along the way to buy some lunch and a little tobacco. "It was warm and the social security checks stretched pretty far here."

Then he found the abandoned icehouse and became fascinated with its history. He recalled Thoreau's description of ice cutting on Walden Pond, how the icemen would drill holes through two feet of ice with hand augers and then insert saws to cut out ten-foot blocks, which were packed in insulating sawdust and hauled by horse team and rail to Boston harbor for shipment to warm places or stored for use locally in the summer. Wilmington's icehouse was one of the destinations of that pond ice described by Thoreau in the 1850s. By the time they arrived here, the ten-foot blocks still measured eight feet or more. The ships would unload in front of the icehouse—the river in those days verged right up against the building—and the blocks would be hauled by slaves along the loading dock (where the musicians now played) and into the warehouse (where the bar now stood). The icehouse's customers would bring their wagons into today's bricked courtyard area to pick up ice for restaurants, hotels, and the homes of those who could afford the extravagance.

Jim had always been intrigued by the idea that something as perishable as ice could be shipped to faraway places and believed that despite modern technology, there was still a fascination with ice. The very name, Ice House, conjured up a mystique that drew people (I could confirm that half a dozen of the cities I had visited from Napa to Burlington had restaurants or bars called the Ice House). But besides making magic out of the Ice House, he also wanted to prove something. "Everywhere I went I met people complaining about lack of opportunity," he declared. "I wanted to prove that you don't have to go on welfare. You can make a living picking money up off the streets. If I could do it at seventy . . ." and he let the rest of the statement speak for itself. So he made a down payment on the icehouse out of his social security and the proceeds from the beer cans he picked up on the way into town every day. He collected brick from demolition sites and began laying the patio himself. He found the tug sunk in the river, its owners happy to give it away to anyone who would remove it. People thought he was crazy, but the project moved ahead and he took a partner, a young bull of a fellow with a bushy beard named Joe Carney. The tug was refitted as a giant refrigerator for twenty-six kegs of beer, and its pilothouse became the establishment's original bar.

Jim and Joe recruited musicians who had followed the film people to Wilmington and offered music without a cover charge every day and night. Like Burlington's Nectar Rorris, Jim Bass became a beloved figure among the music and filmmaking community because he defied business convention and created opportunity. "That's not really what I meant to do," he said. In fact, his project had several consequences exactly opposite of his intentions. If you wanted to find people in Wilmington most in need of Bass's inspiration to get off their rears and do something for themselves, the Ice House was where you would meet them. "At least if they're going to use my place as a setting to flout the example I've tried to set, then they have to listen to my lectures," he said.

Now, after four years in Wilmington, Jim believed that he finally "had his anchor down." Besides maintaining the Ice House as one of the best third places I had ever seen, he enjoyed the occasional stint in films and his local status as consultant for any new waterfront development projects. As he sat on the porch holding court that afternoon, local entrepreneurs and film people alike came through the gate and made a beeline to his chair to chitchat about Wilmington goings on. He learned just that day that he was being considered for the role of lighthouse keeper in *The Birds II.*

I had talked to a lot of directors of various downtown associations during my travels. Usually they were very conventional men or women, extremely careful in their choice of words and so utterly sanitized of regional earthiness that it seemed as if they had all been recruited from the same school of public relations. In Harper Peterson I had already met one exception in Wilmington to this regime, and in Bob Murphery, director of DARE, I met another. Murphery was also that rarity in contemporary Wilmington's public life—he was a native.

I met Murphery at his office in the First Union Bank building. He was white-haired and, after Jim Bass, rather traditional looking, but there was nothing conventional about his pitch to business executives looking to relocate or start up in the Wilmington area. When they asked what they might find out in the suburbs, he would say, "Oh, I don't know, you might fall off the end of the earth or get swallowed by dragons. The world ends at the blue line surrounding the downtown. Now, is there anything we can do for you here in Wilmington?"

"But do I keep close tabs on what's going on out in the suburbs?" he began as we sat down. "You bet I do. It's the enemy." Bob Murphery and DARE possessed a vision for Wilmington as comprehensive as any I had ever seen. It began with some local history that picked up where Bob Jenkins had left off, a familiar story with a radical ending.

In 1977 downtown Wilmington was anticipating a new wave of flight to the suburbs, despite the pioneering efforts of the Cotton Exchange, Chandler's Wharf, Bob Jenkins, and the bohemian youngsters he had told me about earlier. The county's first regional mall was scheduled to open in 1979. After the dismal history of the downtown since World War II, there were a few in local business and government who were ready to consider throwing in the towel once and for all. "Either bulldoze it and start over or let it go to hell and we'll all relocate to the suburbs," they said.

But a majority saw revitalizing the downtown as the key to Wilmington's future, if for no other reason than that it made no economic sense to walk away from an intact downtown infrastructure.

Thus DARE was formed and, funded equally from the public and private sectors, began building a war chest for the battle ahead.

Sure enough, when Independence Mall opened in 1979, the retail action that had remained in the downtown disappeared overnight. DARE, with its well-prepared coffers, stepped in and began buying properties at fire sale prices before they could be turned into topless bars and adult bookstores. With the bottom fallen out of the market and a well-publicized war declared against sleaze, DARE went even farther and bought out places already used for those purposes, evicting the tenants. Soon DARE owned a significant portion of the downtown. It began to resell properties to buyers who would sign covenants forbidding certain kinds of uses in perpetuity. DARE retained the right to reclaim properties whose owners failed to live up to their end of the bargain concerning both renovation and use.

DARE certainly had picked the right acronym. Bob Murphery showed me planning as detailed and aggressive as military strategy. Acknowledging the changed rules under which downtowns of the future would have to operate, DARE had targeted the key groups besides the obvious entertainment and funky retail establishments that it wanted to fill in the empty spaces of the downtown: government, the legal community, the financial community, other professionals, such as architects, engineers, doctors, psychiatrists, dentists, and decorators, and finally residence. If DARE could help it, not one single new proposal for investment in any of these areas would locate outside of the downtown. This was war.

DARE's weapons would be the appeal of Wilmington's riverfront and the old downtown streetscape, both of which would be reclaimed and redeveloped to create a humane urban environment that people would prefer over the sterility of malls and suburbs. Along the riverfront, Wilmington already had the Cotton Exchange and Chandler's Wharf anchoring the two ends of the downtown, with pioneering owners who had kept them alive during even the hardest of years. DARE's job there was to fill in the middle. At its recommendation, the city built the public wooden river walk and pavilion. Individual entrepreneurs, like Harper Peterson and Jim Bass, were encouraged to pursue their private ventures. The idea was to develop a continuous flow of commercial and public focal points linked by the boardwalk along the river. The last remaining gap now was the huge unnecessary parking garage between the Hilton and the courthouse that had been built back in the urban renewal days. In time it would come down; Bob showed me a sketch of the Riverfront Center he hoped would replace it and complete the cycle. On paper it looked like the cluster of commercial, entertainment, and residential quarters that rooted the south end of Tom McCall Waterfront Park in Portland, Oregon, and when I mentioned this to Murphery, he replied, "Exactly."

Concerning the remainder of the downtown inland from the riverfront, the issue DARE had tackled was classic. "We knew the main thing was to make downtown a twenty-four-hour environment for people. You couldn't have downtown shut down and empty out at any point of the day, or you lose your hold on it. To do that you had to create a three-part balance, like a three-legged stool—eight hours as a workplace and market, eight hours as an entertainment and recreation arena, and eight hours for residence."

Maintaining that balance had been the challenge. In acknowledging three different kinds of activity, Murphery realized that the city had taken the first step toward amending the failed zoning practices of the past, in which human life was fragmented into one-dimensional zones far removed from one another. But people simply couldn't be expected to sleep next door to a nightclub hosting rock bands. Thus DARE had successfully advocated microzoning within the city core. Downtown residential areas were encouraged out toward the north end and on the periphery bordering the older, purely residential ring that surrounded the city center. A few blocks had been set aside for business office use, another area could accommodate light manufacturing, and the historic core was open to all uses permitted under historic designation, with an emphasis on retail and entertainment.

The difference between this and traditional practice was mainly a matter of spatial scale. All of the downtown zones were within walking distance of one another; zoning here did not force people into their cars. And by grandfathered practice as well as deliberate definition, a considerable amount of mixed use was allowed in all areas of the downtown.

Thus, Harper Peterson's proposed noise ordinance (aka sound ordinance, according to its opponents at the Ice House) was a manifestation of the strains of success. DARE hadn't anticipated the boom in residence in the core historic area or the popularity of downtown outdoor entertainment. Appointed as mediator in the dispute, Bob Murphery was charged with determining how loud was too loud, where noise was too loud, and at what hours and on what days noise was too loud.

He wasn't particularly happy in the role. "I've always seen myself as a red tape cutter," he complained. "I came to this job with a mission to clear away the crap that prevented Wilmington from coming alive. But now that it has, regulation rears its ugly head as a necessity to protect what we have accomplished." He had a similar problem with hot dog vendors. In the absence of any regulations for their operation, I had witnessed myself how two of them jostled each other physically for position outside the gate of the Ice House in the evenings. "We're going to have to come up with some regs just to keep them from shooting each other," said Murphery.

Still, Bob Murphery took all of this as confirmation of success. "I tell my counterparts in other cities about my problem with the noise ordinance and they moan that they wish they had that problem." The downtown boom had all happened just so much faster than anyone anticipated. If he had been told five years ago that today he'd have 90 percent occupancy of the downtown buildings, Murphery would have scoffed. As a native he was willing to recognize that a considerable factor had been the influence of newcomers, refugees from failed American places who, once they saw what was happening in Wilmington's downtown, began calling him about job possibilities or buildings available for redevelopment. Because locals were always the last ones to change their attitudes about the idea of downtown living, Murphery worked with a Newcomers Club for people who had lived here for less than three years. It wasn't the old welcome wagon, where new residents were assisted in conforming to an established social regime. Rather it was a forum for fast-tracking them into leadership roles and community activism.

Looking out Murphery's office window toward the river, I was struck again by the miracle we hadn't yet discussed, that undeveloped virgin marshland on the opposite shore and the little glades surrounding the battleship. "What about all of that?" I asked him.

He explained that the land wasn't in Wilmington's city limits and so for the moment was out of DARE's jurisdiction. "But a day doesn't go by that I don't think about it." Murphery felt that sooner or later someone would have to do something as aggressive there as had been done on this side of the river to preempt more horrible possibilities. That was the key to DARE's success so far—aggression. Downtowns all across the country needed to get out of their usual defensive stance and go on the offensive. Wilmington's DARE had scouted the way.

I had occasion to visit the New Hanover Medical Center as a patient after something I ate provoked an acute stomach ailment. As I waited in the lobby for a few minutes that busy Sunday night, a young Wilmington cop brought in an injured gang-banger, who eventually ended up in the examining bay next to mine. He had broken his hand and the policeman was charging him with aggravated assault. It could have been assault with a deadly weapon, the cop kept trying to explain as the kid protested vehemently, but he had reduced the charge since it was a first offense. "I told you before, you get in fights, you're gonna do time," the cop patiently went on. "This is not the Bronx. The rules are different. I told you that the first day you got here."

From the conversation, it was apparent that the kid had come here from the Bronx to get out of a gang and make a life for himself. He had been spotted by officers of the youth division of the Wilmington Police Department during his first week here, and the arresting officer had worked with him from day one to help him hold a job and stick to his resolve in leaving the Bronx. But the kid had screwed up, unable to shake the old habits and creed about what it took for a street kid to survive, and now he was going to jail.

Finally my doctor arrived, gave me some vile-tasting green fluid, and let me go, but my encounter with the gang-banger and the compassionate, patient, but firm cop made me aware of Wilmington's police corps henceforth. I began noticing that at some point of every day, police officers went in and joined patrons of each of Wilmington's downtown bars. It was part of a program, I was told by a cop I met in the Barbary Coast, in which law officers were trained to join in the social life of the bars (they drank iced tea) to increase their rapport with the community. Mounted police were omnipresent in the downtown, and neighborhood foot patrols were much in evidence whenever I drove through the residential areas bordering the downtown. The philosophy of the Wilmington Police Department was heavy on prevention through face-to-face contact. That meant getting out of the cruisers and onto the streets.

All of this made me want to talk to the mayor of this enlightened regime. Wilmington's city hall housed more than just government. Here the city had constructed Thalian Hall, the graceful theater and performing arts center I had heard about, on a scale that evoked places far bigger than Wilmington. But that wasn't the only odd presence in city hall.

I found Mayor Don Betz in his office with some spare time to chat shortly after my visit to Bob Murphery. The mayor of Wilmington, North Carolina, was a Yankee who had relocated from Rochester, New York, with Federal Paperboard in 1975. "I guess it says something about Wilmington," he acknowledged. "It's a place of people who come from someplace else who stay on, look at the possibilities, and say, 'Why not?'" There was a constructive chemistry, he believed, between natives and newcomers here. Natives admired the energy and creativity of the newcomers; newcomers respected the heritage and sense of identity provided by the natives. "It's a symbiotic relationship," he said. "The result is a surprising amount of consensus that gets things done."

When he became mayor, he was blessed with a city with very little debt, just the outstanding bonds on the waterfront parking garage and renovations to Thalian Hall. His immediate goal was to quickly fill in some needed infrastructure—eight miles of new streets, installation of underground utilities, a new water treatment plant, and assistance to the Coast Lines project to anchor the north end of the waterfront. He found that these investments by the city were tripled by the investment of private sources like Corning Glass. Again, symbiosis, this time between the public and private sectors.

Annexation was a nastier necessity. There was consensus that Wilmington needed moderate growth if it was to take the next step in community development, guaranteeing a living for the children of those who had done so much to make it a good place to live in the past ten years. Attracting business and industry hadn't been a problem. The challenge was to find places to put them as the area within Wilmington's old city limits filled in. Thus, to avoid losing tax revenue and jobs to the suburbs and to stabilize the rising cost of living, Wilmington embarked on several politically sensitive annexations. "We should handle the growth instead of ceding it to county areas that don't have the infrastructure and planning vision," the mayor believed.

A booming film industry and a city spreading out through annexation—I wondered whether there were disturbing parallels to L.A. here. Mayor Betz was amused at the suggestion. Wilmington was a community with an identity focused on the downtown. The film people who came here did so because it was the antithesis of L.A. If anything, the annexations tended to enfold bordering territory into the humane scale and vision of Wilmington, exactly the opposite of what had happened with the disorganized sprawl of L.A. As I had noted before, in William Whyte's research, minimal peripheral urban expansion *at the same density level as in the heart of town* could accommodate growth that would otherwise gobble up huge tracts of surrounding countryside under the sprawl-inducing regime of most counties.

The mayor cautioned me against overestimating the impact of the film industry. Certainly nearly everyone in the city benefited from its presence and it was an economic engine that required little or no investment in infrastructure by the city. But there were other engines in Wilmington's diversified economy. Major corporations, like Corning Glass, General Electric, and Dupont, had made huge investments in the past five years. Simultaneously, the University of North Carolina at Wilmington had expanded to a student population of fifteen thousand and become a major draw to sophisticated money coming into the city. The New Hanover Regional Medical Hospital had become a significant health center, attracting world-class doctors who liked to do their surgery in the morning and be out on the golf course or in a sailboat in the afternoon. And of course the nearby beaches contributed to the economy at a healthy arm's length. "Wilmington has a tremendously sophisticated professional population that would be here if the filmmakers all moved out tomorrow," the mayor said. "And they will stay here because this is a place where you don't need to get in your car and leave town to take a vacation."

I hung out with some local musicians at the Ice House the last evening of my visit, when the air had cooled and the breeze, as if the river knew it was no longer necessary, had died. Wilmington was a place for healing, they told me. The film community was here because of Dino De Laurentis, but the music community was here because so many musicians were in need of the balm of Wilmington's uncomplicated, neighborly, slow-paced, southern quality of life.

Arthur Shuey, a blues musician who was president emeritus of the Cape Fear Musicians Association, believed that I couldn't understand the underpinnings of Wilmington unless I recognized the importance of its music scene. No matter how reformed were the film community's refugees from L.A., their craft and their contribution to Wilmington were antithetical to those of music, he thought. "Filmmakers are always starting something new from scratch, they're part of the great American way. Musicians are more subversive, because every piece of music is connected to something else, it's an ongoing, organic process, and the whole history of music is a great extended song—just watching the river go by."

It was a great evening for watching the river go by. The music flowed. The neighbors came and went, and some were even beginning to recognize me. At one point a huge freighter ghosted past on the river, obliterating the sky with its bulk, and people clapped and urged the river to "do it again." A petition against the "sound ordinance" was passed around, but when Harper Peterson stopped in he was greeted warmly and with offers to buy him a beer. As the sun set, I didn't even mind the battleship. Santa Fe had its adobe, San Luis Obispo had its Madonna Inn, Charlottesville had Monticello, Burlington had Stowe. So what if Wilmington had a battleship? One look toward the river and you knew exactly where you were.

In the morning I found Harper Peterson, Jim Bass, Bob Murphery, and Mayor Betz conferring collegially with a state senator at the Water Street Market about raising funds for putting in public docks along the riverfront to attract more boat traffic to the downtown. I walked back to the Ice House with Bass afterward, now changed from his usual tobacco-stained work clothes into a clean white shirt. "I like to help the cause," he was saying, "but I don't know that we really need money from the state. Let's throw some fund-raisers, forget the committee meetings, and start pounding nails."

At the Ice House, one of the musicians I had met the night before had left a present for me. It was a cassette recording of a song promoting Wilmington, produced by Brad Thomas and featuring all of the stars of the local music scene. I had heard the dozen spin-offs of "We Are the World" enough to be tired of the genre, but during the car ride back to meet my train at Fayetteville, I played the cassette over and over again. It began with lyrical strings evoking the ageless rolling of the river and then an overlay of electric folk guitars, bass, and vibes conjuring the lively little downtown along its bank.

> There have been so many miles,
> And oh, so many roads now.
> In a life of change and uncertainty
> A man needs a place to call his own now . . .
> We call this place home,
> Here is where we all want to be.

The song could have been about my own journey or about the long journey of Americans from the days of Plymouth onward. It expressed a sentiment that few Americans today could honestly express. But as I boarded my train at Fayetteville, I knew that in the past three years I had met more than my share of those who really did feel that way. They were part of one final migration that had come home at last. Out of the wreckage of North American placelessness, past the interstates, the parking lots, the malls, the commercial strips, the abandoned Main Streets, the city ghettos, the inhumane suburbs, the polluted rivers and lakes and skies, the billboard-strewn hillsides, the satellite dishes, the broken dreams of men and women who lived to watch TV in isolation, and the incessant drone of the twin demons, the auto and the bulldozer—past all of this they had found places salvageable in America. Often without benefit of scholarship or ideology, they had organically developed strategies for reclaiming those places and building real communities.

Perhaps it was still too late. For every Wilmington there were scores of placeless burgs; the buildout into the countryside continued apace; downtowns were still dying; communities were still fragmenting themselves with zoning ordinances that assumed the dominance of the automobile; large cities were in the final throes of disintegration; and the very success of places like Burlington and Wilmington, once they became publicized, threatened to overwhelm them with population numbers that just couldn't be accommodated. What was needed were more Burlingtons, Wilmingtons, Missoulas, and Corvallises. The pioneers had shown that it could be done. Now it was up to the rest of us in places not yet totally defiled to set our lands in order.

EPILOGUE

LESSONS OF THE PIONEERS

Where had we gone so wrong? Part of the problem was certainly our New World restlessness. By continually moving on, by tearing down and rebuilding, by covering up and paving over, Americans had been fouling their nests for generations. But it was more complicated than that, as James Howard Kunstler illustrates so vividly in his recent book *The Geography of Nowhere.* First we exploited our land as a commodity, allowing the buying and selling of it to shape what it became. Millions of market decisions aimed at maximizing the resale value of land, rather than its value for long-term use within a community, had turned our boulevards into sleazy commercial strips, our farms into shopping malls, our meadows into cracker box suburbs.

Communities responded to the devastating consequences of treating land as commodity by concocting zoning codes—which succeeded only in bringing order to the disconnected nature of our towns. Houses had to go here, and shops had to go here and restaurants here, and offices had to go over there. Could you have a grocery store or a restaurant on a corner of a residential neighborhood? Of course not. In rural areas we thought we were preserving our countryside with five-acre-lot minimums. Of course, all it really accomplished was to guarantee that our remaining rural land would be gobbled up at an even faster rate by low-density rural sprawl.

But by far the most disruptive agent in the demise of American places, according to Kunstler and most writers on the subject for the past generation, was the automobile. Cars seduced us into believing that there need be no physical proximity or connection between the places of our lives and, hand in hand with misguided zoning practices, profoundly fragmented the geography of our existence. The grocery store where we bought our food didn't need to be in our neighborhood. It didn't matter if the park was located on the other side of a freeway. We could shop for clothes and hardware at a mall on the outskirts of town that we wouldn't dream of walking to. We could move our workplaces out of town to exurban sites in the middle of what were once cornfields. And, worst of all, we could build our homes in all-residential suburban developments far from downtown —vast, soulless tracts of bedrooms in boxes surrounded by plots of mown grass where life became quiet, lonely, and empty. The downtown itself became superfluous. It was no longer a community focal point or a feature of our daily lives.

At the same time as it disconnected the places in our lives, the automobile also furthered our national antisocial habit of individualism. Alone behind the wheel of two tons of two-hundred-horsepower machinery, American drivers imagined themselves kings of the road, masters of their own destinies. Who needed other people? If you wanted something done right, you did it yourself. Other people were just motorists who cut you off on the highway or slowed you down on a narrow road. The general feeling toward our fellows became one of hostility and aggravation. Eventually we even started shooting at one another on the freeways.

But the damage done by the automobile didn't stop there. At the start of the century, America had a magnificent passenger railroad system and, even more important for community life, thriving electrified trolley systems. In the 1920s it was actually possible to travel almost anywhere, short distances or long, by public conveyance. In Keene you could catch trains leaving three times a day and be in Boston for a ball game two hours later. You could hop a trolley at Central Square and be out at Wilson Pond's band house in less time than it takes to drive today.

The automobile manufacturers won for themselves huge subsidies in the form of highway construction that became one of the chief reasons for the decline of the railroads. But worse, General Motors in particular set out systematically to dismantle the trolley network of the country by buying up systems and ripping up the tracks. By the time Congress investigated in the sixties, the war was long over.

The disruption to American places caused by pavement was obvious. An alien observer looking down at us from another planet might easily conclude that the automobile was the dominant life form in America. What the alien would see is a network of pavement linking shopping malls, commercial strips, interstate highways, and suburban housing tracts to the parking lots where the beasts come to rest. For people, modern highways and the clutter that developed along them divided communities as effectively as the Berlin Wall, and parking lots wasted nearly every open urban space in sight. In the age of auto madness, we paved paradise and put in a parking lot.

Finally, there was the modernist architecture that brought us all the antiseptic glass boxes in our cities. "Let form follow function," Le Corbusier had decreed. That the dictum led to inhumane blockish architecture that turned hostile shoulders to its urban surroundings was less an indictment of the dictum than of the modernists' bullet-headed conceptions of the functions of a building. Take into consideration the role of a building as a habitat for people, as an aesthetic component of the street environment, and as a link in the chain of community infrastructure, and the dictum might still stand in better postmodernist cities.

The modernist trend was so widely embraced largely because of historical coincidence: the Bauhaus originators of these abominations represented the ideological opposite of the fascist regimes we fought against in World War II. Furthermore, developers loved modernism because this kind of architecture was, simply, cheap. It was eminently suited to a culture with a habit of tearing things down and slapping up something new—quick and dirty.

But there are encouraging trends in the nineties. Writers of some of the literature of place, as well as a few far-thinking architects and planners, have begun to develop corrective strategies. Christopher Alexander and others have proposed a new way of looking at architecture and place design as a series of relationships—rather than as an unrelated agglomeration of buildings and byways—which they call a pattern language. An intersection is not just a place where traffic is distributed, but rather it is a nexus of related neighborhoods. A sidewalk is not only a place for pedestrians, it is a fundamental connection between buildings and the street. A front porch is not just a place to get out of the rain before entering a house, but a link between the house and the sidewalk where people pass by. A window is a connection between the indoors and outdoors, and so on.

Architects and planners are finally beginning to heed the thinking of urbanists like Lewis Mumford, William Whyte, and Jane Jacobs, who had collectively rediscovered the art of urban place making. The key is recognizing that constructed environments are just as psychologically important as natural ones. There are certain kinds and shapes of public spaces that make people feel more content. There are principles of place design that promote urges to explore, to linger, to interact, and, yes, also to buy. Many of these principles were well known to an earlier generation of designers of places like Central Park, Grand Central Station, the Mall in Washington, D.C., and the Main Streets of hundreds of turn-of-the-century downtowns. It *was* a lost art. It *is* being rediscovered.

The urban paradigm, especially in small cities, has reemerged as a model for future living. Take crime, inhumane size, and dysfunctional infrastructure out of the city life equation and, as I had seen for myself, people will return to their cities. Our empty downtowns with their multistory buildings are the new frontier of residential housing. And minimal expansion along city peripheries *at truly urban levels of density* could accommodate levels of growth that would otherwise despoil miles of countryside as rural sprawl. Let cities be cities.

Tony Hiss's book *The Experience of Place* identifies a macro-scaled vision, a regional view, of what is needed in American places. He focuses primarily on the exurban sprawl and clutter that makes so much of our land neither town nor country and posits three essential ingredients of a place: a truly urban area of high density where most people live, a working countryside where nature is farmed or otherwise groomed for productive purposes, and primeval lands left in their natural state. According to Hiss, a sense of place requires all three ingredients in reasonable proximity. Exurban, suburban, and rural sprawl of the kind so common today has no place at all in this vision.

The clustering of people and growth into urban areas becomes the key not only to making more integrated communities but also to preserving our precious North American heritage—our land.

In fact, developers have already become accustomed to the general principle of clustering. Increasingly rare is the planning board these days that lets a developer take a two-hundred-acre farm and build two hundred houses, each on a one-acre lot (or worse, forty houses, each on a five-acre lot). Now the developer is often required to cluster the two hundred houses (preferably along with a few key commercial and community amenities) on fifty acres in a true neighborhood and leave the remainder as common parkland or recreational areas or, better yet, as a farm. One might prefer to see the entire farm property left untouched, but the model shows just how far planning boards and developers have come since the days of tract building. Now, with our national sense of place in crisis, how much further might we be able to progress?

I believe I have witnessed over the past three years a new basis for optimism: the groundswell of demand and activism for better places that I have called "the last migration." At the start of these journeys, I thought I would be following a migration of people to a handful of lucky places that had somehow escaped placelessness. Instead I found that people were actively transforming places into renaissance towns. Some sites had the luck of certain preconditions, but the good news is that community revival is happening, and it is spreading. When I started my travels, there was a small collection of places on everybody's shortlist. But the list has grown and continues to grow, not because people are discovering more good places, but because they are making them. Today my itinerary is dreadfully incomplete; there are dozens of renaissance towns either established or in the making that I have not written about, often because, like celestial novas, they have exploded onto the scene overnight.

In searching for and defining renaissance towns, I started with the 10,000 Waves Alternative Places Rated Scale because the qualities it included were those that migrating people kept telling me they sought. It has served me well in targeting sites for study, but I have learned now that it is incomplete. True renaissance centers around the precondition a town has to work with as it embarks on its revival and understanding the process that brings it to fulfillment.

Preconditions. This is not to say that the renaissance phenomenon I have described wasn't possible in places not meeting these criteria. Rather, renaissance *was* possible in those places that *did* meet certain criteria. First was the presence of buildings and a downtown infrastructure that worked during some past time as the human focal point of the community. It needn't be the ancient adobe of Santa Fe, the Jeffersonian layout of Charlottesville, the colonial neighborhood of Strawberry Banke, or even the turn-of-the-century downtown of Asheville. San Luis Obispo's renaissance was built around fifties-era structures. But generally, in the absence of any successful new paradigm of architecture and community layout and the money to build it from scratch, we had to start with the remnants of infrastructure put in place at times when people were better at community making. Such a foundation also provided connection with the past and something authentic about the community for people to rally round. The very term, *renaissance,* demanded that there be something to be reborn.

There were also some very practical considerations accruing from working with a stock of older buildings. Although they had to operate within certain constraints, developers renovating historically designated buildings had distinct advantages in the form of federal or state grant assistance, already existing structures from which to work, probable community support, and a sense of purpose and pride.

Besides a stock of viable downtown buildings, the most successful renaissance towns I visited had a substantial ring of good neighborhoods and well-kept older housing adjacent to the downtown. Not everyone will want to live in downtown apartments or condos, and the presence of neighborhoods from which people could walk downtown was the critical factor, in my observations, to the success of downtown experiments with pedestrian malls.

A second precondition involved natural setting. I'm sure there will be people in the Midwest who will take umbrage at my focus on places with mountains and saltwater. In attempting to maximize my chances of finding success, I took the issue of settings to extremes. But distinctive natural settings exist in almost any part of the country, and what was important was their contribution to a sense of place. From the beginning of time, villages have been located in spots where natural geography provoked settlers to stop, for one reason or another, and say, "This is the place." It may have been a bend in a river, or a hill, or a valley, or the point of transition from one land form to another that inspired the human spirit to linger. The only sites that didn't meet this criterion were those where human-made sprawl had obliterated the surrounding natural setting, as in so many places in the East's "megalopolis" or places where the siting of a community had no relation whatsoever to geographic features.

Beyond the issue of the land as backdrop for community was the related question of the community's relationship to the countryside and *use* of the surrounding land. Besides the obvious example of Napa and the wine country, there were less spectacular linkages in every good place I visited. San Luis Obispo was anchored as much by the fertile broccoli lands as it was by the beaches, Kelowna had its orchards, Burlington had the Vermont country idyll, Charlottesville had the landed gentry still prosperous on their equestrian farms, and of course Santa Fe had the art-inspiring magic that "resided in the dirt." Places where there was no relationship between the town and the functions of the surrounding land, whose identity was not shaped at least in part by something fecund happening in the countryside, seemed most likely to suffer from the malaise of placelessness and the least likely to attract people seeking a home where they could live a complete existence.

The third precondition involved the character of the local people, the natives. I never found a successful renaissance town where an influx of newcomers from other places was not a key in the process. One way or another, the longtime natives of a place had to be ready to accept them and their potential contribution. Here the West Coast had a distinct advantage over other parts of the country, and the South and New England were handicapped. But this was changing as westerners turned hostile to immigrating Californians, and Vermont and North Carolina continued their immigrant-based boom. More important than region might be history and experience. Wilmington's natives had elected a Yankee mayor partly out of frustration with the town's time as a red-light scene. Asheville welcomed exotic outsiders partly because that was how the town had prospered twice in the past. Minneapolis welcomed Asian refugees because of a deeply engrained tradition of economic liberalism. In each place, sometimes through crisis, something happened to make the longtime locals drop their mistrust and prejudice toward outsiders, to instill a sense of humility and openness to new ideas.

Counterbalancing this openness to fresh blood, the people of the good places, both native and newcomer, maintained a sense of what was true to the identity of the place and what was antithetical to it. They had the ability to oppose manifestations of the homogenizing process that made other places look and feel more alike. In this respect, New England and the South had an advantage, and the West Coast, prairies, and Sun Belt were handicapped.

People in renaissance towns often recalled a time of social or even spiritual yearning shortly before their world changed. They felt a void, a hunger for something more than the stagnant auto-based, nuclear family, home-centered life could offer. Of course, what they wanted were the boons of public living, the joys of social congregation and fellowship. With entertainment establishments the mainstay of the renaissance downtown, I suspected that a town might not be ripe for renaissance until this kind of feeling reached a critical mass. After all, public living, with the downtown functioning as everyperson's living room, was the firm constant of the whole renaissance phenomenon.

There seemed to be a fourth precondition involving economics; or maybe it was the seminal first step in the process of becoming. In every renaissance town I visited, there was at least one industry that directly linked economics with the renaissance process. The forms it might take seemed infinitely various the more I traveled. But always there was some potent local economic force with the power to cancel obstacles to excellence and to assist a place in raising its sights above the limitations of Anyplace, USA. In Napa it was wine making; in Corvallis it was Hewlitt-Packard; in Portland it was Nike and Cornerstone Development; in Vancouver it was the Pacific Rim; in Missoula it was the University of Montana; in Ithaca it was Cornell; in Portsmouth it was location and tourism; in Asheville it was mountain convention centers; in Wilmington it was filmmaking. One shouldn't take any one of these examples to make sweeping generalizations. There were lots of places with universities, tourism, shoe manufacturers, or local agriculture that did not benefit from them in the same way. Economic giants could as easily become local tyrants as local benefactors. What the beneficial economic powers all had in common,

though, was that they were uniquely appropriate for their host cities—
and they had muscle. Perhaps the lesson for promoters and recruiters
in good place wannabees was to be clear about their town's identity
and then have the courage to think big.

In addition to their common preconditions, there were also some
similarities in the process by which places made themselves over into
renaissance towns. First, somebody had a vision. It may have been an
idiosyncratic individual leader like Portsmouth's Dorothy Vaughan, a
far-sighted mayor like Missoula's John O'Toole or Dan Kemmis, a
political movement like Ithaca's greens or Burlington's Progressives,
a merchants association like Wilmington's DARE, or an entire community involved in a formal process, as in Corvallis's Vision 2000. If
nothing else, vision provided a place with real leadership. But more
than that, it defined a place by the innovations happening there,
which in turn attracted new people, the key ingredient in the renaissance process. Professional promoters called this "establishing a
niche," but it went further than that in giving planners and developers
a guide for what was appropriate to the place and what was not. It
gave the populace something to rally around. It was the first step
toward becoming Someplace.

Second, it took some money to finance a community renaissance.
It needn't be the wine wealth of Napa Valley or the forty-one-
thousand-dollar average household income of greater Portsmouth, but
there had to be a tax base that could support improvements to community infrastructure and an income level that allowed people to
aspire to things beyond paying their mortgages and keeping bread on
the table. Money came to communities where the people who had it
wanted to live or where the people who wanted to make it saw an
opportunity to do so. Neither could happen without community promotion. The city halls of nearly all of the successful communities I
visited contained some kind of office of community development
whose responsibility it was to aggressively promote the community.
Asheville had ads on CNN, Wilmington had a radio jingle, Missoula
exploited Redford's *A River Runs Through It,* Burlington and many
others placed ads in the *New York Times.* Some of these offices even
went out to actively recruit specific industries, businesses, and cultural
groups that would improve the city's economic standing.

Third, every renaissance town had its renaissance downtown. Usually this was part of the community vision and one responsibility of city hall's office of community development, but in each case there was also an aggressive downtown association that regarded its work as nothing less than a crusade. All associations started by establishing a calendar of community events to get people in the habit of coming downtown, not just to buy things but to experience and celebrate the joys of community. But too many associations stopped there. The really effective ones went on to raise money for property acquisition and amenities projects, to lobby for helpful zoning and regulatory changes, to establish carrots and sticks to guide sometimes laggard merchants into making better business and marketing decisions, and even to hire a professional to function almost as a mall director does.

One of the items typically on the agenda of aggressive downtown associations was to agitate for zoning and other inducements to bring professional offices back into the downtown itself and free up potential residential stock near the downtown for its proper purpose. Leaders who realized that the key to success in the mall era was the presence of large numbers of pedestrian bodies with money in their pockets were on the right track. A welcoming stance and the repeal of blue laws could help attract the entertainment places so critical to downtown public living.

Hand in hand with fostering a resurgence of people in the downtown was finding ways to separate them from their cars. Mixed-use zoning could do a lot to lessen the number of nuisance auto trips. Establishing mass transit and bike paths was clearly helpful. Strategically located parking garages might be a part of the solution mix, but an overreliance on them, as I had seen in Charlottesville, only numbed city leaders to the more fruitful expedient of promoting the nearby neighborhoods. Most important, though, was to establish a pedestrian ethic by guaranteeing that the downtown streets and sidewalks were pedestrian friendly. Pedestrian malls could, under the right conditions, be helpful. But the most successful models of pedestrian friendliness relied on neither parking garages nor streets closed to autos. The Oregon places, Corvallis and Portland, did it sheerly by making the sidewalks of their streets good places to be on foot and by making them easy to walk to from elsewhere in town.

Finally, I never found a renaissance town that didn't have a strong gay, lesbian, or otherwise alternative lifestyle presence. Tolerance and even celebration of diversity seemed to be constants in good places. This is not an expression of political correctness. It is a descriptive, not prescriptive, observation of facts that, frankly, I was surprised to find everywhere I went. Diversity had always been linked with the cultural amenities that were part of what people sought in good places. And the consistent correlation I observed in all of the most flourishing places seemed to vindicate the vision of leaders like President Clinton and Asheville's city councilor Gene Ellison, who stressed America's diversity as a strength and not a weakness.

For nearly a generation, the best minds in community building, people like Jane Jacobs, William Whyte, and Lewis Mumford, had told us what it takes to make places work better: pedestrians and social and entertainment action on Main Streets, residences close to downtown, public gathering places and spaces, mass transit, mixed-use zoning, local ownership of key business and industry, public-private entrepreneurialism, aggressive promotion of the advantages of the urban center, preservation of the integrity of the countryside, and alternatives to life centered around the automobile. What the last migration had done was to discover these things and more—on its own.

My town of Keene, in its little covered-bridge corner of New Hampshire, had not really been discovered yet, either by the forces of degradation or by the forces of renaissance. Though only two hours from Boston, we were just far enough off I-91 that fair and ill winds alike tended to pass us by, as they had in Corvallis and Wilmington up until a decade ago.

What did Keene have going for it? We didn't have Lake Champlain or the Smokies. But we did have Mount Monadnock, the world's second most climbed mountain after Japan's Mount Fuji. We were set in a broad, beautiful valley between forested foothills and dozens of nearby lakes, and our Main Street was lined with a good stock of well-preserved early-twentieth-, nineteenth-, and even eighteenth-century architecture, including a classic white Congregational Church at the head of a grassy New England square. The ring of substantial older housing adjacent to the downtown was still about two-thirds intact, Boston was just two hours away on noninterstate highways, and Vermont's Killington, Okemo, Stratton, and Mount Snow were all about an hour away during ski season. The industries that were already based in Keene were perfect for us; we just needed to expand or replicate them. In fact, we had all of the preconditions for community renaissance except perhaps openness to outsiders and a clear and productive link to the surrounding countryside.

Throughout the time of my travels to other places, Keene had lurched toward crisis. The long-fought proposal to build a regional mall in a cornfield on the outskirts of town had transformed itself, like a mutating alien, into a plan for a Wal-Mart and a Sam's Club. The first closures of stores on Main Street had begun—Goodnow's, a locally owned department store, was now vacant, Sears had left behind an ugly blue facade and boarded-up windows directly opposite the commons, and now Woolworth had announced its intention to depart soon.

Property taxes, because of the lack of any broad-based state taxation and a paucity of industrial property, had soared to among the highest in the country. Our excellent private sector industrial recruiter (we didn't have an office of community development in city hall) was handicapped by local politics. The recession had cost jobs, and wages were lagging behind cost-of-living increases. The callers to the local talk radio station were in an angry mood. Nobody had any figures to prove it, but the prevailing wisdom was that longtime working and retired residents were being forced to sell their homes. City hall and its planning department were under attack as never before for discouraging growth, with the tax-guzzling public school district and tax-exempt Keene State College only a little behind in the pantheon of anger.

Because the development proposals we had gotten for decades tended toward the worst kind—low-end commercial and rural residential sprawl—and because locals had a visceral fear of rampant growth roaring up the Connecticut River valley from megalopolis, city hall had adopted a knee-jerk reticence about new economic activity that earned us a reputation for being unfriendly to developers. The best project done in the past thirty years, the renovation of an old mill as a marketplace, had not been duplicated anywhere else in town. As a hub for a rural Appalachian county, we were identified by the people who forecast retail opportunities as a Kmart rather than Jordan Marsh

market. Keene was on the verge of getting a lot of development attention, but not necessarily the kind we wanted.

One of the most consistent lessons I had learned in my travels was
that times of crisis like ours had often been the crucible out of which
renaissance had frothed. When I returned from Wilmington, I found
encouraging developments in Keene that might yet become the har-
bingers of a renaissance process.

A woman named Nancy Sporborg had almost single-handedly
brought the concept of an activist downtown association to Keene and
was building a calendar of festival events for the town. A property
owners group had created a new public square on a central patch of
land the city had acquired from the departed railroad. Another group
had rescued a dying marquee theater as a performance center, and
there was an active arts council. The city was in the midst of rewriting
a master plan, and a "Mission Committee" appointed by the mayor
was asking questions about the purposes and means of city government that hadn't been asked in years. New proposals, such as the
creation of an office of community development, which earned nothing but scorn a few years ago, were now being seriously discussed by
serious players. Keene State College was embarking on an ambitious
"Vision 2000" plan to become a college of note by the new century.
Philanthropic families and clubs had planted the beginnings of a river
park along the city's northerly stretch of the Ashuelot River, and an
Antioch graduate school professor had come forward to develop a
bicycle path plan like one he had recently designed in another town
nearby. When I spoke on a call-in radio show about the need for more
public living in our downtown third places, a caller trivializing my
suggestion prompted a half dozen others to applaud what I had said
and yearn, over the airwaves, for someplace to go for spontaneous
mingling.

A group of community leaders had formed the Keene Downtown
Revitalization Corporation, a nonprofit private initiative aiming to
attract developers into partnerships to effect a true downtown renaissance in Keene. With the aid of a state tax incentive program, it had
raised $4.42 million from local business and was beginning to plan
how to spend it. As I write, its efforts are controversial and inconclu-
sive, but it has the potential to become Keene's own DARE.

Though currently drowsy, maybe Keene was stirring toward an

awakening. What had never happened in Keene was the achievement of economic, cultural, and social critical mass—what James Howard Kunstler calls "a new community paradigm"—where all of the nascent forces favoring community resurgence *recognize each other* and *come together* to in turn attract more energy from new people and to create renaissance.

Of course, there were some who didn't want that to happen, private interests who preferred to manipulate the community behind the scenes for their own purposes and ends. Many of Keene's people tended to be obsessed with the place as a quiet refuge for children and were fearful of initiatives that would put us on the map. But these things were changing. Community renaissance in Keene was no longer an airy ideal. As our property taxes went up, our earnings went down, and our Main Street storefronts emptied out, it had become a necessity.

We needed to conjure a vision, we needed to land a few hefty economic fish, we needed to add a few thousand new people to our population and give them access to influence, we needed to get out of our cars and begin to live more publicly in our beautiful downtown, we needed to establish a more fruitful link, probably through tourism, with the magnificent surrounding land, and we needed to remember the history of our place—a town of pioneers who trekked just a little farther up the Connecticut valley than those who stopped at the edge of easy land in Massachusetts.

I suspect we were similar in some ways to many American places that were hurting but hadn't yet been totally defiled. We were part of the next wave of Corvallises, Missoulas, Burlingtons, and Wilmingtons. We were America's hope for better places to live in the future.

When T. S. Eliot wrote in *Four Quartets,* "the end of all our explorations will be to arrive where we started and know the place for the first time," he was accurately predicting the twentieth-century movement by the English middle class back to their roots in the rural villages sited in dells throughout the land. It hasn't always worked out so well in England, where a certain antisocial aspect of the migration has exacerbated the nation's ancient class problems. But as America's current homecoming migration brings us back to our Main Streets, back to the center, we have a better chance to get it right this time.

APPENDIX

I have often been invited to speak publicly about the details of the new downtowns, even before this book was finished. The following is a summary of the observations I have shared with groups seeking to promote downtown renaissance in their communities.

The old, strictly retail based downtown is dead. The department stores have moved out to the malls, and until there is actually a divorce between Americans and their automobiles, they are not coming back. The successful new downtowns are built around a different profile. First, some general principles:

• Pedestrian friendliness. People on foot with money in their pockets make a downtown thrive. This means downtown beautification and establishment of sidewalk amenities—benches, gathering spaces, trees, wastebaskets, pocket parks, and attractive window displays.

• Thriving, quality adjacent residential neighborhoods. Successful downtowns almost always have a ring of renovated ("gentrified," if you will) older housing within walking distance of the downtown.

• Ownership of downtown properties by merchants, rather than tenantship. Ownership on Main Street tends to create a whole different mind-set, one that is more vested in the good of the downtown as a whole.

• Parking improvements. Downtowns cannot thrive and compete with malls and plazas through auto traffic alone. But in tandem with residence and pedestrian friendliness, free, easy parking can help.

• Public transit. Anything that gets people downtown without their cars is even better than acres of free parking.

• Redevelopment of the existing stock of buildings under historical designation status rather than "wrecking ball sixties-era urban renewal." People with money in their pockets are attracted to renovations of older buildings, whether or not my ruminations about the reasons for this are correct. It is a fact of downtown economics.

• Use of the tax increment district, rather than special assessment, to finance public amenities and the public side of public-private partnerships in development. The tax-weary public, not to mention the tax-burdened downtown property owners, can swallow the idea of new projects that are financed entirely through tax revenue generated by these projects themselves.

Beyond general principles, the new downtowns are characterized by a new mix of establishments with four critical elements:

• Entertainment establishments. Restaurants, bars, coffee shops, ice-cream parlors, newsstands, bookstores—these are places that attract people wanting simply to gather and experience the joys of community.

• Downtown residence. Condos and apartments in renovated upper floors of downtown buildings are the new frontier of residential development. Again, the goal is get more bodies downtown on foot with money in their pockets.

• Professional and corporate offices in the downtown. Architects, lawyers, dentists, accountants, insurance and travel agents, and so forth—relocating such offices from the surrounding neighborhoods frees up housing as well as provides an additional attractant to people coming downtown. Professionals also form a valuable vested interest to complement the usual downtown merchants. Significant downtown corporate employers put more people on Main Street with money in their pockets and a valuable vested interest.

• Niche retail. Retail that thrives in the new downtowns offers something that can't be found at the mall. That means quality rather than price. That means service rather than convenience. That means creativity and uniqueness rather than staples.

Finally, there are some very specific anchor features of various successful new downtowns:

• The rescue of a marquee-type theater as a performing arts center provides the downtown with a critical cultural and entertainment magnet that generates action on the sidewalks as well as the right kind of spin-off investment.

• A downtown hotel and conference center, often financed by a consortium of local businesses, banks, and city government, pumps new energy into the downtown. The best places always have visitors, even if institutionalized tourism is not a significant feature of the local economy. These establishments need not be grand, and some communities have erred by putting all of their eggs in this basket. But the age-old general principle that a town can be anchored by a place for visitors to stay on its Main Street still holds true.

• The development of a waterfront park with public, residential, business, and commercial mixed uses. Water is a centering feature of local geography. The success stories of waterfront developments across the country are legion.

• The downtown siting of recreational facilities such as ball parks, ice-skating rinks, playgrounds, or traditional public recreation centers. One of the ways to attract people to Main Street with money in their pockets is to get them to play there or to watch others play there.

• Most essential of all is an aggressive downtown association with muscle. The really successful ones think big and operate almost like a mall management. A strong downtown association should perform the following functions:

1. Build a calendar of public events that bring people into the downtown.

2. Analyze the specific needs, opportunities, and deficiencies of the downtown as a commercial entity.

3. Provide promotion and marketing functions for the downtown as a whole, often with a full-time professional heading the effort.

4. Actively recruit appropriate stores and businesses.

5. Provide leadership and incentives to assist merchants to adopt practices good for the downtown as a whole, such as staying open evening and weekend hours, preventing use of Main Street parking by employees, maximizing special opportunities such as Street Fair Days, maintaining standards of appearance, and so forth.

6. Develop a downtown master plan with public consensus to guide the development of the downtown in directions in which the community wants it to go.

BIBLIOGRAPHY

Alexander, Christopher, et al. *A Pattern Language.* New York: Oxford University Press, 1977.

Boyer, Richard, and David Savageau. *Places Rated Almanac.* New York: Prentice Hall, 1989, 1991.

Bryson, Bill. *The Lost Continent.* New York: Harper and Row, 1989.

Calthorpe, Peter, et al. *The Pedestrian Pocket Book.* Princeton, N.J.: Princeton Architectural Press, 1989.

Caplow, Theodore. *The Middletown Families: Fifty Years of Change and Continuity.* Minneapolis: University of Minnesota Press, 1981.

Clapp, James. *New Towns and Urban Policy.* New York: Dunellon, 1971.

Corbett, Michael. *A Better Place to Live.* Emmaus, Pa.: Rodale Press, 1981.

Fitzgerald, Frances. *Cities on a Hill.* New York: Simon and Schuster, 1986.

Gallagher, Winifred. *The Power of Place: How Our Surroundings Shape Our Thoughts, Emotions, and Actions.* New York: Simon and Schuster, 1993.

Garreau, Joel. *Edge City: Life on the New Frontier.* New York: Doubleday, 1991.

Hall, Edward. *The Hidden Dimension.* New York: Doubleday, 1966.

Hardin, Garrett. *Managing the Commons.* New York: W. H. Freeman, 1977.

Helmer, John, and Neil Eddington. *Urbanman.* New York: Free Press, 1973.

Herbers, John. *The New Heartland.* New York: Random House, 1986.

Hiss, Tony. *The Experience of Place.* New York: Knopf, 1990.

Howard, Ebenezer. *Garden Cities of Tomorrow.* Cambridge, Mass.: MIT Press, 1966.

Huxtable, Ada Louise. *Architecture Anyone?* New York: Random House, 1968.
————. *Will They Ever Finish Bruckner Boulevard?* Berkeley: University of California Press, 1988.
Jacobs, Jane. *Cities and the Wealth of Nations.* New York: Random House, 1984.
Kemmis, Daniel. *Community and the Politics of Place.* Norman, Okla.: University of Oklahoma Press, 1992.
Kowinski, William Severini. *The Malling of America.* New York: Morrow, 1985.
Kunstler, James Howard. *The Geography of Nowhere.* New York: Simon and Schuster, 1993.
Lingeman, Richard. *Small Town America, a Narrative History, 1620–Present.* Boston: Houghton Mifflin, 1980.
Lynch, Kevin. *What Time Is This Place.* Cambridge, Mass.: MIT Press, 1972.
Mantell, Michael, et al. *Creating Successful Communities.* Washington, D.C.: Island Press, 1990.
Mumford, Lewis. *The City in History.* New York: Harcourt, 1961.
————. *The Culture of Cities.* New York: Harcourt, 1970.
Oldenburg, Ray. *The Great Good Place.* New York: Paragon House, 1990.
Powers, Ron. *Far from Home, Life and Loss in Two American Towns.* New York: Random House, 1991.
Raban, Jonathan. *Hunting Mister Heartbreak.* New York: Burlingame, 1991.
Rawls, Thomas. *Small Places, in Search of a Vanishing America.* Boston: Little, Brown, 1990.
Roueche, Berton. *Special Places: In Search of Small Town America.* Boston: Little, Brown, 1982.
Rybczynski, Witold. *Home.* New York: Viking, 1990.
————. *Waiting for the Weekend.* New York: Viking, 1991.
Schneider, William. "The Suburban Century Begins," *The Atlantic Monthly,* July 1992.
Schumacher, E. F. *Small Is Beautiful.* New York: Harper and Row, 1973.
Scully, Vincent. *American Architecture and Urbanism.* New York: Henry Holt, 1988.
Smith, Herbert. *Planning America's Communities.* Chicago: American Planning Association, 1991.
Sommer, Robert. *Personal Space.* Englewood Cliffs, N.J.: Prentice Hall, 1969.
Spirn, Anne Whiston. *The Granite Garden.* New York: Harper, 1947.
Stern, Robert A. M. *Pride of Place.* Boston: Houghton Mifflin, 1986.
Stilgoe, John R. *Borderland.* New Haven, Conn.: Yale University Press, 1988.
Thomas, G. Scott. *A Rating Guide to Life in America's Small Cities.* Buffalo, N.Y.: Prometheus Books, 1990.

Van der Ryn, Sim, and Peter Calthorpe. *Sustainable Communities.* San Francisco: Sierra Club, 1986.
Whyte, William. *City: Rediscovering the Center.* New York: Doubleday, 1988.
———. *The Last Landscape.* New York: Doubleday, 1975.

INDEX